Disability Studies:
Enabling the Humanities

Disability Studies

Enabling the Humanities

EDITED BY
Sharon L. Snyder,
Brenda Jo Brueggemann, and
Rosemarie Garland-Thomson

THE MODERN LANGUAGE ASSOCIATION OF AMERICA
New York   *2002*

For information about obtaining permission to reprint material from
MLA book publications, send your request by mail (see address below),
e-mail (permissions@mla.org), or fax (646 458–0030).

Library of Congress Cataloging-in-Publication Data

Disability studies : enabling the humanities / edited by Sharon L. Snyder,
Brenda Jo Brueggemann, and Rosemarie Garland-Thomson.
    p. ; cm.
  Includes bibliographical references and index.
  ISBN 0-87352-980-4 (cloth) — ISBN 0-87352-981-2 (pbk.)
    1. Disability studies. 2. Humanities. 3. People with disabilities in literature.
  4. Sociology of disability. I. Snyder, Sharon L., 1963– II. Brueggemann,
Brenda Jo, 1958– III. Thomson, Rosemarie Garland.
    [DNLM: 1. Disabled Persons—psychology. 2. Disabled Persons—rehabilitation.
  3. Medicine in Literature. 4. Psychoanalytic Theory. 5. Self Concept.
  6. Social Values. WB 320 D6117 2002]
  HV1568.2 .D594 2002
  306.9'08—dc21   2002016698

ISBN-13: 978-0-87352-980-8 (cloth)
ISBN-13: 978-0-87352-981-5 (pbk.)

Cover art (for the paperback edition) by Anne Yanagi

Printed on recycled paper. Third printing 2005

Published by The Modern Language Association of America
26 Broadway, New York, New York 10004-1789
www.mla.org

To Phyllis Franklin, who helped guide us here, and the next generation of disability studies students, who will take us all further

CONTENTS

Enabling Theory

Enabling Pedagogy

ACKNOWLEDGMENTS

This project has been substantially enabled by multiple minds, spirits, and bodies—enablers all. We owe much to the remarkable staff at MLA headquarters who first helped the MLA's Committee on Disability Issues (CDI) become permanent and who also, directly or indirectly, contributed to the development of this volume, which was engendered from preliminary and initial CDI committee meetings: the inimitable Phyllis Franklin; the ever-encouraging, always available Martha Evans; and a team of others who worked with and for the CDI then as now—Karin Bagnall, Karen Susnitsky, and Maribeth Kraus. Carol Zuses kindly suggested ways and means for organizing sessions on disability issues at the 1995 MLA convention in San Diego and the 1996 MLA convention in Chicago; many of this volume's contributors first met as a result. In particular, we wish to acknowledge Terry Ford's counsel on the ways and means to correct for the many bibliographic erasures of disability studies scholarship that have occurred under dated rubrics. Alongside this group are the original CDI members, those fearless (and fun) souls who helped shape the volume long before we had a single submission and who probably, truly, gave us all our best ideas at points and in ways we can hardly trace anymore: Lennard Davis, Tammy Berberi, Georgina Kleege, Nancy Mairs, David Mitchell, and Ellen Stekert. Tremendous thanks also to those who continue to serve disabled academic populations on the CDI: Mark Jeffreys, Michael Bérubé, and Michael Davidson. We are grateful to Harilyn Rousso and Simi Linton, who provided guidance and sage advice as consultants and as members of the "dinner committee." Their expertise and grace surely infuses these pages as well.

The interdependency of relationships is a fact of life most disabled people are quite familiar with; it certainly was a fact with our editorial collaboration. Yet the politics of name order in traditional publishing may work against displaying a sense of interdependent and equal collaboration—especially when three editors, and three names, are involved. While it is not a perfect remedy, we agreed to a game of chance as a means for arriving at name order.

We each are blessed with colleagues and students at our own universities whose presence resonates in our work at large and sometimes sounds itself more precisely on these pages. At the University of Illinois, Chicago, are Carol Gill, Toby Tate, Teresa Garate-Serafini, Larry Voss, Tamar Heller, Yanling "Milly" Li, Sharon Lamp, Teresa Pacione, Sarah Triano, Rebecca Maskos, Carlos Drazen, Sara Vogt, and all the students in the Disabled Students' Union as well as those students from UIC disability studies courses: Histories of the Body (English 590, fall 1998); A History of Disability Representation (Department of Disability and Human Development 570, winter 2000); Visualizing the Body: Disability Film Studies (Department of Disability and Human Development 594, fall 2000); and Interdisciplinary Seminar in Disability Studies (Disability Studies 595, fall 2000). Laura Burt and Theresa Elsey in Michigan provided helpful work-study assistance on the volume. Michelle Jarman in Chicago lent her writing talents not only to the formatting of the volume but also to the devising of a beautifully serviceable index. Anja Tervooren from the University of Berlin provided wonderful feedback on early drafts of the essays. David Mitchell provided editorial guidance, formatting help, and valuable consultation at every step of the way. At the Ohio State University are Andrea Lunsford, Jacqueline Jones-Royster, Jim Phelan, Michal J. Hogan, Johnson Cheu, Amy Shuman, and all the students in OSU disability-centered courses: Representations of (Dis)Ability in Literature and Film (English 575, winter 1995); Disability in Language, Culture, and Literature (Comparative Studies and English 792, spring 1996); Abilities in America (English 110, spring 1998); and Disability Discourses (English 883, winter 1999).

The circle of supportive colleagues ripples in a pool far bigger than just our home institutions. These include many we've worked with in our scholarly areas (disability studies, rhetoric and composition, cultural studies, literature, women's studies, creative writing, African American studies, comparative literature); colleagues at the Society for Disability Studies, which was founded in the mid-1980s by a small, but committed, group of disability academics and professionals; colleagues at conferences we attend where groups similar to the MLA's CDI meet, such as the American Studies Association Disability Studies Caucus, the Conference on College Composition and Communication's Task Force on Disability Issues, and the Teaching about/with Disabilities SIG; and the participants in the NEH Summer 2000 Institute on Disability Studies in the Humanities. Embedded in these enabling locations are significant individuals who deserve being singled out: Sander Gilman, Paul Longmore, Adrienne Asch, Jane Detweiler, John V. VanCleve, Susan Burch, Cindy LaCom, Carrie Sandhal, Jim Ferris. This volume has benefited from the skillful editing of Michael Kandel at the MLA. Finally, there is family—family that believed in us, that believed in this book, and that gave us not just the nod but also the physical space and time to do it in: Jim, Karl, Esther, Bob, Rob, Lena, Cara, David, Cameron, and Emma.

Introduction:
Integrating Disability
into Teaching and Scholarship

Disability as both image and concept pervades language and literature. English abounds with disability metaphors: we have lame ideas, blind justice, dumb luck, paralyzed wills, deaf ears, crippling traffic, and idiotic relatives. Disabled characters people our most canonical literature, from Homer's Polyphemous, Sophocles's Oedipus, William Shakespeare's Richard III, Nathaniel Hawthorne's Roger Chillingworth, Victor Hugo's Quasimodo, Herman Melville's Captain Ahab, Charlotte Brontë's Bertha Mason and Rochester, William Faulkner's Benjy Compson, William Carlos Williams's Elsie, to Toni Morrison's Eva Peace. Many of our most studied authors had disabilities that influenced their writing: Homer and Milton were blind, Byron was lame, Keats was consumptive, Whitman was paralytic, Joan Didion has written of her diagnosis with multiple sclerosis. The centrality of disability to human experience is recorded in our narrative and linguistic records.

This claim to disability's centrality in our lives rests on defining the term broadly, as it has been done in the Americans with Disabilities Act of 1990, known as the ADA. This landmark legislation mandating civil rights for people with disabilities suggests that disability encompasses physical, sensory, and mental impairments; illnesses; congenital and acquired differences thought of as disfigurements or deformities; psychological disabilities; stamina limitations due to disease or its treatment; developmental differences; and visible anomalies such as birthmarks, scarring, and the marks of aging. In this sense, then, disability names the naturally occurring or acquired bodily variations that accrue as we move through history and across cultures. Moreover, the ADA provides civil rights protection for people who have such disabilities (or are perceived as having them). Such an interpretation suggests that being identified as disabled has negative consequences in the social, political, and economic realms. Despite those negative consequences, disability as both a bodily condition and a social category either now or later will touch us all. The fact that many of us will become disabled if we live long enough is perhaps the fundamental aspect of human embodiment.

Yet, in our present collective cultural consciousness, the disabled body is imagined not as the universal consequence of living an embodied life but rather as an alien condition. Thus disability tends to be figured in cultural representations as an absolute state of otherness that is opposed to a standard, normative body, unmarked by either individual form and function or by the particularities of its history. In stigmatizing and distancing ourselves from disability, we participate in late-capitalist culture's relentless attempt to standardize and stabilize the body. Such an effort effectively attempts to reduce both our individual particularities and our experience of bodily vulnerability. Take just these few examples: technology shapes our bodies to conform to norms ranging from straight teeth to generous bust lines; the controlled climate in which our bodies live makes us oblivious to our fragile tolerance for discomfort; pain is to be avoided, illness to be cured, and disability to be corrected or concealed; in the dominant religious iconography of the developed world, the broken, wounded body of Christ has been replaced by the purely symbolic empty cross.[1]

Just as sex was the ubiquitous unspoken subject in the Victorian world, disability—the harbinger of mortality—is the ubiquitous unspoken topic in contemporary culture. Even though disability acts in cultural representation as a magnet for hyperbolic meaning in texts and lives, it has gone largely unnoticed in both teaching and scholarship until recently. Literary and cultural critics are beginning to go beyond disability as a simple metaphor. They are also beginning the process of assessing the implications of disability representations from the perspective of the disability rights movement, as the history of communities and as the record of cultures. At the same time, critics struggle to explain how effacing such a fundamental human experience occurs, since the critical tools, theoretical paradigms, and archival structures that can excavate the influence of disability on all our lives are only now emerging.

This volume provides a guide to studying disability as a subject of critical inquiry and a category of critical analysis. As such, this book constitutes a deliberate, composite rhetorical instrument that demonstrates how disability studies can transform language and literary studies. We now understand that gender and race, among other socially constructed identity categories, inflect literary and linguistic representations and illuminate their meanings in previously unacknowledged ways. These essays demonstrate that disability can and should be interwoven similarly into the critical matrix we use to study and teach literary texts. The representation of disability and of disabled figures has a history that reflects ideological shifts in the perception of the body, of individuality, and of social relations as modernity proceeds. The essays gathered here reveal this critical history. They are exemplary models of the most innovative, rigorous practices and methods currently available in disability studies. Collectively, these essays establish a critical context for teaching and scholarship in literary and language studies.

Disability Studies: Enabling the Humanities is about integration in the widest sense. That is to say, it seeks to redress the exclusion of disability and disabled people from our critical discourses, our scholarly imaginations, and our classrooms. It seeks to *enable* in the way that some of us in disability studies scholarship and activist work have attempted to reclaim *enabling* as a term of our own rather than one rooted in rehabilitation, social welfare, and medical discourses. Appropriating vexed terms like *enabling* to designate power and foster community echoes other acts of renaming in the disability community—taking back, with pride, terms like *Deaf* and *crip* in place of euphemistic tags like *hearing-impaired* and *physically challenged*. (Even "handicapped parking" spaces are now being relabeled as "disability parking"). In the humanities, we now seek an enabling—much like an enlightening—of language and literature that positions disability as a critical, experiential, and pedagogical frame. By enabling the humanities, we strive to make language and literature more accessible to disabled and nondisabled scholars, students, teachers, and readers.

The volume has two purposes: first, to show how to integrate the concept and representation of disability into all our teaching and scholarship; second, to offer strategies for integrating people with disabilities into the classroom and the profession. Disability is indeed a fundamental human experience that is missing from our critical consciousness. As such we need to weave it into all our teaching and scholarship with the self-conscious effort born of rigorous theorizing and interpretation.

This volume, then, has been conceived as a study shelf devoted to the critical analysis of disability in literary and language studies. As such a shelf, it serves as a resource and a reference on integrating disability as a critical category and a system of representation. There are four sets of essays; each set explicates and exemplifies what we take to be one of the fundamental tasks of disability studies in a literary and language context. The first task, undertaken in the section "Enabling Theory," is to show how using disability as a category of analysis transforms major critical discourses. The second section, "Autobiographical Subjects," both implements and studies the first-person narrator's efforts to revise long-inscribed cultural scripts of disability. The third section, "Rehabilitating Representation," illustrates how disability as a critical category produces fresh and provocative readings of literary and artistic traditions. These readings range from classical to contemporary novels, poetry, essays, and oratory as well as figural art and paintings. The fourth section, "Enabling Pedagogy," demonstrates that integrating disability into teaching practices and courses introduces new questions and challenges established assumptions. All the essays in this volume focus on specific texts—literary, visual, or popular—or on pedagogical issues. Each essay exemplifies a disability studies methodology suitable for use in literary study and teaching; at the same time, each essay illuminates texts in which disability appears.

Enabling Theory

The essays in this section demonstrate how disability as a category of critical analysis engages with and transforms the major theoretical discourses that critics use to understand literary works. Collectively they show that our current versions of narrative theory, social constructivism, feminism, psychoanalysis, new historicism, semiotics, and queer theory gain force and range when they account for the differences disabilities make. Disability operates in at least four distinct ways in these essays: it expands our ways of thinking about the form, function, and appearance of the body; it complicates the ways we imagine national, communal, and individual identities; it challenges assumptions about what is normative and what is marginal; it adds further dimension to historical, psychological, and aesthetic inquiries. These essays show how disability serves as a master trope that challenges pervasive social fictions about the experiences of embodiment. They thus attest to the ways that a focus on disability extends and questions current theoretical paradigms that guide our critical analyses.

The first essay, David Mitchell's "Narrative Prosthesis," reveals disability as central to narrative—to the very process of textual production—even though we may not initially recognize that centrality. Mitchell demonstrates that myths from *Oedipus the King* to *The Steadfast Tin Soldier* depend on disabled figures to introduce conflict, initiate difference, and expedite resolution. He reveals how a persistent drive in narrative to anchor meaning to the supposed truth of the body—to make corporeality manifest through disability metaphors—serves to obscure a more socially complex rendering of disabled lives. By exploring the metaphoric potential of disability for literature, Mitchell introduces this volume's most significant cultural work: that is, recognizing disability as a political issue, a social identity, and a community that has historically struggled for equality.

Mark Jeffreys's "Visible Cripple" brings this point home by exploring how the experience of disability exposes the limitations of social constructivism. Jeffreys examines the conflict between constructivism as a "liberation epistemology" and the power of physical disability as an authentic experience. Probing what he calls "the seam where body joins culture," he cautions against the tendencies of constructivist paradigms to neutralize the experience of disability by locating it too fully in the environment and in social relations. His essay contends that one of the primary contributions of disability studies in the humanities is to reconsider bodily experience with respect to current cultural theories of the body.

Jeffreys's essay exemplifies the disability studies practice of situating the critic as a disabled subject, a critical and politicized practice continued in Tobin Siebers's "Tender Organs." Siebers's trenchant critique of the key role of disability in the psychoanalytic theory of narcissism is also a simultaneous examination of how metatheories such as psychoanalysis do the political work of stigmatizing and subordinating groups. By challenging calcified assumptions, such as the accusation of narcissism against disabled people, Siebers shows how disability studies interrogates established critical discourses in productive ways. He thus turns the tables on the hierarchical model of psychoanalysis and places disabled people in the interlocutor's role.

Next, Rosemarie Garland-Thomson's essay on the representation of disabled people in popular photography seeks to historicize rather than metaphorize disability. Her "Politics of Staring" offers a taxonomy of popular disability photography that extends from the earliest commercial freak portraiture and reform movement imagery, through charity poster photographs, and to the use of disabled fashion models in contemporary advertising. Because the politics of disability is in large part about appearance, the visual genres Garland-Thomson elaborates clarify our understanding of the ways that culture imagines and constructs disability.

Michael Davidson's "Hearing Things," like Garland-Thomson's essay, invites us to consider visual genres and the politics of disability as a way of reseeing, rewriting, and reknowing what our culture imagines both as literature and as normal. Davidson aims to extend the concept of Deaf literature-performance (based primarily on sign language and gestures) as he critically analyzes the work of the deaf language-artist Aaron Williamson and the performance of Flying Words Project.[2] The use of speech and vocalization in these performances is a kind of scandal masterfully used to critical ends. As both postmodern poetics and poststructuralist theories, the performance of Deaf literature illustrates the radical potential of disability as critical insight.

In "Compulsory Able-Bodiedness," Robert McRuer explores a productive collaboration between queer studies and disability studies by demonstrating their shared and overlapping critiques of systems of normalcy. Compulsory heterosexuality intertwines with compulsory able-bodiedness in that both produce able bodies and heterosexuality. McRuer shows the radical potential of a disability studies inquiry by explaining what a collaboration of queer theory and disability theory might reveal. He examines popular film representations of disability to excavate an emergent discourse of tolerance and diversity that depends on excising both the queer and disabled body. Along with the other essays in "Enabling Theory," McRuer's demonstrates how disability studies parallels work in other identity-based studies to question mainstream representations of marginalized peoples and experiences.

Finally, Lennard Davis's essay, "Bodies of Difference," shifts this section of the book from particular critical theories to broad historical analysis. Davis focuses on the historical development of the norm in modernity, arguing that democracy, the novel, and ableism emerged historically in tandem as feudalism gave way to modernity in Western culture. His study of how "a national physical type" and its opposite, "an antinational physical type," develop suggests that ableism is not the result of prejudiced people but rather an effect of modernity itself. Davis's concept of the machinery that "enforces normalcy" historicizes and complements the particular readings of texts and genres that follow.

Autobiographical Subjects

The essays in "Enabling Theory" demonstrate how the imperative to normalcy is also the imperative to homogeneity, to a narrow conception of health and embodiment. The essays that follow in "Autobiographical Subjects" build on these insights as a key revolutionary method used by disabled people to narrate their experiences as modes of cultural redress. People with disabilities who write autobiographies face a conflict between self-perceptions and society's view of them. They must rhetorically narrate the vagaries of living within a disabled body while also confronting social stigmatizing of bodily difference. The essays in "Enabling Theory" often articulate a disabled subject as a critical position while they demonstrate how disability has been excluded from traditional studies. Correspondingly, the essays in "Autobiographical Subjects" feature the disabled first-person narrator's efforts to revise long-inscribed cultural scripts. Such efforts begin to challenge the roles disability has occupied historically in traditions of life writing.

G. Thomas Couser's essay, "Signifying Bodies," lays out the possibilities, problems, and practices of teaching disability autobiography. By discussing disability studies and disability narratives within a broader consideration of how areas of scholarship operate in general, Couser provides a critical framework for incorporating disability autobiographies into literary critical paradigms. Along with providing many suggestions and citations, this essay illustrates the critical uses of disability life narratives to explore the variegated nature of disability experience, culture, and identity as well as the rhetorical patterns that recur in such stories. Couser ultimately offers the useful concept of autoethnography as simultaneously a documentation of disability culture and a refutation of prevailing stereotypes and assumptions about disability.

In this same vein, Leonard Cassuto's "Oliver Sacks and the Medical Case Narrative" historicizes disability narratives by tracing the shift in modernity from a wonder narrative to a medical narrative of disability. Such a historical vantage allows him to argue that Sacks's more recent work demedicalizes disability by returning to the model of viewing disability as a source of wonder. In fact, Cassuto suggests, Sacks transforms the medical case narrative into an autobiographical genre of travel narrative that invokes the premodern response of wonder.

The next essay both extends Couser's opening discussion of disability narrative and complicates assertions that ableism primarily developed in modernity. Encarción Juárez examines the spiritual autobiography of a fifteenth-century deaf and disabled Castilian nun,

Teresa de Cartagena, whose *Arboleda de los enfermos* (Grove of the Infirm) focuses on disability as a source for personal insight and literary creation. Juárez finds in Cartagena's narrative the seeds of a social model for disability, in that the nun insists that the hardship of disability lies not so much in her impairments as in the social isolation and stigmatization she experiences. Juárez's analysis establishes Cartagena's autobiography as a predecessor for the many personal narratives of disability that develop as a significant genre.

In "Reconstructing the Posthuman Feminist Body," Diane Price Herndl echoes Jeffreys's essay by speaking autobiographically. From the standpoint of a breast cancer survivor, Herndl engages Audre Lorde in a posthumous dialogue about the feminist politics of breast prostheses and reconstructive-cosmetic surgery. She interrogates feminist and poststructuralist theories about the integrity of the self, the authenticity of the body, the politics of silence, the relation between self and body, and what constitutes a feminist life. She thus illustrates how a disabled perspective complicates feminist theory, even as she articulates the position of a disabled feminist subject as a posthuman one.

Both Herndl's autobiographical exploration and Nancy Mairs's contribution to this collection, "Sex and Death," exemplify how disability autobiography can contest current ideologies about disability. Mairs's influential disability autobiographies and essays have been widely circulated and well received for the past decade. Here Mairs offers her trademark fusion of the critical essay and the personal disability narrative. Her twinned meditation on disabled women's sexuality and the question of so-called physician-assisted suicide invokes the recent politics of disability rights organizations such as Not Dead Yet that contend that physician-assisted suicide directly discriminates against disabled people. Her personal questioning of the controversial limits in this ideological debate powerfully demonstrates autobiography's challenge to pro forma politics and beliefs about the tragedy of disability. She holds out the freedom to choose physician-assisted suicide in her own personal future, while arguing against the superficial understanding of disability by the right-to-die movement.

Rehabilitating Representation

The essays in this section provide examples of how introducing disability as a critical category produces fresh and provocative readings of literary and artistic traditions. The subjects of these studies range from the fifteenth to the twentieth century and represent British, American, French, and German traditions. They consider disability's role in illustrations, figural art, paintings, novels, poetry, and essays. They attest that disability is a fundamental thematic element in a diverse spectrum of literary and artistic works across time, genres, and national literatures. These essays exemplify not only disability's widespread presence but also its potential to expand our understanding of literary and artistic modes.

In "Infinities of Forms," a title drawn from an essay on disability by the fifteenth-century French writer Michel de Montaigne, Sharon Snyder seeks out key figures of disability across artistic traditions. In contrast to Davis's argument that artistic texts reiterate social views of normalcy, she contends that literature and art often contradict stereotypes of disability. Her exploration of literary and artistic archives identifies writers and artists who fashion disability perspectives that overtly contrast with their era's restrictive beliefs. Snyder's cross-cultural catalog is an overview of valuable source materials for further research on disability in history.

Continuing the cross-genre work, Helen Deutsch's "Exemplary Aberration" places the authorial body in history by analyzing eighteenth-century textual and visual representations of Samuel Johnson. Genius, Deutsch argues, was constructed as disability during this period of transition when "exceptional individuality" moved from the category of wonder to the province of science in Western thought. Deutsch's essay, like many others in this volume, exemplifies a scholarly archaeology that "attempts to restore to cultural memory [. . .] bodily difference in all its social and ideological ambiguity."

In the next essay, "Bulwer's Speaking Hands," Jennifer Nelson reveals the influence of sign language on the rhetorical tradition from seventeenth-century British culture. In an analysis of John Bulwer's theoretical treatise on the role of gesture in rhetoric, she demonstrates that Bulwer's familiarity with sign language led him to link gesture and speech within the oral tradition of rhetoric. As Nelson probes Bulwer's complex relation to sign language, she both demonstrates the influence of deafness on rhetorical traditions and reveals the roots of biases against sign language in a form that insists on the primacy of speech as the mark of the civilized and fully human.

Martha Stoddard Holmes's essay, "The Twin Structure," assesses the relation between gender and disability as she explores the use of the device in sentimental Victorian fiction in which one twin is nondisabled and one disabled. Analyzing fiction by Charles Dickens, Charlotte Mary Yonge, and Wilkie Collins, Holmes examines the entanglement among disability, femininity, and the notion of the feeling body in Victorian sentimental ideology. She explicitly identifies disabled characters in these texts as members of a social group with a history and an identity.

In the nineteenth-century American tradition, the next two essays show a crucial disability presence in two of the United States' most canonical authors, Walt Whitman and Mark Twain. First, Christopher Krentz explores Mark Twain's use of deafness as a source of humor. By theorizing the "hearing line" as a liminal site between hearing and deafness where humor can be produced, he unearths Twain's many comic jesters and occasional sentimental figures. This ambivalent, shifting line suggests Twain's own conflict between fascination and envy regarding deafness. Krentz's trenchant analysis of how deafness operates in Twain's writing contributes to the developing critical conversation about passing in American literature.

In a similar vein, "How Dare a Sick Man?" locates a conflict that emerges when Robert Scholnick considers how perfect health operates as a metaphor in Whitman's poetic representation of democracy. The figure of the disabled body, he contends, reveals a collision between Whitman's project of perfectibility and his project of inclusion, creating a paradox at the heart of his poetry. Scholnick mines this tension in Whitman's poetry to suggest the ideological and potentially eugenic assumptions in concepts such as health and fitness.

Carol Poore's essay uncovers a politically radical disability presence in the twentieth-century German exile novel *Das Beil von Wandsbek (The Axe of Wandsbek)*, by Arnold Zweig. Published immediately after the Nazi euthanasia campaign against disabled people, Zweig's novel links the fascist elimination of ethnic populations with the fascist elimination of disabled populations. By analyzing the complex rendering of the disabled figure Tom Barfey in Zweig's realist antifascist novel, Poore contributes to the liberatory project of literary critics who locate characters that challenge stereotypical portrayals of stigmatized groups. Her essay is thus a fine example of the politically engaged critical genre that culls from literary representations liberatory ways of imagining disability and disabled people.

Sander Gilman examines the figure of the fat detective to expand the scope of disability identity to include the stigma of obesity. By tracing the opposing cultural figures of the lean philosopher and the fat detective in late-nineteenth- and early-twentieth-century detective fiction, Gilman finds a shift in how the British and Americans imagined the thinking body. In contemporary detective fiction he uncovers a figure who is mentally acute because of, rather than despite, his obese body. Sensitive and intelligent, this figure, Gilman suggests, is a model for the androgynous new man of the contemporary postfeminist period.

Enabling Pedagogy

The essays in the final section present strategies for integrating disability into teaching practices, particularly in literature and composition courses. They also examine some of the concerns that arise when disability enters such classrooms. Understanding disability as a civil rights issue, an identity group, or a politicized representational system is often new terrain for students and can prove politically and personally fraught, especially in regard to the question of a student's or teacher's disability status. Moreover, because disability is a highly stigmatized identity, it is sometimes imagined as inappropriate or too private for classroom analysis. Like introducing race, gender, and queer theories into classroom discussions and dynamics, discussing disability in other than the expected ways can lead to confusion, guilt, defensiveness, backlash, and silencing in teaching situations. But it can also provide insights, perspectives, challenges, and interchanges that expand understanding and foster innovative learning. These essays offer approaches that capitalize on disability's potential to revolutionize thought and action through new knowledge.

In "Disabilities, Bodies, Voices," Jim Swan examines issues in the teaching of disability from a broad theoretical perspective. In some ways grounding Davis's ideas in "Bodies of Difference," he suggests that teaching might highlight the body as a locus of perception and experience. Probing how disabled bodies both inhabit and create different worlds in contrast to nondisabled bodies, Swan advances a theory of "embodied semantics" as a way to consider disability in the classroom.

James C. Wilson and Cynthia Lewiecki-Wilson's essay, "Constructing a Third Space," presents an extended theoretical and practical paradigm for teaching disability. The authors return to an idea developed in this volume's initial essays: the transformative power of disability as a critical category. Speaking as parents of a disabled child, they show how a disability presence can question deeply entrenched ableist assumptions and exclusionary institutional practices and environments. By marshaling the radical potential of "critical literacy, feminist, and postcolonial studies," the authors—along with all the essayists in *Disability Studies*—"challenge educators to think beyond accommodation, to make their classrooms a third space, one in which teacher, students, and knowledge making are transformed by encounters with disability."

By blending the theory and practice of teaching about and with a disability, Georgina Kleege's essay, "Disabled Students Come Out," offers an account of the complicated issues surrounding coming out as disabled for both teachers and students. Recognizing the complexity of disability identity, Kleege models in her narrative a process of inquiry, including relational strategies and broad ethical as well as political considerations that can serve us all in integrating disability, disabled students, and disabled colleagues into the teaching arena.

Brenda Jo Brueggemann concludes this section with a sustained auto-biographical, pedagogical essay that offers her encounters as a disabled (but invisibly so) teacher in four different courses that centered on disability. Drawing from this wide range of classroom experience, she lays out some of the key goals achieved and issues encountered when disability becomes the primary critical vehicle for reading, writing, and interpreting in language and literature classrooms. In addition, she chronicles the means and ends for inserting disability perspectives in many non-disability-centered courses she teaches. In both kinds of courses and in both pedagogical approaches—whether disability is at the center or on the periphery—Brueggemann aims for disability as insight, a critical and imaginative engagement that reconfigures the concepts of ability and normalcy. Her classroom applications show how, collectively, the topics and concerns of the essays in *Disability Studies* comprise the terms of an enabling pedagogy.

BJB, RG-T, SLS, 2002

NOTES

1. Elaine Scarry's *The Body in Pain* comments on the social implications of the erasure of Christ's body.
2. Distinction is often made between *deaf,* a condition of audiological impairment, and *Deaf,* a cultural and linguistic designation of group membership based on one's use of and affinity with sign language. Contributors in this volume vary in their blended and separate uses of these two terms.

Enabling Theory

DAVID T. MITCHELL

Narrative Prosthesis and the Materiality of Metaphor

Literature and the Undisciplined Body of Disability

This essay develops a narrative theory of shared characteristics in the
literary representation of disability. It also seeks to demonstrate one of a
variety of approaches in disability studies to the problem that disability
and disabled populations pose to all cultures. Nearly every culture views
disability as a problem in need of a solution, and this belief establishes
one of the major modes of historical address directed toward people
with disabilities. The necessity for developing various kinds of cultural
accommodations to handle the problem of physical difference (i.e.,
through charitable organizations, modifications of physical architecture,
welfare doles, quarantine, genocide, euthanasia programs, etc.) situates
people with disabilities in a profoundly ambivalent relation to the cultures and stories they inhabit. The perception of a crisis or a special
situation has made disabled people not only the subject of governmental policies and communal programs but also a primary object of literary
representation.

My central thesis here centers not simply on the fact that people
with disabilities have been the objects of representational treatments
but also on the fact that their presence in literary narrative is primarily
twofold: disability pervades literary narrative, first, as a stock feature of
characterization and, second, as an opportunistic metaphoric device.
Sharon Snyder and I have termed the perpetual discursive dependency

15

on disability in the first instance *narrative prosthesis* (Mitchell and Snyder, *Narrative Prosthesis*). Disability lends a distinctive idiosyncrasy to any characters that differentiate themselves from the anonymous background of the norm. To exemplify this phenomenon, I first analyze the children's book *The Steadfast Tin Soldier* in order to demonstrate that disability serves as an impetus of the storyteller's efforts. I then show that disability also serves as a metaphoric signifier of social and individual collapse.

Physical and cognitive anomalies promise to lend a tangible body to textual abstractions; I term this metaphoric use of disability the materiality of metaphor and analyze its workings in a discussion of Sophocles's *Oedipus the King*. I contend that disability's centrality to these two principal representational strategies establishes a conundrum: while stories rely on the potency of disability as a symbolic figure, they rarely take up disability as an experience of social or political dimensions.

The narrative deployment of disability hinges on the identification of physical and cognitive differences as mutable categories of cultural investment. In literary narratives, disability serves as an interrupting force that confronts cultural truisms. John Limon has argued that, unlike science, literature functions as an "undisciplined discipline" that refuses to adhere to strict laws or established tests of proof (5). Instead, Limon characterizes literature as an upstart in the ranks of the truth-telling discourses of academic or research communities. Rather than legitimize its findings as a product of professional formulas, literature seeks to demonstrate that truth is a variable and contextual phenomenon produced by the convergence of institutional power, ideologies, and influence. Functioning without absolute standards or proof, literature can be said to behave like an unruly sister to the masculine domain of hard science. Limon demonstrates that as a result of this differentiation between literature and science, the literary surrenders its ability to produce truth while also gaining the advantage of flexibility or critique that its antidisciplinarity affords.

Like that of literature, disability's relation to the stable body is one of unruliness. As Sharon Snyder and I discuss in our introduction to *The Body and Physical Difference*, "disability might be characterized as that which exceeds a culture's predictive capacities or effective interventions. [. . . It] defies correction and tends to operate according to its own idiosyncratic rules" (3). Disabled bodies prove undisciplined because they refuse to conform to the controlling narratives of medical or rehabilitative science. In doing so, they are designated as pathological. The inherent vulnerability and variability of bodies serves literary narratives as a metonym for that which refuses to conform to the disciplinary desire for order and rationality so apparent in empirical discourses. In this schema, disability acts as a metaphor and fleshly example of the body's unruly resistance to what Lennard Davis has theorized as the cultural desire to "enforce normalcy" (*Enforcing*).[1] The body's weighty materiality functions as a textual and cultural other—an object with its own undisciplined language that exceeds the text's (and thus culture's) ability to control it.

Disability serves as a symbolic symptom to be interpreted by discourses on the body. Whether a culture approaches the body's dynamic materiality as a denigrated symbol of earthly contamination (as in early Christian cultures), or as a perfectible *techné* of the self (as in ancient Athenian culture), or as an object of social symbolism (as in the culture of the Renaissance), or as a classifiable object of bodily averages (as in the Enlightenment), or as specular commodity in the age of electronic media (as in postmodernism), disability inaugurates the need to interpret human differences both biological and imagined. Whereas the able body has no definitional core (it poses as transparently average or normal), the disabled body surfaces as any body capable of being narrated as outside the norm.

In such a representational schema, literary narratives revisit disabled bodies as reminders of the real physical limits that weigh down transcendent ideals of the truth-seeking disciplines. In this sense, disability serves as the "hard kernel" or recalcitrant corporeal matter that cannot be deconstructed away by the textual operations of the most canny narratives or philosophical idealisms.[2] Representations of disability, then, allow an interrogation of static beliefs about the body while also erupting as the unseemly matter of narrative that cannot be textually contained. The coinage of the phrase "narrative prosthesis" argues that disability has been used throughout history as a crutch on which literary narratives lean for their representational power, disruptive potentiality, and social critique. Yet, at the same time, literature avoids designating disability itself as a source for derisive social myths that need to be interrogated. Instead, disability plays host to a panoply of other social maladies that writers seek to address. Disabled bodies show up in literary narratives as dynamic entities that resist or refuse the cultural scripts assigned to them. The out-of-control body of literature has been historically used to identify the workings of dominant ideology in regard to nearly everything but the social construction of disability itself.

The (In)Visibility of Prostheses

The hypothesis of this discursive dependency on disability at first glance strikes most scholars and readers as relatively insubstantial. During a recent conference of the Herman Melville Society held in Völös, Greece, I met a scholar from Japan interested in representations of disability in American literature. When asked if Japanese literature made use of disabled characters to the same extent as American and European literatures, he honestly replied that he had never encountered any. On further reflection he listed several examples and laughingly added that of course the Nobel Prize winner Kinzeburo Oe wrote almost exclusively about the subject. This surprise about the pervasive nature of disabled images in national literatures catches unaware even the most knowledgeable scholars. Readers tend to filter a multitude of disability figures absently out of their imaginations. For film scholarship on disability, Paul Longmore has perceptively formulated this paradox in his groundbreaking essay "Screening Stereotypes," by asking why we screen so many images of disability and simultaneously screen them out of our minds. This same phenomenon can be applied to literary discourses.

Our current models of minority representation in literature tend to formulate this problem of discursive neglect in the obverse manner. One might expect to find the argument in disability studies that disability is an ignored, overlooked, or marginal experience in literary narrative—that its absence marks an ominous silence in the literary repertoire of human experiences. In pursuing such an argument, one could rightly redress, castigate, or bemoan the neglect of this essential life experience in discourses that ought to have taken up the important task of exploring disability in serious artistic terms. In such an approach, disability would prove to be an unarticulated subject whose real-life counterparts could then charge that their social marginality was the result of a lack of representational interest outside medical discourses. Such a methodology would theorize that disability's absence proves evident a telling cultural repression to escape the reality of biological and cognitive variations. We might answer Longmore's query about screening out disability by pointing a finger at the absence of our images in mainstream and artistic discourses.

Yet disability occupies a rather unusual literary history, one that contrasts with the representation of many other minority identities. Even if we disregard the fact that entire fields of study have been devoted to the assessment, cataloging, pathologization, objectification, and rehabilita-

tion of disability, one comes to be struck by disability's prevalence in discourses outside medicine and the other hard sciences. With regard to
the relation between the social marginality of people with disabilities
and their corresponding representational milieus, disability has suffered
a different representational fate. While racial, sexual, and ethnic criticisms
have often founded their critiques on the pervasive absence of their experiences in the dominant culture's literature, images of disability abound in
literary history. Once readers begin to actively seek out representations
of disability in our literatures, it is difficult for them to avoid being struck
by disability's tendency to proliferate in texts with which they believed
themselves to be utterly familiar.[3] Consequently, as in the above mentioned anecdote about disability images in Japanese literature, the representation of people with disabilities is far from absent or tangential.
Our critical models have failed to attend to questions of the utility of disability to numerous discursive modes, including literature. This failure
to attend to disability's meanings in our critical models provides another,
and more integral, explanation for why disability is so often screened
out of our imaginations even as we consume them.

For the moment let us assume these proliferating images of disability to be fact. If such a characterization turned out to be more true than
false, the historical marginality of disabled people would prove to occupy a much different cultural fate than that of other minority identities
in literary narratives.[4] My working hypothesis is paradoxical: disabled
peoples' social invisibility has occurred in the wake of their perpetual
circulation throughout literary history. This question is not simply a
matter of stereotypes or "bad objects," to borrow Naomi Schor's phrase.[5]
Rather, the representation of disability strikes at the very core of cultural
definitions and values.

What is the significance of the fact that the earliest known
cuneiform tablets contain a catalog of 120 omens interpreted from the
deformities of Sumarian fetuses and irregularly shaped sheep's and
calves' livers? How does one explain the centrality of multiply disabled
gods to Norse myths, such as the blind Hod, the one-eyed Odin, the one-
armed Tyr, and the singular representation of Hephaestus, the crook-
footed god, in Greek literature (see L. Bragg, "Mute God" and "Oedipus")?
Why do our most memorable literary characters so often bear the blemish of a disability—Philoctetes, Richard III, Chillingworth, Captain Ahab,
Holden Caulfield, Wallace Stegner's Lyman Ward, and so on? Why does
the visual spectacle of so many disabilities become a predominating
trope in the print medium of literary texts?

Narrative Prosthesis

What calls stories into being, and what does disability have to do with this most basic preoccupation of narrative? Narrative prosthesis (or the dependency of literary narratives on disability) is the notion that all narratives operate out of a desire to compensate for a limitation or to reign in excessiveness. This narrative approach to difference identifies the literary object par excellence as that which has somehow become out of the ordinary—a deviation from a widely accepted cultural norm. Literary narratives seek to begin a process of explanatory compensation wherein perceived aberrancies can be rescued from ignorance, neglect, or misunderstanding for their readerships. As Michel de Certeau explains in his well-known essay "Montaigne's 'Of Cannibals': The Savage 'I,'" the development of the New World travel narrative in the fifteenth and sixteenth centuries provides a model for thinking about the movement of all narrative. A narrative is inaugurated "by the search for the strange, which is presumed different from the place assigned it in the beginning by the discourse of the culture" from which it originates (69). The very need for a story is called into being when something has gone amiss with the known world, and thus the language of a tale seeks to comprehend that which has stepped out of line. In this sense, stories compensate for an unknown or unnatural deviance that begs for an explanation.

The concept of narrative prosthesis evolves out of this specific recognition: a narrative issues to resolve or correct—to "prostheticize," in David Wills's sense of the term—a deviance marked as abnormal or improper in a social context. A simple schematic of narrative structure might run: first, a deviance or marked difference is exposed to a reader; second, a narrative consolidates the need for its own existence by calling for an explanation of the deviation's origins and formative consequences; third, the deviance is brought from the periphery of concerns to the center stage of the story to come; and fourth, the remainder of the story seeks to rehabilitate or fix the deviance in some manner, shape, or form. This fourth move toward the repair of deviance may involve an obliteration of the difference through a cure, the rescue of the despised object from social censure, the extermination of the deviant as a purification of the social body, or the revaluation of an alternative mode of experience. Since what we now call disability has been historically narrated as that which characterizes a body as deviant from shared norms of bodily appearance and ability, disability has functioned throughout history as one of the most marked and remarked on differences that propel the act of storytelling into existence. Narratives turn signs of cultural deviance into textually marked bodies.

In one of my son's books, entitled *The Steadfast Tin Soldier* (K. Campbell), this prosthetic relation of narrative to physical difference can be quickly exemplified. The story opens with a child's receiving a box of tin soldiers as a birthday gift. The twenty-five soldiers stand erect and uniform in every way, for they "had all been made from the same tin spoon" (1). Each of the soldiers comes equipped with a rifle and pointed bayonet, a blue-and-red outfit signifying membership in the same regiment, black boots, and a stern military visage. The narrator immediately inaugurates the conflict that will propel the story by pointing out a flaw in one soldier that mars the uniformity of the gift: "All of the soldiers were exactly alike, with the exception of one, who differed from the rest in having only one leg" (2). This unfortunate blemish, which mars the otherwise flawless ideal of soldiers standing in unison, becomes the springboard for the story. The missing leg is a locus for attention, and from this imperfection the story ensues. The twenty-four perfect soldiers are quickly left behind in the box, for the very fact of their perfection and uniformity—the ideal or intended soldier's form—promises no story. As Barbara Maria Stafford points out, "There [is] only a single way of being healthy and lovely, but an infinity of ways of being sick and wretched" (284). This "infinity" helps explain the pervasive dependency of literary narratives on the trope of disability. Narrative interest solidifies only in the identification and pursuit of an anomaly that inaugurates the exceptional tale or the tale of exception.

The story of *The Steadfast Tin Soldier* stands in a prosthetic relation to the missing leg of the titular protagonist (fig. 1). The narrative in question (and narrative in a general sense) seeks to rehabilitate or compensate for its lesser subject by demonstrating that the outward flaw attracts the storyteller's—and by extension the reader's—interest. The act of characterization is such that the narrative must establish the exceptionality of its subject matter to justify the telling of a story. A subject demands a story only in relation to the degree that it can establish what Rosemarie Garland-Thomson calls its "extraordinary" circumstances.[6] The normal, routine, average, and familiar (by definition) fail to mobilize the storytelling effort, because they fall short of the litmus test of exceptionality that generates plot. The anonymity of normalcy is no story at all. Deviance serves as the basis and common denominator of all narrative. In this sense, the missing leg preselects the aberrant soldier as the story's

Figure 1

Illustration by David Delamare from *The Steadfast Tin Soldier*. Courtesy of Spiderwebart Gallery

focus, for his physical difference exiles him from the rank and file of the uniform and physically undifferentiated troop. Whereas a sociality might reject, isolate, institutionalize, reprimand, or obliterate this liability of having a single leg, narrative embraces the opportunity that such a lack provides—in fact, narrative wills it into existence—because it is the impetus that calls a story into being.

If we take the story of the tin soldier as exemplary (and I'm arguing that we should), the law of disability in narrative can be summed up by the formula "Difference demands display. Display demands difference" (Snyder). The arrival of a narrative must be attended by the unsightly eruption of the anomalous (often physical in nature) in the social field of vision. The (re)marking of disability begins with a stare, a gesture of disgust, a slander or derisive comment on bodily deviance, a note of gossip about a rare or unsightly presence, a comment on the unsuitability of deformity for the appetites of polite society, or a sentiment about the unfortunate circumstances that bring disabilities into being. This ruling out-of-bounds of the socially anomalous subject engenders an act of violence that stories seek to rescue or reclaim as worthy of narrative attention. Stories always perform a compensatory function in their efforts to renew interest in a previously denigrated object. While there exist a myriad of inroads to the identification of the anomalous—femininity,

race, class, sexuality—disability services this narrative appetite for difference as often as any other constructed category of deviance.

The politics of this recourse to disability as a device of narrative characterization demonstrates the importance of disability to the storytelling
act itself. Literary narratives support our appetites for the exotic by posing disability as an alien terrain that promises the revelation of a previously uncomprehended experience. Literature borrows the potency of
the lure of difference that a socially stigmatized condition provides. Yet
the reliance on disability in narrative rarely develops into a means of
identifying people with disabilities as a disenfranchised cultural constituency. The ascription of absolute singularity to disability performs a
contradictory operation: a character stands out as a result of an attributed blemish, but this exceptionality disqualifies the character from possessing a shared social identity. As in *The Steadfast Tin Soldier,* a narrative
disability establishes the uniqueness of a character, a uniqueness that is
quickly seen as more than a purely biological fact. Disability marks a
character as unlike the rest of a fiction's cast, and once singled out, the
character proceeds to become a case of special interest who retains originality to the detriment of all other characteristics. Disability cannot be
accommodated in the ranks of the norm(als), and thus there are two options for dealing with the difference that drives the story's plot: a disability is either left behind or punished for its lack of conformity.

In *The Steadfast Tin Soldier* we witness the exercise of both options to
the visible difference that the protagonist's disability poses. Once the soldier's incomplete leg is identified, that difference is quickly nullified.
Nowhere in the story does the narrator call attention to a difficult nego-
tiation that must be attempted as a result of the missing appendage. In
fact, like the adventurer of Certeau's paradigmatic travel narrative, the
tin figure undergoes a series of epic encounters without further reference to his limitation. After he falls out of a window, his bayonet gets
stuck in a crack; a storm rages over him later that night; two boys find
the figure, place him into a newspaper boat, and sail him down the gut-
ter into a street drain; he is accosted by a street rat who poses as gate-
keeper to the underworld; the newspaper boat sinks in a canal, where
the soldier is swallowed by a large fish; and finally he is returned to his
home, when the family purchases the fish for dinner and discovers the
one-legged figure in its belly. The series of dangerous encounters recalls
the adventure of the physically able Odysseus on his way home from
Troy. The tin soldier endures the physically taxing experience without

any further remark made on the incomplete leg in the course of the tale. The journey and ultimate return home embody the cyclical nature of all narrative (and the story of disability in particular)—the identification of deficiency inaugurates the need for a story but then is quickly forgotten once the difference is established.

Yet a marred appearance cannot ultimately be allowed to return home unscathed. Near the end of the story the significance of the missing leg returns when the tin soldier is reintroduced to his love—the paper maiden who pirouettes on one leg. Because the soldier mistakes the dancer as possessing, like him, only one leg, the story's conclusion hinges on the irony of an argument about human attraction based on shared likeness. If the maiden shares the fate of one-leggedness, then, the soldier reasons, she must be meant for him. However, in a narrative twist of deus ex machina the blemished soldier is inexplicably thrown into the fire by a boy right at the moment of his imagined reconciliation with the one-legged maiden. One could read this ending as a punishment for his desiring someone physically perfect, unlike him. Mary Shelley's Frankenstein tale ends with the monster's promise of self-obliteration by fire in the wake of the villagers' misinterpretation of him; the tin soldier fable reaches its conclusion in a similar manner. Disability inaugurates narrative, but narrative inevitably punishes its own prurient interests by overseeing the extermination of the object of its fascination.

The Materiality of Metaphor

The problem of disability representation is not the search for a more positive story of disability, as it has often been formulated in disability studies, but rather the thoroughgoing challenge that disability invites of the undergirding authorization to interpret. There is a politics at stake in the fact that disability inaugurates an explanatory opportunity that the unmarked body eludes by virtue of its physical anonymity. Because disability has served primarily as a metaphor for things gone awry with bodily and social orders (as opposed to the inherent mutability of bodies themselves), there is a cumulative material impact on cultural attitudes toward disabled people in general. Disability proves an exceptional textual fate in that it is deployed in literary narrative as a master metaphor for social ills; thus the characterization of disability provides a means through which literature performs its social critique while simultaneously sedimenting stigmatizing beliefs about people with disabilities.

Representations of the body provide a foundation for grounding abstract meanings in the specifics of an individual story. Whereas physical or cognitive differences identify an exceptional character in need of a compensatory narrative, metaphors of disability serve to extrapolate the meaning of a bodily flaw into cosmological significance. Blindness may represent the incapacity of humanity to see into the future; lameness can designate the crippling effects of social ideologies; physical deformity may symbolize corrupt corporate policies; deafness may represent a refusal of leaders to listen to their constituencies; diabetes might conjure up images of a gluttonous commodity culture; amputation can provide evidence of an unchecked medical industry; and so on. While disability as an experience is rarely narrated in terms of its own significance, disability as a metaphor allows writers to access concerns on a metaphysical scale. Literary portrayals of disabled bodies move between the specificity of a character's overriding identifying feature and the larger concerns of social disorder. In either case, the social navigation of stigma or the physical demands of a disability are slighted in favor of gesturing toward a symbolic register of commentary on the conditions of the universe.

Like the cycle of dramas surrounding the figure of Oedipus (another renowned disabled fictional creation), cultures thrive on solving the riddle of disability's rhyme and reason (fig. 2). When the limping Greek

Figure 2

Oedipus and the Sphinx. Detail. By Gustave Moreau (1826–98). Oil on canvas, 1864. Courtesy of the Metropolitan Museum of Art

protagonist overcomes the Sphinx by supplying the answer "Man who walks with a cane" as the concluding puzzle piece to her three-part riddle—"What walks on four legs in the morning, two in the afternoon, and three at night?"—we must assume that his own disability served as an experiential source for this insight. The master riddle solver in effect trumps the Sphinx's feminine monstrosity with knowledge acquired from his experience of inhabiting an alien body. Oedipus taps into disability as an interpretive source for his riddle-solving methodology. Whereas disability usually provides the riddle in need of a narrative solution, in this instance the experience of disability momentarily serves as the source of Oedipus's interpretive mastery.

Yet Sophocles's willingness to represent disability as a mode of experience-based knowledge proves a rare literary occasion and a fleeting moment in the play's dramatic structure. While Oedipus solves the Sphinx's riddle in the wake of his physical experience as a lame interpreter and an interpreter of lameness, his disability remains inconsequential to the myth's plot. Like the tin soldier's missing leg, Oedipus's disability—Laius pinned his infant son's ankles as he sent him off to die of exposure—marks Oedipus's character as distinctive and worthy of an exceptional tale. Beyond this physical fact, Sophocles neglects to explore the relation of the body's mediating function to Oedipus's subjectivity. The disability remains a physical fact of Oedipus's character that the text literally overlooks once this difference is established; the disability is little more than a repressed remnant of his childhood. Perhaps those who share the stage with Oedipus have learned to look away from his disability in order to avoid commenting on the existence of the protagonist's physical difference.

Yet, without the pinning of Oedipus's ankles and his resulting lameness two important aspects of the plot would be compromised. First, Oedipus would falter at the riddle of the Sphinx like others before him and fall prey to the voracious appetite of the she-beast; second, Sophocles's protagonist would lose the physical sign that literally connects him to an otherwise inscrutable past. In this sense Oedipus's physical difference secures key components of the plot that allow the riddle of his identity to be unraveled. At the same time, his disability provokes no substantive commentary in the course of the drama. Beyond establishing the literal source of Oedipus's ability to solve the baffling riddle, the earlier pun about Oedipus as a lame interpreter allows the dramatist to metaphorize humanity's incapacity to fathom the dicta of the gods. Lameness (and, later in the drama, blindness) serves as a symbol for the tragedy of hubris or the limits of human knowledge. This movement exemplifies the literary oscillation between micro (personal) and macro (social) levels of metaphoric meaning supplied by disability.

What is of interest for a narrative theory of disability in this ancient text is the way in which one can read the text's representational strategy as a paradigm for literary approaches to disability in general. The ability of disabled characters to allow authors the metaphoric play between social and individual registers of meaning making establishes the role of the body in literature as a critical bridge between concrete experience and abstract commentary. In his study of editorial cartoonings and caricatures of the body leading up to the French revolution, Antoine de Baecque argues that the corporeal metaphor provided a means of giving the abstractions of political ideals an embodied power. To provide a visual correlative to a political commentary, French cartoonists and essayists deployed the body as a metaphor because the body "succeeds in *connecting* narrative and knowledge, meaning and knowing" in a visible and visceral manner (5). For de Baecque, textual embodiment provides a concrete visible form to an otherwise abstract idea. To give an abstraction a literal body allows an ideology to simulate a foothold in the material world that it would otherwise fail to procure.

Whereas an ideal such as democracy signifies an abstracted notion of governmental and economic reform, de Baecque argues, that the embodied caricature of a hunchbacked monarch overshadowed by a physically superior democratic citizen, for example, proves more powerful than any ideological argument. Instead of political harangue the body offers an illusion of fixity to a textualized belief:

> [Body] metaphors were able simultaneously to describe the event and to make the description attain the level of the imaginary. The deployment of these bodily *topoi*—the degeneracy of the nobility, the impotence of the king, the herculean strength of the citizenry, the goddesses of politics appearing naked like Truth, the congenital deformity of the aristocrats, the bleeding wound of the martyrs—allowed political society to represent itself at a pivotal moment of its history. [. . .] One must pass through the [bodily] forms of a narrative in order to reach knowledge. (4–5)

Such a process of giving body to belief exemplifies the corporeal seductiveness of the body for textual mediums. The desire to access the seeming solidity of the body's materiality offers representational literatures a way of grasping that which is most unavailable to them. For de Baecque, representing a body in its specificity as the bearer of an otherwise intangible concept grounds the reality of an ideological meaning. The passage through a bodily form helps secure a knowledge that would otherwise drift away of its own insubstantiality. The corporeal metaphor offers narrative the one thing it cannot possess—an anchor in materiality. Such a process embodies what I term the materiality of metaphor. Like cartooning, literature functions as a written form of expression that aims to give body to the abstractions of theory through accounts that are dependent on the effective evocation of physical and sensory life far more than on espoused beliefs.

Yet, while de Baecque's theory of the material metaphor argues that the attempt to harness the body to a specific ideological program provides the text with an illusory opportunity to embody Truth, he overlooks the fact that the same process embeds the body in a limiting array of symbolic meanings: crippling conditions equate with monarchical immobility, corpulence evidences tyrannical greed, deformity represents malevolent motivation, and so on. While delineating his corporeal catalog of bodily metaphors, the historian depends for his readings almost exclusively on the potent symbolism of disabled bodies in particular without commenting on the meaning of this dependency. In the above quotation, for instance, visible degeneracy, impotency, congenital deformity, festering ulcerations, and bleeding wounds all provide the contrastive bodily coordinates to the muscular, aesthetic, and symmetrical bodies of the healthy citizenry. One cannot narrate the story of a healthy body (or, apparently, of a national reform movement) without the contrastive device of disability to bear out the symbolic potency of the message. The materiality of metaphor via disabled bodies gives all bodies a tangible essence, in that the healthy corporeal surface fails to achieve its symbolic effect without its disabled counterpart.

As Georges Canguilhem has pointed out, the body calls attention to itself only in the midst of its breakdown or disrepair (209). The representation of the process of breakdown or incapacity is fraught with political and ideological significance. To make the body speak its experience, one must give a language to it. Elaine Scarry argues that "there is ordinarily no language for [the body in] pain" (13). I would argue that the body itself has no language, since language is foreign to its materiality. The body must be spoken for if its meanings are to prove narratable. The narration of the disabled body allows a textual body to mean through its long-standing historical representation as an overdetermined symbolic surface; the disabled body also offers narrative the illusion of grounding abstract knowledge in a bodily materiality. If the body is the other of text, then textual representation seeks access to that which is most outside its ability to grasp. If the nondysfunctional body proves too ordinary to narrate, the disabled body becomes a paramount device of characterization in this process. Narrative prosthesis or the dependency on disability proves essential to, even the essence of, the story of difference.

NOTES

1. There is an equivalent problem to the representation of disability in literary narratives in our own critical rubrics of the body. The disabled body continues to fall outside critical categories that identify bodies as the product of cultural constructions. While challenging a generic notion of the white, male body as ideological proves desirable in our present moment in the realms of race, gender, sexuality, and class, there has been a more pernicious history of literary and critical approaches to the disabled body. In the introduction to *The Body and Physical Difference*, Sharon Snyder and I argue that minority discourses in the humanities all tend to deploy the evidence of "corporeal aberrancy" as a means of identifying the invention of an ideologically encoded body. Yet, "while physical aberrancy is often recognized as constructed and historically variable it is rarely remarked upon as its own legitimized or politically fraught identity" (5).

2. In his book *The Sublime Object of Ideology* (98), Slavoj Žižek extracts the notion of the hard kernel of ideology from the theories of Jacques Lacan. For Žižek, the notion of the hard kernel represents that underlying core of belief that refuses to be deconstructed away by even the most radical operations of political critique. More than merely a rational component of ideological identification, the Žižekian hard kernel represents the irrationality behind belief that secures the interpellated subject's illogical participation in a linguistically permeable system.

3. A brief catalog of disabled representations in literature includes some of the most influential figurations of suffering humanity across periods and cultures: the crippled Greek god Hephaestus; Montaigne's sexually potent limping women; Shakespeare's hunchbacked king, Richard III; Frankenstein's deformed monster; Charlotte Brontë's madwoman in the attic; Melville's one-legged, monomaniacal Captain Ahab; Nietzsche's philosophical grotesques; Hemingway's wounded war veterans; Morrison's truncated and scarred ex-slaves; Borges's blind librarian; Oe's autistic son.

4. The documentation of disability's proliferation in literary texts is evidenced in new works, including Davis's *Enforcing Normalcy*, Garland-Thomson's *Extraordinary Bodies*, and Mitchell and Snyder's *The Body and Physical Difference*.

5. For Naomi Schor a bad object is a discursive object that has been ruled out of bounds by the prevailing academic politics of the day or one that represents a "critical perversion" (xv). My use of the phrase implies both these definitions in relation to disability. The literary object of disability has been almost entirely neglected by literary criticism in general, until the development, in the mid-1990s, of disability studies in the humanities; and disability as a topic of investigation still strikes many as a perverse interest for academic contemplation. To

these two definitions I would also add that the labeling of disability as a bad object nonetheless overlooks the fact that disabilities fill the pages of literary interest.

6. Her *Extraordinary Bodies: Figuring Physical Disability in American Culture and Literature* forwards the term *extraordinary* in order to play off of its multiple nuances. The word can suggest the powerful sentimentality of narratives of overcoming so often attached to stories about disabled people; it can also suggest people whose bodies are the products of overdetermined social meanings, where physical differences are exaggerated or performed as a way of enhancing their exoticness, In addition, I share with Garland-Thomson the belief that disabled bodies prove extraordinary in how they expose the variety and mutable nature of physicality itself.

MARK JEFFREYS

The Visible Cripple
(Scars and Other Disfiguring
Displays Included)

One of the defining difficulties for disability studies scholars
is going to be a grappling with ideas and experiences of
physicality in a historical moment of constructivism.
—David T. Mitchell and Sharon L. Snyder

Cultural constructivism is the reigning epistemology of
the humanities. Like scientific empiricism, which is
its dominant rival and frequent target, constructivism is more than just
a way of knowing: it's a way of debunking, a siege engine for the subversion of fortresses of unexamined assumptions and received opinions.
Despite wide variances in theory and application, constructivist approaches are united by the assumption that all knowledge and all ways
of knowing, including the most mathematically rigorous findings of empiricism, are historically confined, ideologically inflected, and culturally
specific. Of course this assumption is self-reflexive, but the danger of
epistemological self-destruction can be reduced by the Socratic strategy
of claiming self-knowledge about one's limitations. Constructivist arguments are conventionally prefaced by some ritual acknowledgment of
their own historical contingency and cultural biases, thus shielding
themselves somewhat from reactions to their forcefulness.

Linked to historical method, constructivist epistemology can be
used to question even the most entrenched assumptions about human
nature, by exposing the cultural foundations of those assumptions and

31

by providing compelling moral narratives explaining how those assumptions evolved to serve the interests of elite segments of societies
and particularly of patriarchal, Eurocentric, colonial, and capitalist societies. Many of the most egregiously oppressive and even genocidal
practices of the modern era, including race laws, eugenics, and the
Holocaust, have been buttressed and defended by the authoritative
rhetoric of objective science.

The power of constructivism, as a liberation epistemology, is that it
tunnels under the claims to transcendent truth that are used to univer-
salize and thus eternalize, as invariant laws of nature, mere social hierarchies such as those that privilege male over female, European over
African, heterosexual over homosexual, normal over abnormal. By under-
mining the very epistemological certainty of empiricism, by exposing the
historically and culturally specific grounds on which such claims to certainty are based, constructivist humanism forcibly reopens closed questions about human nature. Without the engines of constructivist theory
and scholarship laying bare the foundational historical biases of empiricism, the current campaigns of humanist cultural studies would never
have got under way.

Nor, without constructivism, could there have emerged the
humanities-based inquiry into disability. Constructivism opens up the
study of disability, previously the exclusive domain of the biological,
medical, and rehabilitative professions, as a new field of cultural studies.
In particular, constructivism makes possible the argument that disability
is itself not so much a pathological or even biological condition as it is a
cultural condition, a marginalized group identity that has a history of
oppression and exclusion, a stigmatized category created to serve the interests of the dominant ideology and its privileged classes. As Rosemarie
Garland-Thomson writes:

> The "physically disabled" are produced by way of legal, political,
> cultural, and literary narratives that comprise an exclusionary dis-
> course. Constructed as the embodiment of corporeal insufficiency
> and deviance, the physically disabled body becomes a repository
> for social anxieties about such troubling concerns as vulnerability,
> control, and identity. [. . .] Disability is a representation, a cultural
> interpretation of physical transformation or configuration, and a
> comparison of bodies that structures social relations and institu-
> tions. Disability, then, is [. . .] not so much a property of bodies as
> a product of cultural rules about what bodies should be or do.
>   (*Extraordinary Bodies* 6)

However, just as we in disability studies rely heavily on constructivism to justify our preoccupation with the forms, functions, and representations of bodies as cultural artifacts, we are also vulnerable to constructivism's backfiring on us and damaging the activist project of empowering people with disabilities. From the strong constructivist standpoint, as David Mitchell and Sharon Snyder note, "physicality is a fiction embodied by a normative frenzy to make unacceptable cultures visible and, therefore, recognizably different" (*Body* 27n). The body that is a fiction cannot be false or falsely represented, all representations being equally fictive, except if the body is represented as not fictive. What then of the other emphasis of disability studies, that of giving voice to physical disability as authentic experience through the privileging of first-person narratives by the disabled themselves? The constructivist invalidation of physicality is no more helpful to the person with a disability than the empiricist objectification of it.

Garland-Thomson suggests alternating "strategic constructivism" with "strategic essentialism," the former to destigmatize disability and denaturalize "so-called 'normalcy,'" the latter to validate "individual experience and consciousness," build community, and facilitate "self-naming" (23). But if deploying an epistemology is a matter of rhetorical convenience, then it begs the question of what unexamined, a priori assumptions are actually driving the arguments. "Extraordinary bodies," asserts Garland-Thomson, are "invested with meanings that far outstrip their biological bases" (8), but perhaps the most important implication of her carefully phrased, constructivist claim is that bodies actually do have biologically based meanings, however culturally overdetermined. Bodies and cultures, organisms and ideologies interact in complex ways, but no theoretical construction of the body as textual object or any autobiographical construction of the self as mythic subject can set out to completely rewrite the body and ignore those "biological bases" without quickly running up against the body's surprisingly stubborn resistance to reinvention.

At the seam where body joins culture, every construction of the body begins and ends. On the efforts of cultures to hide that seam, every oppression depends. Jim, my brother, has no legs. Jim has wheels. Jim has both wheels and legs. Jim has neither wheels nor legs. All this is true.

Jim was born without legs, none at all, in Seoul, South Korea, in 1967 and left in a basket at the door of an orphanage. When my parents were contacted about adopting him, it was because they had already adopted a Korean girl. Furthermore, not only was my mother a registered nurse but my father himself had an unusual genetic condition, osteogenesis imperfecta, aka brittle-bone disease, which had also been passed on to one of his children, me. The adoption agency must have reasoned that such a family might be uniquely willing and qualified to adopt a congenital double amputee. In any case, they were eager to get him adopted, as he was already four years old and in Korea would have been multiply stigmatized as disabled, an orphan, and a Eurasian.

They had to make sure, however, that we knew not just who but what we were adopting. They sent us the usual winsome portrait photos of Jim (then Kim Byung Chul) but also pictures of his naked bottom, in stark black and white, taken from multiple angles, like mug shots. We sat around the kitchen table one day when I was eight and looked at them. The pictures seemed sinister to me, alien. I had never seen any human body portrayed like that before, and the high contrast of the prints and the Korean lettering on the back only emphasized their harsh otherness. But I was fascinated by the croissant-shaped button of smooth flesh that capped one buttock and by the single baby toe, complete with toenail, that capped the other. His otherwise unremarkable body had been neatly tied off at the hips.

Garland-Thomson employs the term "extraordinary bodies" to include all "the related perceptions of corporeal otherness we think of variously as 'monstrosity,' 'mutilation,' 'deformation,' 'crippledness,' or 'physical disability'" (5). That was how my brother was first presented to me: a documented body, ordinary enough in most respects and utterly healthy but, in that one direction, extraordinary. Obviously, his body had been textualized, pathologized. The pictures were meant to contain its extraordinariness by their unblinking, comprehensive documentation, reducing what was "wrong" with him to authoritative illustrations, as if to say, You see, this is how it is, we have hidden nothing, this is the whole truth of it, "Only this, and nothing more."

I have an educational toy stuck on a shelf in my office, a partially assembled plastic anatomic model, one of those kits that have been marketed for decades as the Visible Man and the Visible Woman. The appeal of the toy is that it standardizes the internal, biological reality of the human body and renders it visible and accessible through a removable, translucent outer shell. The shell itself is stamped with the normative features of a young white adult. In some sense, those first photographs presented my brother as the Visible Cripple, a presentation enhanced by numerous X rays taken soon after his arrival in the States, revealing a complete pelvic bone but no hips, only the tiny floating bones of the single small toe. The reality of his extraordinary body, once seen and seen through, was no longer mysterious but understood, and once understood, manipulatable.

No sooner had my parents completed the medical surveys of the reality of my brother's extraordinariness than they began to think how best to conceal it. The decision of the adults, including my father in his wheelchair, was that to mainstream Jim as much as possible necessarily meant making him appear as normal as possible. Before long the family was making regular road trips to Delaware to have Jim fitted by the DuPont prosthetic specialists. Jim hated those trips, as all his siblings did, but he most hated the times when he was left with the doctors over a weekend or a week. I hated the boredom of the place, the smell of the prosthetics, all the things that reminded me of the hospitals my own traumas took me to from time to time. And what was accomplished by all this effort, alienation, and expenditure? The most inappropriate and useless deception possible, my brother marooned on stilts. Culture was doing its damnedest to construct his body as it pleased, and my parents were doing their damnedest to appease the demands of culture by making their boy as unobtrusive in his difference as possible.

What strikes me now as awful about all this was not that culture constructed us. Culture could take my brother's healthy, nimble leglessness and make it into a dark comedy of monstrosity, a nearly immobilized boy cyborg, one half flesh, one half mechanism. But if culture was as omnipotent as constructivist theory would have it, and the body was entirely culture's fiction, then culture could have also succeeded in erasing the difference it could not tolerate. Instead, Jim's body, and Jim, resisted. Well enough to talk about making our culture accommodate physical difference; but only in acknowledging that there is some physical reality beyond culture can that accommodation be reached. The refusal to make such an acknowledgment can only result in betraying and torturing the body in a futile attempt to erase it.

Jim made constant requests, every birthday and Christmas and anytime in between, for action figures, macho dolls with guns and biceps and articulated limbs. When he got them, he pried off all their macho legs. Stripping the camouflage pants, he figured out how the rubber-band device concealed in the torso hooked up the swiveling hips, or he discovered that this particular doll had simpler joints that could be un-screwed or popped loose. Either way, he eventually pulled off the legs. He has since told me that he simply couldn't relate to the legs. His fantasy was to have enormously powerful arms, but the legs, far from enhancing the fantasy, destroyed it. Culture could offer him guns and biceps, but the experience of legs was literally unimaginable and therefore unassimilable.

I can't remember whether he ever tried to put back on the soldiers' pants, and neither, he says, can he. He himself wore shorts with the leg holes sewn shut, at least when he wasn't swaying precariously in his custom-fitted bucket atop his latest pair of DuPont artificial legs, all their straps and plastics cloaked in slacks, the idea being to make him look as standardized as possible, even though the contraption imprisoned him.

He was much more comfortable in his wheelchair, of course, but our parents, once again including our wheelchair-using father, insisted that he learn to walk. He had to wear the legs to school, as I recall, until he went to public high school, where the long hallways and tight schedule demanded the wheelchair's speed. He recently told me that Mom tried to insist he use his legs at school, arguing that all the time, money, and practice put into acquiring an upright posture would be wasted otherwise. Jim held firm, and the compromise, apparently, was that he could go to school in his chair for his safety and convenience but that he would have to wear the legs while sitting in the chair. Thus the true, dissembling purpose of the legs becomes clear. In his freshman year, few classmates knew he had no legs. Only when he joined the wrestling team did the reality of his body become obvious. Not long after that, he says, he started making friends, began acting like himself, and soon stopped wearing the legs to school altogether.

Even then, he continued to wear the legs for formal occasions. At our sister Alleene's wedding, someone took away his crutches while posing the family portrait. He stands there between us, his four-limbed brothers, shoulder to shoulder for balance, suited and propped like FDR for a publicity still. Except for the ironic perfection of his machine-tooled stance and the slightly odd forward lean of his counterbalancing torso, the illusion is perfect: the invisible cripple.

Not that his was the only illusion in that photograph; it was only one of the more successful. The least successful was probably Dad's. Having never walked without prosthetic support in his life, in the photo Dad stands petrified with pride, dressed in a custom-tailored suit purchased for the purpose, his wheelchair out of sight and my mother's hand clutching his in apparent affection but actually to support him. The pose was foolhardy on two counts. Given a lifetime history of more than a hundred fractures, he knew that he could break a bone just supporting and balancing his own weight, to say nothing about what would happen if he toppled over. And whatever invisibility he thought he was achieving was delusory; if anything, his four-foot-tall inverted triangle shape looks more unusual when upright. It was as if he felt that if he stood still enough, somehow his bodily difference would disappear into the traditional patriarchal role of father of the bride.

Nor did the dissembling end with Dad. The brothers propping Jim up hid their own disabilities. In the picture, Peter, born with spina bifida, stands so that his partial paralysis looks more like a casual, hipster's slouch. Clark, who had polio as a child in Korea, stands in the second row so that his legs cannot be seen. My own brittle bones were at that time supporting me fairly well, so I stand in the front with a smug look on my face, perhaps because I knew I could pass, or perhaps because I had been mischievously teasing Jim about leaning on him and causing the whole house of cards to tumble. Oddly enough, even our able-bodied youngest sister, Alice, who was coincidentally recovering from a broken leg, had her crutches taken from her and stands awkwardly, her weight on her good leg.

The whole arrangement was both mundane and unique. Other families pose with smiles to approximate whatever they believe a normal happy family should look like. They pose to disguise the ordinary, daily frictions of their household. We did too, but we also posed to disguise the ordinary, daily realities of our bodies. We were used to being stared at; we just wanted to look our "best" for such a special occasion. We understood how people look at photographs. We understood that if our disabilities were framed, our disabilities would frame us, and we wanted to exclude them so we wouldn't vanish behind them. But to understand the full nature of our dissembling, we would have had to understand also both the cultural construction of that ideal normality to which we aspired—physical, familial, matrimonial, ritual—and the physical existence that, by being only partially reconstructable, testified to a reality outside that construction. And that's an understanding that disability studies is just beginning to attempt.

By the time Jim himself got married, he almost never wore the artificial legs, having completed college and gone to work for years in his chair. Yet, something about the magic of matrimony brought out all the old props once more for his wedding, where I served as best man. During the course of the ritual, both of us literally risked our necks to walk in, climb steps, stand, and descend steps. For reasons I don't at all remember, the charade extended beyond the posing of photographs and became an absurd, utterly unnecessary kind of high-wire act. At one point we both stood with our backs to the congregation, high on a platform, the edge of which was just inches behind our heels, while the minister droned through some laborious homily that neither of us could hear above the buzzing of terror in our ears. Jim was swaying slightly, one of his crutches having again been taken from him, and I was certain that he would lose his balance and grab me, and that we'd both go backward over the edge. I would land with six or seven fractures, and he would sit there looking dazed, half his tuxedoed form in one place, the other half still hanging off the stage.

And what, I asked him years later, was the point of that whole performance? Hadn't Cathy, his bride, fallen in love with him as a man in a wheelchair? Ah, another cultural appeasement was at work: Cathy was unusually tall, and her dream of her wedding ritual demanded that her groom not make her look like a giantess. If Jim got married in his legs, they could stand together in front of the preacher, just as she had always imagined. When Jim told me about this, a comment that Cathy had made later at the reception made better sense to me. Her sister, who was her maid of honor, was even taller than she, as was their brother, the other groomsman, whereas I could barely top five feet. When we readied ourselves to enter the reception hall in pairs, we violated one small tradition for the sake of Cathy's sense of symmetry, and rather than the maid of honor and best man traipsing in together, the maid of honor came in on her brother's arm, led by the shorter bridesmaid on the best man's arm and followed by the bride and her groom. As we walked in, Cathy joked awkwardly, "Here we come, the dwarves, the giants, and the freaks."

Cultural studies in general and disability studies in particular have already done much to expose, historicize, and explain the constructedness of both the visible and the invisible cripple. Both constructions are built from anxiety, hostility, and hubris. They ritually demonstrate the power of post-Enlightenment technoscience to control, cure, or erase the extraordinary body, and they unintentionally illustrate that power's limitations. That some extraordinariness refuses to be hidden or cured generates much of the anxiety and hostility of the culture at large toward persons with such bodies; it also generates much of the embarrassment and hunger for appeasement experienced by those persons, whether they have functional impairments or are ill, scarred, or simply inappropriately shaped or sized. The extraordinary body is precisely that body whose resistance to cultural constructions cannot be dissolved except by deception or destruction.

Now, however, the constructivist epistemology that has powered disability studies thus far needs to be more critically examined. Outright hostility to biology and to the natural history of our flesh all too easily plays into mind-body, theory-matter dualism and may turn out to be just another effort at erasure of the body by culture. Just as society needs to learn how to accommodate rather than stigmatize those of us with unusual and extraordinary bodies, so too humanist cultural theory needs to learn how to accommodate rather than demonize the study of the biological aspects of our bodies.

The difficulty for disability studies scholars that Mitchell and Snyder identify in the epigraph to this essay is also our great opportunity: to grapple "with ideas and experiences of physicality in a historical moment of constructivism" (*Body* 27n). Beyond alternating epistemological frames at our convenience, we have a chance to make a unique contribution to cultural studies by producing a thoroughgoing critique of those frames, perhaps even reframing future inquiry. Any epistemology born of both the cultural materialism of historicist constructivism and the biological materialism of naturalist empiricism may offer a new materialist praxis that is less prone to either cultural or biological determinism.

Only if we insist on the conjoined material reality of both culture and biology, even while recognizing it as only partially knowable and never wholly objective, can we then hope to identify deceptive representations of that reality. And only if we identify deceptions can we hope to end the oppressions that inevitably depend on deceptions left undiscovered.

TOBIN SIEBERS

Tender Organs, Narcissism, and Identity Politics

We of the tender organs are narcissists. Tender of the eye—closeted in a dark little world. Tender of the ear—imprisoned within a soundless castle. Tender of the limb—the radius of our associations short and incestuous. Tender of the brain—thrown down into a well of private imaginings.

To theorize disability requires that we understand not only the history by which the accusation of narcissism is leveled against people with disabilities but the centrality of disability to the concept of narcissism itself. This is because there may be no more powerful example of the logic of blaming victims for their own pain than the accusation of narcissism.[1] Narcissism is a psychological concept that defines social withdrawal, suffering, and demands for attention as the direct result of the psychopathology of the victim. Its structure allows no room for the idea that the accuser might be an interested party in the process of accusation. Narcissists, the theory goes, cease to love everyone but themselves. They turn away from society in favor of self-gratification, suffer the consequences, and then require others to take the blame for sorrows they have themselves created. Positive and negative attention alike contributes to a sense of their grandiose self, while indifference only increases feelings of narcissistic injury. In fact, injury is said to augment the feelings of self-importance felt by narcissists. This is even more powerfully the case with the narcissist than with the masochist, since masochism as a psychological concept relies on the more foundational theory of narcissism. (In theory there is no masochist who is not already a narcissist.) A critique of narcissism is vital to disability studies, then, because narcissism summons the metapsychology by which the isolation, suffering, and claims to attention of people with disabilities are turned against them and by which their reaction to their own disability becomes the proof of even greater defects than visible ones.

My primary goal here is to probe the metapsychology supporting the accusation of narcissism and to show how it relies on the idea of disability itself, but the politics of the moment obliges me to comment briefly on how the accusation of narcissism has been used to attack the emerging discipline of disability studies. In a culture said to be increasingly narcissistic, pockets of self-interest seem to be thriving, and disability studies is apparently the newest one—at least this is the position of its opponents. The most egregious attacks summon the specter of identity politics—those centers of hyperindividuality, supposedly bent on greater self-awareness and self-esteem, that have produced black studies, women's studies, and now disability studies. "Disability studies," Nora Vincent pronounces, is a form of "self-righteous goodspeak" and "the newest branch of social theory and its ignominious bedfellow, identity politics" ("Disability Chic" 40). Camille Paglia calls disability studies "the ultimate self-sanctifying boondoggle for victim-obsessed academic-careerists" (qtd. in Vincent 40). "You can't win," complains Walter Olson, a conservative commentator who blames the Americans with Disabilities Act for paralyzing the workplace in the United States. "Call attention to disability and you're oppressing them, ignore the disability and you're making them invisible" (qtd. in Vincent 40).

People with disabilities have forgotten how to suffer and be still. They want to raise the consciousness of others to their plight, to have their oppression recognized and brought to an end, and to feel good about themselves, even though other people cannot. For critics of disability studies, these goals are without merit. They prove merely that American society is suffering a breakdown, since people are more interested in pursuing self-gratification than in contributing to a common cause. That identity politics is thriving is supposedly proof that American society is a culture of narcissism.

It is wrong to study what you are. This allegation is familiar after more than thirty years of attack against black studies and women's studies.[2] In this light, disability studies appears to be only the latest example of moi criticism because it privileges the special needs of a small group.[3] The most urgent objection is supposedly to the politics of advocacy. Critics, especially in the sphere of higher education, object that identity politics substitutes political advocacy for intellectual substance. The introduction of black studies, women's studies, disability studies, and other forms of consciousness-raising, they claim, has diluted the content of higher education, bringing about the current state of decline in the American university system.[4]

And yet politics is not really the problem. *Identity,* not *politics,* is the vexed term in *identity politics.* For the ultimate purpose of any minority politics is self-identification. There can be nothing like an identity politics without a strong sense of identity because individuals would not be motivated by political action if they did not want to be in control of their identities and if they did not feel that this opportunity had been denied them by groups more dominant than theirs. In this sense, identity politics is no different from any other form of political representation, since politics always implies the existence of a coalition whose membership is defined by ideological, historical, geographic, or temporal borders.[5] The objection that identity politics differs from other forms of politics because it derives identity from a singular subjectivity or organizes itself single-mindedly around suffering only carries negative connotations because suffering has been linked so successfully to narcissism. But if limited ideas of identity are properties of all forms of political representation—and if suffering and disability have been inappropriately linked to the psychology of narcissism—then we should distance ourselves from such objections to identity politics. The political psychology applied in current debates about identity politics is deeply flawed, and we need a more enlightened discussion about how questions of identity and suffering contribute to the political as such.

If critics of identity politics value the capacity to generalize from experience, the necessity of representing the individual experiences of unique human kinds is clearly the goal of black studies, women's studies, and disability studies. An enlightened concept of the political cannot exist in the absence of either purpose, which is why the choice between them is hardly clear-cut and why arguments for and against them have relied on misinformation and debilitating accusations. It would be worth tracking how the preference for general over individual experience—or disinterestedness over self-consciousness—achieved prominence and then lost its persuasive power, but this history is too complex to recount here. My goal is to interrogate the metapsychology that associates minority discourses like disability studies with narcissism and to show that disability is a major component of this metapsychology, for it is precisely this metapsychology that represents acts of self-consciousness as negative by definition. My point is that the accusation of narcissism is one of the strongest weapons used against people with disabilities (and other minorities who pray that consciousness-raising will bring an end to their suffering). In fact, the psychological character attributed to people with disabilities and that of narcissists are more often than not one and the same.

Narcissism and Disability

The introduction of narcissism into the literature of psychoanalysis is also its first major link to disability, although the association between excessive egotism and pain appears earlier and so plays a significant part in Freud's metapsychology. The "study of organic disease," Freud argues in "On Narcissism: An Introduction," may help launch a "better knowledge of narcissism" (14: 82). Disability and the state of sleep are the two analogies used by Freud to introduce the idea of narcissism, and disability is more primary and enduring. "It is universally known," he explains, "and we take it as a matter of course, that a person who is tormented by organic pain and discomfort gives up his interest in the things of the external world, in so far as they do not concern his suffering. Closer observation teaches us that he also withdraws *libidinal* interest from his love-objects: so long as he suffers, he ceases to love" (82). In short, we of the tender organs are narcissists. Freud's prototype of the "painfully tender" organ is, of course, the penis, which is "the seat of a multiplicity of sensations" when "congested with blood, swollen and humected" (84). He coins the term "erotogenicity" to name this tenderness but recognizes it as a general characteristic of all organs and not only of the male member. For the tendency to erotogenicity produces a damming up of libido in any tender organ. More important, it induces a parallel change of libidinal investment in the ego. The greater the attention given to a tender organ, the more energy flows to the ego. This parallel effect accounts for "the familiar egoism of the sick person" (82). It also makes physical disability the model for narcissistic self-interest.

Beyond the Pleasure Principle broadens Freud's theory of tender organs. Here his primary concern is the relation between neurosis and the general anxieties produced by living in human society. Generalizing from his experience of soldiers suffering from battle fatigue, he asks why patients continue to relive painful traumas, even though the entire psyche is supposed by his theories to be organized around pleasure.

Freud discovers that soldiers wounded in battle adjust to psychic trauma better than those who are merely frightened: a "wound or injury inflicted," he states, "works as a rule *against* the development of a neurosis" (18: 12; Freud's emphasis). This is the case because any injury strikes at both the body and the ego. The defenses of the body and mind are penetrated, and large amounts of energy are invested in repairing the intrusion. When only the psyche is wounded, the trauma is repressed, and the patient must relive it whenever it fights its way back to consciousness. When the body is wounded, however, the injury remains in the conscious mind; the trauma is not repressed but symbolized by the damaged body. Consequently, not only do injured people not develop a neurotic symptom as a result of trauma, they are protected by their wounds against neurosis in general. This is because neurosis in Freud's conception arises as a result of the ambiguity of social existence. We grow anxious because life is full of uncertainties, and we blame ourselves for our failure to adjust, but we blame ourselves for a thousand and one reasons. The inability to manage many reasons is neurosis. People with disabilities, according to this theory, have one good reason for all their failures—the tender organ—and so the radical uncertainty of human existence disappears or at least becomes more manageable.[6] Freud gives a hint of this process in his case study of Dora, although it precedes by a decade his work on neurosis and disability:

> Let us imagine a workman, a bricklayer, let us say, who has fallen off a house and been crippled, and now earns his livelihood by begging at the street-corner. Let us then suppose that a miracle-worker comes along and promises him to make his crooked leg straight and capable of walking. It would be unwise, I think, to look forward to seeing an expression of peculiar bliss upon the man's features. No doubt at the time of the accident he felt he was extremely unlucky, when he realized that he would never be able to do any more work and would have to starve or live upon charity. But since then the very thing which in the first instance threw him out of employment has become his source of income: he lives by his disablement. If that is taken from him he may become totally helpless.   (7: 44)

The fortunate fall of people with disabilities does not really guarantee a healthy mental existence. There are worse things in life than neurosis, according to Freud, and these are the narcissistic disorders. Bodily scars may serve as a protection against neurosis, but the sufferer's extreme investment in the body produces a parallel exaltation of the ego. The self inhabits the disabled body like an armored fortress. It is protected but alone—and its own dear self becomes its most cherished prize.

Freud conceived of the ego as a body ego. It exists on the surface of the skin. It may be more accurate to say that he thought of the self as a scar, as a wound healed over. As scar tissue accumulates, the self becomes less and less flexible. The initial mending of pain provided by scarification gives way to a rigidity more disabling than the original wound. We of the tender organs apparently have a guaranteed protection against the sorrows of social existence, but we pay for it with the tendency to narcissism, which is the more serious disorder because it has no cure.[7] Narcissists are beyond the reach of therapy because they refuse to invest energy in other people. So long as they suffer—and they suffer always—they cease to love.

If narcissism seems an extreme model for thinking about people with disabilities, the model nevertheless dominates the psychological literature.[8] Like narcissists, people with disabilities are said to be beyond the reach of therapy. It would seem impossible at this moment in history that such prejudice would exist, but it is widespread. "Much psychoanalytic literature on disability," Adrienne Asch and Harilyn Rousso show, "supports the contention that the disabled are inherently unanalyzable" (4). Any number of case studies try to prove this conclusion. Melvin Bornstein argues that the intense involvement of a congenitally blind musician with his art mobilizes "a grandiose self in the self-centered repetitive material having to do with his music and trumpet," placing him beyond the reach of therapy (33). William Niederland associates "compensatory narcissistic self-inflation" with even "minor physical anomalies or imperfections" (519, 522). Some of the features accompanying narcissistic injuries, he explains, are self-aggrandizement, heightened aggressiveness, bisexuality, sadomasochism, and "florid birth-rebirth fantasies." According to Niederland, people with disabilities convert "defectiveness into a mark of distinction and a seat of power" (523, 526). People with disabilities, it seems, demonstrate a conspicuous resistance to reality, taking flight into an active fantasy life where their disabilities justify special privileges.[9] As one analyst sums it up, "The clinical problems presented during the psychoanalytic treatment of patients with disabilities are legion" (Yorke 187). Psychoanalysis treats disability almost exclusively as a symbol of narcissistic injury; disability has little meaning beyond this symptomology.[10]

The ordinary rules of life apparently do not apply to people with disabilities. Nor do the rules of psychoanalysis. The narcissism of patients with disabilities supposedly inhibits the transference, and thus the efficacy of therapy.[11] They seek revenge for their disabilities or demand compensation, it is said, and they refuse to place trust in their therapists.

A closer look, however, suggests that countertransference may be the real cause of therapeutic failures. A recent essay by Kenneth R. Thomas makes the absurd but telling case that "physical disabilities, largely because of the close developmental connection between the body and the ego, will tend to evoke specific types of countertransference responses from therapists" (151). In other words, analysts cannot bear to work with patients with disabilities. The sight of disability apparently evokes the threat of castration—the classic example of narcissistic injury—and the training of the analyst unravels. "Therapists may experience a variety of reactions" to patients with disabilities, Thomas explains, "including 'imaginary' pangs of pain in the genital area, headaches, dizziness, or other physical symptoms" (152). Nevertheless, he counsels therapists not to ignore or to evade these symptoms. Rather, they should use them to formulate hypotheses concerning what the patient is feeling about the loss of bodily integrity. The "therapist has identified with the patient," Thomas concludes, and these "reactions are accurately mirroring what the patient is feeling" (153). In short, the threat to the therapist's self-integration becomes an analytic tool used to think about the patient's disability. These threats do not belong to the psychology of the therapist; they spring from the patient. For the patient's narcissism contaminates the therapist. A clearer case of concealing the role of the accuser could not be imagined. It is simply assumed that the therapist cannot resist the psychopathological condition of the patient, who bears the responsibility for the therapist's reactions—and this despite the enormous gulf supposedly existing between the psychological states of the expert doctor and the narcissistic patient.

On the one hand, people with disabilities are supposedly unable to extend themselves emotionally to others. On the other hand, the sight of a person with a tender organ disables able-bodied people. Nor are people with disabilities acceptable as therapists, according to this logic. A number of experts have made the case over the years that narcissistic people should not work as therapists. A 1964 study of candidates rejected for psychoanalytic training reported that people with constricted patterns of defense and those considered narcissistic, controlling, isolated, and withdrawn are not suitable as analysts (Fox, Daniels, and Wermer). But Asch and Rousso argue that psychoanalytic literature often maintains that disability itself causes such undesirable characteristics (4–11). Studies of face-to-face interaction between able-bodied and dis-able-bodied individuals tend to support these findings. They show that able-bodied people focus in face-to-face encounters more on their own anxiety than on the feelings of the person with the disability and that their acceptance of disability lessens as narcissistic regression increases.[12] These studies give some indication of the potential problems faced by therapists with disabilities.[13]

While this material gives us a clear view of the prejudices in psychology against people with disabilities, it is actually more revealing about American culture at large. Psychoanalytic theory and practice may have formalized the association between narcissism and disability, but the connection exerts a powerful and terrible influence well beyond that sphere. The same arguments that demonstrate that people with disabilities make bad patients and analysts suggest that they make bad citizens. This last argument about citizenship is actually being made in attacks against disability studies and the Americans with Disabilities Act. The accusation of narcissism rages just below the surface in current debates about disability in higher education and in American culture. Most important, this accusation is a major impediment to reform in health care and other areas of concern crucial to the lives of people with disabilities.

The Narcissism of Small Differences

Despite the use of narcissism to attack identity politics, it is in fact incompatible with group psychology. Freud establishes in *Group Psychology and the Analysis of the Ego* (vol. 18) that solitary leaders are more likely than groups to have narcissistic attributes. Group psychology requires the suppression of individual narcissistic urges, he maintains, but for this reason people in groups tend to be fascinated by individuals whose narcissism sets them apart. Freud is also aware that this fascination may turn into violence. The murder of the primal father by the primal horde provides the classic example of collective attack against the solitary narcissistic figure.

What Freud and the entire tradition surrounding narcissism miss, however, are the similarities between his description of group psychology

and the history of collective violence. Narcissism is a collective accusation that isolates one member of a community as completely different
from everyone else. Whether this difference represents excessive ability
or disability counts for little in the final analysis because negative and
positive valences of difference shift suddenly whenever group psychology is involved. The only constant is the fact that the community turns
against one individual and holds special properties of that individual responsible for its actions. In short, this is the logic: we killed him but he
made us do it. Narcissism promotes a structure of blame where collective violence is concealed and victims are described as people divided
against themselves. Narcissists bring themselves down, and we know
nothing and can know nothing about it. A more sinister masking of violence could not be imagined.

Narcissism is a form of violent hyperindividualization imposed on
victims by political bodies and other groups. That people with disabilities
are automatically assumed to be narcissistic reveals not only that they
are being victimized but that the perception of their individuality is itself
a form of violence. The major interpretations in this country relentlessly
individualize disability. This applies to health-care reform and rehabilitation, special education, the struggle for civil rights, as well as to attacks
against disability studies and the ADA (see Linton 134). The disability of
individuals is always represented as their own personal misfortune.
Treatment isolates what is individual about the disability, only rarely relating it to the conditions of other people in a way that identifies a political problem, such as the denial of constitutional rights guaranteed to
every citizen (Hahn 192). Instead, the disability symbolizes not a suffering group but one person in his or her entirety: the crippled senior citizen in the park, the deaf boy on the bus, the blind student in the hall.
This means, of course, that the deaf boy on the bus may be entitled to
individualized educational planning and medical services, but this special treatment, since it is based on special rights and not civil rights, exposes him to great isolation and suffering because it ends by symbolizing
his individuality as such.

The narcissism of people with disabilities, then, is a political formation that inhibits their ability to act politically. It isolates them in their
individuality, making a common purpose difficult to recognize and
advance as a political agenda. Disability activists have made the case that
prejudices against people with disabilities and discrimination based on
race and sex are analogous. But this analogy always fails because racism

and sexism lead easily to political action based on the recognition of a particular advocacy group, while discrimination against a person with a disability seeks the same kind of solution used in health care and rehabilitation. It designs an individual remedy that addresses one person's particular problem or a small subclass of problems.[14] In short, political action is based on the individualization of disability. Indeed, the association between narcissism and disability makes it almost impossible to view people with disabilities as anything other than absolutely different from each other. Physical and mental disability are more difficult to overcome than prejudices against race and sex not only because people are less likely to identify with a blind person, for example, but because the perception of the individual with a disability is antithetical to the formation of political identity—which is to say that individuality itself is disabled for political use in the case of people with disabilities.

Identity politics in the United States emerged over the last few decades in the struggle for rights. Special rhetorical points were scored by coining the phrase "special rights." This rhetoric drew attention to the groups using it, made their individual agendas more visible, and gave them additional political currency. But it also separated them from a broader definition of rights, which is precisely why they have been attacked as special-interest groups too preoccupied with self-gratification, self-esteem, and separatist agendas. It is ironic that the word *special* has particular usage in the representation of mental and physical disability because people with disabilities are the one group that does not need to individualize itself. People with disabilities need, if they are ever to form political coalitions, to reverse the general perception that they are so unique or special that they can expect neither to serve as citizens nor to possess the rights that come with citizenship.

The argument that individualization victimizes people with disabilities is crucial to the theorization of disability because it unravels the accusation of narcissism. The narcissism of small differences does not apply to disability because "small differences" is the excuse used to defeat general claims for the rights of the disabled. We need to challenge the reigning idea that rights of the disabled are not possible because each person with a disability is different. My point has been that this idea has taken hold in large part because of the association between narcissism and disability, with the consequence that individuality itself, a foundational concept in American politics, has been transformed from a principle enabling political action into an impediment.

A Personal Conclusion, However Narcissistic

Disability studies, like black studies and women's studies before it, has relied in its first phase on a literature of witnessing. The autobiographical account has been the preferred method of representing disability to a wider public. But if disability studies is susceptible, beyond other minority discourses, to the accusation of narcissism, it is to be expected that this strategy will backfire. Personal accounts of suffering and injury will only convince the opponents of disability studies that "the person who is tormented by organic pain and discomfort," in Freud's words, "gives up his interest in the things of the external world, in so far as they do not concern his suffering." Disability activists have made the case that we need to move beyond the narcissism of first-person narratives to other paradigms if we are to be successful in revising the cultural understanding of disability. David Mitchell and Sharon Snyder, for example, argue that personal narratives invite reactions of pity and sympathy from readers rather than educating them about the social and political meanings of disability (*Body* 11). This is an important argument, especially for the future of disability studies, because the lives of people with disabilities will never be improved if we do not change the current political landscape. But I also think that people with disabilities need to resist the suggestion that their personal stories are somehow more narcissistic than those of able-bodied people. If we cannot tell our stories because they reflect badly on our personalities or make other people queasy, the end result will be greater isolation. For human beings make lives together by sharing their stories with each other. There is no other way of being together for our kind.

More pragmatically, we of the tender organs need to think about ways of telling our stories that will communicate the truth of our existence as a group facing prejudices and other barriers, often physical, put in place by society at large. Disability has served throughout history to symbolize other problems in human society. Oedipus's clubfoot signifies his hubris and political overreaching. Teiresias's blindness symbolizes his gift of prophecy. No one ever sees Sophocles's play as a drama about a cripple and a blind man fighting over the future of Thebes. The *Iliad* shows the crippled Hephaestus being cast out of Olympus, but no one asks whether Achilles's isolation from his Greek brothers relates to his vulnerable heel. The heel merely symbolizes his mortality. But isn't every warrior in the *Iliad* mortal? Why, then, is Achilles so different? Shakespeare's Richard III is a hunchback, but his disability represents deceitfulness and lust for power, not a condition of his physical existence.

Disability is the other other that helps make otherness imaginable. Throughout history, it has been attached to other representations of otherness to grant them supplementary meaning, sharper focus, and additional weight.[15] In providing this service, however, disability has lost the power of its own symbolism, and it is now time for disability activists to recapture it. By symbolism, I understand a political process through which private emotions and thoughts are made compelling to the public imagination.[16] The political cannot exist in the absence of such symbolism, for it describes the dynamic by which individuals are recognized by others and gather together into communities. Disability has provided the public imagination with one of its most powerful symbols for the understanding of individuality, but it always symbolizes something other than itself. Now we of the tender organs need to introduce the reality of disability into the public imagination. And the only way to accomplish this task is to tell stories in a way that allows people without disabilities to recognize our reality and theirs as a common one. For only in this way will we be recognized politically.

And so I tell one of my stories.[17] The first time my legs buckled under me as an adult, I experienced a shock of recognition. I suppose a psychoanalyst would say that I was reliving the trauma of falling to polio at age two. But I remember distinctly that my thoughts were drifting in a different direction. I could not believe it was the first time my legs had failed me because my memories were saturated with the experience. This was obviously as bewildering to me as the fact that I found myself hugging a lamppost to hold myself up. Suddenly, I remembered a recurring nightmare that has plagued me all my life. I am walking on my way home at night when an overwhelming sense of fatigue strikes my legs. I am forced to the ground, and I crawl through the darkness on my hands and knees—and once my knees fail, flat on my belly—until I reach my house. Then I drag myself up the stairs—there are always stairs, even though I have lived most of my life in one-story houses—and throw myself into bed. I wake up the next morning amazed that I have so quickly recovered the ability to walk.

Now the strange thing is that I realized that this dream was not part of my reality only when I was hugging that lamppost. It existed as part of my experience, but I had no understanding that it was experience given by nightmares rather than reality. The dream occurred so often and with such vividness that I had always assumed, until the moment I lost the ability to walk beyond short distances, that I had already lost that ability a long time ago.

I have tried to understand this dream since I first realized that I have been having it. My current interpretation is that it is a screen memory composed of many fragments of the experience of coping as a person with a disability with my physical and social environment. I cannot walk very far anymore, so I spend a lot of time counting blocks and gauging distances, trying to think about easier routes, avoiding stairways, spacing tasks throughout the day and the week to conserve energy. But now that I am doing this so consciously, I have come to realize that I have always done it, because I have been disabled since I was two years old. I was always compensating for my disability, just like I was always dreaming that dream. I just never knew it.

But I knew it when I was having the nightmare. That is what my nightmare is: the knowledge that it is difficult for me to take one step after another. It is also the knowledge that I am totally alone in my dilemma and pretty much in the dark about what to do about it. The nightmare is also about the fact that, despite all this, I am going to get out of bed every morning and go through it all over again. But I am not going to think too much about it, at least with my conscious mind. The nightmare collects all my fears about my environment and serves them up to me, and now that I am more conscious of what those experiences are, I can describe them to myself and to you.

Here are some day fragments that just might be the stuff that dreams are made of. During my freshman year in high school, I joined the other boys in my gym class in a physical fitness campaign based on running. We spent a week at the track being timed by the track coach in the 60- and 100-yard dashes, the 220- and 440-yard runs. My most vivid recollection is of the 440-yard run because it lasted the longest. The slowest boy ran across the finish line about 220 yards ahead of me. The coach signed up the fastest boys for the track team. He asked me to be the team manager.

I approach a building for the first time. From my car, I try to scout out the location of the handicapped entrance. I spot a little blue sign with a wheelchair on it. I circle the block for twenty minutes, waiting for a parking space to open up near that little blue sign. I park and walk over to the door. But under that wheelchair is a tiny arrow pointing to the left. No other writing. It seems that this is a sign telling me that this is not the handicapped entrance. The real handicapped entrance is somewhere to the left of me.

I am going to lunch with some friends. We are in animated conversation. We come to the stairs, and my friends, all fitness buffs, instinctively head for them. The elevator is in view. I fight my way up the stairs because I am too embarrassed to ask the others to take the elevator with me and too much in love with good conversation to take it alone.

Let it be recognized that physical barriers are each and every one of them psychic barriers as well. That is because people with disabilities travel in groups, although not necessarily always, and these groups are composed mostly of the able-bodied. When we come to a barrier, we realize that our perception of the world does not conform to theirs, although they rarely have this realization. This difference in perception is a social barrier equal to or greater than any physical barrier—which introduces my final point about the accusation of narcissism. Narcissism is profoundly incompatible with the reality of disability because we of the tender organs have to rely so often on other people. Studies show, for example, that blind people are terrified of their aggressive impulses because they are afraid that able-bodied people will also get angry and abandon them (see Burlingham 131–32). People who rely on caregivers have to be diplomats. They also need a form of identity politics unlike any other.[18] To rewrite Freud, "The person who is tormented by organic pain knows that all things of the external world concern his suffering. So long as he suffers, he needs the love of others." This is why it is so alarming when we see the solitary woman in a wheelchair in the middle of town fighting repeatedly to get her chair to jump a curb. This is why we wonder at the common sense of a blind man who goes to the shopping mall alone on a busy weekend. The sighting of these creatures is the equivalent of seeing a giraffe in a parking garage. People with disabilities do not often put themselves in such situations because they are at risk when they are alone. We of the tender organs need to be in groups. We need a community to support us.

Some of you have disabilities. Some of you do not. Most of you will someday. That is the reality of the human mind and body. Remember what you already know about people with disabilities, so the knowledge will be useful to you when you join us. The blind do not lead the blind. The lame do not want to walk alone. We do not love only our own kind or ourselves. You others are our caregivers—and we can be yours, if you let us. We of the tender organs are not narcissists.

NOTES

1. In *The Mirror of Medusa*, I trace the peculiar logic of narcissistic accusation from its appearances in classical mythology to its use in psychoanalysis and anthropology.

2. The most famous attacks against black studies and women's studies are the most exaggerated, but their exaggeration is only rhetorical, not an exaggeration of content, since the same arguments are made by feverish and subtle commentators alike. Frequently, the accusation of narcissism is just below the surface of the attack. William Bennet blasted the educational community for giving in to "special interests" such as ethnic studies and women's studies, while Lynne Cheney called for a return to a past in America untainted by intrusive discussions of race and gender. "Just at the moment," Allan Bloom has said of black studies, "when everyone else has become a 'person,' blacks have become blacks. [. . .] They stick together" (92). Nathan Glazer, another critic of affirmative action, understands that multiculturalism is about race relations in the United States, but he makes his case against it by arguing that multiculturalism inflates certain parts of the self at the expense of others. "There are multiple selves," he concludes. But only one self is dominant in multiculturalism. "Consequently, it is not necessary to represent the musical, athletic, regional, class, or religious self, because the racial or ethnic self is central and decisive" (49). For Camille Paglia, black studies, women's studies, and gay studies are only about self-interest: "each has simply made up its own rules and fostered its own selfish clientele, who have created a closed system" (*Vamps* 99–100). Paglia singles out women's studies in particular as narcissistic: "Women's studies is a comfy, chummy morass of unchallenged groupthink [. . .] sunk in a cocoon of smug complacency"; it is a "prisoner of its own futile, grinding, self-created discourse" (*Sex* 242, 243).

3. Certainly, disability studies owes a large debt to recent trends in identity politics, for good and for ill. It has learned lessons from black studies and women's studies in particular, embracing the desire for empowerment, the strategy of representing marginality through first-person accounts, and the need to criticize practices of cruelty and injustice. But, of course, critics of disability studies have also profited from the negative rhetoric developed by critics of black studies and women's studies, with the result that disability studies, while new to the scene, finds the rhetoric of its enemies fully formed, even while its self-description is not.

4. Christopher Lasch, among others, makes this point in *The Culture of Narcissism* (253).

5. In *The Subject and Other Subjects*, I discuss political subjectivity at greater length. One point is worth restating here. Politics always operates according to exclusionary principles insofar as it requires borders: "Politics justly lays down the limits of inclusion for communities, whether it involves groups internal to its borders or whether it is policing external borders. There can be no political community without a serious conception of borders" (132).

6. Turner and McLean show more recently that, contrary to Freud's views, people with disabilities do experience heightened anxiety.

7. Freud admits that narcissists "become inaccessible to the influence of psychoanalysis and cannot be cured by our efforts" (14: 74). He compares narcissists to "primitive peoples," in addition to people with disabilities, especially in their capacity to consider their thoughts omnipotent (14: 75).

8. A selection of reading in which the connection between disability and narcissism is suggested includes Coleman and Croake; Cubbage and Thomas; Fichten and Amsel; Greenacre; Jacobson; Lussier; Niederland; Ogden; K. Thomas; and Yorke.

9. I derive my language here from another case study, where Edith Jacobson analyzes the narcissistic behavior of both people with disabilities and beautiful able-bodied women with respect to the idea of "the exception" derived from Freud's 1915 essay "Some Character-Types Met with in Psychoanalytic Work."

10. Harris and Wideman make this point (117). They also note that the impact of the psychoanalytic approach for people with disabilities has been largely punitive (121).

11. In Yorke's words, for some patients, "physical disability is hypercathected and becomes a physical coat-hanger on which to put a whole psychopathological wardrobe" (188).

12. See, for example, Kleck, Ono, and Hastorf; Stiller; and Fichten and Amsel. Grier comes at the difference of the therapist from a different but related angle.

13. Asch and Rousso conclude that patients are more accepting of therapists with disabilities than their own colleagues (10–11). A development parallel to that between therapist and patients with disabilities exists in the relation between a mother and a child with a disability and between able-bodied children and parents with disabilities. The psychological literature tends to conclude that greater narcissistic injury results from having a child or parent with a disability than from having a disability oneself. For example, Lussier finds that "the psychologically weak father is not a condition creating a traumatic impact, no matter how frustrating and anxiety provoking, while the crippled father does in some way, at one stage or another" (184). See also Greenacre.

14. My discussion here relies on Funk's succinct analysis (esp. 26).

15. "The most common methodological approach to the question of disability in the humanities," note Mitchell and Snyder, "is the analysis of cognitive and physical differences that symbolize other social conditions" (21).

16. I explore this symbolism in, among other places, "Kant and the Politics of Beauty."

17. For more first-person narrative see "My Withered Limb."

18. The right and the left misunderstand the relation between disability and identity politics as a result. The underlying assumption on the left is that groups create false ideals of the unified self. In short, the left's attacks against identity politics are individualistic. The right, of course, counters that identity politics is too individualistic. Disability studies requires a form of identity that resists both models because the left's insistence on lone-wolf ideals of the self reproduces the medicalized view of disability and the right's refusal to acknowledge difference leaves people with disabilities without any position from which to speak about their civil rights. See Bickford for a discussion of this problem in the context of feminism.

ROSEMARIE GARLAND-THOMSON

The Politics of Staring: Visual Rhetorics of Disability in Popular Photography

The history of disabled people in the Western world is in part the history of being on display, of being visually conspicuous while politically and socially erased. The earliest record of disabled people is of their exhibition as prodigies, monsters, omens from the gods, and indexes of the natural or divine world. From the New Testament to the miracles at Lourdes, the lame, the halt, and the blind provide the spectacle for the story of bodily rehabilitation as spiritual redemption that is so essential to Christianity. From antiquity through modernity, the bodies of disabled people considered to be freaks and monsters have been displayed by the likes of medieval kings and P. T. Barnum for entertainment and profit in courts, street fairs, dime museums, and sideshows.[1] Moreover, medicine has from its beginnings exhibited the disabled body as what Michel Foucault calls the "case," in medical theaters and other clinical settings, in order to pathologize the exceptional and to normalize the ordinary (*Birth of the Clinic* 29). Disabled people have variously been objects of awe, scorn, terror, delight, inspiration, pity, laughter, or fascination—but they have always been stared at.

Staring at disability choreographs a visual relation between a spectator and a spectacle. A more intense form of looking than glancing, glimpsing, scanning, surveying, gazing, and other forms of casual or uninterested looking, staring registers the perception of difference and gives meaning to impairment by marking it as aberrant. By intensely telescoping looking toward the physical signifier for disability, staring creates an awkward partnership that estranges and discomforts both viewer and viewed. Starers gawk with abandon at the prosthetic hook, the empty sleeve, the scarred flesh, the unfocused eye, the twitching limb, but seldom does looking broaden to envelop the whole body of the person with a disability. Even supposedly invisible disabilities always threaten to disclose some stigma, however subtle, that disrupts the social order by its presence and attenuates the bond between equal members of the human community. Because staring at disability is considered illicit looking, the disabled body is at once the to-be-looked-at and not-to-be-looked-at, further dramatizing the staring encounter by making viewers furtive and the viewed defensive. Staring thus creates disability as a state of absolute difference rather than simply one more variation in human form. At the same time, staring constitutes disability identity by manifesting the power relations between the subject positions of disabled and able-bodied.

The rapid flourishing of photography after 1839 provided a new way to stare at disability. In our ocularcentric era, images mediate our desires and the ways we imagine ourselves.[2] Among the myriad, often conflicting, and never indifferent images modernity offers us, the picture of ourselves as disabled is an image fraught with a tangle of anxiety, distance, and identification. As a culture, we are at once obsessed with and intensely conflicted about the disabled body. We fear, deify, disavow, avoid, abstract, revere, conceal, and reconstruct disability—perhaps because it is one of the most universal, fundamental of human experiences. After all, we will all become disabled if we live long enough. Nonetheless, in representing disability in modernity, we have made the familiar seem strange, the human seem inhuman, the pervasive seem exceptional. By the beginning of the twentieth century, for example, public displays of disabled people became inappropriate in the same way that public executions and torture came to be considered offensive. Disabled people were sequestered from public view in institutions and the private sphere as middle-class decorum pronounced it impolite to stare. Photography, however, has enabled the social ritual of staring at disability to persist in an alternate form.

Photographs seem to be transparent windows onto reality that ensnare truth. But like all representations, photographs organize our perceptions, shaping the objects as they depict them by using conventions of presentation that invoke cultural ideas and expectations. Photographs evoke the familiar only to make it seem strange, eliciting a response Alan Trachtenberg describes as "astonishment mingling with recognition" (*Reading* 4). Because disability has such potent cultural resonances, our capitalist democracy has enlisted its imagery to manipulate viewers for a wide range of purposes. Popular photography catapults disability into the public sphere as a highly mediated image shorn from interactions with actual people with disabilities. Photography's immediacy, claim to truth, and wide circulation calcifies the interpretations of disability embedded in the images, at once shaping and registering the public perception of disability.

Photography authorizes staring. Photos are made to be looked at. With the actual disabled body absent, photography stylizes staring, exaggerating and fixing the conventions of display and eliminating the possibility for interaction or spontaneity between viewer and viewed. Photos absolve viewers of responsibility to the objects of their stares at the same time that they permit a more intense form of staring than an actual social interchange might support. Disability photography thus offers the spectator the pleasure of unaccountable, uninhibited, insistent looking. This license to stare becomes a powerful rhetorical device that can be mobilized to manipulate viewers. By exploring some of the purposes to which popular photography's "dialectic of strange and familiar" has been put, I aim here to suggest how modern America imagines disability and disabled people (Trachtenberg, *Reading* 4).[3]

To look at the way we look at disability, I elaborate a taxonomy of four primary visual rhetorics of disability. They are the wondrous, the sentimental, the exotic, and the realistic. This template of visual rhetorics complicates the often restrictive notion of images as being either positive or negative, as communicating either the truth of disability or perpetuating some oppressive stereotype. Thus, I analyze more than evaluate. These visualizations of disabled people act as powerful rhetorical figures that elicit responses or persuade viewers to think or act in certain ways. The wondrous, the sentimental, the exotic, and the realistic converge and inflect one another in individual pictures as well as across all genres of disability photography. These visual rhetorics seldom occur discretely; rather, the photographs blend together in individual photographs. They wax and wane, shift and combine over time as they respond to the purposes for which the photographs are produced. Moreover, these rhetorics constitute part of the context into which all representations of disabled people enter. Not only do these representational modes configure public perception of disability, but all images of disabled people either inadvertently or deliberately summon these visual rhetorics and their accompanying cultural narratives. None of these rhetorical modes operates in the service of actual disabled people, however. Indeed, almost all of them appropriate the disabled body for the purposes of constructing, instructing, or assuring some aspect of a putatively nondisabled viewer.

The first visual rhetoric is the wondrous. The oldest mode of representing disability, the wondrous continues to find a place in modernity's framing of disability. This genre capitalizes on physical differences in order to elicit amazement and admiration. The antecedents of the wondrous disabled figures are the monsters of antiquity, who inspired awe, foretold the future, or bore divine signs, and freaks, who were the celebrities in nineteenth-century dime museums and sideshows (Garland-Thomson, "From Wonder"). The rhetoric of the wondrous springs from a premodern interpretation of disability as either augury or marks of distinction, whether representing good or evil. Oedipus, Teiresias, monsters, giants—even Shakespeare's Richard III—were imposing if ominous disabled figures.

A nineteenth-century example is Charles Tripp, the famous Armless Wonder (fig. 1), pictured eating with his toes in a carte de visite, one of the exceedingly popular photographic portraits commonly sold to augment and promote live appearances. This carefully choreographed portrait includes samples of his calligraphic skills, paper figures he's cut out, as well as the pen and scissors he used to accomplish such remarkable tasks. The silver tea set in the picture refers to other photos of him drinking from a cup with his toes. The composition is a visual résumé documenting Tripp's supposedly amazing accomplishments. The spectacle tries to elicit awe from the viewers, whose sense of their own clumsy toes makes Tripp's feet feat seem wondrous.

Photography introduced into the rhetoric of wonder the illusion of fusing the ordinary with the extraordinary. This picture invites a relation of identification and differentiation between Tripp and his viewer, making him seem simultaneously strange and familiar. Viewers see a typical man engaged in the quotidian acts of writing, eating, or drinking tea, but—to those with arms—he does this in a most extraordinary manner. Only the single detail of eating with feet rather than hands marks this scene as distinctive. Disability operates visually by juxtaposing the singular (therefore strange) mark of impairment in a surrounding context of the expected

Figure 1

Surrounded here by the products of his agile feet, the famous nineteenth-century freak show entertainer,
Charles Tripp, one of the many "armless wonders," is
presented as amazing and yet ordinary. Courtesy of the
Robert Bogdan Collection, Syracuse, NY

(therefore familiar). By telescoping the viewer's eye to the mark of impairment, the picture instructs viewers to stare and coaches them to understand impairment as the exception rather than the rule. Orchestrated
and provoked by the photo, staring creates a particular relation between
the viewer and the viewed that gives meaning to impairment.

Modernity secularized wonder into the stereotype of the supercrip,
who amazes and inspires the viewer by performing feats that the nondis-

Figure 2

This photograph for adventure vacations invokes wonder by inviting the viewer to look up in admiration and awe at the person who can scale rocks while using a wheelchair. Courtesy of Wilderness Inquiry

abled viewer cannot imagine doing. Contemporary wonder rhetoric emphasizes admiration rather than amazement, in part because bourgeois respectability now deems it inappropriate to delight in staring at disabled people. One example is a recent ad for adventure tours that features a rock climber using a wheelchair (fig. 2). Here the photographic composition literally positions the viewer as looking up in awe at the climber dangling in her wheelchair. By making the disabled figure exceptional rather than ordinary, the wondrous can estrange viewer from viewed and attenuate the correspondence that equality requires.

Sentimentality has inflected the wonder model, producing the convention of the courageous overcomer, contemporary America's favorite figure of disability. Even though armless calligraphers are no longer an acceptable form of middle-class entertainment, photos of disabled people who have adapted tasks to fit their bodies still ask their viewers to feel a sense of wonder. An advertisement for Habitat for Humanity, for example, pictures a disabled volunteer worker building a house (fig. 3). Like Tripp, this man is portrayed as entirely ordinary except for the detail of the fingerless hands holding the hammer, which occupies the center of

Figure 3

This photograph of a volunteer worker for Habitat for
Humanity, an organization that builds homes for the
needy, utilizes the narrative of overcoming to elicit admiration for working despite having a disability. Courtesy of
Habitat World

interest, at once inviting and authorizing the stare. As is typical in disability photography, the text instructs the viewer how to respond to the
picture, with a headline that says, "Extraordinary Volunteer, Unstop-
pable Spirit." The picture thus combines the narrative of admiration for
overcoming disability with the narrative of empowerment characteristic of a post–disability rights movement consciousness. By making disabled subjects masters of ordinary activities such as climbing rocks,

drinking tea, or using hammers, these photos create a visual context that elicits adulation for their accomplishing what the normalized viewer takes to be a superhuman feat.

———————

The second visual rhetoric is the sentimental. Whereas the wondrous elevates and enlarges, the sentimental diminishes. The sentimental produces the sympathetic victim or helpless sufferer needing protection or succor and invoking pity, inspiration, and frequent contributions. The sentimental disabled figure developed as a part of the larger nineteenth-century bourgeois culture of fine feelings.[4] The pathetic, the impotent, and the suffering confirmed the Victorian bourgeoisie by arousing their finest sentiments. As the increasingly empowered middle class imagined itself capable of capitalizing the world, it began to see itself as responsible for the world as well, a stewardship that launched humanitarian and reform movements to which today's telethons are heir. This discourse of middle-class noblesse oblige operates on a model of paternalism, often trafficking in children and alluding to the cute, the plucky, the long-suffering, and the courageous.

The rhetoric of sentiment found an effective home in the photographic conventions of the poster child of mid-twentieth-century charity campaigns. The 1946 March of Dimes poster child (fig. 4) echoes the spunky cuteness of freak figures such as General Tom Thumb. But where Tom Thumb delighted with his miniature adulthood, this poster child breaks hearts as he is propped vulnerably up in a corner of his crib in the before-and-after format. In order to catalyze the adult, to whom the photo addresses itself, this March of Dimes poster presents disability to the middle-class spectator as a problem to solve, an obstacle to eliminate, a challenge to meet. In such appeals, impairment becomes the stigma of suffering, transforming disability into a project that morally enables a nondisabled rescuer. The viewer's dimes, the poster suggests, will literally catapult the unhappy little fellow trapped in braces in his crib into a smiling and spirited tyke, striding with determination and gratitude toward the viewer. Sentimentality makes of disabled people occasions for the viewers' own narratives of progress, improvement, or heroic deliverance and contains disability's threat in the sympathetic, helpless child for whom the viewer is empowered to act. Whereas earlier sentimental literature accentuates suffering to mobilize readers for humanitarian, reform, or religious ends, the poster boy's suffering is only the background to his restoration to normalcy that results from "your

Figure 4

The March of Dimes 1946 poster boy appeals to the rhetoric of sentiment, which often employs pathetic, courageous, or cute children to elicit the viewers' sympathy and
money. Courtesy of March of Dimes

dimes." The optimism of cure thus replaces the intensity of sympathy,
testifying to an increasing faith in clinical treatment and scientific
progress as modernity increasingly medicalizes and rationalizes the body.

The rhetoric of sentiment has migrated from charity to retail in late
capitalism's scramble to capture markets. For example, the cover of a
1998 Benetton public relations brochure (fig. 5) distributed in stores
employs a chic sentimentality in documenting a school for developmentally disabled children Benetton supports and outfits. This cover girl

Figure 5

Sentimental cuteness and high fashion come together in this public relations brochure's presentation of a developmentally disabled child in a school supported and outfitted by Benetton clothing stores. Concept: O. Toscani. Courtesy of United Colors of Benetton

with both Down syndrome[5] and a stylish Benetton hat fuses sentimental cuteness with high fashion to produce the conviction in the viewer-shopper that Benetton is humanitarian rather than solely commercial. In anticipation of its patron's skepticism, the brochure instructs its viewers that Benetton launched this campaign as social commentary, although people are apt to see it as "cynical advertising." Benetton devotes a whole introductory page to assuring its customers that this brochure is about "the gift of love" (United Colors 3). So while commercial fashion marketing demands a certain sophistication and sleekness that precludes the gushy sentiment of the 1940s poster child, Benetton still assures its viewers of their tolerance and allows them to fantasize rescuing this child from the stigma of being disabled by dressing her smartly and supporting her school.

The third visual rhetoric is the exotic. The rhetoric of sentiment domesticates the disability figure, making it familiar and comforting. In contrast, the visual rhetoric of the exotic presents disabled figures as alien, distant, often sensationalized, eroticized, or entertaining in their difference. The exotic reproduces an ethnographic model of viewing characterized by curiosity or uninvolved objectification and informed by the proliferation of popular ethnographic photography that accompanied the era of Western imperialism. For example, nineteenth-century freak photography often transformed disabled people into "wild men" or other exotic "savages," whose impairments were translated into marks of alien ethnicity (Garland-Thomson, "From Wonder" 5). The exotic demedicalizes, fascinates, and seduces with exaggeration, creating a sensationalized, embellished alien.

The introduction of disabled models has exploded the contemporary fashion world in the last several years, returning the rhetoric of the exotic into disability photography. Where the sentimental makes the disabled figure small and vulnerable in order to be rescued by a benevolent agent, the exotic makes the disabled figure large, strange, and unlike the viewer. Ever straining for novelty and capitalizing on titillation, the fashion arm of the advertising world was sure to discover the power of disabled figures to provoke responses from viewers. Advertising has learned that disability sells in two ways. One is by making consumers feel good about buying from a company that is charitable toward the supposedly disadvantaged, which is the Benetton brochure's pitch. The other is to capture the disability market, which is 54 million people and growing fast as the baby boomers age and as their spending power is estimated to reach the trillion-dollar mark in 2000 (J. Williams 29).

The exotic serves this commercial aim by upsetting the earnest, asexual, vulnerable, courageous image of disability that charity rhetoric has so firmly implanted. One image advertising wheelchairs presents a tattooed biker figure brandishing a hockey stick (fig. 6). The image alludes at once to the strong men and tattoo kings of the sideshows and then inflects it with a hyperphallic sexuality, completely rewriting the cultural script of the emasculated invalid and the male who becomes feminized by disability. As is typical with much popular disability photography, the text instructs the viewer on how to read this photo. The exaggeration characteristic of exoticization here marshals ironic hyperbole to mount a brazen, sensational parody, provocatively challenging the viewer by lewdly commanding, "Lick this!" Such representations preclude even a trace of the sentimental or the wondrous, insisting instead on the empowerment of the transgressive, even at the expense of distancing the spectator from the spectacle.

Another venue for disability as the exotic is emerging in the high-fashion market, which is always desperate to keep its edge. These advertisements and magazine features present disabled models in a dual

Figure 6

The rhetoric of the exotic in this ad for wheelchairs "with an attitude" employs the tattooed biker-jock figure to create a transgressive, hypermasculine image for the wheelchair user. Courtesy of Colours Wheelchairs

attempt to capture a market and to novelize high fashion by introducing bodies that at once depart from and conform to the exhausted image of the high-fashion body. Alexander McQueen, known in England as the bad boy of fashion design, recently collaborated with other designers and the fashion photographer Nick Knight for a shoot called "Accessible," featuring eight disabled models. Knight's shots fold the models' impairments into a context of exoticism that extends to the entire frame, as in

Figure 7

The high-fashion layout of the model, sports star, and double amputee Aimee Mullins emphasizes rather than conceals her prosthetic legs, exploiting the exotic mode to make disability seem chic. Courtesy of *We Magazine*. Photograph by Nick Knight.

the shot of Aimee Mullins, the double-amputee celebrity cover girl, rendered as a kind of high-tech bionic mannequin (fig. 7). No attempt is made to disguise her cosmetic prosthetic legs—so she can pass for nondisabled; rather, the entire photo thematically echoes her prostheses and renders the whole image chic. As a gorgeous amputee, Mullins becomes an embodied contradiction. Her prosthetic legs parody, indeed proudly mock, the very idea of the perfect body that has been the mark of fashion until now, even while the rest of her body conforms precisely to fashion's impossible standards. Rather than conceal, normalize, or erase disability, these photos use the hyperbole and stigma traditionally associated with disability to quench postmodernity's perpetual search for the new and arresting image. These transgressive juxtapositions of disability and high fashion, such as the macho chair user and the athletic but legless Mullins, produce a fresh, attention-grabbing brand of exotic radical chic that redefines disabled identity for the disabled consumer.

The fourth visual rhetoric is the realistic. Where the exotic mode cultivates estrangement, realism minimizes distance and difference by establishing a relation of contiguity between viewer and viewed. The wondrous, sentimental, and exotic modes of representation tend to exaggerate the difference of disability to confer exceptionality on the object in the picture. The rhetoric of the realistic, however, trades in verisimilitude, regularizing the disabled figure in order to avoid differentiation and arouse identification, often normalizing and sometimes minimizing the visual mark of disability. Realism domesticates disability. Realist disability photography is the rhetoric of equality, most often turned utilitarian. The use of realism can be commercial or journalistic, and it can also urge the viewer to political or social action.[6]

Realism emerged as a property of portraiture, documentary, and medical photography of the nineteenth century. Documentary photography such as that made famous by Lewis Hine and Jacob Riis aimed photographic realism at the progressive obsession with social reform.[7] Documentary and journalistic photographies differ from charity and commercial photographies in that they do not solicit the exchange of money so directly but rather aim to democratically disseminate information intended to shape the viewers' actions and opinions. Hine and Riis recorded the fabric of the American underclass, exposing the supposed truth of the conditions in which it struggled. Hine photographed wounded workers whose disabilities robbed them of the male privilege and duty of work (fig. 8), and he featured children whose disabilities he felt stole their childhood. The caption below an amputee worker reads, "When a man's hand is mutilated, he keeps it out of sight" (Stange 60). The implied message is that the social mandate to hide disability precludes entry into the workplace. Hine enlists disability in documentary photos ultimately to tell a cautionary tale: disability is a scourge that can and should be avoided in a world that works right. In spite of the political support and social acceptance the picture confers, the photo-

AN ARM GONE AT TWENTY
This young brakeman when last seen was studying
telegraphy in order to stay in the service

Photo by Hine

THE WOUNDS OF WORK
When a man's hand is mutilated he keeps
it out of sight

Figure 8

Lewis Hine documented wounded workers in 1907-08 by using
the rhetoric of realism as a form of social protest against excluding
disabled men from the privileges of labor.

graph nevertheless marks this worker as a person the viewer does not
want to be.

A more sensationalized use of realism recently provoked controversy and roused political protests over what constitutes unacceptable looking at women's breasts. The Breast Cancer Fund, a San
Francisco–based nonprofit organization dedicated to education about
and funding of breast cancer research, mounted a public awareness
campaign in January 2000 called Obsessed with Breasts, featuring three
posters showing women boldly displaying mastectomy scars. The
posters parodied a Victoria's Secret catalog (fig. 9), a *Cosmopolitan* cover,
and a Calvin Klein perfume ad, all of which typically parade women's
breasts in soft-porn modes that have become an unremarkable staple of

Figure 9

This controversial 2000 Breast Cancer Fund poster employs the sensationalism often characteristic of realism to
protest inadequate breast cancer research and to expose
the cultural effacement of mastectomies. Courtesy of the
Breast Cancer Fund

commercial magazine advertising. The posters disrupt the visual convention of the female breast as sexualized object for male appropriation
and pleasure by replacing the now normative, eroticized breast with the
proscribed image of the amputated breast. The powerful visual violation
produced by exchanging the spectacle of the eroticized breast, which
has been desensationalized by its endless circulation, with the medicalized image of the scarred breast, which has been concealed from public
view, was so shocking to viewers that many demanded that the images

be removed. Of course, the censuring and censoring of images that demand a recognition of the reality of breast cancer ignited a vibrant controversy. The images intensify this forbidden version of the disabled breast by ironically juxtaposing it with the commonplace but virulently sexist eroticization of the breast. The posters thus advance a potent feminist challenge not only to sexism in medical research and the treatment for breast cancer but also to the oppressive representational practices that make erotic spectacles of women's breasts an everyday thing while erasing the fact of the amputation that one woman in eight will have. By mocking the tired sensationalism of pornography, these pictures protest against the refusal of contemporary America to literally and figuratively look at breast cancer.

The visual rhetoric of the ordinary has emerged in a climate of integration and diversity created by the disability rights movement and resulting legislation such as the Americans with Disabilities Act of 1990 (ADA). While the post-ADA era is not without resistance and backlash to the integration of people with disabilities, the social environment is filling with disability in the popular press. Disability not only appears in the sensationalist underbelly of the press, where it always has, but also is tucked with various degrees of conspicuousness into the fabric of common visual culture. Department store and catalog advertising, for instance, has adopted the rhetoric of the ordinary both to appeal to disabled people as a market and to suggest an ethic of inclusion. L. L. Bean promotes a wheelchair backpack in its catalog; Walmart and many other stores feature disabled models and mannequins in everything from frumpy jog suits to evening gowns. Toy lines like Barbie and the upscale American Girl have wheelchair-using dolls. Such routinization of disability imagery not only brings disability as a human experience out of the closet, it also enables people with disabilities—especially those who acquire impairments as adults—to imagine themselves as a part of the ordinary world rather than belonging to a special class of untouchables and unviewables. Images of disability as a familiar, even mundane, experience in the lives of seemingly successful, happy, well-adjusted people can reduce the identifying against oneself that is the overwhelming effect of oppressive and discriminatory attitudes toward people with disabilities.

The most radical reimagining of disability offered by the realist mode is, ironically, the least visually vivid of the images discussed here, perhaps because it is the only mode with no commercial purpose. The genre of disability photography I conclude with is the official portrait,

Figure 10

The contrast between this official portrait of Assistant Secretary Judith E. Heumann sitting in her wheelchair and the many photos of FDR that hid the wheelchair he used daily during his presidency marks the difference between a pre- and post–civil rights era. Courtesy of United States Department of Education.

exemplified by the Department of Education's simple photographic portrait of Judith E. Heumann, assistant secretary of education during the Clinton administration (fig. 10). The conventions that govern such pictures strive for the effect of the everyday, inflected with enough dignity and authority to communicate the importance of the position but not enough to separate the official from the constituency. In a democracy, official portraits depict public servants, after all, in no-nonsense black and white, with standard costuming and poses, and flanked unpretentiously by flags. Unlike commercial photographs, these portrayals are neither generalized nor stylized; rather, they are particularized. The photo suggests that here is a real, recognizable person responsible for certain official duties. The radical aspect of this common visual rhetoric is that part of this woman's particularization is the wheelchair that is clearly an aspect of her identity, an integral element of who and what the photograph says she is. The glimpse of her chair is descriptive, as fundamental to her image as the shape of her chin, the cut of her hair, or the tint of her skin. In its ordinariness, the photograph discourages staring without prohibiting it. Indeed, it encourages forms of looking such as glancing, if the viewer is not very interested in the secretary, or perhaps beholding, if the viewer is interested in her. By depicting Secretary Heumann as an ordinary person who has a position of official status in the society, the portrait encourages both viewers who consider themselves disabled and those who consider themselves nondisabled to identify with her. The photograph suggests neither that her accomplishments are superhuman nor that she has triumphantly overcome anything. She thus becomes more familiar than strange. Most important is the picture's message that a woman with a disability can occupy such a position.

Secretary Heumann's picture sits in bold historical opposition to the many now-controversial official photos of President Franklin D. Roosevelt that hide the wheelchair he used daily.[8] Authorized by the cultural changes the civil rights movements wrought, Heumann's official portrait exemplifies one of several genres in contemporary photography that familiarize disability rather than defamiliarize it. Indeed, such representations banish the strange and cultivate the ordinary, radically reimagining disability by installing people with disabilities in the realm of human commonality and dismantling the assumption that disability precludes accomplishment.

This taxonomy of four primary visual rhetorics of disability provides a way to see the way we see disability. These pictures choreograph a social dynamic of looking, suggesting that disability is not simply a natural state of bodily inferiority and inadequacy. Rather, it is a culturally fabricated narrative of the body, similar to what we understand as the fictions of race and gender. Disability, then, is a system that produces subjects by differentiating and marking bodies. Furthermore, this comparison of bodies legitimates the distribution of resources, status, and power in a biased social and architectural environment. As such, disability has four aspects: first, it is a system for interpreting bodily variations; second, it is a relation between bodies and their environments; third, it is a set of practices that produce both the able-bodied and the disabled; fourth, it is a way of describing the inherent instability of the embodied self. The category of disability exists as a way to exclude the kinds of bodily forms, functions, impairments, changes, or ambiguities that call into question our cultural fantasy of the body as a neutral, compliant instrument of some transcendent will. Moreover, *disability* is a broad term in which cluster ideological categories as varied as sick, deformed, ugly, old, crazy, maimed, afflicted, abnormal, or debilitated—all of which disadvantage people by devaluing bodies that do not conform to cultural standards. Thus *disability* functions to preserve and validate such privileged designations as beautiful, healthy, normal, fit, competent, intelligent—all of which provide cultural capital to those who can claim such status, who can reside within these subject positions. Thus, the various interactions between bodies and world make disability from the raw material of human variation and precariousness.

All visualizations of disability are mediations that shape the world in which people who have or do not have disabilities inhabit and negotiate together. The point is that all representations have social and political consequences. Understanding how images create or dispel disability as a system of exclusions and prejudices is a move toward the process of dismantling the institutional, attitudinal, legislative, economic, and architectural barriers that keep people with disabilities from full participation in society.

NOTES

1. For a historical account of the display of disabled people as monsters and freaks, see Altick; Bogdan; Dennett; Garland-Thomson, "From Wonder"; and D. Wilson.
2. For an account of the ocularcentric in Western culture, see Barthes; Crary; Debord; and Jay.
3. I am not including medical or artistic photography here, although both genres inform the visual construction of disability. I am limiting this analysis to popular photography, which I take to be the primary register and shaper of public consciousness. For an analysis of images of insanity, see Gilman.
4. For a discussion of the development of middle-class feeling as a form of distinguishing respectability, see Halttunen; for a discussion of how sentimentality uses disabled figures, see Garland-Thomson, "Crippled Little Girls."
5. The term "Down syndrome" is now preferred over "Down's syndrome" by more politicized parents and guardians looking to mark some distance from the English physician John Langdon Down, who first described the syndrome's characteristic features (i.e., they are challenging his "ownership" of Down syndrome). See, for example, Richards.
6. To use the term *realistic* does not suggest that this visual rhetoric is more truthful, accurate, or real than the other modes discussed here. Realism's function is to create the illusion of reality, not to reproduce or capture reality's elusive and complex substance. Although more subtle perhaps, the rhetoric of realism is just as constructed and convention-bound as the rhetorics of the wondrous, sentimental, or exotic.
7. For further discussion of Hine, see Rosenblum, Rosenblum, and Trachtenberg.
8. For a discussion of Franklin Roosevelt's disability, see H. Gallagher.

MICHAEL DAVIDSON

Hearing Things:
The Scandal of Speech
in Deaf Performance

In the film version of Mark Medoff's play *Children of a Lesser God,* James (William Hurt) is a speech instructor at a deaf school who believes that his students must be educated into oral culture by being taught to lip-read and speak. He falls in love with Sarah (Marlee Maitlin), who is deaf but who refuses to participate in his pedagogical project. She signs throughout the film, insisting on her right to remain silent, until one climactic scene when, under James's badgering, she suddenly screeches out a stream of speech. It is a powerful scene, because it is the first time the hearing audience has experienced her voice and realizes that she *can* speak but prefers not to. It is also powerful because instead of achieving the desired result, Sarah's vocalizing illustrates the coercive force of an educational system based around speech rather than manual signing. What James witnesses is a kind of Deaf performative—a form of speech that enacts rather than describes—its meaning contained not in the content of Sarah's words (most of which are unrecognizable) but in the results the performance achieves in shaking his oralist bias. In Henry Louis Gates's terms, it signifies *on* speech as a much as *by means of* it (44–88). For the hearing educator, speech is the key to normalization in hearing-based culture; for the Deaf signer, speech is the sign of an alienating process that only performing can make evident.

I want to extend the concept of a Deaf performative to describe the work of Deaf language artists for whom the use of speech and vocalization is a kind of scandal and who utilize that scandal to critical ends. By scandal, I mean that the eruption of speech in Deaf performance challenges the conventional opposition of signing and speech and allows for more complex, hybrid combinations. In the wake of the Deaf President Now protests (DPN) of 1988 at Gallaudet University and the launching of a powerful political movement for the empowering of Deaf persons, the use of speech-based pedagogies represents the continuing authority of hearing culture. (On the DPN protests, see Brueggemann, *Lend Me* 151–200; Christiansen and Barnartt; and Lane.) The attempt to reinforce oralist values by audiologists, psychologists, educators, and legislators has been combated by an increasingly politicized social movement of the Deaf, who regard themselves not as a handicapped population but as a linguistic minority with distinct cultural and historical traditions. (For this reason I capitalize *Deaf* when referring to deaf persons as a distinct culture and use a small *d* when speaking of the physiological condition of deafness.) As Dirksen Bauman, Harlan Lane, Douglas Baynton, Tom Humphreys and Carol Padden, and others have observed, audism—the ideological replication of humans as hearing subjects—has influenced treatment of Deaf persons from the outset. The incarceration of the deaf in institutions, the denial of American Sign Language (ASL) as a language, the imposition of medical aids (cochlear implants, hearing aids), mainstreaming in education, punishment of children for manual signing—all constitute what Lane has called a "colonial" subjugation of the Deaf (31–38). A postcolonial regime is very much under way, and performance is one of its key venues.

Humphreys and Padden refer to the portmanteau ASL sign for "think-hearing," which transfers the sign for "hearing" (a finger rotating near the mouth) to the region of the head in order to describe someone who "thinks and acts like a hearing person" or who uncritically embraces the ideology of others (53). ASL poets like Clayton Valli, Ella Mae Lentz, Debbie Rennie, and others have made "think-hearing" a subject of aesthetic critique while using ASL as a powerful counter-discourse to phonocentric models for literature. In their work, "performing the text" means utilizing ASL signing to establish community (the Deaf audience understands a sign as multiple meanings) and politicize the occasion (the hearing audience cannot rely on acoustic prosodic models). Thus a key meaning in every Deaf performance is a set of shared cultural values implicit in the use of ASL. One might say that in addition to the four categories foregrounded in Deaf performance—space, body, time, language—a fifth must be added: that of Deaf culture itself.

But to speak of Deaf culture as a single entity is to generalize a rather broad continuum of persons variously positioned with respect to deafness. The phrase would include children who are deaf but whose family is hearing or hearing children of deaf parents (CODA) as well as persons who have become deaf later in life or who still retain some hearing. (A good introduction to the situation of hearing children of deaf parents can be found in Lennard Davis's memoir, *My Sense of Silence: Memoirs of a Childhood with Deafness.* See also his *Enforcing Normalcy: Disability, Deafness, and the Body.*) In descriptions of Deaf performance, such differences often become obscured in a more general celebration of an authentic (i.e., soundless, textless, ASL-based) poetry. The decision by Lentz and others not to have their ASL works voice-interpreted is an understandable refusal of hearing culture, but it has limited the venues in which they may participate and audiences they might reach. I would like to look at two performers, Peter Cook and Aaron Williamson, who violate such authenticity and in doing so comment suggestively on issues of language and communication in general, insofar as language and communication are based on a phonocentric model. In my conclusion I suggest some of the implications that such performers pose for the intersections among performance, disabilities, and multiculturalism.

Peter Cook is the deaf half of Flying Words Project, a collaborative performance group; the other half is Kenny Lerner, who hears but also signs. The two create performances that draw on several vernacular Deaf traditions, including mime, deaf ventriloquism, and storytelling. Where Flying Words differs from Deaf poets like Valli and Lentz is in its use of sound and collaboration. Not only does Lerner occasionally vocalize (speak over) Cook's signs, Cook sometimes vocalizes while he signs. For Deaf nationalists, such collaboration with the hearing world is problematic, to say the least, but for these two poets it is a way of extending the gestural potentiality of ASL into what we might call an immanent critique of audist ideology. Furthermore, Lerner's vocalization is seldom used to translate or interpret Cook's signing. Often, Lerner is silent while Cook punctuates his signing with words or parts of words— as in "I Am Ordered Now to Speak," a performance that dramatizes pedagogical tensions between oralist and manualist learning. The two performers, standing on either side of a stage, render a poem recounting Cook's oralist education at the Clarke School. Cook speaks the poem while Lerner signs, thus reversing the usual interpreter and interpreted roles.[1] In the absence of commercially available tapes by Deaf performers, the student of sign literature must rely on a few videos circulated in an ad hoc manner among friends and colleagues. While this situation limits the number of performances available for commentary, it points to the limits of video documentation and to the site-specific nature of such performances. The important interactive character of Deaf performance can hardly be rendered in a video. Cook's voice is, as Brueggemann points out, "loud, monotone, wooden, 'unnatural,' nearly unintelligible," while Lerner's signs are "a bit stiff and exaggerated as well" (*Lend Me* 205). The unsettling nature of oral delivery is reinforced by the poem's violent denunciation of oral education, which is compared at one point to a kind of lobotomy, "for the sake of ma bell." Cook's repeated version of the speech instructor's refrain "you/must/ now/talk" becomes increasingly agitated as the poem moves to its conclusion. At one point, the two performers come together, Lerner standing behind Cook, posing as the "speech freako" who, in demanding vocal articulation from his deaf student, imitates a brain surgeon. Cook, as patient, warns:

Don't stare at me
I was on that cold metal table
that speech freako wants me
as example for the society
rip my brains with
peanuts buttered spoon
scream with blackboard trick:

B IS NOT P
D IS NOT T
S IS NOT Z   (206)

Like James in *Children of a Lesser God*, the oral instructor wants to make an example of the deaf student by asking him to pronounce phrases like "peanuts buttered spoon." Such phrases are replete with phonemes that, for a lip reader, are difficult to distinguish. The oralist teacher's corrections, "B IS NOT P / D IS NOT T / S IS NOT Z," are counterpoised to Lerner's signing, in which the verbal distinctions among phonemes become spatial and readable distinctions among manual signs. Cook's unintelligible speech suggests the limits of oralist education, while Lerner's signing, however tentative, provides a corrective. Both performers utilize a language foreign to their usual cultural milieu and in this way embody the alienation thematized in the poem. The deaf student is forced to speak under orders; the hearing person translates into readable signs a speech that is all but incomprehensible.

Figure 1

Peter Cook (in front) and Kenny Lerner (behind), from "I Am Ordered Now to Speak." Photo by Roy Sowers

Before beginning their performance, Lerner announces that Cook will sign briefly—without vocal interpretation—to the deaf audience. Lerner points out that Cook "will be focusing on hearing people. So, please, feel paranoid" (205). Such framing of multiple constituencies creates a certain edginess that reverberates throughout the performance. It also foregrounds the *audio* in *audience,* because for most performers *audience* implies a homogeneous (hearing) entity. For Cook to speak the poem is to show the ideology of think-hearing at its most flagrant. But by collaborating with Lerner, who remains silent, he does something more. He illustrates a fruitful comixture of sound and sign contributing to a critical as well as aesthetic performance.

Interaction with the audience is a key feature of the Flying Words Project's best-known performance, "Poetry around the World," in which Cook and Lerner play a series of variations ("transformations," they call them) on signs for poetry and language. Their primary metaphor is the global extensiveness of poetry, but the means by which they develop this message suggests certain limits to a universalist aesthetics. In one segment, Cook quite literally throws the sign for "language" (the fingerspelled letter *l*) around the world like a baseball, while Lerner, standing behind him, assists. According to Brueggemann, the use of two signers signing, one behind the other in a mask, is a standard "deaf ventriloquist" act used in many forms of Deaf storytelling (207).

The two primary signs used here, "language" and "poetry," are given cosmic dimensions by being thrown through space, yet the circular pattern of the signing (Cook watches his extended sign circling his body) is broken by moments when Cook gestures outward at the audience. At one point, while the hand shape "p" for text-based poetry bounces among three of the performers' four hands, Cook waves at someone in the audience and drinks from a cup. Although it is a small gesture, it breaks the circle in which signs are produced and acknowledges the larger space of signed communication. It also addresses the audience, whether deaf or hearing, as a component in the signing process.

To address these multiple audiences, Cook mixes three signs for poetry: the sign for ASL poetry, a gesture of the hand out from the heart; the sign for written English, based on the finger-spelled letter *p;* and, finally, the finger-spelling p-o-e-t-r-y. The three together indicate the Deaf poet's multilingual, multicultural identity, suggesting that if poetry is to achieve truly global resonance, it must utilize all the resources of language—including the cultural specificity of its dissemination. Cook also utters the plosive \p\ as he bounces the sign for poetry off Lerner's hands, a gesture that Brueggemann regards as a reference to an "oral school exercise." As she points out, this sound establishes a rhythm— "like a train gathering speed"—and thus enhances the metaphor of travel (207). It also frames the pedagogical implications of oral learning in which, for the deaf child, an abstract sound is molded into a word through rote repetition. Against this form of cultural coercion, embodied in Cook's utterances, the audience experiences the rich, multifaceted background of a poetry constructed through manual signing.

The heat generated by such transformations is illustrated by the way the two performers exchange signs, quite literally bouncing the sign for "poetry" from hand to hand. Such sharing of signs in real time is, of course, at the core of Deaf communication, but this performance literalizes the fact by having four hands signing. The links between hearing and Deaf culture are established in the collaborative nature of performance, yet by placing the hearing Lerner behind in a mask, Cook stresses the ghostly presence of hearing culture—assisting but invisible. In this sense, Flying Words redirects the paternalist hierarchy of hearing to nonhearing persons by placing the deaf performer in front, reversing the spatial (and audiological) proximity.

The spatial positioning of hearing and deaf, English and ASL, interpreter and interpreted in Flying Words performances maps an indeterminate space between and in audist culture. Lerner and Cook utilize their bodies and their bicultural experiences to define and critique a world that must be spoken to be known. What would a world look like in which sound follows rather than precedes signs created by the body? A contrasting view might, in Owen Wrigley's terms, "see a world built around the valence of visual rather than aural channels" (3). This is the subject of work by Aaron Williamson, a British performance artist who began to lose his hearing at a young age and who was profoundly deaf by his mid-twenties. Although he has been deaf for most of his adult life, he retains a strong connection to hearing culture and makes his bicultural condition a major theme in his performances. Like Cook, he often collaborates with other performers, including musicians and drummers (he has appeared in punk bands since the mid-1970s).

In several of his performances, Williamson utilizes musicians and dancers. In a recent collaboration, he worked with the drummer Craig Astill, "a kind of Beckettian reduction of my capacity to hear or sense music. Craig played a frame drum directly into the floor (we insisted on hollow wooden stages only), and I picked up a barefoot vibrational signal from varying distances from the drum, thus stimulating degrees of animation in the improvised performance" (E-mail). But in contrast to many Deaf performers—including Flying Words—signing is not a prominent feature of his work. Rather, it is among the arsenal of gestures that he uses to confront the liminal situation of the late deafened: those with one foot in the Deaf and the other in the hearing community.

A good introduction to Williamson's work is his 1999 performance "Phantom Shifts," a series of lyrical reflections on the authority of the ear. In one sequence, the ear, in the form of a large plaster sculpture, is carried on the performer's back. Williamson has said that the inspiration for this image came less from an attempt to represent the burden of hearing than from an attempt to impede routinized movement. To some extent, all his work involves the imposition of limits to normalized action, constructing a "law of diminishing referentiality" that he shares with a wide range of contemporary performers (Lecture). The title of this segment, "Breath," refers to the sound track that features Williamson's labored breathing as he bears his physical (the plaster ear is in fact quite heavy) and ideological burdens. But the sound track often cuts out, leaving silences that impose their own acoustic burden on the hearing viewer, who expects some continuity between image and sound.

The second segment, "Wave," takes the metaphor of breathing another step by introducing vocalization in the form of a single syllable. Thus "Phantom Shifts" shifts from breath to the beginnings of significant sound. The performer stands facing us at the end of a long room, wearing a white shift. Before him and extending toward the camera is a long piece of translucent white material. In the foreground the plaster ear is faintly outlined beneath the material. It is, in British slang, covered by cloth or "cloth-eared," meaning mute or stupid. Williamson takes a series of deep breaths, approaches the white sheet, raises it, and suddenly lowers it, creating a wave that rolls from him to the ear. The material is flexible enough to create a continuous unfolding wave or ripple the full length of the room until it reaches the ear. On one level, the wave seems to emanate from Williamson's breath, exhaled at the moment the material is lowered. On another level, the wave is a dramatization of sound waves traveling through space to strike the tympanum. For the Deaf performer, however, Williamson's gesture is about the separation of breath from sound, of sound from sense. The ear is less an extension of the body than a prosthesis to which the body aspires. Williamson's breathing exercises resemble a kind of ritual gesture made toward the fetish at the opposite end of the room, but instead of animating the fetish with significant speech, his breath simply creates a wave.

Figure 2

Aaron Williamson, "Wave," from "Phantom Shifts" (1999). Photo by Tertia Longmire

In the final seconds of the brief performance, Williamson comes to speech, uttering a loud "Ha" before lowering the sheet. This time, the ensuing wave uncovers the ear, permitting the performer to leave the space. In a discussion of "Phantom Shifts," Williamson has said that he uses this open-throated "Ha" because it is the most expressive and primal of sounds, employed equally in laughter and crying (Lecture). Thus the sound that lays bear the device of the ear is one that defies the purely semantic features of speech and calls attention to the body's expressive functions. If he cannot hear his own voice, Williamson can represent the scene of its emergence, the agon of its production. Moreover, by cutting the sound track off and on, he may embody for the viewer the discontinuity of images detached from their animating sounds.

What animates this and other performances by Williamson is a recognition of the constitutive force of speech and hearing in the production of knowledge. In Western theology and philosophy, the Logos or reason is represented as a voice, the spirit as breath. Such metaphors have been active in constructing much postwar poetics, from Charles Olson's projective verse and beat testimony to the anthropological oralism of Gary Snyder or Jerome Rothenberg to sound poetry and spoken word performance. For Williamson, the Logos is figured not as a voice but as an ear, the agent of reception in a Saussurean communicational diagram. The poet short-circuits the Judeo-Christian model of the Logos as voice by treating the ear as a fetish, a stony recipient of cryptic messages that wash up on its shore.

This same deconstruction of a logo- and phonocentric tradition can be seen in Williamson's recent work, "Hearing Things" (1999). This performance is a kind of cybernetic meditation on the oracle at Delphi. According to the story, the oracle purportedly delivered cryptic messages that were then decoded by her acolytes. Williamson's Artaudian version utilizes a technological interface to turn himself into a cyborg creature: half oracle, half scribe, part technology, part human. In order to effect this synthesis, he utilizes voice recognition software to generate a text that becomes the focal point for the performance. In its most recent manifestation, "Hearing Things" uses software that picks up the sounds of audience members who are encouraged to speak into a microphone placed in the gallery space. In an earlier version, on which I focus here, the sounds are produced by Williamson himself, converted by the software into a text of recognizable English words. That text is then projected from the ceiling onto the floor and reflected in two transparent autocuing glasses behind the performer. He moves around the text, gaz-

Figure 3

Aaron Williamson, from "Hearing Things" (1999). Photo by
Tertia Longmire

ing at the words and making a variety of whoops, cries, chatters, and
moans—the indecipherable words of the oracle.

Although he cannot hear his voice, he may see its representation in
words generated by it, the computer acting as an interpreter of the deaf
speaker's sounds. Thus by a curious inversion of agency, Williamson
may encounter his own words as alien—which for the deaf person living in an audist world is precisely the case. Moreover, Williamson performs on and within the text, the words occasionally projected onto his
white shift, making him both the reflector and creator of the text to
which he gives birth, his status as poet confirmed by the laurel wreath
he wears on his head. And since he is wearing a dress, gender confusion
reinforces the mixed nature of this originary word, half female oracle,
half male amanuensis. Against the Judeo-Christian model of a male
Jehovah speaking from the whirlwind, we have a female oracle whose
signs have yet to be learned by a patriarchal scribe.

The title, "Hearing Things," is elaborately unpacked in this performance. On one level it refers to language as unreality—"I must be hearing
things"—a phrase that refers to the phantasmal quality of words when

encountered as alien forms. For a late-deafened person, words have become wraiths of their former semiotic bodies. Willamson literalizes this aspect by seeing them projected on his body from some outside source. But at an epistemological level, "hearing things" refers to the binary opposition by which humans are measured in hearing culture—in which an originary Logos (the oracle) must be heard in order to be incarnated in flesh. As Jacques Derrida has pointed out, via Jean-Jacques Rousseau, hearing subjects are granted human status by their ability to hear, but as such they become merely things that hear, objects whose only claim to identity is their possession of an intact auditory nerve (*Grammatology* 165–268).

Although Derrida does not refer to deaf persons in his various critiques of phonocentrism, he might well consider a population that relies on non-phonetic means to signify and that bases its meaning production on visual rather than audible information. Derrida's phonocentrism is usually equated with speech, but Williamson foregrounds voice as a multifaceted producer of meaning, not limited to the production of strictly linguistic signs. (For further discussion of deafness and Derrida, see Bauman.) The title fuses persons and things, the fusion made palpable by Williamson's use of a series of objects—a large plaster-of-paris ear, a navel stone, and a metal tripod (as used by the Delphian Pythia)—that he attempts to animate. At three points in his performance he moves offstage to bring these objects into view, moving them around, attempting to animate them much as Beckett's characters interrogate stones, bicycles, and biscuits. The objects become similar to the projected words themselves, inert, contextless, and foreign. Yet in Williamson's interrogation, they gain new life and function.

Williamson poses a number of problems for any consideration of Deaf literature, beyond the fact that he utilizes voice in his performances. The recursive manner by which text and body, computer and script interact frustrates the idea of creativity as something that gives voice to some prior meaning. As an allegory of deafness, such recursiveness embodies the ways that deafness is inscribed in what Michel Foucault, in another context, has called "technologies of the self" (*Technologies*). For Williamson, speaking of his use of technology,

> the biological becomes fused with the digital as normal relations between cause and effect—between human and computer—are broken down. [. . .] As the digital and biological circulate with each other, the boundaries of linguistic agency and textual authority erode as both components—computer and performer—desperately try to interpret, respond to, and prompt each other's cracked, inauspicious stimulation.   ("Hearing" 18)

This "cracked" or fractured relation between human and machine suggests a fissure in the edifice of postmodern performance based, as it often is, on the authenticity of the body and gesture in an increasingly technologized world. One dream of modernism was to return the text to its materiality, to make the text speak authentically by removing it from the instrumental purposes to which speech is linked. For postmodern d/Deaf performers, this materiality can no longer sustain its purely aesthetic focus. In this sense, Flying Words and Aaron Williamson could be aligned with Chicano interlingual poets such as Gloria Anzaldúa or Lorna Dee Cervantes and with feminist performance artists such as Laurie Anderson or Eleanor Antin, for whom performing or materializing the text always implicates the word as a problem, not a conduit, in which cultural identity is hybrid, not unitary.

As Williamson's "Hearing Things" makes evident, alienation from the text and from textuality is literal; words appear on the ground like exotic flora and fauna in some new, cybernetic Eden. Williamson may step on them, point at them, and give them meaning, but he is removed from their production. His nonsemantic roaring, like that of Sarah's in *Children of a Lesser God*, is a speech act that challenges the ordinariness of ordinary language, making strange not only sounds but also the discursive arena in which speech makes sense. Similarly Flying Words, by treating the sign as a process of community building, reinforces the collective qualities of meaning production on a global scale. Cook and Lerner's complex use of sound and sign, far from uniting sound and sign in a gesture of multicultural unity, illustrates the continuing divide between speech-based and Deaf pedagogies. Cook and Lerner's metatextual references to both hearing and deaf audiences challenge the idea that ASL is an invented or iconic language, ancillary to English. Rather, in their hands, it becomes a rich, polyvalent structure, capable of containing the container. The "scandal of speech" in Deaf performance is not that it appears in concert with signing but that its use calls into question the self-evident nature of speech-based communicational models. At the very minimum, such performers make "think-hearing" a phrase that, once seen, can never be heard the same way twice.

NOTE

1. Brenda Brueggemann has provided an excellent reading of this performance, as she has of many other ASL poets. I am indebted to her readings of both performances, as I am to the videotapes she and Lerner loaned me.

ROBERT McRUER

Compulsory Able-Bodiedness and Queer/Disabled Existence

Contextualizing Disability

In her famous critique of compulsory heterosexuality Adrienne Rich opens with the suggestion that lesbian existence has often been "simply rendered invisible" (178), but the bulk of her analysis belies that rendering. In fact, throughout "Compulsory Heterosexuality and Lesbian Existence," one of Rich's points seems to be that compulsory heterosexuality depends as much on the ways in which lesbian identities are made visible (or, we might say, comprehensible) as on the ways in which they are made invisible or incomprehensible. She writes:

> Any theory of cultural/political creation that treats lesbian existence as a marginal or less "natural" phenomenon, as mere "sexual preference," or as the mirror image of either heterosexual or male homosexual relations is profoundly weakened thereby, whatever its other contributions. Feminist theory can no longer afford merely to voice a toleration of "lesbianism" as an "alternative lifestyle," or make token allusion to lesbians. A feminist critique of compulsory heterosexual orientation for women is long overdue. (178)

The critique that Rich calls for proceeds not through a simple recognition or even valuation of "lesbian existence" but rather through an interrogation of how the system of compulsory heterosexuality utilizes that existence. Indeed, I would extract from her suspicion of mere "toleration" confirmation for the idea that one of the ways in which heterosexuality is currently constituted or founded, established as the foundational sexual identity for women, is precisely through the deployment of lesbian existence as always and everywhere supplementary—the margin to heterosexuality's center, the mere reflection of (straight and gay) patriarchal realities. Compulsory heterosexuality's casting of some identities as alternatives ironically buttresses the ideological notion that dominant identities are not really alternatives but rather the natural order of things.[1]

More than twenty years after it was initially published, Rich's critique of compulsory heterosexuality is indispensable, the criticisms of her ahistorical notion of a "lesbian continuum" notwithstanding.[2] Despite its continued relevance, however, the realm of compulsory heterosexuality might seem to be an unlikely place to begin contextualizing disability.[3] I want to challenge that by considering what might be gained by understanding "compulsory heterosexuality" as a key concept in disability studies. Through a reading of compulsory heterosexuality, I want to put forward a theory of what I call compulsory able-bodiedness. The Latin root for *contextualize* denotes the act of weaving together, interweaving, joining together, or composing. This essay thus contextualizes disability in the root sense of the word, because I argue that the system of compulsory able-bodiedness that produces disability is thoroughly interwoven with the system of compulsory heterosexuality that produces queerness; that—in fact—compulsory heterosexuality is contingent on compulsory able-bodiedness and vice versa. And, although I reiterate it in my conclusion, I want to make it clear at the outset that this particular contextualizing of disability is offered as part of a much larger and collective project of unraveling and decomposing both systems.[4]

The idea of imbricated systems is of course not new—Rich's own analysis repeatedly stresses the imbrication of compulsory heterosexuality and patriarchy. I would argue, however, as others have, that feminist and queer theories (and cultural theories generally) are not yet accustomed to figuring ability/disability into the equation, and thus this theory of compulsory able-bodiedness is offered as a preliminary contribution to that much-needed conversation.[5]

Able-Bodied Heterosexuality

In his introduction to *Keywords: A Vocabulary of Culture and Society,* Raymond Williams describes his project as the record of an inquiry into a vocabulary: a shared body of words and meanings in our most general discussions, in English, of the practices and institutions which we group as culture and society. Every word which I have included has at some time, in the course of some argument, virtually forced itself on my attention because the problems of its meaning seemed to me inextricably bound up with the problems it was being used to discuss.   (15)

Although Williams is not particularly concerned in *Keywords* with feminism or gay and lesbian liberation, the processes he describes should be recognizable to feminists and queer theorists, as well as to scholars and activists in other contemporary movements, such as African American studies or critical race theory. As these movements have developed, increasing numbers of words have indeed forced themselves on our attention, so that an inquiry into not just the marginalized identity but also the dominant identity has become necessary. The problem of the meaning of masculinity (or even maleness), of whiteness, of heterosexuality has increasingly been understood as inextricably bound up with the problems the term is being used to discuss.

One need go no further than the *Oxford English Dictionary* to locate problems with the meaning of heterosexuality. In 1971 the *OED Supplement* defined *heterosexual* as "pertaining to or characterized by the normal relations of the sexes; opp. to homosexual." At this point, of course, a few decades of critical work by feminists and queer theorists have made it possible to acknowledge quite readily that heterosexual and homosexual are in fact not equal and opposite identities. Rather, the ongoing subordination of homosexuality (and bisexuality) to heterosexuality allows heterosexuality to be institutionalized as "the normal relations of the sexes," while the institutionalization of heterosexuality as the "normal relations of the sexes" allows homosexuality (and bisexuality) to be subordinated. And, as queer theory continues to demonstrate, it is precisely the introduction of normalcy into the system that introduces compulsion. "Nearly everyone," Michael Warner writes in *The Trouble with Normal: Sex, Politics, and the Ethics of Queer Life*, "wants to be normal. And who can blame them, if the alternative is being abnormal, or deviant, or not being one of the rest of us? Put in those terms, there doesn't seem to be a choice at all. Especially in America where [being] normal probably outranks all other social aspirations" (53). Compulsion is here produced and covered over, with the appearance of choice (sexual preference) mystifying a system in which there actually is no choice.

A critique of normalcy has similarly been central to the disability rights movement and to disability studies, with—for example—Lennard Davis's overview and critique of the historical emergence of normalcy (*Enforcing* 23–49) or Rosemarie Garland-Thomson's introduction of the concept of the "normate" (*Extraordinary Bodies* 8–9). Such scholarly and activist work positions us to locate the problems of able-bodied identity, to see the problem of the meaning of able-bodiedness as bound up with the problems it is being used to discuss. Arguably, able-bodied identity is at this juncture even more naturalized than heterosexual identity. At the very least, many people not sympathetic to queer theory will concede that ways of being heterosexual are culturally produced and culturally variable, even if and even as they understand heterosexual identity itself to be entirely natural. The same cannot be said, on the whole, for able-bodied identity. An extreme example that nonetheless encapsulates currently hegemonic thought on ability and disability is a notorious *Salon* article attacking disability studies that appeared online in the summer of 1999. Nora Vincent writes, "It's hard to deny that something called normalcy exists. The human body is a machine, after all—one that has evolved functional parts: lungs for breathing, legs for walking, eyes for seeing, ears for hearing, a tongue for speaking and most crucially for all the academics concerned, a brain for thinking. This is science, not culture" ("Enabling").[6] In a nutshell, you either have an able body or you don't.

Yet the desire for definitional clarity might unleash more problems than it contains; if it's hard to deny that something called normalcy exists, it's even harder to pinpoint what that something is. The *OED* defines *able-bodied* redundantly and negatively as "having an able body, i.e. one free from physical disability, and capable of the physical exertions required of it; in bodily health; robust." Able-bodiedness, in turn, is defined vaguely as "soundness of bodily health; ability to work; robustness." The parallel structure of the definitions of ability and sexuality is quite striking: first, to be able-bodied is to be "free from physical disability," just as to be heterosexual is to be "the opposite of homosexual." Second, even though the language of "the normal relations" expected of human beings is not present in the definition of able-bodied, the sense of normal relations is, especially with the emphasis on work: being able-bodied means being capable of the normal physical exertions required in a particular system of labor. It is here, in fact, that both able-bodied identity and the *Oxford English Dictionary* betray their origins in the nineteenth century and the rise of industrial capitalism. It is here as well that we can begin to understand the compulsory nature of able-bodiedness: in the emergent industrial capitalist system, free to sell one's labor but not free to do anything else effectively meant free to have an able body but not particularly free to have anything else.

Like compulsory heterosexuality, then, compulsory able-bodiedness functions by covering over, with the appearance of choice, a system in which there actually is no choice. I would not locate this compulsion, moreover, solely in the past, with the rise of industrial capitalism. Just as the origins of heterosexual/homosexual identity are now obscured for most people so that compulsory heterosexuality functions as a disciplinary formation seemingly emanating from everywhere and nowhere, so too are the origins of able-bodied/disabled identity obscured, allowing what Susan Wendell calls "the disciplines of normality" (87) to cohere in a system of compulsory able-bodiedness that similarly emanates from everywhere and nowhere. Able-bodied dilutions and misunderstandings of the minority thesis put forward in the disability rights movement and disability studies have even, in some ways, strengthened the system: the dutiful (or docile) able-bodied subject now recognizes that some groups of people have chosen to adjust to or even take pride in their "condition," but that recognition, and the tolerance that undergirds it, covers over the compulsory nature of the able-bodied subject's own identity.[7]

Michael Bérubé's memoir about his son Jamie, who has Down syndrome, helps exemplify some of the ideological demands currently sustaining compulsory able-bodiedness. Bérubé writes of how he "sometimes feel[s] cornered by talking about Jamie's intelligence, as if the burden of proof is on me, official spokesman on his behalf." The subtext of these encounters always seems to be the same: "In the end, aren't you disappointed to have a retarded child? [. . .] Do we really have to give this person our full attention?" (180). Bérubé's excavation of this subtext pinpoints an important common experience that links all people with disabilities under a system of compulsory able-bodiedness—the experience of the able-bodied need for an agreed-on common ground. I can imagine that answers might be incredibly varied to similar questions—"In the end, wouldn't you rather be hearing?" and "In the end, wouldn't you rather not be HIV positive?" would seem, after all, to be very different questions, the first (with its thinly veiled desire for Deafness not to exist) more obviously genocidal than the second. But they are not really different questions, in that their constant repetition (or their presence as ongoing subtexts) reveals more about the able-bodied culture doing the asking than about the bodies being interrogated. The culture asking such questions assumes in advance that we all agree: able-bodied identities, able-bodied perspectives are preferable and what we all, collectively, are aiming for. A system of compulsory able-bodiedness repeatedly demands that people with disabilities embody for others an affirmative answer to the unspoken question, Yes, but in the end, wouldn't you rather be more like me?

It is with this repetition that we can begin to locate both the ways in which compulsory able-bodiedness and compulsory heterosexuality are interwoven and the ways in which they might be contested. In queer theory, Judith Butler is most famous for identifying the repetition required to maintain heterosexual hegemony:

> The "reality" of heterosexual identities is performatively consti-
> tuted through an imitation that sets itself up as the origin and the
> ground of all imitations. In other words, heterosexuality is always
> in the process of imitating and approximating its own phantas-
> matic idealization of itself—and failing. Precisely because it is
> bound to fail, and yet endeavors to succeed, the project of hetero-
> sexual identity is propelled into an endless repetition of itself.
>
> ("Imitation" 21)

If anything, the emphasis on identities that are constituted through repetitive performances is even more central to compulsory able-bodiedness—think, after all, of how many institutions in our culture are showcases for able-bodied performance. Moreover, as with heterosexuality, this repetition is bound to fail, as the ideal able-bodied identity can never, once and for all, be achieved. Able-bodied identity and heterosexual identity are linked in their mutual impossibility and in their mutual incomprehensibility—they are incomprehensible in that each is an identity that is simultaneously the ground on which all identities supposedly rest and an impressive achievement that is always deferred and thus never really guaranteed. Hence Butler's queer theories of gender performativity could be easily extended to disability studies, as this slightly paraphrased excerpt from *Gender Trouble* suggests (I substitute, by bracketing, terms having to do literally with embodiment for Butler's terms of gender and sexuality):

> [Able-bodiedness] offers normative [. . .] positions that are in-
> trinsically impossible to embody, and the persistent failure to iden-
> tify fully and without incoherence with these positions reveals

[able-bodiedness] itself not only as a compulsory law, but as an inevitable comedy. Indeed, I would offer this insight into [able-bodied identity] as both a compulsory system and an intrinsic comedy, a constant parody of itself, as an alternative [disabled] perspective.

(122)

In short, Butler's theory of gender trouble might be resignified in the context of queer/disability studies as what we could call "ability trouble"—meaning not the so-called problem of disability but the inevitable impossibility, even as it is made compulsory, of an able-bodied identity.

Queer/Disabled Existence

The cultural management of the endemic crisis surrounding the performance of both heterosexual and able-bodied identity effects a panicked consolidation of hegemonic identities. The most successful heterosexual subject is the one whose sexuality is not compromised by disability (metaphorized as queerness); the most successful able-bodied subject is the one whose ability is not compromised by queerness (metaphorized as disability). This consolidation occurs through complex processes of conflation and stereotype: people with disabilities are often understood as somehow queer (as paradoxical stereotypes of the asexual or oversexual person with disabilities would suggest), while queers are often understood as somehow disabled (as an ongoing medicalization of identity, similar to what people with disabilities more generally encounter, would suggest). Once these conflations are available in the popular imagination, queer/disabled figures can be tolerated and, in fact, utilized in order to maintain the fiction that able-bodied heterosexuality is not in crisis. As lesbian existence is deployed, in Rich's analysis, to reflect back heterosexual and patriarchal "realities," queer/disabled existence can be deployed to buttress compulsory able-bodiedness. Since queerness and disability both have the potential to disrupt the performance of able-bodied heterosexuality, both must be safely contained—embodied—in such figures.

In the 1997 film *As Good As It Gets,* for example, although Melvin Udall (Jack Nicholson), who is diagnosed in the film as obsessive-compulsive, is represented visually in many ways that initially position him in what Martin F. Norden calls "the cinema of isolation" (i.e., Melvin is represented in ways that link him to other representations of people with disabilities), the trajectory of the film is toward able-bodied heterosexuality. To effect the consolidation of heterosexual and able-bodied norms, disability and queerness in the film are visibly located elsewhere, in the gay character Simon Bishop (Greg Kinnear). Over the course of the film, Melvin progressively sheds his sense of inhabiting an anomalous body, and disability is firmly located in the nonheterosexual character, who is initially represented as able-bodied but ends up, after he is attacked and beaten by a group of burglars, using a wheelchair and cane for most of the film. More important, the disabled/queer figure, as in many other contemporary cultural representations, facilitates the heterosexual romance: Melvin first learns to accept the differences Simon comes to embody, and Simon then encourages Melvin to reconcile with his girlfriend, Carol Connelly (Helen Hunt). Having served their purpose, Simon, disability, and queerness are all hustled offstage together. The film concludes with a fairly traditional romantic reunion between the (able-bodied) male and female leads.[8]

Critically Queer, Severely Disabled

The crisis surrounding heterosexual identity and able-bodied identity does not automatically lead to their undoing. Indeed, as this brief consideration of As Good As It Gets should suggest, this crisis and the anxieties that accompany it can be invoked in a wide range of cultural texts precisely to be (temporarily) resolved or alleviated. Neither gender trouble nor ability trouble is sufficient in and of itself to unravel compulsory heterosexuality or compulsory able-bodiedness. Butler acknowledges this problem: "This failure to approximate the norm [. . .] is not the same as the subversion of the norm. There is no promise that subversion will follow from the reiteration of constitutive norms; there is no guarantee that exposing the naturalized status of heterosexuality will lead to its subversion" ("Critically Queer" 22; qtd. in Warner, "Normal and Normaller" 168–69n87). For Warner, this acknowledgment in Butler locates a potential gap in her theory, "let us say, between virtually queer and critically queer" (Warner 168–69n87). In contrast to a virtually queer identity, which would be experienced by anyone who failed to perform heterosexuality without contradiction and incoherence (i.e., everyone), a critically queer perspective could presumably mobilize the inevitable failure to approximate the norm, collectively "working the weakness in the norm," to use Butler's phrase ("Critically Queer" 26).[9]

A similar gap can be located if we appropriate Butler's theories for disability studies. Everyone is virtually disabled, both in the sense that able-bodied norms are "intrinsically impossible to embody" fully and in the sense that able-bodied status is always temporary, disability being the one identity category that all people will embody if they live long enough. What we might call a critically disabled position, however, would differ from such a virtually disabled position; it would call attention to the ways in which the disability rights movement and disability studies have resisted the demands of compulsory able-bodiedness and have demanded access to a newly imagined and newly configured public sphere where full participation is not contingent on an able body.

We might, in fact, extend the concept and see such a perspective not as critically disabled but rather as severely disabled, with *severe* performing work similar to the critically queer work performed by *fabulous*. Tony Kushner writes:

> *Fabulous* became a popular word in the queer community—well, it was never unpopular, but for a while it became a battle cry of a new queer politics, carnival and camp, aggressively fruity, celebratory and tough like a streetwise drag queen: *"FAAAAABULOUS!"* [. . .] *Fabulous* is one of those words that provide a measure of the degree to which a person or event manifests a particular, usually oppressed, subculture's most distinctive, invigorating features.
>
> (vii)

Severe, though less common than *fabulous,* has a similar queer history: a severe critique is a fierce critique, a defiant critique, one that thoroughly and carefully reads a situation—and I mean reading in the street sense of loudly calling out the inadequacies of a given situation, person, text, or ideology. "Severely disabled," according to such a queer conception, would reverse the able-bodied understanding of severely disabled bodies as the most marginalized, the most excluded from a privileged and always elusive normalcy, and would instead suggest that it is precisely those bodies that are best positioned to refuse "mere toleration" and to call out the inadequacies of compulsory able-bodiedness. Whether it is the "army of one-breasted women" Audre Lorde imagines descending on the Capitol; the Rolling Quads, whose resistance sparked the independent living movement in Berkeley, California; Deaf students shutting down Gallaudet University in the Deaf President Now action; or ACT UP storming the National Institutes of Health or the Food and Drug Administration, severely disabled / critically queer bodies have already generated ability trouble that remaps the public sphere and reimagines and reshapes the limited forms of embodiment and desire proffered by the systems that would contain us all.[10]

Compulsory heterosexuality is intertwined with compulsory able-bodiedness; both systems work to (re)produce the able body and hetero-sexuality. But precisely because they depend on a queer/disabled existence that can never quite be contained, able-bodied heterosexuality's hege-mony is always in danger of being disrupted. I draw attention to criti-cally queer, severely disabled possibilities to further an incorporation of the two fields, queer theory and disability studies, in the hope that such a collaboration (which in some cases is already occurring, even when it is not acknowledged or explicitly named as such) will exacerbate, in more productive ways, the crisis of authority that currently besets heterosexual/able-bodied norms. Instead of invoking the crisis in order to resolve it (as in a film like *As Good As It Gets*), I would argue that a queer/disability studies (in productive conversations with disabled/queer movements outside the academy) can continuously invoke, in order to further the crisis, the inadequate resolutions that compulsory hetero-sexuality and compulsory able-bodiedness offer us. And in contrast to an able-bodied culture that holds out the promise of a substantive (but paradoxically always elusive) ideal, a queer/disabled perspective would resist delimiting the kinds of bodies and abilities that are acceptable or that will bring about change. Ideally, a queer/disability studies—like the term *queer* itself—might function "oppositionally and relationally but not necessarily substantively, not as a positivity but as a positionality, not as a thing, but as a resistance to the norm" (Halperin 66). Of course, in calling for a queer/disability studies without a necessary substance, I hope it is clear that I do not mean to deny the materiality of queer/disabled bod-ies, as it is precisely those material bodies that have populated the move-ments and brought about the changes detailed above. Rather, I mean to argue that critical queerness and severe disability are about collectively transforming (in ways that cannot necessarily be predicted in advance) the substantive uses to which queer/disabled existence has been put by a system of compulsory able-bodiedness, about insisting that such a sys-tem is never as good as it gets, and about imagining bodies and desires otherwise.

NOTES

1. In 1976, the Brussels Tribunal on Crimes against Women identified "compulsory heterosexuality" as one such crime (Katz, "Invention" 26). A year earlier, in her important article "The Traffic in Women: Notes on the 'Political Economy' of Sex," Gayle Rubin examined the ways in which "obligatory heterosexuality" and "compulsory heterosexuality" function in

what she theorized as a larger sex/gender system (179, 198; qtd. in Katz, *Invention* 132). Rich's 1980 article, which has been widely cited and reproduced since its initial publication, was one of the most extensive analyses of compulsory heterosexuality in feminism. I agree with Jonathan Ned Katz's insistence that the concept is redundant because "any society split between heterosexual and homosexual is compulsory" (*Invention* 164), but I also acknowledge the historical and critical usefulness of the phrase. It is easier to understand the ways in which a society split between heterosexual and homosexual is compulsory precisely because of feminist deployments of the redundancy of compulsory heterosexuality. I would also suggest that popular queer theorizing outside the academy (from drag performances to activist street theater) has often employed redundancy performatively to make a critical point.

2. In an effort to forge a political connection among all women, Rich uses the terms "lesbian" and "lesbian continuum" to describe a vast array of sexual and affectional connections throughout history, many of which emerge from historical and cultural conditions quite different from those that have made possible the identity of lesbian ("Compulsory Heterosexuality" 192–99). Moreover, by using "lesbian continuum" to affirm the connection between lesbian and heterosexual women, Rich effaces the cultural and sexual specificity of contemporary lesbian existence.

3. The incorporation of queer theory and disability studies that I argue for here is still in its infancy. It is in cultural activism and cultural theory about AIDS (such as John Nguyet Erni's *Unstable Frontiers* or Cindy Patton's *Fatal Advice*) that a collaboration between queer theory and disability studies is already proceeding and has been for some time, even though it is not yet acknowledged or explicitly named as such. Michael Davidson's "Strange Blood: Hemophobia and the Unexplored Boundaries of Queer Nation" is one of the finest analyses to date of the connections between disability studies and queer theory.

4. The collective projects that I refer to are, of course, the projects of gay liberation and queer studies in the academy and the disability rights movement and disability studies in the academy. This chapter is part of my own contribution to these projects and is part of my longer work in progress, titled "De-composing Bodies: Cultural Signs of Queerness and Disability."

5. David Mitchell and Sharon Snyder are in line with many scholars working in disability studies when they point out the "ominous silence in the humanities" on the subject of disability (*Body* 1). See, for other examples, Simi Linton's discussion of the "divided curriculum" (71–116) and assertions by Rosemarie Garland-Thomson and by Lennard Davis about the necessity of examining disability alongside other categories of difference such as race, class, gender, and sexuality (Garland-Thomson, *Extraordinary Bodies* 5; Davis, *Enforcing Normalcy* xi).

6. Disability studies is not the only field Vincent has attacked in the mainstream media; see her article "The Future of Queer: Wedded to Orthodoxy," which mocks academic queer theory. Neither being disabled nor being gay or lesbian in and of itself guarantees the critical consciousness generated in the disability rights or queer movements or in queer theory or disability studies: Vincent is a lesbian journalist, but her writing clearly supports both able-bodied and heterosexual norms. Instead of showing a stigmaphilic response to queer/disabled existence, finding "a commonality with those who suffer from stigma, and in this alternative realm [learning] to value the very things the rest of the world despises" (Warner, *Trouble* 43), Vincent reproduces the dominant

culture's stigmaphobic response. See Warner's discussion of Erving Goffman's concepts of stigmaphobe and stigmaphile (41–45).

7. Michel Foucault's discussion of "docile bodies" and his theories of disciplinary practices are in the background of much of my analysis here (*Discipline* 135–69).

8. The consolidation of able-bodied and heterosexuality identity is probably most common in mainstream films and television movies about AIDS, even—or perhaps especially—when those films are marketed as new and daring. The 1997 Christopher Reeve–directed HBO film *In the Gloaming* is an example. In the film, the disabled/queer character (yet again, in a tradition that reaches back to *An Early Frost* [1985]) is eliminated at the end but not before effecting a healing of the heteronormative family. As Simon Watney writes about *An Early Frost*, "The closing shot [. . .] shows a 'family album' picture. [. . .] A traumatic episode is over. The family closes ranks, with the problem son conveniently dispatched, and life getting back to normal" (114). I am focusing on a non-AIDS-related film about disability and homosexuality, because I think the processes I theorize here have a much wider currency and can be found in many cultural texts that attempt to represent queerness or disability. There is not space here to analyze *As Good As It Gets* fully; for a more comprehensive close reading of how heterosexual/able-bodied consolidation works in the film and other cultural texts, see my forthcoming article "As Good As It Gets: Queer Theory and Critical Disability." I do not, incidentally, think that these processes are unique to fictional texts: the MLA's annual *Job Information List,* for instance, provides evidence of other locations where heterosexual and able-bodied norms support each other while ostensibly allowing for tolerance of queerness and disability. The recent high visibility of queer studies and disability studies on university press lists, conference proceedings, and even syllabi has not translated into more jobs for disabled/queer scholars.

9. See my discussion of Butler, Gloria Anzaldúa, and critical queerness in *Queer Renaissance* 149–53.

10. On the history of the AIDS Coalition to Unleash Power (ACT UP), see Douglas Crimp and Adam Rolston's *AIDS DemoGraphics.* Lorde recounts her experiences with breast cancer and imagines a movement of one-breasted women in *The Cancer Journals.* Joseph P. Shapiro recounts both the history of the Rolling Quads and the Independent Living Movement and the Deaf President Now action in *No Pity: People with Disabilities Forging a New Civil Rights Movement* (41–58, 74–85). Deaf activists have insisted for some time that deafness should not be understood as a disability and that people living with deafness, instead, should be seen as having a distinct language and culture. As the disability rights movement has matured, however, some Deaf activists and scholars in Deaf studies have rethought this position and have claimed disability (that is, disability revalued by a disability rights movement and disability studies) in an attempt to affirm a coalition with other people with disabilities. It is precisely such a reclaiming of disability that I want to stress here with my emphasis on severe disability.

LENNARD J. DAVIS

Bodies of Difference: Politics, Disability, and Representation

When thinking about normality, we in disability studies have generally made the error, I would say, of confining our discussions more or less exclusively to impairment and disease. But there is really a larger picture that includes disability along with any nonstandard behaviors. Language usage, which is as much a physical function as any other somatic activity, has become subject to an enforcement of normalcy, as have sexuality, gender, racial identity, national identity, and so on. As Georges Canguilhem writes, "There is no difference between the birth of grammar [. . .] and the establishment of the metric system. [. . .] It began with grammatical norms and ended with morphological norms of men and horses for national defense, passing through industrial and sanitary norms" (150).

Let me backtrack here for a moment and rehearse the argument I made in *Enforcing Normalcy* so that I can make clear to readers of this essay the direction in which I am going. In that book, I claimed that before the early-to-mid-nineteenth century, Western society lacked a concept of normalcy. Indeed, the word *normal* appeared in English only about 150 years ago, and in French fifty years before that. Before the rise of the concept of normalcy, there appears not to have been a concept of the normal; instead the regnant paradigm was one revolving around the word *ideal*. If people have a concept of the ideal, then all human beings fall below that standard and so exist in varying degrees of imperfection. The key point is that in a culture of the ideal, physical imperfections are seen not as absolute but part of a descending continuum from top to bottom. No one, for example, can have an ideal body, and therefore no one has to have an ideal body. Around the beginning of the nineteenth century in Europe, we begin to see the development of statistics and of the concept of the bell curve, called early on the normal curve. With the development of statistics comes the idea of a norm. In this paradigm, the majority of bodies fall under the main umbrella of the curve. Those that do not are at the extremes—and therefore are abnormal. Thus, there is an imperative placed on people to conform, to fit in, under the rubric of normality. Instead of being resigned to a less than ideal body in the earlier paradigm, people in the past 150 years have been encouraged to strive to be normal, to huddle under the main part of the curve.

Is it a coincidence, then, that normalcy and linguistic standardization begin at roughly the same time? If we look at that confluence in one area in particular, we see that language and normalcy come together under the larger category of nationalism. As Benedict Anderson has pointed out, the rise of the modern nation took place largely in the eighteenth and nineteenth centuries, when the polyglotism that had existed in a politically controlled area was standardized into a single national language. Without this linguistic homogeneity, the notion of the modern nation-state would have had great difficulty coming into being. In addition, national literatures, both in prose and poetry, were made possible through the standardization of languages, the prescriptive creation of normal language practices.

While few now object to Anderson's thesis that language practices had to be standardized, homogenized, and normalized to allow for the creation of the modern nation-state, I think that the next step, which I propose in this essay, might be more objectionable: that for the formation of the modern nation-state not simply language but also bodies and bodily practices had to be standardized, homogenized, and normalized.[1] A national physical type, a national ethical type, and an antinational physical type had to be constructed. We see much work done in the nineteenth century on racial studies, studies of pathology, deviance, and so on—all with the aim of creating the bourgeois subject in opposition to all abnormal occurrences.

We need to think through ableism in a somewhat different way than we have in the past. Rather than conceptualize it as a trait or habit of thought on the part of certain somatically prejudiced people, we can consider it to be one aspect of a far-ranging change in European and perhaps global culture and ideology that is part of Enlightenment thought and part of modernization. Further, we can begin to move away from the victim-victimizer scenario, with which ableism, along with racism, sexism, and the other isms, has been saddled and which leaves so little room for agency. Instead, one can see ableism as an aspect of modifications of political and social practice that have both positive and negative implications.

Let us look at the development of bourgeois representative democracy as an example of how ideological structures can shape notions of the body. The feudal model of society encouraged, for its own ends, the notion of inequality, that the king or queen represented an ideal below which all subjects fell. The feudal system was based on the hierarchical notion of perfection, power, and wealth massed at the top of the social and political pyramid, in less abundance among the aristocracy, and even less among the peasantry. This model looks to a justification of such inequality in religion, in the patriarchal family, and in the violence inherent in visible trappings of state. Enlightenment writers like Jean-Jacques Rousseau, Voltaire, Adam Smith, and Thomas Jefferson rejected the concept of an idealized ruler holding all the power and wealth in favor of a representative government that postulated individuals who were equal to all other individuals. Thus the ruling entity, whose power derived from a social contract, was theoretically made up of individuals who were not different in kind from one another. Thus, for example, a well-known statue of George Washington can show a button missing on his coat without fear of diminishing his authority, which derives not from his embodying an ideal but from the delegated power of a social contract.

Yet the notion of an individual equal to other individuals, as expressed in the phrase of the Declaration of Independence for the United States of America that "all men are created equal," has at base several contradictions. First, how is it possible that someone can be an individual and yet be the same as other individuals? This paradox is contained in the word *identity*, which signifies both individual existence and similarity with others. In order to postulate a government, at least theoretically, in which citizens are individuals equal to other individuals, you need a notion of the average citizen. This being is seen as representative of all citizens. Likewise, in a representative democracy, you have to postulate that the elected officials represent each of these equal individuals.

The word *represent* conveys the next paradox. If the elected representative is a stand-in for any citizen, then he or she must act to convey the opinion of the individual. So the representative must both convey and literally be, or represent the existence of, the citizen. But for a government to be truly representative, there would have to be one elected official for each citizen. The notion of an individual representative representing groups of citizens contains the fundamental paradox of representative democracy: How is it possible to represent an individual citizen when you are elected by a majority or plurality of a segment of voters?

None of these issues were a problem for feudal or monarchical governments, since no representation of citizens had to take place. You had to postulate not individuals but rather groups, classes, realms of control. But in order to represent a citizen—as a painter or a novelist would, for example—you must visualize, create, postulate a simulacrum of that citizen.

Here is where we see the development of the average citizen in the literary form, of the average character in the novel, a genre that is devoted to the depiction of daily life, the quotidian: the average citizen as hero rather than the epic hero as larger-than-life victor. Thus the novel is a form centrally concerned with the norm.

We may say of the norm, as a concept, that it is the perfect ideological and technical solution to the paradox of the early modern individual. The norm provides an efficient explanation that reconciles the contradiction required in representative democracy concerning the notion of the represented individual. The problem of how is it possible to be an individual equal to other individuals and the further problem of how to represent such individuals are solved through the concept of the norm and the bell curve. Instantiations of individuals become statistically possible. Each entry has an existence and integrity, each person is an individual with his or her place on the bell curve. Yet, at the same time, each person is part of a continuum and fits into the whole. In addition, there is an average, a normal citizen who can be described. These are the hypothetical people whose cumulative characteristics fall under the center of the curve. Thus, the concept of the norm permits the idea of individual variation while enforcing a homogeneous standard or average.[2]

Further, with the concept of a norm, representation is made possible, since the average citizen can be seen, postulated, consulted in this way. Individuals can be represented in government as a collective. Indeed, the very idea of voting in an election for a representative has much to do with the formulation of an ideology of the norm. A collective voting decision is nothing more than the tabulation of individual variations. When the vote is taken, the result is the election of a person who represents a

norm of opinion or sentiment. Thus the majority or plurality vote describes a kind of bell curve whose distribution can be graphed. The House
of Representatives in the United States, for example, is supposed to be a
kind of living embodiment of the norm. Representative democracy is
normalcy or, to try a neologism, normocracy.

Bourgeois, representative democracy implies normalcy—the two are
really one form of government. As Canguilhem writes, "Between 1759,
when the word 'normal' appeared [in French], and 1834, when the
world 'normalized' appeared, a normative class had won the power to
identify [. . .] the function of social norms, whose content it determined, with the use that that class made of them" (151). Democracy
needs the illusion of equality, and equality needs the fiction of the equal
or average citizen. So with the creation of representative democracy
comes the need for an ideology that will support and generate the aims
of normalcy.

If democracy fosters notions of individualism, equality, and liberty, it
also requires an ideology that reconciles those aims with the aims of
capitalism, under whose watchful eye democracy is shaped. Capitalism
conceptualizes equality as equality among workers rather than as financial equality—since the latter would eliminate the difference in capital between ruling classes and workers and therefore eliminate
capitalism. But there is a fundamental paradox in Enlightenment thinking. Enlightenment philosophers have argued for equality, freedom, and
liberty in an ethical sense, hoping to have a society in which all people
are theoretically free as regards rights. However, the unequal distribution of wealth required by capitalism starkly contradicts that ethical
goal. So capitalism must explain logically or through ideology why it is
just and fair that some people have so much wealth and by virtue of that
wealth so much power to influence government.

The concepts behind normalcy allow such an explanation. If you
take the bell curve as a model, you notice that all variations fall into the
unremitting logic of this distribution. Indeed, even random instantiations fall into a bell curve, as Francis Galton demonstrated through his
construction of the quincunx, a device that allowed steel balls to fall
randomly through a series of pegs and accumulate at the bottom. Galton
could demonstrate that because the balls always accumulated in the
form of the bell curve, the normal curve was in effect a law of nature.
Therefore, it is logical to say that something like individual wealth will
conform to the curve of normal distribution—on the one side will be the
poor; in the middle, people of means; and on the other extreme, the

very wealthy. So the very theory that allows the individual to be instantiated in the collective on an equal basis also allows for wealth to be unequally distributed. Equality and normalcy demand, by the unbending laws of mathematics, that there will always be inequality.

Equality among citizens is therefore based not on an ethical notion but on a quasi-scientific one. Once the ethical is reconditioned by the statistical, equality is transformed. Indeed, the operative notion of equality, especially as it applies to the working classes, is really one of interchangeability. As the average man can be constructed, so can the average worker. All working bodies are equal to all other working bodies, because they are interchangeable. This interchangeability, particularly in nineteenth-century factories, means that workers' bodies have been conceptualized as identical. And able-bodied workers came to be interchangeable with able-bodied citizens. This ideological module has obvious references to the issue of disability. If all workers are equal and all workers are citizens, then all citizens must have standard bodies to be able to fit into the industrial-political notion of democracy, equality, and normality. Clearly people with disabilities pose problems to work situations in which labor is standardized and bodies conceptualized as interchangeable.[3]

The patient or citizen governed by the norm of representation and by the hegemony of normalcy passes, in one lifetime, through a series of institutions—day-care; primary, secondary, and higher educational facilities; corporate employment; hospitals; marriage and family; managed care; and finally nursing homes—all of which are based around legally, juridically, medically, and culturally normalizing concepts. The interlocking demands of these normalizing institutions are overwhelming and even totalitarian. Has there ever been such total control of people in history? Arguably even in the most unfair feudal rule by a single all-powerful despot the ability to control all aspects of the mind and body seems trivial compared with the rule of normalcy as it has developed over the past two hundred years.

In the midst of this system, the person with disabilities is only one casualty among many. Under normalcy, no one is or can be normal, just as no one is or can be equal. All have to work hard to make it seem that they conform, and so the person with disabilities is singled out as a dramatic case of not belonging. This identification makes it easier for the rest to think they fit the paradigm.

As the media unfold endless tales of people with disabilities, take alone many Academy Award nominees: *Shine, The English Patient,*

Slingblade, A Beautiful Mind, and *I Am Sam,* all disability films—for the examination and comfort of people who believe themselves to be able-bodied. Society continues, groaning, to single out disability as the other and to define itself by that other. Whether we are talking about AIDS, low-birth-weight babies, special education issues, euthanasia, and the thousand other topics listed in the newspapers every day, the examination, discussion, anatomizing of this form of difference is nothing less than people's desperate attempt to consolidate their normality. If more effort was spent on describing the variety of human experience and less in trying to categorize into forms (literary and visual) that proscribe anomalous states of physical identity, we would be able to explore the ways that society, narrative, and politics work to oppress bodies of difference.

NOTES

1. I am following Foucault's lead in this claim. Foucault talked about the control of deviant bodies—criminal, sexual, and medical (*Discipline, Birth,* and *History*). He never fully accounted for why these bodies were considered deviant, never really explained the ontology of deviance. My emphasis here is to speak of deviance as pressured by concepts of the norm. In other words, the creation of the modern sense of deviance for bodies is located in the work of statisticians, medical doctors, and eugenicists attempting to normalize physical variation.

2. You can see how easily the ideology of the norm then permits a management of individual variation into ideas of biodiversity that make up the theory of evolution. As soon as some variation becomes dominant, the bell curve just shifts over. So, for example, as giraffes' necks get longer through evolution, the data on giraffes shift, with shorter-necked giraffes being seen as anomalous rather than the norm.

3. It is interesting that this formulation of an average worker is a necessity not only for capitalism but also for socialism and communism. Marx, for example, used Quetelet's idea of the average man to come up with his formulations of labor value or average wages. For more on this, see Davis, *Enforcing* 28–29.

Autobiographical Subjects

G. THOMAS COUSER

Signifying Bodies: Life Writing and Disability Studies

In 1980, James Olney noted that "autobiography has become the focalizing literature for various 'studies,'" such as American studies, black studies, women's studies, and African studies, because "autobiography—the story of a distinctive culture written in individual characters and from within—offers a privileged access to an experience [. . .] that no other variety of writing can offer" (13). Autobiography deserves a prominent place in the rapidly developing discipline of disability studies by the same logic that has made it essential to other area studies. Autobiography warrants study not just as all too rare first-person testimony about disabling conditions but also as potentially powerful counterdiscourse to the prevailing discourse of disability. Olney's paradigm may also be attractive and useful for disability studies because of its idea that autobiography reveals a distinctive culture. As a medium perhaps unique in its registration of the nexus of the individual, culture, and the body, autobiographical literature can provide a valuable component to humanities courses on disability.

The value of disability narrative is illustrated by an incident reported in Anne Finger's *Past Due*, itself a model narrative—a politically self-conscious, humorous, and candid account of living with disability. Finger reports a disability activist as saying, "The difference between what I imagined disability to be like and what it actually was like was enormous" (30). Unlike most cultural representations of disability, which issue from nondisabled parties and which may reinforce stigma and marginalization, disability autobiography issues from the perspective of someone living with the condition in question. Written from inside the experience of disability—and in some instances from inside a distinct disability culture—autobiography may represent disability in ways that challenge the usual cultural scripts.

Those who teach disability autobiography should be aware of hostility to the genre from (at least) two directions. On the cultural right, those opposed to the idea that disability is a proper subject of academic inquiry are likely to feel that it is also not a proper topic or occasion for autobiography, which should reflect instead the distinction of accomplishment. For example, writing in the *Times Literary Supplement,* A. M. Daniels attributes the recent proliferation of narratives of illness and disability "to the death of humility as a social virtue; at one time, after all, only people of great or exceptional achievement, or with an extraordinary or exemplary tale to tell, would have written an autobiography." Conservative culture critics may be quite outspoken in their attempts to perpetuate the silence of people with aberrant bodies. At the same time, there are critics on the cultural left who are skeptical of narrative of any sort as a medium for challenging conventional discourse about disability. Their suspicion is generated by a long history of Gothic, sentimental, and heroic narratives—in various media, including fiction, film, and personal narrative—in which disability is represented as alternately terrifying, pitiable, or inspiring. Whatever the particular valence assigned to disability, such narratives are all merely variations of the symbolic paradigm, which reads a physical difference as a sign of some underlying moral condition; furthermore, all represent disability as fundamentally an individual problem. Thus, one of the leading theorists of disability, Lennard J. Davis, has claimed with some justification that "by narrativizing an impairment, one tends to sentimentalize it and link it to the bourgeois sensibility of individualism and the drama of an individual story" (*Enforcing* 4). Those on the cultural right may see disability autobiography, then, as excessively transgressive and counterdiscursive; those on the cultural left may see it as insufficiently so. It appears that teachers cannot assume that the work of countering the dominant discourse of disability will be done by the narratives themselves. One aim of this essay is to suggest how to use personal narrative to expose and deconstruct the often seductive, because apparently positive, popular portrayals of disability.

The situation of those teaching disability autobiography is analogous to that of those writing it, insofar as it is fraught with the risk of reinforcing conventional views. On the one hand, there is the danger of sentimentalizing, as Davis notes; on the other, there is the risk articulated by Finger: "It is my old fear come true: That if you talk about the pain, people will say, see, it isn't worth it. You would be better off dead" (33). That is, the presumed advantage of firsthand testimony may be offset by the danger that candid representation of some aspects of a condition may serve only to reinforce the assumption that disability is necessarily, wholly, and universally a negative experience. Indeed, there is no shortage of narratives that may backfire in this manner.[1]

The reason is not far to seek: disability has been so stigmatized and marginalized that it finds its way into even that most democratic literary genre, autobiography, only on condition; the prose license granted to the disabled autobiographer involves restrictions. One aim of teaching autobiographical testimony of disability is presumably to counter objectifying scenarios of display in other media. Yet most of the rhetorical patterns of autobiographical display preferred by publishers, if not by the reading public, are themselves suspect. The rhetoric of triumph, in which individuals narrate their success in overcoming adversity, is, first of all, not available to many disabled people; the narrative of triumph is thus an exclusive subgenre. In addition to being somewhat atypical, the narrative of triumph tends, at best, to remove stigma from the autobiographer, leaving it in place for others; that is, it reinforces the idea of disability as primarily misfortune. Examples of this subgenre are too numerous to list, but a classic one is Helen Keller's *The Story of My Life*. Narratives of disability acquired late in life—as represented by Jean-Dominique Bauby's popular and critically acclaimed *The Diving Bell and the Butterfly*—may employ what I call the rhetoric of nostalgia to wistfully evoke the predisability past. Such rhetoric tends to reinforce the divide between ability and disability, representing disability essentially as loss. In Gothic rhetoric—exemplified by Oliver Sacks's *A Leg to Stand On*—disability is characterized as a literally dreadful condition, to be shunned or avoided. The rhetoric of spiritual compensation—exemplified by Reynolds Price's *A Whole New Life*—represents physical disability as needing to be offset by gains in a transcendent dimension of life. And so on.[2] Thus, the personal narrative of disability is by no means guaranteed to offer positive, progressive, and counterdiscursive portrayals of disability.

All the more need, then, to provide students with a critical framework. One way to do this is give them, through reading or lecture, a critical perspective from body theory or the emerging discourse of disability studies in the humanities. Such an approach would, at a minimum, establish the differences among the ancient symbolic paradigm of disability; the modern medical or individual model of disability; and the contemporary social, political, and cultural model. According to the first, disability is a sign of a moral condition or divine disfavor. According to the second, disability is a defect or deficit in the individual body that medicine attempts to fix or compensate for (e.g., through rehabilitation or the fitting of prostheses). As should be evident, most of the prevailing rhetorical patterns suggested above in one way or another subscribe to the symbolic or individual paradigms. According to the third, disability is a social and cultural construct, analogous to race and gender, that characterizes as deviant certain arbitrarily selected physical or cognitive differences. By this paradigm, disability needs to be addressed not in the individual body but in the body politic, which may require rehabilitation in the form of legislation, modification of the physical environment, and so on, to ensure equality of access and opportunity. More generally, recognizing disability as a cultural construct enables us to understand and deconstruct the procedures by which some bodies are privileged over others.

Like race and gender, disability is multifarious in its manifestation. It may affect the form or the function of the body or both; it may be invisible or manifest; it may be static, intermittent, or progressive in its manifestation; it may be acquired at birth or later in life; it may affect physical, sensory, or cognitive function; and it may be moderate or severe in degree. Any of these differences may have powerful implications for the way a disability is represented in narrative. As much as one needs to insist on the reality of the category of disability and its power to construct our lives, there is a danger in thinking of disability as a single condition. One risk built into teaching disability autobiography is that constraints on the syllabus will result in overgeneralization from a single instance of disability.

Another risk is that insofar as disability is often epitomized in the popular mind by a few conditions—primarily sensory impairment and mobility impairment (as represented in the international symbol of the person in a wheelchair)—it will be rendered less visible than it should be, less common than it really is. Thus, the extent of disability in society is underestimated; it is thought to pertain only to people with a small number of paradigmatic conditions. A way to counter this tendency is to take class time to generate a list of as many disabling conditions as students can think of and then categorize them according to aspects suggested above. This exercise will help students see how widespread, as well as how various, disability is and how all people are normed on a variety of bases or axes. Students will suddenly become aware of disabilities in their own circles of family and friends—and thus of the immediacy and ubiquity of disability. The exercise also serves to establish a larger matrix of conditions in which to place any particular disability. This strategy may be reinforced, if time allows, by your presenting narratives in contrasting pairs—for example, narratives of different kinds or degrees of disability. The matching of texts will help counter the tendency to think of disability as a monolithic status represented by a few paradigmatic conditions.

A second strategy would be to examine, side by side, narratives that differ significantly even though they seem to concern the same condition; thus, you might teach a narrative of an oral deaf person (like Henry Kisor's *What's That Pig Outdoors?*) against one by a culturally Deaf person (like Bernard Bragg's *Lessons in Laughter,* which Bragg signed to a collaborator). Here the distinction between viewing a disability as a deficit to be overcome and as a condition of identity will be very clear. Alternatively, one might teach side by side an autobiography and a memoir of the same condition.[3] Doing so would permit discussion of what difference point of view makes: How does a nondisabled person's view of a disability, say, differ from a disabled person's—and why? The literature of deafness is particularly rich in this regard, offering accounts of a single condition from a number of different perspectives. For example, both Ruth Sidransky and Lou Ann Walker write as daughters of deaf parents; both Paul West (*Words*) and Thomas Spradley (Spradley and Spradley) write as fathers of deaf daughters. (And, after reading her father's book about her at a deaf school, Lynn Spradley wrote an epilogue to his account of her childhood.)

Such juxtapositions would raise a number of instructive questions: What sorts of relationships do memoir writers have to their disabled subjects, and how do these relationships inflect their narratives? To what extent do memoir writers mimic the ethnographic scenario in which the story of the other is written by a professional expert? What ethical questions arise when disability is narrated by a close relative or friend that do not arise in autobiography—at least not in solo autobiography? For example, what is the proper role of parents of disabled children? (Michael Bérubé, Michael Dorris, and Juliet Cassuto Rothman differ radically in their stance toward their children's disabilities— Down syndrome, fetal alcohol syndrome, and quadriplegia, respectively. Bérubé acts as an advocate for his son; Dorris takes up the cause of preventing people like his adoptive son from being born; Rothman supports her son's decision to die.) In the case of deafness, what investment do hearing parents have in reproducing in a deaf child their own oral culture?

A third approach is to consider collaboratively produced narratives of disability. One reason to include this form of life writing is that it affords an opportunity to question what might otherwise be taken for granted—the accessibility of autobiography as a genre to disabled people. Assistive technology—such as voice-recognition word-processing software—makes the print medium much more accessible to people with some disabilities, but there are other conditions (e.g., neurological impairments) that this technology does not so readily compensate for. And some severe disabilities may effectively prevent individuals from representing themselves in this medium. Here are questions that address the print medium: To whom is print entirely and easily accessible? What conditions present particular difficulties of self-representation? What are the implications of representation in print as compared with aural or visual media? What are the consequences of the fact that, as a nonvisual medium, print simultaneously represents disability and conceals it from the reader? In the case of visible disability, does the blindness of print allow reader and writer to meet in a zone where their interaction is less likely to be determined by visual cues? Does print permit disabilities to be performed in ways not possible in visual media—or in everyday life? (To take a specific example, which aspects of Tourette's syndrome are displayed, which masked, in print? One might compare Lowell Handler's *Twitch and Shout* to the documentary film by the same title [Chiten]. Does print allow a reader to get beyond the most obvious, but superficial, manifestation of Tourette's in a way that film makes difficult? Or is the film preferable precisely because it so vividly portrays the tics that characterize Tourette's?) In collaborative narrative, what issues does collaboration raise in terms of the authority of the narrative and the authenticity of its voice? If an autobiography is collaborative in authorship, whose life is it, anyhow?

An especially interesting instance of collaborative autobiography is *I Raise My Eyes to Say Yes*, by Ruth Sienkiewicz-Mercer and Steven B. Kaplan, an account of the life of a woman with cerebral palsy who was institutionalized early in life but who moved into a residence of her own with the advent of the disability rights movement. Insofar as it speaks for others in her previous condition of near invisibility, and insofar as its production involves the assistance of an advocate, it becomes a kind of disability *testimonio*. It articulates the situation of a large number of people who are marginalized and muted—not by their impairments but by their institutionalization (a function of the medicalization of their conditions). And yet the voice of the narrator is in some significant sense not that of the subject herself, who was unable to speak or write. Although the book is apparently an authoritative record of the life of Sienkiewicz-Mercer, its voice is necessarily a simulation, generated by an extremely labor-intensive, collaborative process of composition. Representation in the mimetic sense (speaking about) and representation in the political sense (speaking for) seem somewhat at odds here: in his desire to speak *for* her, Kaplan speaks *as* her in a way that may misspeak her.

While my primary purposes here are to explore what I see as the usefulness of life writing to disability studies—including some problems built into the medium—and to suggest ways of teaching disability narrative, rather than to construct a canon of such narratives, I would argue that the selection of texts is made both easier and harder as a result of the recent proliferation of disability narratives: easier, because more good books are available; harder, because the richness of the literature complicates choices. The literature in recent years has increased not only in quantity but also in sophistication. To return to Davis's complaint that narrating disability tends to sentimentalize it and render it as an individual's problem or challenge, I might point out that among the best personal accounts of disability are some that do not merely or primarily narrate the conditions in question. Rather, they reflect critically and politically on disability and culture. As Kenny Fries puts it, after centuries of being stared at, today "writers with disabilities [. . .] are staring back" (Introduction 1). Some examples of these accounts are Finger's *Past Due,* Robert Murphy's *The Body Silent* (which can be easily excerpted, because it is not organized primarily on narrative principles), Irving Zola's *Missing Pieces,* and Nancy Mairs's essays, especially those in *Waist-High in the World.* (I would include Mairs's prose under the general rubric of disability narrative or testimony. But the personal essay has the advantage of not confining itself to the telling of a story; rather, it is expected to reflect and analyze as well. This added dimension does not mean that essays will automatically be superior to more narrowly narrative forms, but essays are likely to include higher-order thinking, to present arguable propositions and not only existential truths.)

To return to Olney's paradigm of interdisciplinary area studies, an additional aspect of the political-cultural paradigm is that it recognizes that disability may, like race and gender, generate distinctive cultures. The most obvious instance of this is Deaf culture, but other ways in which disability generates distinctive cultural attitudes, artifacts, and communities are currently being researched. One important issue in disability autobiography, then, is the way in which and the extent to which the narrative depicts the protagonist as involved in a distinctive disability-based culture or a community of people with disabilities.

The degree to which writers identify as disabled is a crucial issue for discussion. Françoise Lionnet has defined a term that may be useful in this context, "autoethnography": "the defining of one's subjective ethnicity as mediated through language, history, and ethnographical analysis; in short, [. . .] a kind of 'figural anthropology' of the self" (99). Stimulated by the progress of the disability rights movement, disability autobiography is more likely in the future to take the form of autoethnography; that is, disability autobiography is more likely to explore the positive ways in which identity and life narrative are shaped by disability, the ways in which disability may create culture. (Of course, in a limited sense, self-representation by disabled people itself constitutes a form of disability culture.) Already we can see something of this development in the books by Bragg, Finger, Murphy, and Zola, in that they address membership in a larger community or culture of disability; they are first-person plural accounts of disability, in part because they reflect the growth of disability consciousness.[4] Zola's narrative of his research sojourn in Het Dorf, a Dutch community for the disabled, focuses on his recovery, or acceptance, of his identity as disabled. Living among disabled people for the first time in his life, he found a kinship based not in ethnicity or language, which he did not share with them, but rather in a shared sense of disability as an identity. His book is, then, in effect a coming-out narrative.

Such books may be autoethnography also in the rather different sense used by Mary Louise Pratt, who defines autoethnographic texts as "instances in which colonized subjects undertake to represent themselves in ways that engage with the colonizer's own terms. If the ethnographic texts are a means by which Europeans represent to themselves their (usually subjugated) others, autoethnographic texts are those the others construct in response to or in dialogue with those metropolitan representations" (7). (Lionnet's use of the term "autoethnography" is a variant of *autobiography;* Pratt's is a variant of *ethnography.*) Obviously, the analogy with non-European cultures needs to be adapted here, in the manner of Harlan Lane's chapter "Representations of Deaf People: Colonialism, 'Audism,' and the 'Psychology of the Deaf,'" in *The Mask of Benevolence,* which makes the case that deaf people have in effect been treated like colonial subjects. In *Missing Pieces*, the postcolonial dimension is evident in the way in which Zola's identification with the disabled inhabitants of Het Dorf puts him increasingly at odds with the nondisabled administrators of the community. The point is that narratives that are autoethnographic in Lionnet's sense, because they foreground the roots of identity in disability culture, are often autoethnographic in Pratt's sense as well, because they resist or undermine objectification by some presumptive medical or medicalizing authority.

To frame the issue differently, the problem of disability autobiography lies in the fact that what Western autobiography has valued (that which distinguishes the individual from others) the medical model of disability has devalued (some deviation from normality in the individual's body). Autoethnography may offer a way out of this bind for life writers, critics, and teachers, because it speaks of disability as a condition that is affirmative rather than destructive, defining rather than confining. It is this subgenre that is most likely to realize the counterdiscursive potential of disability narrative. Disabled bodies have long been cultural signifiers whose meaning has been largely determined by nondisabled people; today disabled people are signifying on their bodies in their own ways with their own voices. Their testimony should be an integral part of the exploration of disability in the humanities.

NOTES

1. In fact, I have come across one narrative that quite deliberately makes this argument: *Saying Goodbye to Daniel: When Death Is the Best choice*, by Juliet Cassuto Rothman, a mother's account of her son's high spinal cord injury. The book's title and its Library of Congress subject listing—quadriplegia, medical ethics, DNR orders, life-support systems, and euthanasia—suggest its thrust, which is to rationalize her son's decision to discontinue treatment rather than to live with severe disability.
2. For further discussion of these rhetorics, see my essay "Conflicting Paradigms."
3. The terms *autobiography* and *memoir* are often used interchangeably, even by scholars in the field, but *memoir* in a stricter sense denotes a narrative that focuses on someone (or something) other than the writer. I maintain a distinction between the terms in this essay, so that "disability autobiography" means a narrative by a person with a disability, while "disability memoir" refers to a personal narrative about but not by a person with a disability.
4. For more on B. Bragg, Kisor, Murphy, Price, Sacks, Sidransky, the Spradleys, Walker, West, and Zola, see Couser, *Recovering Bodies*.

Oliver Sacks and the Medical Case Narrative

Oliver Sacks has been the target of various slings and arrows from disability studies scholars in recent years. I come not to bury him but rather to praise him—as someone who is trying to open a new authorial space for talking about disability. In the process I hope to address some of the criticism of him as "the man who mistook his patients for a writing career."[1] In responding to this charge, I center on the paradoxical way that Sacks uses his primary genre, the medical case study. The case study is the creation of Western rationality and the province of the medical practice that arose from it. It's a discourse that has medicalized disability and frequently objectifies disabled people. When Sacks loses control of his material, he can objectify them too. But when he's on his game, his case studies generate the very wonder and mystery that the genre was designed precisely to explain away. This quest for wonder animates all of Sacks's work. In contrast to the rationalistic teleology of the case study—which seeks to identify disease in order to cure it—he uses the case study not to detect but to discover, and to marvel.

This risk-laden effort makes Sacks a tremendously useful figure to study in relation to the vexed question of authority in disability studies—who should talk about disability and how. The evolution of Sacks's writing over time illuminates both the sordid past and the hopeful future for the writing of disability from its borders. His most recent work focuses self-consciously on those borders and suggests a new direction toward the study of communities that illuminates his earlier work in positive ways. I compare Sacks's earlier and later work—in conjunction with a close look at one of his least cited books, *A Leg to Stand On* (1984)—to get to my main point, which centers on how he injects himself into his case narratives and on how his interventions affect both the narratives and the way we read them.

The Doctor, the Case Study, and Disability

Sacks's paradoxical use of the case study is part of a multifaceted project that deconstructs the genre (within which much of his work can be fairly classified). He does this in a variety of ways, but his most effective tool is his I. His first-person narrative case studies put a staple of modern medical practice to new use.

The case study is one of the most powerful tools of the Western medical profession. As a genre with tendentiously objective connotations, it became the vehicle by which rationally based medical science turned the disabled person into a medical narrative. The case study also helped turn the doctor into an authority on such narratives—in part through its impersonal character, which effaces the I.

The medical case study emerged in American medicine as doctors gained an authority they never had before. The buildup of medical authority in the United States took place as part of a larger professionalization, or incorporation, of America in the later decades of the nineteenth and into the twentieth century. But as Paul Starr has shown, the rise in the professional and social mobility of doctors drew on many broad social trends, such as urbanization, the growing prestige of science, and the increasing intellectual stature of the university. In consolidating their profession and establishing its authority, doctors drew on these concurrent social changes to improve their social, intellectual, and professional status. Fueled by these changes, medicine rocketed from the lower middle of the United States social strata into its higher reaches. Through canny management of their work and image, doctors achieved a corporate authority built on laypeople's deference to their expertise and an institutional dependence on their services.[2]

As the doctor gradually turned into the authority figure we recognize today, the relation between doctors and patients became more hierarchical and the social distance between them increased. In a manual written for doctors near the beginning of this shift in power relations, for example, Dr. D. W. Cathell warned that a doctor should not appear as "an ordinary person" (qtd. in Starr 86). He recommended that his colleagues engage in pleonastic subterfuge (such as the use of arcane Latin names for commonly prescribed medicines) to keep patients and other nondoctors from knowing what doctors were doing. The result of such maneuvers was to draw doctors together, into an "us" that was necessarily opposed to a "them" composed of those outside the profession. The norming of medical education was crucial to this process. By standardizing licensing procedures and the medical school curriculum, the profession erected secure gates to prevent unauthorized entry into its midst.

Clinical practice rose against this backdrop at around the turn of the century. Perhaps the single most distinctive attribute of the modern medical profession, clinical medicine was surrounded by "an aura of scientific discovery" (Hunter 117) whose foundation had been built during the previous decades. Centered on "the gaze"—in this instance the hierarchical scrutiny of the patient by the doctor—clinical medicine quickly standardized and quantified this objectifying, "calculating" practice.[3] As new diagnostic hardware was invented in the early twentieth century, precise measurement became standard in medical education, consultation, and practice. These new measurements became "part of a movement to identify statistical norms of human physiology and behavior" (Starr 137). This collection of averages created a quantifiable idea of the normal. Such measurements became the reified vision of what Rosemarie Garland-Thomson has termed the "normate," the figure opposed to the disabled person "through which people can represent themselves as definitive human beings" (*Extraordinary Bodies* 8).

It was in this setting that the case study took its place as the narrative tool designed to convey medical knowledge, typically by juxtaposing the particular case against the general, the average, the expected—or the normate. As a narrative account (frequently couched in technical language) that enabled doctors to talk to one another about patients, the genre reinforced power relations within the profession and toward patients. The case study thus stands as both a cause and a result: it both arose from and contributed to the new forms of authority that doctors claimed for themselves.

The Doctor Enfreaking Himself

"I have always regarded [case histories] with especial affection," writes Sacks (*Awakenings* xxxiv). And well he should, for his case studies become the vehicle by which he conveys not the usual medical narrative of pathology and diagnosis but rather his open fascination with people and their conditions. Simply put, Sacks is writing narratives of wonder at a time when wonder is hard to generate.

Stephen Greenblatt calls wonder "ravishment [. . .] an overpowering intensity of response [to . . .] something amazing. [. . . It is] a primary or radical passion that precedes, even escapes, moral categories. [. . .] When we wonder, we do not yet know if we should love or hate the object at which we are marveling; we do not know if we should embrace it or flee from it" (*Marvelous Possessions* 16, 17, 20). Garland-Thomson has described freak narrative as the result of linking the narrative of pathology to the narrative of wonder ("From Wonder")—but by explaining the amazing, science has made wonder a scarce commodity in the Western world and deprived this equation of its most crucial element. Consequently, medicine has been fairly credited with killing the freak show.[4]

Wonder has been central to Sacks from his first stirrings as a writer. His first book, *Awakenings*, began with some letters he wrote about his patients to *The Lancet* "that allowed me to convey the wonder of the clinical experience" (xxxi). *Awakenings* is constructed around a series of case studies designed to convey that wonder. But wonder—this awestruck response to the amazing and mysterious—is the opposite of the traditional goal of the case study, which is to bring the unknown (the disease, the pathogen, the defect) into the province of the known and understood. Sacks's case studies spotlight the mystery, not the solution. Though a doctor, Sacks stands in opposition to the long-standing movement led by doctors to medicalize (and therefore pathologize) the anomalous human body. He represents an important countertrend.

This paradoxical use of the case study to create wonder hinges on Sacks's narrative presence in his stories. In his highly self-conscious effort to create "disability as sensibility," he employs a number of unusual rhetorical strategies to create authority for himself. The most important of these connects to another significant paradox in his work: he builds himself up by effacing himself consistently. Departing from the medical posture of detached and objective professional authority, he depicts himself as a frequently flawed, often wrong, and thoroughly eccentric character. Related to this stance is his unusually open identification with his subjects—who increasingly cannot be considered patients in any traditional sense, since he does not always have a professional relationship with them and he's usually not even trying to "cure" them.

In order to study this identification more closely, consider two of Sacks's most famous books, *The Man Who Mistook His Wife for a Hat* and *An Anthropologist on Mars*. The case studies in *Hat* are sketchy freak-show exhibits of human oddities. Though not gratuitously cruel, they appear insensitive, not so much displaying people as turning them into wondrous displays of the spectacular conditions they possess. They mark Sacks's low point. The case studies in *Anthropologist*, on the other hand, are portrayals of human beings in unusual situations that evoke sympathy and identification as well as wonder. One uncomplicated reason for the difference is length. The case studies in *Anthropologist*—there are only seven, against twenty-four in *Hat*—allow more space for a fully articulated portrait of a human being, not just an oddity that happens to be attached to a person.

The second, more compelling, difference in each case study in *Anthropologist* is mediation. And for Sacks, that difference is himself. His own presence as an eccentric in his depictions of others softens the display of a collection of people who ultimately become his group, his people.

Sacks's critics are immensely irritated at what has been described as his "intrusive authorial presence" (T. Shakespeare 138), but this intrusion is precisely the point. Sacks likes to tell stories about himself. He knows that they make him appear weird and compulsive, but he evidently doesn't care. Here are some of the things he has allowed to be known about him:

He imitates Tourette's syndrome. He was a drug user. He writes during concerts and in restaurants. He stammers. He has never married or lived with anyone. He describes his house—at which he rarely entertains—as "a machine for work." He eats cereal with bananas every day for both breakfast and lunch, and for dinner he always has fish and rice with tabbouleh, which his housekeeper prepares each week in labeled daily batches. He eats standing up. Every day he visits the baby gorillas in the Central Park Zoo.

And he swims. Oh, does he swim—for hours at a time in very cold water off the shore of City Island, where he lives, and anywhere else he happens to be. A friend of mine tells me that when Sacks came to southern California for a lecture not long ago, he insisted on swimming in every pool on the linked campuses of the five Claremont colleges.[5]

It's not hard to glean such peculiarities from reading Sacks's books; he puts his strangeness on display.[6] He also puts himself on display. Consider *A Leg to Stand On*, a personal account of his recovery from a severe injury. While he's lying crippled by a fall on a mountain, he talks to an imaginary audience, describing his injury as "a fascinating case!" Ingested as a patient by the medical machine, he experiences what he calls "the dread of degradation" at being "no longer a person." He bonds with the other patients, seeing them—and himself—avoided "like lepers" and "outcasts," with their white gowns creating "a complete gulf between us and them, [. . .] the reduction to a generic status and identity" (22, 46, 163–64). In refusing "to play the role of doctor to himself" (Frank 110), he feels disabled and objectified: like a freak.[7]

But freakishness in Sacks's work is a state that has value, because it inspires wonder—and when the mysterious reawakening of his leg begins, sure enough, something ineffable overwhelms his feelings of objectification. "I felt terror, but also awe and exhilaration of spirit. Within me there seemed to be the working of a cosmic mathematics, the establishment of an impersonal microcosmic order." This reawakening helps reaffirm his life's mission to practice "a person medicine" that will combine scientific reasoning and romantic feeling. He is, he says, "filled with gratitude, with wonder, with hope" (*Leg* 141, 210).

A Leg to Stand On is Sacks's case study of himself. The case study is by nature a doubled narrative (Hunter 51): the patient's account is folded into the physician's. Sacks makes this doubling into an act of community by folding his own foibles into it, leveling the field by questioning its hierarchies. In effect, he turns the case study—and himself—into a rhetorical bridge between wonder and rationality, between the worlds of the disabled and the able-bodied. This is a bridge for others to cross—in both directions.

The case study arises from the relation in medicine between the individual and the general, and this relation is uniquely powerful when the individual is a human being. The genre is the literal embodiment of a doubling and a paradox: an expression of general knowledge relating to the "science" of medicine and of the universality of disease and death but also a story of a person whose humanity is independent of the narrative. The case study thus stands at the border between the need to generalize and the refusal to do so. It acts as the concrete embodiment confirming general medical postulates (that a hard blow to the head will often lead to unconsciousness, for example) and the story of a person whose symptoms might or might not conform to this general rule (for instance, there is a documented case where a man took himself to a doctor after a freak accident drove a crowbar through his skull).[8] The genre has a dual capacity then—it sucks the patient into the clinical system of knowledge and practice, but it also distinguishes the patient as an individual case.

The case study relies on this continuing tension between the abstract (and general) and the concrete (and individual), but in narrative practice the genre can list toward one or the other, with important consequences for the positions of doctors and patients. When the individual becomes subordinated to the general, the patient can be subsumed. In such instances, the case study becomes the tool that draws patients—in their humanity still—into the discourse that colonizes that humanity, making the body part of the general fund of knowledge and rules. In this light, then, the case narrative captures the patient. In the medical profession, the scientific emphasis effaces individuality more often than it distinguishes it. Human anomaly—whether disease, disability, or both—turns into a plot that activates a scientific teleology in which the patient becomes little more than a vessel for the condition being studied. When does human anomaly become part of a life story instead of a deviation from the norm? The key, I would say, lies in which ends the author of the case narrative seeks to serve and in what kind of story the case study turns into.[9]

One of the most important master narratives underlying the case study is the detective story: that is, the case study documents a scientific exercise in detection, with disease as the villain. Sacks shows that this sustained analogy—which informs even studies that stress the patient's humanity, like Hunter's *Doctors' Stories*—is simply wrong, because it separates the person from the condition. Nowhere is this distinction clearer than in Sacks's portrayal in *Anthropologist* of Franco Magnani, a painter who devotes his life to painting photographically accurate landscapes of the Italian town of his birth, a place he has not seen in many decades but whose details he can summon when he is overtaken by intense, trancelike states. Sacks suggests that Magnani's trances most likely arise from a form of epilepsy, but this diagnosis, or "solution" to the case, is essentially irrelevant, as the subject has no intention of treating himself for an "affliction" that is part of who he is and who he wants to be.

Sacks's intensely personal memoir, along with his other work, suggests an effort to bend the case study away from scientific taxonomy and toward the use of medical methodology to liberate human diversity and individuality. "Only when we hear *both* the doctor's and the patient's voice," says Ann Hunsaker Hawkins, "will we have a medicine that is truly human" (161). Sacks's willingness—even eagerness—to do to himself what he does to others suggests that he understands this necessity. He clearly sees the wonder of his cases as overwhelming any dehumanizing associations attached to the case study genre. His cases have an untraditional trajectory: the condition is an inextricable part of the person. There's no disease to isolate or any cure to search for. These are stories of people who just are—in wondrous ways.

The Authority of Doctors and Travelers

A Leg to Stand On makes the nature of Sacks's project especially clear: he's deconstructing the case study. His wonder narratives merge self and other—and thus doctor and patient. They erode the authority boundary that modern medicine erected as part of its professionalization. They lay open the opposition between the particular and the general that is a foundation of standard case-study narrative. They dismantle the assumptions—one might say the myths—of medical determinacy and precision that underlie the oppressive form that the case study has taken since its emergence in modern medical practice.[10] In doing all this, Sacks's best case studies undermine the traditional authority position of the doctor. With each of his works, Sacks discards more of the trappings of authority conferred on him by his profession; for years now he has been stepping further away from being doctor. (It is worth noting that only two of the seven cases in *Anthropologist* are medical patients.) In the place of doctor, Sacks has written himself into a new position, that of visiting narrator. His case studies are written by a spectator—literally, a viewer of a human spectacle.

There has been considerable pressure brought to bear by many medical professionals in recent years to make the case study more like a scientific document, not less (Hunter 160). Sacks is battling these forces in his quest for a romantic medicine, a practice that provides space for disabled people as something other than problems and failures. Rather than follow established case-study narrative practice of flattening the patient and pursuing an objective gaze (162), Sacks is trying to redeploy the genre's basic elements to re-create it as something else, an explicitly subjective project that takes its place in a broad humanistic inquiry that encompasses medicine—not the other way around.

It is therefore both consistent and important that Sacks begins *Anthropologist* with another account of himself as patient, this time a temporarily left-handed one who is recovering from surgery on his right arm. He compares his effort to develop a limited sort of "different identity" as a lefty with the activities of the seven people whose stories make up the book (xvi). This rhetorical gesture points to what is finally the most important difference between *Hat* and *Anthropologist*: while the first book centers on the subjects themselves, the second features autobiographical accounts of Sacks's meeting and knowing these subjects. This change suggests his evolving emphasis as a writer, where he calls more and more attention to himself and his position relative to the people he writes about.

Sacks is everywhere in *Anthropologist*. We know that the doctor as well as the patient is folded into the case presentation (Hunter 63), but Sacks underscores this inclusion again and again. All the cases in the book are filtered through his impressions. One constantly encounters the phrase "I felt," and these feelings run a range: we see him blushing, struck, horrified. He relates his first encounter with marijuana, allows his house to be sketched by an autistic art prodigy, and tries out a mechanical hug machine designed by an autistic engineer who can't bear physical human contact (*Anthropologist* 120, 212, 265). More than a clinical voice, Sacks becomes a physical presence in the lives of his subjects, visiting them and weaving their stories together with his own. He flies with a surgeon who has Tourette's syndrome; goes to Russia with Stephen, an autistic artist; goes to a slaughterhouse with the autistic agricultural engineer Temple Grandin; and goes to a Grateful Dead concert with Greg, a young man whose sight and short-term memory have been totally destroyed by a brain tumor, leaving him living permanently in the 1960s (104–06, 214–21, 277–80, 72–76). Physicians, Hunter explains, seek closure, which "fixes meaning." They see the patient's story as "a text produced by the illness," to be shaped into a "diagnostic plot" (128). With his explicit emphasis on his presence as an observer in the lives of his subjects, Sacks turns the shaping agency into a collaboration of the sort that exists between a journalist and an interview subject.

These accounts are not intrusions into the lives of disabled people; they are connections with them. Sacks's case narratives implicate and intertwine him with the subjects he's studying. It is no coincidence that *Anthropologist* ends with a hug. Sacks reaches out to Temple Grandin, the inventor of the hug machine, and embraces her. "(I think)," he writes, "she hugged me back" (296). This hug is worth close reading in terms of the book's title: as Sacks observes, the "anthropologist on Mars" job description applies to Sacks and Grandin both (292)—and the hug merges them too. The hug is a self-aggrandizing gesture, certainly (why does he think she will appreciate it? and if he doesn't, then he's imposing it on her), but it's also a symbol of what Sacks is trying generally to depict: the embrace of one prodigy by another.

Sacks's interest in the idea of the prodigy is evident throughout *Anthropologist,* and his use of the term (it's the title of chapter 6) engages its long history of associations with religious views of the world. The category of "prodigy" dates from the early modern period, when it encompassed "monstrous" births and people with odd bodies (the "freaks" of later generations) along with then-inexplicable natural phenomena such as earthquakes and comets. By the early sixteenth century, the general lesson conveyed by prodigies, drawn from Saint Augustine, was that nature acts in unusual and mysterious ways that reflect the will of God.[11] The prodigy has gained exclusively positive connotations during the last couple of centuries, but it has retained its connection to the category of people and phenomena that lie beyond human understanding. Sacks is the rare doctor who acknowledges this vast uncharted territory and remains humble before it. The cover design of *Anthropologist* invokes the older associations of the word and underscores Sacks's appreciation of individual human mystery.

In his best work Sacks is (covertly) writing an autobiography to go with his biographical displays of wonder. Chunks of his experience accrete as he goes on.[12] Unlike the colonialist who supports the construction of the normal without questioning it, Sacks is deconstructing normality—through the display of himself on the stage and his framing of uniquely wondrous disabilities. In the terms devised by Arthur W. Frank, Sacks's cases are not traditional "restitution narratives" of disease and cure that celebrate doctors and medical practice. Instead, Sacks conveys "testimony," frequently forming it into modified "quest narratives," a genre in which the teller is given something important to be

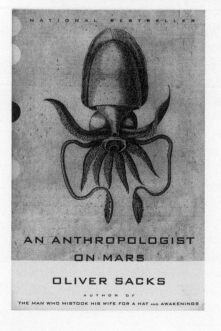

Figure 1

Anthropologist cover reproduced by permission of Alfred A. Knopf Publishers, Inc.

shared with others (118).[13] Thus, I would argue that Sacks's writings wind up creating a uniquely collaborative space in which disabled people can express themselves—instead of one that closes them off. Not only does Sacks give sympathetic voice to some who cannot speak for themselves (such as the autistic artistic prodigy Stephen), he also helps amplify the voices of those who can—and do—tell their own stories (like the well-known Temple Grandin). The overarching goal is to illuminate mystery rather than penetrate it, for mystery is, as Albert Einstein has said, "the fundamental emotion which stands at the cradle of true art and true science" (5).

Sacks's writing presents an implicit argument with some of the neo-essentialist positions in disability studies today. Sacks's work aims at an integrative ideal that embraces not only human difference but also the human desire to look upon this difference. By pointing to the wonder that such difference can inspire, he shows it to be spectacular in the most positive sense. His work argues that people will want to stare, and the best way to counter this desire is not to forbid it but to shape and direct it, to make the gaze into a mutual look, a meeting of two worlds.

Where Sacks has lately been going helps confirm where he's been. Two of his recent books, *Seeing Voices* (1990) and *Island of the Colour-Blind and Cycad Island* (1996), and his recent television series show him moving to the study of communities—a logical destination for one who is so concerned with the border between the disabled and the normate. Moreover, when he moves into these communities, he becomes the outsider (for example, when he writes about the Deaf, he highlights his lack of fluency in sign language). The paradigm underlying his writing is changing, moving from the many (the community of doctors) studying the one to the one studying the many. This is another level on which he deliberately undermines the concept of "normal."

This important shift in position transforms Sacks from a doctor writing case studies into a travel writer writing himself in exotic locales—which is, in a sense, what he has been all along. The external transformation is clearest in his recent PBS television series, appropriately named *The Mind Traveler*. In this four-part presentation, Sacks chooses to efface (if not obliterate) his identity as a doctor. In effect, he exchanges the medical theater—a place where the doctor performs and the patient is a living prop—for a place in the audience, where he watches his extraordinary subjects perform the drama of their lives in their own home places. In the place of Dr. Sacks strides Mr. Sacks, an informed and idiosyncratic traveler to strange communities: of the deaf-blind, the color-blind, the autistic, those with Williams syndrome (whose possessors have heightened musical and social skills but diminished spatial and conceptual ability). Entering the Williams syndrome community, he confesses his shyness, and his awkwardness is assuaged by the members of a summer camp for people possessing this rare genetic condition. He's the one out of place, as the title of the episode, "Don't Be Shy, Mr. Sacks," abundantly shows.

This television series makes clear Sacks's abiding preoccupations: to show how disability can be sensibility, depending on where you're standing; to show how wondrous such human diversity can be; to write himself into a bridge between communities that need to understand each other; and to convey the voices of those who need to be heard but aren't always in a position to be heard. Doing these things means trading in the authority of the doctor for the studied innocence of the traveler. And it means working within a travel-writing tradition that, as Mary B. Campbell has shown, originated in early modernity as a wondrous journey to where the monsters are. Sacks shows that the monsters aren't monsters and the doctors aren't hierophants. In offering a different way of looking, he shows that they, and everyone else, are all connected.

NOTES

1. The phrase is Tom Shakespeare's (137); the charge is repeated by Linton (141).

2. For the documentation of these broad trends, see Starr; Trachtenberg, *Incorporation*.

3. See Michel Foucault, *The Birth of the Clinic* 89. Foucault notes the inherently objectifying aspect of case study generally: "In the hospital, the patient is the *subject* of the disease, that is, he is a *case*" (59). For a critique of the assumptions behind the quantitative approach to the ideas of norm and average, see Canguilhem 151–79. For an excellent social history of the idea of the normal body, see Davis, *Enforcing*.

4. For a fuller elaboration of this argument, see Bogdan; Garland-Thomson, "From Wonder." For a discussion of Sacks's work in relation to the freak show, see Cassuto.

5. This list is drawn in part from Shakespeare's review of *Anthropologist* (139, where Shakespeare draws on various interviews that Sacks has given) and Kirk Johnson's "Looking Inward, Understanding Strange Worlds."

6. For example, his obsessions with water frame the narratives in *Anthropologist* (where he thanks "lakes, rivers, and swimming pools everywhere" in his acknowledgments [xii]). At one point, he "impetuously" runs toward a river without seeing the hydroelectric dam ahead of it (294–95).

7. I am disagreeing here with G. Thomas Couser, who argues in his interesting reading of *A Leg to Stand On* that Sacks "fails to reckon with, much less to

counter, the stigmatization that accompanies disability" (*Recovering* 186)—in large part because Sacks eventually recovers his mobility and subsequently distances himself from his disabled condition. Arthur Frank offers a more sympathetic reading centering on Sacks's creation of a quest narrative, in which the author "tells self-consciously of being transformed" (118). Similarly, Ann Hunsaker Hawkins reads Sacks's account in anthropological terms, as a rite of passage (82–87).

8. I am referring here to the famous 1848 case of Phineas Gage, recounted by Sacks in *Anthropologist* (59–61).

9. I have relied in this paragraph on Hunter (esp. 38–48) for her description of the teleological scientific model. Foucault also argues that the case study enforces a systemic hegemony, drawing the individual case into the larger organization of knowledge and power (*Birth*).

10. Hawkins argues that the pathography genre offers a kind of countermyth to the case study, one written by patients, in which their stories reclaim and reconfigure their experience according to recognizable mythic paradigms.

11. This description of prodigies draws on Park and Daston, esp. 23–24.

12. The recently published memoir of his childhood, *Uncle Tungsten*, continues this process of unfolding himself.

13. Testimony, says Frank, emphasizes communication and creates community (140–45). The quest narrative "speaks from the ill person's perspective and holds chaos at bay" (115). I am arguing that Sacks implicates the ideas informing quest narrative with his own integrative project.

ENCARNACION JUAREZ

The Autobiography of the Aching Body in Teresa de Cartagena's *Arboleda de los enfermos*

In the second half of the fifteenth century, a Castilian nun of Jewish origin, Teresa de Cartagena, writes the spiritual treatise *Arboleda de los enfermos* (Grove of the Infirm), and later, a defense of her gender and her capacity as a writer, *Admiraçión operum Dey* (Wonder at the Works of God). The initial rubric of *Arboleda* informs us that it was composed in a state of pain and disability: "[Teresa] being afflicted with grave ailments and, in particular, having lost completely her sense of hearing" (23).[1] The rubric also indicates that the objective of her work was to praise God and to find spiritual consolation for herself and for all who suffer illnesses. However, the text presents a much more complex personal circumstance, since Teresa remarks that her pain is not only caused by her illness and impairment but also provoked by social rejection:

> [O]ur afflictions and physical suffering not only scourge and wound our bodies, causing our heads, eyes, and arms to ache, but even more harshly cause our hearts to ache and afflict our spirit and inner feelings. It is not that our physical suffering alone completely causes these inner pains; rather, they are caused by this aforementioned talent of humiliation and contempt. For when the invalid sees himself so humiliated and despised by his neighbors, there is no doubt that his heart is stung with great affliction and feeling, so that, depending on the quality of the contempt and the person who receives it, someone can be more tormented by this type of anguish than by his many physical pains. (69)

In discussing this social rejection and the humiliation and contempt it inflicts, the fifteenth-century nun presents a phenomenon that concerns us deeply in our contemporary intellectual discourse: the social creation of the other based on corporeal, gender, racial, or class differences. This construction of others defines the social norm and supports the legal practices of the groups in power; it also produces the segregation and discrimination of the less favored.[2] If we approach the treatise from this perspective, Teresa de Cartagena's voice is of double interest: not only is the author one of few women writers in medieval Spain but also *Arboleda* is the only known text, written in the first person during the premodern period, that explores issues of disability, corporeal pain, and social rejection of the different.[3]

Given the historical and personal circumstances of Cartagena, we need to study her work by taking into account her triple marginalization as a woman writer, a conversa (her grandfather and father converted from Judaism to Christianity in either 1390 or 1391), and a deaf person (Vicente García 97; Howe 139; Seidenspinner-Núñez, *Writings* 3). While there are valuable essays that study the first two aspects, her gender and ethnicity,[4] the examination of the most obvious, her deafness and illness, has been neglected. I approach the text of *Arboleda de los enfermos* as a woman's autobiography that denounces and bears witness to the problem of disability, as a woman's attempt to resolve her personal dilemma. I show that the text follows the basic confessional pattern of fall and redemption and that Teresa de Cartagena's disability explains the genesis as well as the content of her work.[5] Through her writing she explores her experience of deafness, body pain, and stigma and finds understanding and the answer to her existence.

This focus on her disability as an impulse for literary creation and personal insight relates *Arboleda* to personal narratives in our time written by women with disabilities.[6] Autobiographical confession is therefore a key concept that needs to be defined for the analysis of a work that lacks the formal design of this genre.[7] I argue that although *Arboleda* follows various discursive literary sources and models of Cartagena's time (consolatory treatises, sermons, exempla, the Bible),[8] her text should be interpreted as an inner exploration of the self, since the doctrine expounded is based on her intimate experience.[9] This emphasis on the inner self is typical of spiritual confessions. Moreover, that she reflects on her deafness and chronic pain makes *Arboleda* a predecessor of self-referential accounts of disability and illness written by marginalized people (Couser, *Recovering Bodies* 4; Mitchell and Snyder, *Body* 9–10). According to Thomas Couser, people who contend with their corporeal problems have the need to write as an act of self-consolation and the desire to secure the fraternity and the understanding of others in the same situation (xi), which makes the personal become decidedly social. Such narratives resemble spiritual conversion autobiographies because the writers situate themselves in a position in which their problem has been either accepted or resolved. From this site they explore their problematic personal past in the text by detaching it from themselves. Referring to this phenomenon of split self, John R. Rosenberg affirms that "the essence of confession rests in the sense of being different, in the awareness of change wrought upon the past from the present, and in the deepened consciousness of transcendent transmutation." This type of confessional writing, he adds, follows the circular design of the history of Christianity: paradisiacal state, fall, estrangement and exile, and eventual redemption through Christ (16).

This basic circular pattern appears in *Arboleda de los enfermos,* where a double rupture—within the self as well as between the individual and the community—exists. In effect, Cartagena examines her other self in pain, which longs to enjoy again the lost pleasures; she creates through her writing the answer to her existential situation of corporeal pain, psychological anguish, and social isolation. The text, written in the rigid prose of medieval form and thought and using a codified Christian rhetoric (Vicente García 96), traces a unique journey of self-knowledge and acceptance through which Cartagena resolves her private problem of twenty years of deafness. It is precisely her deafness and her physical pain that give her license to write and insight for that writing. With her imagination she tries to impose an order on her aching existence. She compares the positive consequences of her sickness with the negative ones to elaborate a transformation through language. The painful identity of Cartagena appears divided in the treatise and reaches unity in a new being that emerges from difficult tests that take place through the act of writing. In addition, her personal case, extended by her use of the pronoun *we,* ultimately merges with a community of sufferers. Finally, she prepares for redemption, not by recovering her former healthy state but by accepting her present condition and by expecting final integration in resurrection. After resurrection, she hopes to find a fulfillment superior to her lost happiness, "so that, just as we are equal in our suffering, we may be equal in our resurrection where [. . .] temporal and human happiness have no place" (43). Her preoccupation with the body in distress and her hope of redeeming body and soul after death are characteristic of medieval religious specialists, who, according to Caroline Bynum Walker, "assumed the flesh to be the instrument of salvation" ("Why" 15). For Bynum Walker the spirituality of medieval women owed its intense bodily quality in part to the association of the female with the fleshly and in part to the prevalent concept of a person as a psychosomatic unity and the belief that the body as well as the soul would be resurrected at the end of time (*Fragmentation* 183). The intensity of Cartagena's detailed examination of her situation has a cathartic effect that propels Cartagena to communicate her discovery of hope and acceptance. In this sense, *Arboleda* is an exemplary book that presents her case and her consciousness of pain and disability as a consolatory paradigm for the destitute sick and disabled community.[10]

Although the exploration of the suffering self and the need to reach others in *Arboleda* are goals shared with disability narratives today, the treatise lacks a chronologically linear organization. The author's experience demonstrates her thesis that body weakness brings positive changes and spiritual fortitude. In effect, she declares that her impairment has transformed her condition as a human being, her personality, her association with the world, and, most of all, her relationship with God. In the text, she analyzes the physical and social consequences of being disabled and in pain and develops a program of action to reach a superior spiritual state. The motifs of body weakness that deprives her of desirable worldly pleasure and of the spiritual fortitude obtained through suffering appear throughout her writing. This repetition creates intensity and drama to her inner conflict, resolved at the end of *Arboleda* when she embraces her disability and renounces human pleasures in exchange for a profound faith in God's will and in a reward in eternal life. In doing so, she not only redeems her soul but also her rejected imperfect body, since it becomes the site for her enlightenment and final salvation. The writer's transformation, like that of Saint Augustine in his *Confessions*, evolves from her own readings and is accomplished through her writing. Furthermore, like Augustine, her last state is not complete but consists of a progressive movement toward a final and postponed union, since Cartagena still lives with suffering and rejection (J. Rosenberg 18).

In the fifteenth century, deafness condemned Cartagena to marginalization and isolation (Sacks, *Seeing* 9; Davis, *Enforcing* 51–52) and probably caused her to enter the convent (Plann 13).[11] Once she loses her hearing, she testifies that oral exchange ceases to have its communicative role ("[S]peech without hearing is worth nothing and only increases one's torment" [27]), and she palliates that torment by centering her communicative activities on reading and writing. These activities are called by Lennard Davis the "deafened moment," the "process that does not involve speaking or hearing" (101). Unlike most medieval women condemned to silence, ironically Cartagena can now develop a new voice because of her deafness; this impulse can be realized because of her excellent intellectual formation and the privacy of the convent, conducive to retreat and reading.[12]

Seidenspinner-Núñez indicates that deafness deprives Cartagena of the oral culture of women (*Writings* 113). However, although the texts she reads are written by men, her separation from the spoken word and from the authority of intermediary males (preachers, confessors) places her in a very privileged situation. Silence lets her hear God's voice with "the ear of my understanding" (29),[13] and in this act she gains authority and greater freedom of interpretation. For Saint Augustine, silence constitutes the highest value for grasping the eternal and intelligible reality (Mazzeo 193). In addition, Jacques Derrida points out the preference in the Western philosophical tradition for the metaphysics of presence and the word, which favors, as Toril Moi summarizes, "speech over writing precisely because speech presupposes the *presence* of the speaking subject, who thus can be cast as the unitary *origin* of his or her discourse" (107). For Derrida, in writing, to the contrary, the word is liberated from the authority of presence, of the voice, and acquires infinite displacements of meanings.[14] Therefore, reading and writing in silence can be transgressive, as Davis argues in his elaboration of "deafness as a critical modality." According to Davis, in the Western tradition blindness is used as a metaphor for insight, yet "deafness has the potential to reassign the critic away from the cultural construction of system to a more transgressive role" (*Enforcing* 105). We can apply this critical modality to the writer's activity in connection with deafness to underline its liberating, transgressive, and insightful effects when confronting established systems.

We see in Cartagena's text this liberation of meaning and the search for deciphering experience through writing. The nun is forced by her deafness to separate herself from speech and the presence and to look for communication in the written word, which is more open to interpretations. She violates the rules of convention through her labor of exegesis and writing—customary activities of men in the Middle Ages—but she also concentrates on deciphering the text of her body and, by doing that, remains in the domain of women's preoccupation. She universalizes her discourse and places it among other consolatory treatises through the use of numerous biblical quotations and through oblique self-references (Seidenspinner-Núñez, *Writings* 123); at the same time, she uses her hermeneutic work to control and support her experience. In addition, she goes beyond writing when she decides to open the ear of her soul to God, who speaks directly to her; hence she annuls human authority and gains greater autonomy as a writer.[15]

Writing brings Cartagena freedom to assert her experience; further-more, in this activity she overcomes her physical and emotional isolation and constructs a site of security and ease. In the introduction to *Arboleda de los enfermos,* Cartagena explains that the emotional circum-stances of her life during her twenty years of deafness have reduced her to total isolation from the community on an "ynsula" called "Oprobrium hominum et abiecio plebis" ("The Scorn of Mankind and Outcast of the People" [23n3]). Though the convent separates her spatially from soci-ety, her impairment places her in a more difficult situation of abjection and human rejection, in an "exile and shadowy banishment" where she feels "more in a sepulcher than a dwelling" (23) and severed from hu-man pleasures. But for the writer this long exile is also a place of trans-formation where she procures the ideal requisite of solitude and leisure to accomplish her reading and writing activities: "[Y]ou will see me more alone in the company of many than when I retreat to my cell all by myself" (25). In this solitude, with the advice she finds in books and with divine help and guidance, her deserted island full of affliction is transformed into a grove (*arboleda*) abounding with solace for her soul. Later in the text, in addition to the grove image, she represents the idea of isolation by means of a fictitious convent where she situates herself together with a community of fellow sufferers.[16] In this convent gov-erned by the virtue of Patience, abbess of the congregation, the com-munity counters their physical weakness with spiritual fortitude through prayer. Cartagena's objective in creating these imaginary spaces of the grove or cloister, where she and the disabled can commune, may be compared with that of Nancy Mairs, who writes her memoirs "to conceptualize not merely a habitable body but a habitable world: a world that wants me in it" (*Waist-High* 63).

Her isolation is not only socially enforced but also constitutes a per-sonal choice. According to Cartagena, after frustrated attempts to continue with her habitual oral communication, she imposes a voluntary silence on herself, more because of the lack of understanding of people than because of her incapacity to communicate. The others are placing her slowly in the group of the different. She complains that people do not understand the phenomenon of her disability and the complexity of her situation when they insist that she speak, "knowing as I do that speech is pointless without hearing" (27). Her frustration and lack of enjoyment during conversations lead her to the decision of avoiding the company of people and embracing the alternative of silence.

Her adaptation to her new state of silence, seclusion, and solitude is a long and difficult process, because, according to Cartagena, human obstinacy is powerful when we have to give up corporeal pleasures to which we are naturally inclined. Therefore, even though the writer accepts her physical condition as a divine decision and emphasizes its spiritual advantages, her disability exists against her wishes: "And I, silenced by force, did not willingly listen to what I should hear" (27). It is not surprising that, after losing her hearing, her thoughts remain entangled for a long time with former concerns: "What I do want is to involve myself in worldly activities, and what I do not want is solitude or isolation from them" (35). The memory of hearing, together with resistance and rebellion toward this loss, explains her divided self. It is only in mature age that she finds that her afflictions bring her a platform of spiritual stability and purgation of her faults. In this moment of her life, in the act of writing, when she declares that she has accepted her condition, the struggle still echoes: "And I, who up until now desired but was not able to spend my time in worldly conversations, am no longer able nor inclined to have the power to fulfill such a harmful desire" (29). When she renounces the recovery of her lost paradise and embraces her pain, she achieves an integrated identity.[17]

Cartagena's journey toward a final resolution through her body in pain is a means to subdue her soul and gain insight.[18] According to Cartagena, corporeal suffering functions as penance and punishment for our sins and as a bridle or restraint for other sins. It is a force that impedes her from fulfilling her desires of hearing, talking, and getting involved in worldly business and thereby forces her into solitude. But it is also an instrument of experience that makes her wiser and leads her to a realm unexplored by healthy and able people. Paradoxically, the acceptance of her deafness opens for the writer a new capacity to hear spiritual voices. Like the work of this medieval nun, present accounts of disability or chronic illness also testify that physical pain influences and modifies corporeal and spiritual acts and opens other possibilities of experience.[19] Cartagena believes that her disabled body places her in a superior position. Furthermore, she doubts the differences that separate her from the able and healthy, since their security is a dream, an illusory and temporary condition, and death is the reality where all bodies become equal: "Here let those blessed with physical health beware, lest the dream of their invulnerability deceive them" (34). Her affirmation coincides with recent disability analysis that questions the "assumption that society at large is intact, normal [. . .] undamaged" (Davis, *Enforcing* 14–15). In her new position Cartagena develops unexplored aspects of her personality.

Susan Wendell comments that often for those who live with pain or with other problems, it is an effective psychological strategy to identify more with intellectual or emotional experiences, or with other activities or relations (176)—like writing books, as Mairs suggests (*Waist-High* 63). In the same way, the fifteenth-century nun forges her new identity by concentrating more on a spiritual, virtuous happiness: "And to this spiritual happiness I invite the infirm and I wish to be invited" (43). Her new project accepts a moderate corporeal sadness as her permanent human condition; nevertheless, in the text, through reflection and analysis, she separates herself from that sadness (*dolença*) and renders it a means for attaining a superior level of spirituality.

To reach this level, Cartagena elaborates a spiritual plan based on her own experiences and supported by quotations from sacred texts. This plan opposes the lifestyle of the normal, because the longing of the disabled for living that way eliminates any possibility of a satisfactory life in earth. She postulates that "all the blessings of this world are food reserved for the healthy; so let us leave what we cannot have and get accustomed to our own diet" (46). The only option for disabled and sick people is to reject everything that alienates them and find alternative modes of experience and spiritual rewards. In order to accomplish this objective, the nun points out that, given the unpleasant conditions that surround the disabled, it is important to create other comforting and useful expectations:

> And I do not know why we infirm should want anything from this world, for as much as we may wander, we shall never find anything in it that loves us well. Worldly pleasures despise us, health forsakes us, friends forget us, relatives get angry, and even one's

own mother gets annoyed with her sickly daughter, and one's father despises the son who with chronic afflictions dwells in his
home.   (46)

The negative description of the sick, abandoned by their own parents, may be self-referential, although this is not entirely clear. What is
clear is Cartagena's strong testimony of the marginality of the different
in the fifteenth century, not unlike their situation today. Her solution to
overcome this marginality, however, is quite characteristic of her time.
She recommends accepting pain and rejection with patience, as the path
that leads us to God: "Therefore, let us who languish in hunger for physical health in this strange land seek Him with fervent desire" (47). This
intense longing of the body or "yearning stuff," as Bynum Walker calls
it, is a trait of Cartagena's identity that conforms to the concept of identity for "singers, preachers, and lovers of the fourteenth century" for
whom the "body is not only instrument, expression, and locus of self,
but in some sense self itself" ("Why" 32–33). But Cartagena shifts the
object of the body's desires from worldly pleasures to the postponed
eternal happiness of divine union.

To elaborate on her longing and the model of consolation aligned
with it, first she reflects on the source of pain and the condition of the
disabled, taking into account both personal and social reaction to the
phenomenon of human suffering. Her lucid and detailed analysis exposes the social construction of disability and the consequences of such
a construction; the stigma and social signs imposed on the creation of
otherness; the grief, impotence, rebellion, and lack of control of the sufferer over her corporeal changes; and society's response to those
changes. She also points out the advantages that one can discover in
such a situation: a change of personality since "the mortification of our
outward strength makes our inward thoughts faint and completely
powerless" (65), greater self-confidence, experience, and spirituality.
This analysis is carried out by a characteristic methodology of the medieval literary tradition: the allegory of the five talents, where she develops the idea that corporeal suffering is a kind of commodity in which
one exchanges pains and privations for spiritual benefits.

In her exegesis of the second, third, and fourth talents of corporeal
pain, Cartagena unveils the cultural construction of disability in her
time, which has many elements in common with our present conceptu-
alization (cf. Wendell 42–43; Davis, *Enforcing* 23–49). For example, disabled and sick people cure the sin of pride, because they are deprived of

the most appreciated and desirable attributes in medieval society. When people have a sickness or an embarrassing plague, they are abandoned by friends and parents, thrown out from home, disinherited, and even scorned by servants. Moreover, sickness or deficiency saps corporeal strength and deforms proportion; it transmutes beauty into ugliness and youth into old age; graceful eloquence converts to whining complaints, even more so if one has lost the capacity of hearing and talking. Dignity and human honor flee from the invalid, "since his own dignity is lacking" (60). Finally, disability drives away wealth. In the same manner that disabled and sick people cure the sin of pride, they avoid the remaining capital sins: more by force than by will.[20] Cartagena reveals that, just as today, fifteenth-century society conceives disability in the negative term of dichotomies such as strength/weakness, beauty/ugliness, youth / old age, poverty/wealth, and ability/disability.

In addition to psychological, social, and moral challenges, Cartagena also refers to the stigmata and body marks that change, separate, and differentiate the body of the afflicted: "This mortification is like the source or stamp of our suffering, for just as the seal placed over wax leaves its own impression, so afflictions with the stamp of mortification impress on the body and face of the sufferer the seal of its own coat of arms" (63–64). These are the visual or perceptible signs of the disabled person that, according to Erving Goffman, "turn those of us whom he meets away from him" (*Stigma* 5).[21] They transform people, Cartagena indicates, and function like a suit or livery that aggregates and makes equal to one another those who suffer and converts them into others. In this state of separation and physical inactivity, the power of imagination and desire is the only means of union for the incapacitated with a world denied to them. To mitigate this pain, Cartagena's goal is to arrive voluntarily to a position where "our temporal desires, fears, and cupidity diminish little by little until they are level with the impotence and weakness of our bodies" (66). The only desire she considers just is our natural inclination of wanting to improve our health. She recommends asking God "health for our body, salvation for our soul" (79). In her program of consolation, she asserts that the lack of control over our bodies—"one of the most powerful symbolic meanings of disability," according to Wendell (61)—and over our social rejection offers us paradoxically a control over the inner self, over the occult. It is through this power that one can find liberation and spiritual consolation. The spirit fortifies the weak flesh, and the mortification of flesh elevates the spirit in the project of *Arboleda*.

Despite this elevation, the experience that seems to hurt the most is social alienation. Cartagena declares that the pain is difficult to express, as "experience can describe it better than tongue or pen" (68). To ameliorate this damage, she again suggests that we avoid struggling against the situation and accept it with true humility (88–89). To escape the great affliction that social repulsion causes, we must renounce the values on which we have formerly based our security and self-esteem: "Therefore, to have voluntary humility we must be pleased with the contempt that others show us, for this contentment in received scorn is the basis of true voluntary humility" (70). By abandoning cultural values that are no longer viable and through a transformation of identity, one can construct a protective building of humility, an alternative place of comfort for the disabled body.

In a period with a rigorously hierarchical society that lacks our modern notions of individuality, Cartagena cannot advocate social justice or individual rights as disability activists do today. She considers the pain and abjection of the different a condition that evades human control and comprehension, that needs to be resolved at a spiritual and personal level. She seems to accept that her body is inferior to the normal one; however, the doctrine of bodily resurrection redeems it. She ends her treatise recommending that we accept with patience God's secret designs and have faith in a future reward. For Cartagena, God controls and is responsible for our suffering and is also the source of our health, since pain can be explained only by his hidden and inherently good purpose.

Arboleda de los enfermos is an important document for the study of the history of marginalization due to body differences. As in modern testimonies on disability, Teresa de Cartagena denounces the abjection and the social creation of the other. She considers her deafness a circumstance that paradoxically situates her in a privileged position for enlightenment and hope. Like many writers of today's memoirs related to disability, pain, and chronic diseases, this medieval writer not only finds in her text consolation for her personal suffering but also validates alternative forms of living that equally fulfill human experience.

NOTES

I would like to thank Brenda Jo Brueggemann, Tom Couser, and Dayle Seidenspinner-Núñez for reading this paper and for their valuable suggestions.
  1. I quote from Seidenspinner-Núñez's English translation, *The Writings of Teresa de Cartagena*. The Spanish text is edited by Lewis J. Hutton.

2. Rosemarie Garland-Thomson defines norms as "a hypothetical set of guide-lines for corporeal form and function arising from cultural expectations about how human beings should look and act" (*Extraordinary Bodies* 6–7). Lennard Davis explains in chapter 2 of *Enforcing Normalcy* the construction of normalcy and its hegemony in Western thought and how "the application of the idea of a norm to the human body creates the idea of deviance or a 'deviant' body" (34).

3. For a review of Castilian medieval women writers, consult Deyermond, "Writers" and "Las autoras." See also López Estrada.

4. The implications of being an intellectual woman and a *conversa* in fifteenth-century Spanish society are examined by Seidenspinner-Núñez; Vicente García; and Deyermond, "El convento."

5. Deyermond, in a pioneering study of the work of Cartagena, indicates that the decisive factor that generated this extraordinary text is precisely her physical impairment ("'El convento'"). For Vicente García, *Arboleda* is the fruit of the writer's social isolation, due to her deafness, that would predispose her to introspection and the need for communication (97).

6. See Couser, "Autopathography" and *Recovering Bodies*. In addition, Mary Burgan, in her study of Katherine Mansfield, and Nancy Mairs in her works ("On Being Crippled" and *Waist-High*) expose the link between trials of the body and women's creativity.

7. Philippe Lejeune defines autobiography as "retrospective prose narrative written by a real person concerning his own existence, where the focus is his individual life, in particular the story of his personality" (4).

8. For her literary sources and models, see Hutton 17–18; Deyermond, "El convento" 23; and Seidenspinner-Núñez, *Writings* 2. In addition, Irene Alejandra Molina studies the sermon structure of *Arboleda*, while Gregorio Rodríguez Rivas places the work among the literary ascetic prose of the fifteenth century.

9. Seidenspinner-Núñez proposes that *Arboleda* is an oblique autobiography for its emphasis on the private, for its fragmentation, and for self-representation in relation to another (God or healthy people), all characteristics of narratives written by women (*Writings* 117, 119).

10. The ideas of J. Rosenberg (1–24) have greatly helped me elaborate this section.

11. Susan Plann in her recent book on deaf education in Spain leaves out the study of the medieval period. She nevertheless suggests, quoting *Arboleda*, that in earlier periods wealthy families "concealed their 'defective' children [. . .] in convents and in monasteries" (13).

12. The nun acquires an excellent education because she belongs to a notable family of intellectuals and writers (Vicente García 97–98; Howe 133–34; Seidenspinner-Núñez, *Writings* 10). She receives additional instruction at the University of Salamanca (*Writings* 80) and by the teaching of sermons (*Writings* 75; López Estrada 16; Howe 139).

13. For the role of understanding (*entendimiento*) in the works of Cartagena, see Howe.

14. Derrida develops these concepts in *Writing and Difference* (3–30) and *Of Grammatology* (6–26).

15. Her capacity as a woman writer is defended in her second treatise, *Admiración*. See the analysis of Vicente García; Howe; and Seidenspinner-Núñez, "El solo" and *Writings* (113–38).

16. For the structural role of the cloister image, see Surtz 300.

17. Five centuries later we observe similar personal stories of struggle confronting body losses and achieving redemption. For example, Susan Wendell, in her meditations on her chronic pain, affirms, "[M]y experience of illness has been profoundly meaningful, but only because I accepted my body as a cause" (175). In the same fashion Mairs, from the perspective of her wheelchair, confirms her present state of satisfaction: "[Th]e languid, pensive state in which I now live much of the time has calmed me and expanded my contentment immesurably" (*Waist-High* 37).

18. She talks frequently about her corporeal pain. Apparently she suffered chronic ailments in addition to losing her hearing.

19. Wendell, for instance, affirms, "[I]llness has forced me to change" (175). Such change seems to be a general experience with disability, as we can see in Mairs's compilation of testimonies from other women (*Waist-High* 124–45).

20. Interestingly enough, Mairs talks about a similar experience in relation to the Catholic Church, to which she belongs: "[M]ine must be just about the same ideal state: too helpless even for the sins other flesh is heir to" (61).

21. For the concept of "visibility," "perceptibility," or "evidentness," consult Goffman, *Stigma* 48–51.

DIANE PRICE HERNDL

Reconstructing the Posthuman Feminist Body Twenty Years after Audre Lorde's *Cancer Journals*

[F]eminist cultural criticism is not a blueprint for the conduct of personal life (or political action, for that matter) and does not empower (or require) individuals to "rise above" their culture or to become martyrs to feminist ideals. It does not tell us what to *do*. [. . .] Its goal is edification and understanding, enhanced *consciousness* of the power, complexity, and *systemic* nature of culture, the interconnected webs of its functioning. It is up to the reader to decide how, when, and where (or whether) to put that understanding to further use in the particular, complicated, and ever-changing context that is his or her life and no one else's.

—Susan Bordo, *Unbearable Weight*

This is an essay about the feminist politics of visibility, silence, and the body. I warn you up front that there is a distinct possibility that it is a theoretical version of self-justification, a meditation on a fall from one version of feminist politics, a confession. I warn you up front that it is about the conflict of finding myself at odds with a feminism that I greatly admire and about coming to terms with not living up to Audre Lorde. I warn you up front that today, three months after my mastectomy and breast reconstruction, may be too soon for me to achieve academic distance from the body of the breast cancer patient and the politics of prosthesis, reconstruction, disability.

Invisibility and Silence: Audre Lorde and the Voicing of Breast Cancer

I wanted to be glad I was alive, I wanted to be glad about all the things I've got to be glad about. But now it hurts. Now it hurts. Things chase themselves around inside my eyes and there are tears I cannot shed and words like cancer, pain, and dying.

Later, I don't want this to be a record of grieving only. I don't want this to be a record only of tears. I want it to be something I can use [. . .] something I can pass on [. . .]. My work is to inhabit the silences with which I have lived [. . .].   (Lorde 45–46)

Twenty years ago, Audre Lorde was diagnosed with breast cancer and underwent a mastectomy; *The Cancer Journals* is the book that came out of that experience. In addition to recording some of her actual journals, her meditations on her fury and mourning, it includes essays about the silence that surrounded breast cancer and mastectomy at that time and about the falseness of prosthesis and reconstructive surgery. The essays articulate a theory of prosthesis as a means of silence, as a way of hiding women with breast cancer from one another and therefore keeping them from being able to share their sense of rage and the knowledge they have gained from the experience. She argues further that prosthesis hides breast cancer from public awareness, allowing people to ignore its politics. She claims that prosthesis works as a lie, a way for a woman to pretend cancer did not happen to her, a way to avoid the reality of amputation. Finally, she states that the emphasis on looking normal after mastectomy works to keep women within a stereotypical femininity, treating their bodies as aesthetic objects.

As did other feminists of her generation, Lorde begins the work of giving voice to women and to women's issues that had remained hidden, shameful, unspoken.[1] For her, that silence is the silence over breast cancer. Her confrontation with mortality drives her to think of her silences and of the ultimate silence, death: "In becoming forcibly and essentially aware of my mortality, and of what I wished and wanted for my life, however short it might be, priorities and omissions became strongly etched in merciless light, and what I most regretted were my silences. Of what had I *ever* been afraid?" (19). Her fear about that complete silence brings her to speak out about cancer and to reveal to the world the consequences of her amputation. She decided both to speak out about cancer and to exhibit her body's difference; she decided on an ethical course of action that would turn her private experience of fear, pain, and mourning into politics. Lorde related voice to the visual and, in doing so, made the personal political.

Emerging from surgery, she realizes that one of the greatest difficulties for her is her lack of role models, the lack of a tradition that will guide her, that will tell her what to do. She asks, "Where are the models for what I'm supposed to be in this situation?," and laments, "Where were the dykes who had had mastectomies?" (29, 50). The silence surrounding breast cancer even as late as the 1970s was startling. Cancer itself in the late 1970s was being attributed to a particular—and bad—personality type. Depression, repressed emotions, and succumbing to stress were designated as causes of cancer; thereby the patient was blamed for her illness (see, e.g., Sontag 50–57). Breast cancer carried the added weight of being not only gender-specific (though men do get breast cancer) but somehow sexual as well. Even today, some men are embarrassed about the disease (I have male colleagues who have not yet said the word *cancer* to me although I taught all the way through chemotherapy and surgery and they saw me almost daily). Women's breasts, the object of such obsession in our culture, were nonetheless still unspeakable. Breast cancer, even among women, was unspoken. Lorde writes, "I needed to talk with women who shared at least some of my major concerns and beliefs and visions, who shared at least some of my language." Her painful conclusion, though, was, "But there were none. This is it, Audre. You're on your own" (42, 29).

Lorde enters a world of ethical narration and becomes a model for other women facing cancer. She goes public as the dyke with the mastectomy, to talk about the experience of cancer and of living one-breasted. She undertakes a writing project that Arthur Frank, in *The Wounded Storyteller*, contends is at the heart of the postmodern illness narrative: claiming a voice. Frank argues that the medical experience is essentially colonizing, that the patient is forced to be passive, to leave the work of healing to the heroic physician. The person telling her illness narrative, though, demands "to speak rather than [be] spoken for and to represent [herself] rather than [be] represented or, in the worst cases, rather than [be] effaced entirely" (13). It was a sense of being effaced that Lorde encountered in the few women who did talk to her about the experience of cancer. When a representative of Reach for Recovery visited her in the hospital, it was to deliver a pink lamb's-wool prosthesis; when Lorde visited the surgeon's office without the prosthesis, the nurse told her she should wear it, because she was bad for morale in the office. In both cases, the women were urging her to deny the reality of her loss, were suggesting that she not only could but should efface the change. Lorde writes of her visitor from Reach for Recovery, "Her message was, you are just as good as you were before because you can look exactly the same. Lamb's wool now, then a good prosthesis as soon as possible, and nobody'll ever know the difference. But what she said was, '*You'll* never know the difference,' and she lost me right there, because I knew sure as hell *I'd* know the difference" (42). Frank writes, "Telling stories is a form of resistance" (170), and Lorde's story is precisely that: resistance against the effacement of her disease and loss.

Her choice to live without a prosthesis or a reconstruction is to make visible her difference. Instead of wearing a prosthesis, she chooses to wear breast cancer, to wear difference. But she makes it clear that even though such a choice is not an easy one, for her to make another choice would be a denial of who she has become:

> I looked at the large gentle curve my left breast made under the pajama top, a curve that seemed even larger now that it stood by itself. I looked strange and uneven and peculiar to myself, but somehow, ever so much more myself, and therefore so much more acceptable than I looked with that thing stuck inside my clothes. For not even the most skillful prosthesis in the world could undo that reality, or feel the way my breast had felt, and either I would love my body one-breasted now, or remain forever alien to myself.
>
> Then I climbed back into bed and cried myself to sleep, even though it was 2:30 in the afternoon. (44)

Refusing to acknowledge one's difference, she argues, is to remain alien to oneself.

Perhaps this is the point at which much of contemporary feminist theory departs from Audre Lorde. Guided by poststructural theories, many feminists now see all subjects as essentially alien to themselves. That alienation is a condition of postmodernity, a condition of the subjectivity that is always different from itself. The earlier feminist politics that urged an acceptance of self, an embrace of self, and a move toward self-loving did not always recognize that internal difference. Lorde's is not an unsophisticated position, but it is grounded in an understanding of self in which one can eventually know the self and not be alien to oneself and in which one can make decisions about a relation to the body that may not be comfortable for many postmodern feminists.

"I Am Talking Here about the Need for Every Woman to Live a Considered Life": Reconstructing the Feminist Body

Twenty years after Lorde was diagnosed with breast cancer, so was I. I had options she didn't have, including the opportunity to just have the lump removed rather than to lose the whole breast. It was an obvious choice for me. But ten months after that first surgery and after nine months of chemotherapy, the cancer came back, and I had no choice but to have a mastectomy. What I did have a choice about (again, one unavailable to Lorde) was whether to have reconstructive surgery done, not with silicon implants but with my own body tissue. In early February, I sent this e-mail message to the group of women on whose support I depend:

> At a couple of crisis points in my life, I've found myself singing in the shower without really stopping to think about what I'm singing. The first time was in grad school, the morning I was to start doing my written exams. Carl noticed that I was singing the Roches' "You're being weeded out" at the top of my lungs. Well, one morning this week I caught myself singing Laurie Anderson— "I want stereo-FM installed in my teeth, / And take this mole off my back and put it on my cheek, / And while you're at it, why don't you give me some of those high-heeled feet?"
>
> Which is to say that after an agonizing weekend of decision-making, I've decided to subject myself to plastic surgery, and to do it at the same time as the mastectomy (next Friday, on February 19). They'll be taking my belly off and moving it up, to build a new "breast." As the plastic surgeon put it, the silver lining to this is that one gets a free tummy-tuck. Which probably should come under the rubric of "be careful what you wish for," as any number of times I've looked in the mirror and wished that someone could just cut that belly fat off. Ooops. Ah, chemotherapy and steroids giveth and surgery taketh away.
>
> And medical subject I am, now, thoroughly. Part of the ritual humiliation of this is the "examination" at the plastic surgeon's: my breasts and belly were hefted, measured with calipers, compared to plastic forms. Then I was photographed, naked but for my socks

and a pair of paper "modesty" panties—elastic and blue paper, every designer's dream—but, to comfort me, the doctor and his assistant assured me that my face wouldn't be in the pictures. Though I did have to hold up a card for the first one that identified me by name and patient number. Mug shot, indeed.

But the choice I've made is interesting to me on a couple of levels. First, I've had to put my beliefs about the relationship between mind and body into practice in a way I never really expected to. But I believe that mental healing is as important as physical and I believe that having the surgery done right away, so that by May I'm recovering from both surgery and radiation, means that I can get on with my life sooner. And I believe that is important. Second, I've had to assess my limits. I've had to measure how much loss I can stand. And all the theorizing about the body that I've ever done didn't prepare me for how I'd choose. At the same time that I've chosen in favor of my mind, my spirit, my emotions, I've also chosen to preserve as much of my physicality intact as I can, and it turns out that is important to me. It is just too Lacanian to imagine my body parts being removable. That image in the mirror is whole, after all.

To enhance the lighter side of all this, the university payroll office made a mistake on my W-2 form, and checked the box for "deceased" instead of "pension plan."

Which may be, to conclude, a comment on just how postmodern all this is.

Looking back on this message, I don't know if the " agonizing" in the second paragraph half covers what that week of decision making was like. (One problem with breast cancer surgery is that such decisions need to be made relatively quickly, usually within two weeks, if only because of the terror of it; I wanted that tissue out of me.) I had always assumed, before I had breast cancer, that I would choose what I thought was the feminist alternative: refusing reconstruction or prosthesis, Lorde's choice. Things have changed since her experience—in part because of her experience. Now, living without a prosthesis is an alternative that is open, out there, always mentioned as one possibility.[2] I thought it was the right choice. I thought it was the feminist choice. And I couldn't do it. Feminist theorist fails, I told myself at first.

Then I rethought what I meant by feminist theory and realized that feminist relations to the body are different now than they were twenty years ago for Lorde and that feminist relations to breast cancer are different. I am not often in the position of thinking that feminism has made great strides; too often I look at the sexism of the world around me, at the disavowal of feminism by a younger generation, and fall into the trap of thinking that we've achieved so little. But when it comes to breast cancer, the difference that feminism has made is undeniable. Lorde's refusal to wear a prosthesis was an open avowal of something that had remained hidden; the result, I realized, was that I didn't have to wear breast cancer in the same way.

Lorde's resistance made possible many other acts of resistance, so that today breast cancer is no longer silent. Books on it have become widely available, and almost all encourage survivors to become vocal about the disease—about environmental toxins that are almost certainly to blame for the rising incidence of the disease, about the politics of funding research, and about the emotional issues of survival. Other artists have begun speaking out about breast cancer, about both the experience of the disease and the politics of it, often at once. For example, in a move in the visual arts that was analogous to Lorde's literary one, the *New York Times Magazine* put a photograph on its 15 August 1993 cover of the photographer Matuschka, with her mastectomy scar exposed. "You Can't Look Away Anymore," the cover declared. The collection *Art. Rage. Us: Art and Writing by Women with Breast Cancer* similarly includes photographs like Diana Young's self-portrait, *One in Eight* (a reference to American women's chances of being diagnosed with breast cancer). In the photograph, Young—whose scars reveal a double mastectomy—is seated with six other women and one little girl, all of whom are topless. One doesn't have to look far for women who have had breast cancer and who are willing to reveal it. There are breast cancer foundations, support groups, Web sites;[3] there is Race for the Cure; the post office has even issued a breast cancer stamp. Lorde's mission to make breast cancer visible, to give it voice, has succeeded.

My (almost) unconscious evocation of Anderson's postmodern music was an indicator of some of the marks of that change. The 1990s have seen the emergence of the "posthuman."[4] While in 1979 Lorde could choose to love her one-breasted body as an alternative to remaining alien to herself, postmodern art and theory during the 1980s and 1990s have challenged the idea that any of us are ever anything but alien to ourselves; in fact, they celebrate the alien within us. Donna Haraway's "Cyborg Manifesto" is a call not to return to the pretechnological body but to embrace the simulacrum body:

> From one perspective, a cyborg world is about the final imposition
> of a grid of control on the planet, about the final abstraction em-

bodied in a Star Wars apocalypse [. . .], about the final appropriation of women's bodies in a masculinist orgy of war [. . .]. From
another perspective, a cyborg world might be about lived social
and bodily realities in which people are not afraid of their joint
kinship with animals and machines, not afraid of permanently
partial identities and contradictory standpoints. (155)

It is both, of course, but accepting that doubleness is to embrace partiality and contradiction. My choice to have reconstruction was to leap with
both feet into the posthuman, the partial, and the contradictory. My
new "breast" reflects that: it is me to the extent that it is my own tissue,
but it is alien because it has been moved, reshaped, and changed by
technology. I am now partial, because a part of me is missing—I keep using scare quotes around "breast" as an indicator that this flesh is not an
actual breast, doesn't feel like one now and never will—and because my
choice reveals a partiality for a normal appearance.

Of course, to say that I chose to become posthuman is a lie. From the
moment that I began my interaction with technology (And when was
that? I ask myself. When I had the first mammogram? When they did
the first surgery? When they installed a plastic fitting under my skin to
do chemotherapy more easily? When I was born?), I was already
posthuman. Is my new "breast" any less a visible sign of my interaction
with technology than a mastectomy scar would be?

To a certain extent, yes. It is certainly less visible to other people
when I am wearing clothes. This invisibility of what happened to me is
at the heart of Lorde's resistance to prosthesis. Hiding the amputation of
mastectomy is, she argues, a way to deny what has happened, to try to
pretend that nothing has happened:

After a mastectomy [. . .] there is a feeling of wanting to go back,
of not wanting to persevere through this experience to whatever
enlightenment might be at the core of it. And it is this feeling, this
nostalgia, which is encouraged by most of the post-surgical counseling for women with breast cancer. This regressive tie to the past
is emphasized by the concentration upon breast cancer as a cosmetic problem, one which can be solved by a prosthetic pretense.
(56)

For the posthuman feminist, Lorde's claims have a double edge.

First, although I had what might be called by some cosmetic surgery,
cancer was never a cosmetic problem to me. The treatment for cancer
was the cosmetic problem. Covering my bald head while I was under-
going chemotherapy was a cosmetic issue. Deciding whether to present

myself to the world as one-breasted or not was a cosmetic choice. But cancer, with or without reconstruction, goes to the bone. It cannot be solved or cured by a visible change in my body. Prosthesis is technology, and it never lets me forget. Its artificiality is palpable. I am alien to myself forever. I will never be able to pretend this didn't happen to me.

Second, despite my alienness to myself, I do have to confront the fact that what I have done makes it easier for other people to dismiss the reality of cancer or at least to think that it is something that can be taken care of easily. Cancer will never and can never be cosmetic for me, but that doesn't mean that other people can't miss that.

I thought when I made the choice to have the reconstructive surgery that I could still follow part of Lorde's lead and make breast cancer visible by talking about it, by claiming the identity of a woman with breast cancer, and that would outweigh my choice to make cancer less manifest to others. I thought that my voice would outweigh the visible. And so I openly talk about breast cancer to lots of women. I describe what has happened to me and talk about the statistics, the state of cancer research, what we know and don't know about prevention. That voicing of breast cancer, though, doesn't always work.

After I had surgery, I was in the beauty shop and talking about it. One of the cosmetologists was listening eagerly. (The importance of setting and character has not escaped me, by the way.) I thought she was with me, understanding how it felt to live posthumanly, to have one's skin lifted, to have tissue removed and rearranged, to have over nineteen inches of scars across my abdomen and "breast." I thought she heard me talking about the pain, about spending five weeks on narcotics, about the fact that two months later I still couldn't use my stomach muscles to sit up. Instead, what she said was "Maybe I could get that surgery. They could cut off all this flab on my belly and make my boobs bigger!" The guilt I spiraled into was overwhelming. What had I done? Had my belief that the voice could belie the visible been self-delusion? Had I let my secret wish for a tummy tuck and a cosmetically enhanced body rule my choices? Was I that wrong?

Forever Alien to Myself: Aesthetics, Disability, and the Feminist Body

Cancer is not a cosmetic issue, but prosthesis and reconstruction are. For Lorde, a statement like this one is a lie, a misunderstanding of the interconnection between cancer and the placebo of replacement. Worse, it is a delusion that keeps women within a certain stereotype of femininity: "This emphasis on the cosmetic after surgery reinforces this society's stereotype of women, that we are only what we look or appear, so this is the only aspect of our existence we need to address. Any woman who has had a breast removed because of cancer knows she does not feel the same" (Lorde 58). Looking the same, feeling the same, self-knowledge: for Lorde, these issues are intimately connected. She believes in an integrity of self, in which, when one knows one's difference, one lives it, reveals it. Voice and visibility are the same for her.

In the twenty years since she wrote *The Cancer Journals*, we have come to think about bodies differently, to see bodies as produced, as, in fact, forever alien to ourselves. The challenge for me personally and for feminism more generally, I think, is to find a way to understand the difference between a postmodern, posthuman view of the body and an earlier feminism's view without having to regard either as entirely wrong. Each is historically situated, responding to different cultures, different crises in women's embodiment. Does reconstructive surgery fall prey to this culture's insistence on feminine beauty at any cost? Of course it does. Does it also help rethink the borders of the natural, sexual, and what counts as feminine beauty? Yes, it does that too.

Audré Lorde looked at her one-breasted body and decided to love it as it was. She staged a kind of feminist self-claiming that was and still is crucial. But there are other scenes of self-loving. I made my decision standing in a dressing room at my favorite countercultural clothes shop, looking in the mirror. Michel Foucault (and Lorde) might well describe my moment of self-regard as the instant when I gave in to the self-disciplining of our culture, when I decided to give in to the demand that I look normal. I see that moment as one in which, like Lorde, I decided to love my body but in the full realization that, one way or another, it would never be normal, that I would always be alien to myself. In the full postmodern, posthuman realization that all bodies are constructed, that all bodies are a production—of gender, of the normal, of beauty, of ability—I really had no choice. Mastectomy scar or reconstructed breast, neither would leave me untouched.

The myth most of us embody is that we get a choice. The myth is that we are born, not made, that being abled or disabled, male or female, visibly different or normal is something real. The myth is that there is a right way of doing things, that there are right choices about the body, that all bodies are the same. Disability studies questions the lines we draw to make ourselves believe in that myth. Is the visible embodiment of difference what it takes to make one different? Is the choice of a cosmetically created normality a sign that one is giving in to the cultural demands for a specific femininity, or is it a disavowal of the whole idea of the normal? In *Extraordinary Bodies,* Rosemarie Garland-Thomson writes:

> My intention is to [. . .] disclos[e] how the "physically disabled" are produced by way of legal, medical, political, cultural, and literary narratives that [comprise] an exclusionary discourse. Constructed as the embodiment of corporeal insufficiency and deviance, the physically disabled body becomes a repository for social anxieties and such troubling concerns as vulnerability, control, and identity. [. . .] I intend to counter the accepted notions of physical disability as an absolute, inferior state and a personal misfortune. Instead, I show that disability is a representation, a cultural interpretation of physical transformation or configuration. [. . .] Disability, then, is the attribution of corporeal deviance—not so much a property of bodies as a product of cultural rules about what bodies should be or do.   (6)

Disability studies challenges that myth of the "is" as well as the myth of the "should." In the era of the posthuman feminist body, there cannot be a "blueprint for the conduct of personal life" (Bordo 30).

Paula Rabinowitz, in an essay on the posthuman and the feminist, has argued that the voices of posthuman bodies are "only accessible through vast networks of mediation prone to recuperation and misinterpretation at best," that "the posthuman, alien and marginal [. . .], probably cannot speak because it is always spoken through stories that someone else has already told" (98). This may be true. Certainly my own attempt to speak the posthuman at the beauty shop was subjected to misinterpretation. But that experience will not keep me from continuing to try to speak it. Lorde is right: "Any woman who has had a breast removed because of cancer knows she does not feel the same." And the ethical imperative of breast cancer is that I must continue to try to voice that difference, from myself and from the normal.

When Lorde made her choice to live one-breasted without the mask of the prosthesis, she wrote, "I must consider what my body means to me. I must also separate those external demands about how I look and feel to others, from what I really want for my own body, and how I feel to my selves. [. . .] Every woman has a right to define her own desires, make her own choices." I like to think that even though she added to this the caveat "But prostheses are often chosen, not from desire, but in default" (67), she would understand what I did, she would see that I am living my difference and that the difference between my voice and my visible self is part of that difference.

June 1999

NOTES

1. I am comparing Lorde's work on silence with that of Tillie Olsen in *Silences* and Adrienne Rich in *On Lies, Secrets, and Silences*.

2. Admittedly, though, it is an option that is often mentioned but then immediately marked as different. For instance, Susan Love (in the book usually thought of as the bible of breast cancer, *Dr. Susan Love's Breast Book*) quotes Audre Lorde, mentions the artists Matuschka (whose photographic self-portraits reveal her mastectomy scars) and Deena Metzger (who covered her amputation with a tattoo of a tree), and writes: "Having the self-confidence to feel comfortable without the appearance of a breast is wonderful, but most of us are products of our culture and need to feel that we are cosmetically acceptable to the outside world. In some cases, there are actual penalties for failing to appear 'normal.' If your nonconformity will cost you your job, for example, you're likely to want to wear a prosthesis [. . .] at least part of the time or choose reconstruction" (385–86).

3. There are too many breast cancer resources on the Internet to list them all. Here are a few of the better sites. The NABCO (National Alliance of Breast Cancer Organizations) site is a good repository of information and links to other sites (www.nabco.org). The *New York Times* site *Women's Health* includes many links about breast cancer and other women's health issues (www.nytimes.com/specials/women/whome/). Though I share many of Lorde's reservations about the American Cancer Society's politics, its site, the *Breast Cancer Network* (www2.cancer.org), provides some good information about the disease and about activism. A good site for women's stories about breast cancer is the *Breast Cancer Lighthouse* (commtechlab.msu.edu/sites/bcl/). The breast cancer support group Y-Me has an excellent site listing resources for both women with the disease and for survivors (www.y-me.org/). One thing that almost all these sites have in common is an activism component; I take that as sign that feminism has made a difference in women's relation to the disease.

4. The term *posthuman* comes from an exhibit curated by Jeffrey Deitch in 1992. In *Bad Girls and Sick Boys*, Linda Kauffman defines the term: "*Posthuman* signifies the impact technology has had on the human body. Any candidate for a pacemaker, prosthetics, plastic surgery, or Prozac, sex reassignment surgery, in vitro fertilization, or gene therapy, can be defined as posthuman" (2). In their collection, *Posthuman Bodies*, Judith Halberstam and Ira Livingston locate the posthuman body in postmodern, poststructural theory and claim, "Posthuman bodies are the causes and effects of postmodern relations of power and pleasure, virtuality and reality, sex and its consequences. The posthuman body is a technology, a screen, a projected image; it is a body under the sign of AIDS, a contaminated body, a deadly body, a techno-body; it is, as we shall see, a queer body" (3).

NANCY MAIRS

Sex and Death and the Crippled Body: A Meditation

All bodies function under social constraints of various sorts, but none more inexorably than bodies distinguished by disability. People whose disabilities are absent or not yet detected, made anxious by conditions they cannot experience, ascribe limitations (some accurate, others wildly wide of the mark) to those with disabilities; and since the view of these people has conventionally predominated, even among the disabled themselves, their ascriptions take on considerable force. Cast as either permissions (even obligations) or denials (even prohibitions), the ascriptions are seldom promulgated; they lie too deep to require lip service.

Many of them, though they may stir an outcry among militants, are relatively harmless, little more than nondisabled solecisms: referring to a wheelchair user as "confined," for instance, or patting a guide dog without permission. Others, however, lie at the very roots of human existence. And what could be more radical than sex and death? Here, the (often subconscious) attitudes and assumptions of the nondisabled may threaten the well-being of anyone whose mental or physical circumstances diverge from a norm defined without reference to them. From both reading and experience, I have learned that I had best refrain from sex while seriously entertaining my death.

Sex and the Gimpy Girl

The other day, I went into a tizzy. As a rule, I avoid this state, not merely because it violates the reticent courtesy demanded by my Yankee upbringing but also because it reinforces the misperception that people with disabilities are difficult to deal with. But to be honest, sometimes I get sick of acting the Girl Scout of cripples, and I fall out of (or perhaps into my true) character.

On this day, I had scheduled a Pap smear at a clinic new to me, on the eighth floor of the hospital at the heart of the Arizona Health Sciences Center. In this building, I can't reach higher than 3 on the elevator buttons, so I must make sure someone else gets on with me. When I arrived at the clinic, the doors weren't automated: another wait till some other woman came along. The counter was too high for me to reach the sign-in sheet—so high, in fact, that I couldn't see the receptionist to ask for her help. After a thirty-five-minute wait, a nurse escorted me into a windowless cubicle with a standard examining table, although I had specified when booking the appointment that I required a model of table that can be lowered and tilted.

"I can't use that," I said.

"You can't?" She sounded skeptical and slightly aggrieved.

"No, my legs are too weak to climb up. That's why I use a wheelchair. Surely I'm not the only woman ever to have come in here in a wheelchair."

"Well, we don't get many."

"I don't wonder," I said with an asperity I now regret, "if this is the kind of treatment they receive."

She skedaddled, sending back the head nurse, who assured me that they had one of the tables I needed, though it was being used and wouldn't be available for some time. So I settled down with the book I'd brought, took my turn, and left, pretty well exhausted. The ten-minute procedure had consumed two hours, but I'd survived a classic example of the reproductive care women with disabilities are all too apt to receive.

Although, when I first consulted Harvey W. Buchsbaum, MD, in 1972, I hadn't yet presented the symptoms "disseminated in space and time" (a standard phrase in the medical literature) necessary for a diagnosis of multiple sclerosis, he had no doubt that my body had gone neurologically awry. "Not to get pregnant," he scribbled in my chart. "Not to take birth control pills." He did not, of course, suggest how I was to accomplish the former without resorting to the latter. He was a neurologist. Modern doctors chop their patients into pieces and parcel them out like so many cuts of beef, and this one wasn't about to have anything to do with my reproductive system.

I betook myself to a gynecologist, who suggested that I have my uterus removed. Uh-uh, said Dr. Buchsbaum: all my innards should remain in place, a decision with which I rather concurred. I consulted another gynecologist, who recommended tubal ligation. Nope, said Dr. Buchsbaum: I ought to avoid anesthesia. If any tubules were to be prevented from transporting their reproductive cargo, they ought to reside in George's simpler anatomy. A little Xylocaine, a couple of snips, and our worries would be over. This didn't strike me as a fair deal. Although, owing to Rh incompatibility, we had decided not to produce more children, he was only in his early thirties; if anything happened to me, he would almost certainly marry again, and he might well want to have children with his new wife. So we resorted to barriers until, after a pregnancy scare a few years later, he decided that he really didn't want more children with anyone and elected to have a vasectomy.

It didn't strike me as odd, in those days, to have a bunch of guys dictating orders about my reproductive system. As I recall, one of them was female, so I'm using the word *guys* loosely. But since some medical schools continue to pride themselves on inculcating traditionally masculine attitudes and behaviors in their students—the problematic ones like arrogance and competitiveness right along with the noble ones like bravery and self-discipline—a good many of the doctors I have met have been "real men" regardless of gender. And I was reared a good girl, deferential to authority and expertise. Even though my docility had made my son's early life as an anti-Rh baby into something of a tragedy, since I accepted their decrees instead of following my instincts, I continued to do as I was told.

Nor did it occur to me until some years later that my experience might be generalizable in any way. I had a habit of assuming that whatever happened in my life happened to me alone, not that my experiences might typify those of other women in similar circumstances. I didn't much think of myself (or think much of myself) as a woman then, and I didn't think of myself as a disabled woman at all, since, early on, my MS was more a nuisance than a handicap and I seldom encountered others like me. As I worked my way into graduate studies, and particularly into feminist theory, my perspective began to shift, until I came to recognize not merely that I was far from unique but that there wasn't an original word in my life story. The details were distinctive, of course, because I was myself and not some other woman of my age and heritage, but the structure recapitulated many of the features that had marked females as women from time immemorial.

Despite the real progress generated by feminists, female and male, over the past century or so, for example, our society persists in construing women as commodities. In this we are hardly singular. Several years ago, when I visited my daughter in Zaire, I was entertained by Tata Nzulu, a farmer of about sixty. Over a dinner of mfumbwa (peanut-flavored grass clippings) and tilapia freshly harvested from his pond, he counseled me to accept in exchange for Anne's hand in marriage nothing less than a cow, a Coleman lantern, and ten thousand zaires (worth about $300 at the time). He was not trying to mock or offend me. On the contrary, he was trying to convey just what a treasure this young Peace Corps worker was to the village of Mfuatu. I was flattered.

Nevertheless, on her return to the States, I didn't ask a bride price for my daughter. We don't do that here. Perhaps we ought. If all those pregnant fourteen-year-olds at the alternative school where my husband teaches had believed themselves to have some authentic value (though I don't think being traded for a cow would do the trick), maybe they'd have thought twice before hopping into the backs of pickup trucks with one acned lothario or another swearing love for all eternity, or at least until orgasm, whichever comes first. As it is, we commodify women—the models, the movie stars, the pretty little girls in beauty pageants, and the millions who, willingly or unwillingly, are held to their standards—without investing them with any specific worth. In the information age, ours is an economy of images, not of substance, and a woman's situation may be worse—or at least no better—than it was in the days when she could feel certain that, as long as she behaved herself, her price would be far above rubies.

If you view women as commodities (and being social products, none of us can altogether escape such an unconscious assumption), then a disabled woman must inevitably be damaged goods. How many people do you know who would willingly take home a television set that displayed only snow or a loaf of bread that had fallen from a shelf under the wheels of a shopping cart? Interestingly, my son would do so, on the grounds that a little tinkering might restore at least a moderately visible image to the screen, and the nutritional value of bread remains the same whether the loaf is six inches or pita-flat. His partners have been similarly the worse for wear—one obsessed by the certainty that she had a brain tumor and so agoraphobic that she couldn't leave the house, another a heroin-addicted prostitute, now on methadone—and I have often wondered to what extent his choices have resulted from his being reared by a disabled mother.

Unlike Matthew, most people would send the broken television or the crushed loaf straight to the dump, an outcome that may help explain the high level of anxiety triggered in people with disabilities by the question of physician-assisted suicide (of which more in a moment). And indeed, many disabled women might have an easier time finding someone to help them end their lives, lives assumed by their very nature to lack quality, than enlisting the corps of medical personnel required to resolve my daughter's infertility. Anne was an ideal matrix—didn't drink, didn't smoke, ate little fat and lots of complex carbohydrates—and no one could figure out why she didn't get pregnant. She just didn't. Finally, on the second try, intrauterine insemination did the trick, and soon we were all awaiting the birth of Colin James Mairs Peterson, who has burgeoned from the cutest little fetus in the world into the cutest little toddler in the world and doubtless will become, before we know it, the cutest little college graduate in the world.

No one ever questioned the appropriateness of Anne's desire for a baby. In fact, she'd have raised more eyebrows had she chosen not to reproduce. Suppose, however, that she was exactly the same woman except with cerebral palsy. Would the nurse practitioners and doctors who considered Anne's inability to conceive a treatable problem and mustered their arsenal of scopes and dyes and hormones and catheters be just as eager to rush to her aid? I have my doubts. Her infertility might even be viewed as a blessing. If such a woman—Chloë, let's call her—insisted, health professionals might try to reason with her. How can you change an infant's diaper with so little control of your hands? they might ask. How will you chase down a toddler with your unsteady gait? How can your child acquire normal language skills listening to your slurred speech? I don't mean to suggest that hard questions ought not to be asked of a disabled woman. In fact, I think one of the deepest troubles of our society is that we don't ask enough questions, hard enough, of everybody. But those asked of Chloë are less authentic questions than veiled judgments—not so much "How can you . . . ?" as "You can't possibly . . . "—and as such they reveal not merely medical caution but also some dubious premises about disability.

Medical professionals tend to pathologize disability, assuming that people whose bodies or minds function in abnormal ways have something wrong with them. People with disabilities certainly do have something—demyelination of the single nervous system, seizures, a severed spinal cord, inflamed joints, an extra chromosome; the possibilities seem endless and pretty unpleasant—but the wrongness of that something depends on one's point of view. From a doctor's perspective, a disability is wrong because it deviates from the ideal norm built up during years of training and practice. But for the patient, disability simply is the norm. There is nothing wrong with me. In fact, for a fifty-five-year-old woman with multiple sclerosis, I'm just about right. I am occasionally ill, of course, being a mere mortal, but my disability itself is not a sickness. It's part of who I am. And I'm far more likely to thrive if you don't regard me as sick at my very core.

In another misconception, society as a whole tends to infantilize those with physical or mental limitations, and none do so more readily than doctors and their adjuncts. To some extent, paternalism infects their relations with all their patients—*patient* is a word that doesn't share its root with *passive* by accident—because doctors' apparent (and often real) power over life and death reduces us all to a childlike dependency on their superior knowledge. We reinforce their dominance through our docility. My father-in-law swallowed blood-pressure medication for years, never knowing—indeed, refusing to ask—what his blood pressure actually was. If I were a doctor, I think that sort of quiescence would drive me nuts, but I can also see its allure. Not only does it endow the practitioner with an almost shamanistic force but also it makes treatment much more efficient. Patients who demand explanations for every detail of their care eat up time; and time, as HMOs know only too well, is money.

The tendency for doctor and patient to slip into a parent-child relationship is exacerbated in the case of people with disabilities by the fact that they are usually, in some way, genuinely helpless. I, for instance, can no longer walk or even crawl; I must be dressed and undressed; I manipulate eating utensils with an overhand grasp; when the sole of my foot is scratched, instead of curling under, my toes flare in the Babinski response characteristic of newborns. In short, my central nervous system is, quite literally, regressing toward its infantile state. Understandably, others may have trouble remembering that these neurological deficits are not accompanied by spiritual, emotional, or intellectual regression. But even if they were—as they appear to be in Alzheimer's, for example—the end product would be not an infant but an adult, damaged, to be sure, but fully mature.

In no area of human experience does it better suit the general population to think of the disabled as children than in the sexual. On the
whole, we are a society fixated on sexual images and issues without
ever feeling quite at ease with them. Shortly before a melanoma was
discovered in his small bowel, my husband became impotent—a word I
have never heard uttered in ordinary social discourse, even though the
condition is shared by a good ten million men in this country. When
George mentioned his state to his oncologist, Dr. Ralph waved it off as
the least of our worries. Only after George raised the matter over a period of months did Dr. Ralph finally refer him to a urologist.

One day, I mentioned George's persistent impotence to my mother.
"Good heavens," she said briskly, "you can live without *that*!"

"I know I can," I replied. "I just don't *want* to."

She shrugged. What else could she do? As her response and Dr.
Ralph's suggest, plenty of people dismiss sexual enthusiasm in fifty-
year-olds as at least a little silly. Perhaps the only person who can sym-
pathize with me is my eighty-six-year-old mother-in-law. Her libido
continues to flourish, and she has the boyfriend to prove it.

When it comes to sexuality in the disabled, dismissal is apt to turn
into outright repression. Made uncomfortable, even to the point of excruciation, by the thought of maimed bodies (or, for that matter, minds)
engaged in erotic fantasy or action, many deny the very possibility by as-
cribing to them the innocence of the very young. (In this, of course, they
are as wildly mistaken about immature as about adult sexuality.) Perhaps
this disgust and denial stem, as the sociobiologists would probably have
it, from the fact that such bodies are clearly less than ideal vehicles for the
propagation of the species. Whatever its origin, the repulsion lies buried
so deeply in consciousness as to seem natural rather than constructed. As
a result, even someone with the best intentions in the world may fail to
see a disabled woman whole. The parents of a congenitally disabled
daughter may rear her to believe that she will never enter a sexually intimate relationship like the one that they enjoy themselves, may with-
hold information about reproductive inevitabilities like menstruation,
may perhaps punish her for the sexual acting out that adolescence
brings. Those responsible for her health may forget that she requires reproductive care or provide it in a manner so cursory that she is left baf-
fled and ashamed.

All the same, in most cases she will long for intimacy, since desire
arises not "down there," in an area that may possibly be numb, but "up
here," in the libidinous brain. If she is heterosexual, she will likely dis-

cover that, although she may make close male friends, most men will not think of her as a romantic object. I am fortunate in having found a partner before I became disabled who has elected to remain with me for thirty-five years. Nevertheless, I can speak with some authority here, because in order to prepare an article for *Glamour,* I read several hundred letters from readers with disabilities. I can't report as confidently about lesbian women with disabilities because they didn't write in, although several respondents naively contemplated trying lesbianism as a solution to their sexual frustration. Anyone who cannot accept as normal both a disabled woman's desire and the grief she feels when it is thwarted will never see her as fully human.

In condemning some of the social attitudes toward women with disabilities that may increase their difficulty in receiving optimal care, I don't propose that such a woman should instead be treated just like a nondisabled woman. To do so would be neither practical nor ethical. Disability does set one apart from the general population, impinging on every decision. Only when we define these differences frankly, instead of politely ignoring them, can we discern the ways in which they do—and do not—matter.

When a young friend of mine, already blinded and crippled by juvenile rheumatoid arthritis, suffered a stroke, she was found to be eight weeks pregnant. Although she and her husband, also severely disabled, wanted nothing more dearly than a baby, she bravely underwent an abortion and a tubal ligation, knowing that her future health would never be certain enough for the long-term commitment child rearing requires. Those in charge of her care botched the emotional dimension of her case, I think, brushing aside her desolation at the loss of this baby and the hope of any others, although I do not doubt that they did what her circumstances required them to do. They simply could not see her whole. They grasped the medical fact that her disability prevented her from bearing a child without acknowledging the emotional fact that, like ordinary women throughout the world, she wanted to do just that.

I'll concede the strain involved in balancing a disabled woman's significant differences from the general female population with her equally significant similarities to it—in the reproductive sphere as in all areas of human experience—but I also believe, true to my Yankee roots, in the virtue of hard work. Women with every kind of disability must learn to speak forthrightly about their needs and appetites, even when society appears to ignore or repudiate their feelings. The nondisabled must accustom themselves to hearing the utterances of such women without judging the rightness or wrongness of their realities. I am always dismayed when a parent snatches a curious child away from my wheelchair or shushes her when she asks, "Why do you use that?" I see in the making yet another adult who will, in the name of politeness, pretend there is nothing the matter with me while simultaneously but surreptitiously regarding me as an escapee from *The X-Files*. Neither of these views is accurate, but she'll never find that out unless we talk.

Rethinking Who Lives, Who Dies

Open communication is equally urgent when the issues surround the end of life, where medical misperception may run just as rampant. Indeed, physicians who assume that disability disqualifies one from sexual activities may readily leap to the conclusion that without them one is better off dead. The view from inside the disabled body is seldom so romantic or so extreme.

A year or so ago, I met one of my husband's colleagues, who, like me, has multiple sclerosis. Complaining of the fatigue that is perhaps the peskiest symptom of this disease, he said he was so exhausted at the end of a teaching day that he fell into bed as soon as he got home and didn't drag himself out again until the next morning.

"Why don't you get a wheelchair, Jay," I asked, "so you'd have some energy left for important things?" Like your wife and children, I thought, who must be reaping small joy from your prone and suffering form.

"You'll see me dead first," he replied. I was startled and a little amused. This man had just looked straight at me and said, in so many words, that I'd be better off dead than tooling around campus in my little black power chair. Some days I might well agree with him, but this didn't happen to be one of them. I felt a frisson of fear for him.

"You sound awfully depressed," I said. "Have you tried any medication?"

"I can handle my life without relying on pills." This stiff-upper-lipness, characteristic of but hardly exclusive to men who have invested heavily in manly attitudes and activities, ill befits either cripples or depressives. Jay always prized himself as an athlete, George has told me. Now, instead of forging a new identity to replace the one "spoiled" by MS (to use Erving Goffman's term), Jay seems intent on quitting the game altogether.

"Maybe so," I reply, "but without antidepressants I wouldn't be alive today." This statement always sounds overblown to me, but it happens to be true. Because I am a clinical depressive with suicidal tendencies, I tried to kill myself more than once, but not in the eighteen years since I began to take mood-elevating drugs. These, despite the hopeful phraseology, don't make me high. Indeed, I can't tell that I'm taking them at all. More dangerously, I can't tell that I'm not taking them. George can pick up the earliest signals—a flattened tone, an indirect gaze—but these are so subtle, and I've grown so accomplished at masking them, that those who know me less well would likely have no chance to intervene.

For this reason, I have come to think of taking antidepressants not as a failure to handle my life but as a means of taking responsibility for it and for the well-being of those, like George, who sometimes seem to value it more dearly than I do. I have never made peace with the fact that I once came perilously close to killing myself when my children were more than old enough to pick up the unspoken message that their mother was willing to die and leave them. If I require pills to keep me from sinking into the kind of pathological self-absorption that act reflects, hand me the bottle.

But can I be trusted with the bottle? It contains the same antidepressant that nearly killed me once, and, although it has proved remarkably efficacious when taken at appropriate dosages, it isn't foolproof. More important, should I be trusted with it? If not, whose task is it to see that I take my medication as prescribed and don't squirrel it away "just in case"? Are my guardians at fault if I elude their vigilance and kill myself despite it? What should they do if I tell them my life has become unbearable, because of MS or some other physical deterioration, and I would like their assistance in ending it? Are they guilty of cruelty if they deny me surcease? Of complicity if they uncap the bottle my hands are too weak to grasp, shake out the pills, pour me a glass of water, hold it to my lips? Should they be punished? How, and by whom?

The very asking of these questions might be deemed heretical in some quarters, among them the Catholic Church, whose faith I embraced more than twenty years ago. For centuries self-murderers have been denied burial in consecrated ground and consigned (though surely not by God) to eternal damnation. My qualms about suicide don't spring from fear for my immortal soul, however, since I am one of those commonly sneered at as cafeteria Catholics. In view of the outrages committed in God's name throughout church history (burning women as witches, leading little children to certain death, condemning Jews as Christ killers, whipping oneself bloody) and of the glories of art, architecture, music, and literature produced in God's praise, I think one ought to pick and choose among the church's doctrines with considerable care. I make no apology, then, for believing that God expects us, as what the theologian Matthew Fox calls God's cocreators, to sort through moral issues one by one, teasing out their full consequences and implications rather than following, like docile children, a set of rules, obedience to which may sometimes, but not invariably, result in right action. As attested by incidents like the shootings of doctors who perform abortions, adherence to a moral absolute can lead just as easily to atrocity.

We would all like our moral lives to be far simpler than they are. This desire, like so many others, is a holdover from our earliest days, when we relied on parents to reward us consistently for good behavior and chastise us for bad. The infant in us, though overlaid by later developmental stages, remains alive and squalling in our deepest recesses, impulsive, easily startled, uncertain how to behave in unfamiliar circumstances, frantic for structure in a world wholly beyond our control. Small wonder that we create God in the image of the large and mysterious beings whose dictates calm our chaos. But unless we are cognitively damaged, we grow beyond this state. Indeed, many of us loom large and mysterious in the psychic lives of new beings, whom we give what direction we can, until they, too, achieve adulthood. We are none of us helped in this process by worshiping an Almighty Father who so regiments our spiritual lives that we can fly on automatic pilot straight through them to salvation.

I cannot say absolutely, then, that suicide is either right or wrong but only, "It depends." Like other major choices, it is difficult; and, since human nature at an inchoate level shies away from ambiguity, we endeavor to reduce such dilemmas to a simpler, more definite structure. To this end, we become legalistic, placing our trust in an external Word instead of our own powers of discernment. Recent controversies over whether to pass laws permitting physician-assisted suicide clearly illustrate this urge to specify publicly a single clear-cut rule that will relieve us of the anguish of thinking through, and then bearing full responsibility for, decisions about life's most fundamental issues (death too is a life issue).

I'm not recommending that we abolish or flout laws. I'm awfully glad, for instance, that we've all (well, almost all) agreed to stop our vehicles at red lights rather than weigh the merits and consequences of our actions at every intersection. I object only when I perceive the law proliferating in areas that belong properly in the moral domain, thereby constricting and occasionally perverting our capacity for justice. The Jesus of the Gospels illustrates the transition I have in mind from Mosaic law to individual conscience—recapitulated in the psychic dimension of each of us—in the narrative of the woman caught in adultery. "In the law Moses commanded us to stone such," the scribes and the Pharisees say to him, challenging him to say otherwise. Without disputation, Jesus replies, "Let the one among you who is without sin be the first to throw a stone at her" (John 8.7). At issue is not the adultery itself, against which he cautions in several other Gospel passages, but the locus of responsibility. When the law enforcers have to scrutinize their own souls, they slink away. Jesus neither condemns the woman nor condones her deed. Instead, he places the power of right action squarely with the wrongdoer: "Go, and do not sin again." Does she comply? Who knows. But in his parting injunction, Jesus has conferred on her (a woman, no less!) moral adulthood, the capacity to choose, in future, to refrain from iniquity.

Is suicide—one's own or aid in another's—similarly sinful? After all, the Mosaic code forbids killing as plainly as it forbids adultery. But is all bringing to death killing? Apparently not, since many people, among them the most fervent Christians, decry abortion as the killing of unborn children yet hail execution as justice. Since both measures are lawful, obviously legality cannot determine their propriety. Once again, every deed must be scrutinized in its own context. In some instances, killing might constitute an act of mercy, even of love.

Many seem to think that assisted suicide is a recent development, but of course it has occurred throughout human history, and doubtless prehistory as well. What's novel about it, as about so many personal matters, is its emergence into the public sphere. In a society where the dimensions and distinguishing characteristics of the president's penis can be speculated on not merely in the boudoir or at intimate dinner parties, where gossip has always abounded, but by self-appointed or self-serving pundits in the national media, so that the complexion of all the press has turned a sickly yellow, no issue is presumed to be handled more appropriately in private. As my writing demonstrates, I don't oppose public discussion of all kinds of subjects if clearer understanding promotes the general welfare. But public decision making is quite different from discussion. If at some point I choose to end my life, I want to do so in consultation with my family, my doctors, and my spiritual advisers, but I want lawyers and newsmongers kept strictly outside the loop.

The possibility of choosing to end my life implies the equal and opposite possibility of choosing not to, and I am exquisitely aware that there are those who find the positive side of that choice puzzling at the least, downright improper at the most. As a person with a disability, I am assumed by many to lead a life without worth, and plenty would be glad to help me end my misery. Medical personnel, trained to heal bodily ills, are especially apt to view people like me, who have chronic, often incurable conditions, as hopeless. Some neurologists, for instance, refuse to take patients with MS or voice their distaste for such patients, as though the neurological syndrome were equivalent to the person. People with disabilities report being required to sign do-not-resuscitate forms in order to receive treatment in hospital.

Since many of us can't hold jobs and those who can are too rarely offered them, in a culture that commonly confounds social value with economic productivity our lives are often considered worthless. More chillingly, they are characterized as drains on resources, both public and private, that could better be spent on projects more deserving than the upkeep of our wretched bodies. One of Jack Kevorkian's clients, I've heard, was told repeatedly by her husband that she was a vampire sucking his blood. In most cases, such verbal assault would be deemed a type of domestic abuse. In hers, it led to justification for her suicide.

Dr. Kevorkian's name comes up in my deliberations because his actions have rendered rational discourse about assisted suicide all but impossible. To begin with, he is a pathologist by training and inclination, a man who appears to have been fascinated from an early age by death. Though without credentials in psychotherapy, pastoral care, or even medicine (having lost his license years ago), he claims to counsel those who put themselves into his hands. The longest he has known one of these is a couple of months; in one case, he provided his service in less than twenty-four hours. He does not consult physicians, counselors, or spiritual advisers, on behalf of either his clients or himself. His messianic zeal for his self-appointed task (and perhaps for the attendant publicity) has earned him the moniker Dr. Death. (See *Suicide Machine*.)

Of the hundred people he has helped die by various means, most have been women, many with multiple sclerosis. Hardly surprising, then, that I find his work particularly alarming. Even more unsettling, some people had no clear diagnosis at all. In his determination, however, the quality of these sufferers' lives became nil and he was merely terminating their misery. That their misery might have been terminated by other means—mood-elevating drugs and painkillers, financial aid, adequate assistance with personal care, meaningful day-to-day activities, a supportive community, even in some cases a pet—isn't likely to occur to a pathologist, who prefers his bodies dead. Indeed, some of Kevorkian's remarks reveal a sense of himself as a social hygienist, purging humanity of waste matter.

A great many people with disabilities like their lives a lot. I happen to be one of them. We tend to repudiate the medical model of disability, which views us as sick and in need of a cure, and the mechanical model, in which we are broken and require repair. We see disability rather as a social construction, in which the assumptions and insensitivities of the majority assign limits, not merely differences, to bodies and minds that work in deviant ways. Some would go so far as to say that society at large is responsible for dis-abling us, that with plenty of ramps, braille, interpreters, and other modifications, we would live just as easily in the world as anyone else.

In my experience, a certain amount of suffering attends disability regardless of how well it is accommodated. I have an infant grandson, for instance, and I long to the point of pain to scoop him up, cuddle him, rock him, play patty-cake and peekaboo, trot him on my knee to Boston, to Lynn, just as my Granna did with me. No anodyne can ease my grief that my arms and legs have grown too weak for romping, though I did take some comfort the other day in spooning half a jar of strained carrots into him without dyeing both of us entirely orange. Some of my limitations stem from nothing except my MS, and I must come to terms with them or . . . die.

Perhaps because I have embraced a faith with crucifixion at its heart, I do not consider suffering an aberration or an outrage to be eliminated at any cost, even the cost of my life. It strikes me as an element intrinsic to the human condition. I don't like it. I'm not asked to like it. I must simply endure in order to learn from it. Those who leap forward to offer me aid in ending it, though they may do so out of the greatest compassion, seek to deny me the fullness of experience I believe I am meant to have.

I'm not a masochist. I do not wish to end my days in teeth-gnashing excruciation. I have no reason to expect to do so, however. Because of my intimate association with cancer patients, many of whom I have helped escort through their dying, I know that with responsible pain management and responsive companionship, we tend to leave life with rather more dignity than we entered it. Part of the public hue and cry over assisted suicide springs from sheer ignorance about death, resulting in such terror that we seek to bring it on prematurely and under our own control so as not to risk either pain or helplessness. Because we ship the dying off to "health-care facilities" instead of keeping them among us, most of us never learn to view death as one of life's major events, to be planned for and seen through with a different spirit but no less care than a wedding, a birth. We need to spend time with the dying in order to gain the wisdom to go through the same process ourselves— as every one of us will do—with grace.

To comfort the dying is one of the seven corporal works of mercy, but no particular manner of death is specified or excluded. Those who are ready and determined to die on their own terms, then, should have their will. "Take her home," the psychiatrist told George after my last suicide attempt. "I think she'll be all right. But if she wants to kill herself, she will no matter what. They always do." We don't need to legalize assisted suicide. We need simply to acknowledge it as a choice that depends on moral conviction, discuss it openly and with the gravity it deserves, trust people—patients and doctors alike—to make decisions appropriate to their circumstances without public interference, leave them to carry these out in peace, bless those who choose to die in order to escape suffering, bless equally those who choose to live even if they suffer, let no one ever live or die without our consolation.

Rehabilitating Representation

SHARON L. SNYDER

Infinities of Forms: Disability Figures in Artistic Traditions

This essay traces varied operations of disability in literary and artistic traditions.[1] My aim is to identify the contours of an intertextual conversation across generations where significations of disability alter key directions in figurative possibilities. In doing so, I offer brief analyses of factors in the representation of disabled people in Western canons as well as chart some important examples of artists whose disability perspectives influence their imaginative output.

First, let's take up the question, What has happened to the interpretation of disability in art created by those who lived their lives as artists and as disabled people? Frequently, corporeal otherness is viewed as an impediment to art. As a result, disabled artists have been often (mis)understood as succeeding despite rather than as a result of disability experiences. Think of the lingering consumption of the poet John Keats, who had his companion assist him down four flights of stairs to draw material for his poetry. Or remember the multiple disabilities of Frida Kahlo, whose sketches and paintings transform her bodily wounds and disorders into a haunting tapestry of personal introspection (fig. 1). In scholarship, celebrity and influence have often eclipsed the lived corporealities that inform artistic production, and they never eclipsed them more than in artwork and writing by people with disabilities.[2]

Yet disability experiences do influence the nature of artistic achievement and figurative expression across traditions. A prime example is the American author Henry James, who indicated that his commitment to

Figure 1

Frida Kahlo. *Tree of Hope, Stand Fast*. Oil on masonite,
1946. Private collection

literary work could be traced to disabling back problems that kept him
sidelined from the physical life of boys. Beyond the confusing biographical versions of James's personal disablement lies the fame of his
father's wooden leg and the many, typically pathologizing, biographical
and historical studies that view James's work (and that of his brother
William) as a matter of compensation for his father's amputation.[3] In
critical studies, a disability source will often anchor explanations for
artistic origins even as it will seem to explain away other motives.

In *The Sun Also Rises* (fig. 2) Ernest Hemingway reflects on the disability issues that permeate James's creative life by having disabled veteran
Jake Barnes discuss them. Jake's companion Bill Gorton introduces the
topic on the morning of their first fly-fishing venture:

Figure 2

Book jacket for the first-edition printing of Ernest Hemingway's *The Sun Also Rises* (1926). Courtesy of Charles Scribner's and Sons

"You are an expatriate, see? You hang around cafes."

"It sounds like a swell life," I said. "When do I work?"

"You don't work. One group claims women support you. Another group claims you're impotent."

"No," I said. "I just had an accident."

"Never mention that," Bill said. "That's the sort of thing that can't be spoken of. That's what you ought to work up into a mystery. Like Henry's bicycle."

He had been going splendidly, but he stopped. I was afraid he thought he had hurt me with that crack about being impotent. I wanted to start him again.

"It wasn't a bicycle," I said. "He was riding horseback."

"I heard it was a tricycle."   (115)

Jake rejects Bill's suggestion that he work up his disability into an opportune mystery in order to represent his altered body. While Bill would reference James's accident as a humorous example of literary myth-making, Jake soberly contemplates wounds as a constitutive feature of postwar identity. Hemingway makes these facts of a literary predecessor's disability status most important to Jake, who insists on physically different bodies as a social reality, not as an opportunity for metaphor.

At the heart of Jake's self-definition reside issues crucial to the lives of many disabled people: work and identity, erased sexuality, enforced silence, social impropriety, misunderstanding by one's friends, contrived mystery, mundane impairment, and the biological basis of cultural seg- regation. How ironic to critique the penchant for making disability little more than a shadowy rumor that enhances personal celebrity—partic- ularly in a work that admiringly promotes the physical agility of bull- fighters. What might it mean to point out that Hemingway's character's contemplations of impaired bodies stem from Hemingway's own life- long struggles with inherited depression and a shrapnel wound received during his stint as an ambulance driver in World War I? How might the story predict his inability to accept his physical debility following two plane crashes in the 1950s?[4] How does this parallel of a maimed biology between Jake and the author serve as a challenge to criticism's insis- tence on the robust masculine mystique of the Hemingway hero? From just such questions can one begin to comprehend disability as integral to critical insights—and as more than another metaphor for cultural col- lapse in modernism.

As the work of disability studies in the humanities intensifies, this elucidation of disability's many artistic incarnations provides us with ev- idence of disability as yielding significant social perspectives. For in- stance, one can find Lord Byron's recasting of Shakespeare's villainous hunchback Richard III in his own Faustian drama *The Deformed Trans- formed.*[5] Byron claimed that the source of his dramatic effort stemmed from an incident in his childhood when his mother called him a "lame brat" in a moment of rage. According to the dramatist, the outburst plunged him into a self-conscious worry over the visibility of his "def- ormity" (*Poetry* 477; fig. 3). The plot of *Deformed* centers on the yearnings of a disabled lead named Arnold, who believes his humped back de- prives him of love from family and women alike. While Arnold con- templates thoughts of suicide as a means to alleviate his social predicament, a Stranger materializes and offers to take his soul in ex- change for the apparently ideal body of Achilles. After Arnold takes on the form of Achilles (oblivious to the hero's vulnerable heel) and the Stranger perversely dons Arnold's discarded disabled form, Arnold finds that his beloved, Olimpia, spurns his new physique for the misshapen one acquired by the Stranger. Such an outcome underscores Byron's in- terest in distancing disability from its limited associations with failure and rejection.[6]

Resignifying strategies in *The Deformed Transformed* bear a family re- semblance not only to Shakespeare's "humpback'd king"—with the provocative possibility that *Richard III* may have been penned by the

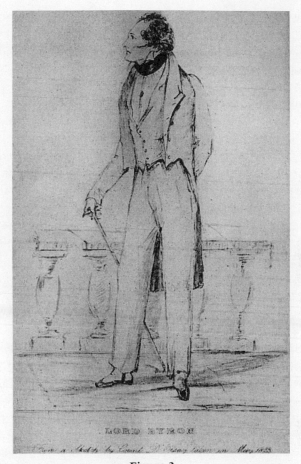

Figure 3

Sketch of Lord Byron by Count d'Orsay (1823). Victoria and Albert Museum, London

lame earl of Oxford—but also to some of the ironic signifying strategies of the Enlightenment poet Alexander Pope, who endured numerous insults slung at him by his literary rivals. The Pope biographer Maynard Mack excerpts songs and a fifteen-page insult entitled *A True Character of Mr. Pope* that was read in coffeehouses: "Tis the mark of God and Nature upon him, to give us warning that we should hold no Society with him, as a Creature not of our Original, not of our Species" (300). Pope scholarship from the Victorian era shows a similar squeamishness about disability insults. A scholar typically comments, after citing disability metaphors of Pope by Lady Mary Worley Montagu, "the remainder of the passage is too coarse to quote" (Pope 263n). The importance of Pope's life as a disabled person, and his crafting of a poetical verse that sought aesthetic symmetry in the strictures of fixed forms and rhyming heroic couplets, revises critical understanding of the relation between Pope's physical life and poetic form. The Enlightenment's most celebrated poet viewed poetry as an escape from "this long disease my life," but he also used verse to rebuff stigmatizing beliefs ("Epistle to Dr. Arbuthnot" [line 132]).

To fully interpret Pope's influential life and poetical canon we need to conceive of disability, like other social rubrics of devaluation imposed from the outside, as a source of stigma that can be navigated from the inside as a mode of social redress.[7] Disability experiences led both Byron and Pope to literary achievement, not as mere compensation for physical differences but as a necessary resignification of their bodies in the social register of art. The critical contexts of disability studies revise scholarship that disputes an author's biographical disability as a slander, as with Byron, or psychologizes an author's disability as transparent motive, as with Pope. (An example of transparent motive can be found in Mack: "[Pope] longs desperately—as he did in all his relationships with women, and as we know today that cripples and other afflicted persons regularly do—to know the degree and nature of his acceptance" [306].)

As a counter to historical oblivion to disability identities, we find writers who openly seek out the exemplary work of disability thought and concerns in other writers. Disability quests for predecessors have been recognized and understood before; likewise, scholars with disability identifications have explained the necessity of assessing, for an aesthetic or cultural purpose, the implications of disability as critical insight. Literary studies such as Eleanor Gertrude Brown's *Milton's Blindness* (1934), reissued in 1968 as a landmark in Milton studies, grounds readings of John Milton's poetry in developed interpretations drawn from her experiences as a blind woman. With a fully essentialist claim for her methodology, Brown examines how Milton's declining vision provided an analytic dimension to his poetics that had gone unarticulated by sighted critics. Seizing on Milton's adoption and rewriting of figures for blindness such as the biblical Samson, Brown outlines her critical methodology: "To the interpretation of Milton's life and writing after the loss of sight, I add my knowledge of blindness. And on account of this bond of union, I bring to the task an interest such as Milton must have given to the writing of *Samson Agonistes. Thus by similarity of experience alone, I am rendered a more able critic*" (i; emphasis added). With a mocking inversion of sighted rhetoric, Brown applies an early example of a disability studies paradigm to the criticism of Milton's verse as she acclaims Milton for his disability poesis in representing Samson.

One of her contentions is that Milton, like the later Pope, immerses himself in a writing life as a viable response to detractors' claims that his blindness was a sign of divine disfavor. In addition to her readings of Milton's disability metaphorics, including a critical history of sonnet 19 on his blindness, Brown probes the blind claims that emerge in the final line "They also serve who only stand and wait." She offers disability contexts for Milton's poetry by arguing that the poet drew on citations of monstrosity from a classical canon in order to resignify his body's depreciated value in seventeenth-century literary circles. Such an approach lends dimension and accuracy to the life and work of one of Britain's great poets. Milton masterfully grapples with literary traditions in order to refigure the many lethal metaphysical meanings ascribed to figures of disability.

In literary history a search for precedents and predecessors often crosses cultures and borders to take the form of an international comparative effort. Disability-identified writers from one culture will look to the work of artists from other cultures for creative incentive and disability insights. The Japanese writer Kenzaburo Oe, whose public role and writings issue from his vantage as the father of a cognitively disabled son, reclaims the work of Flannery O'Connor, an author who wrote eloquently out of her experience of lupus (fig. 4). Readings of O'Connor's posthumously published letters enable Oe to argue that the basis of her originality sprang from her narrative navigation of her disabling condition: "I am sure it [disability] results in the same accumulated practice that comes into play when the obstacles encountered by all those who labor in the fields of art are somehow—by trial and error—cleared to reveal a landscape no one has seen before" (57). Oe's interpretation of O'Connor through a lens of disability results in his analysis of her fiction for an originality that issues from her articulation of suffering as a social, meaning-laden predicament.

Oe's cross-cultural championing of O'Connor's deliberately misshapen characters bears witness to a writer who would see disability as part and parcel of an absurdly designed universe—rather than as biological deviance. Suffering, according to O'Connor, brought a nobility to life that should not be too easily depreciated. As the hardened character of the Misfit in "A Good Man Is Hard to Find" argues, "Jesus thrown

Figure 4

Flannery O'Connor feeding peacocks. Courtesy of Joe Mc-
Tyre / *Atlanta Journal-Constitution*, 1962

everything off balance [. . .] because he was the only one that ever
raised the dead" (2157). For O'Connor, the promise of Christian resurrection, with suffering alleviated by a utopian afterlife, makes earth-
bound existence dangerously disposable. In her era, the eugenics
rhetoric of expendability had resulted in the sterilization of those labeled
unfit in the United States and the mass murder of "defectives" under the
Third Reich.[8] Oe's interpretive frame for O'Connor demonstrates that
if one is cut off or isolated from a community of like-minded and like-
stigmatized people, literary archives can operate as an imaginative
refuge for alternative discourses of physical and cognitive differences.

Disability reading and viewing audiences remember works that es-
pouse an open cure-or-kill mind-set in order to comprehend disability's

absence or unspeakability. (For an analysis of the cultural logic of eugenics that underpins a narrative imperative to cure or kill disabled figures, see Finger, "Helen"; Longmore; Pernick; Mitchell and Snyder,
Narrative Prosthesis [ch. 6].) Cure-or-kill story endings frequently connect to logics of eugenics where disabled people represent a soon-to-be
eradicated group whose promised erasure will better society. A pointed
example of this mind-set can be found in the explanatory reassurance
tacked onto Tod Browning's *Freaks* (1932) (fig. 5). In an effort to remar-
ket Browning's film to 1930s audiences that had rejected its freak-
culture vantage on the nondisabled, the film begins with a lengthy
scrolled message: "Never again will such a story be filmed, as modern
science and teratology are rapidly eliminating such blunders of nature
from the world." Historical violence shows up most clearly in United
States legal texts, eugenics-era legislative argument, confinement dicta,
forced-labor asylums, disabled forced-labor industries, and medical textbook exhibits. Eugenics-era ordinances include "unsightly" laws such
as that reconfirmed by the city of Chicago in 1911: "Any person who is

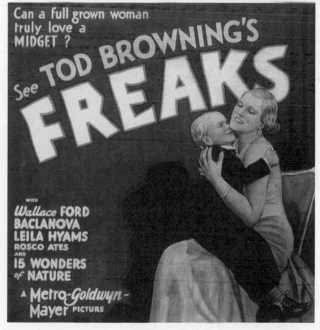

Figure 5

Promotional poster for Tod Browning's film *Freaks* (1932).
Courtesy of MGM Studios

diseased, maimed, mutilated or deformed in any way so as to be an unsightly or disgusting object is hereby prohibited from exposing himself
to public view."[9] Disability histories can be located in the texts that seem
to demand eradication through the promise of restorative cures or banishment from public arenas.

Disability figures are also concealed as spectral presences in the attic,
such as the burdensome madwoman Bertha Mason in Charlotte
Brontë's *Jane Eyre;* or enclosed in sickrooms and charity wards, as in the
work of the Victorian writers Harriet Martineau and Charles Dickens.
Literary works such as Sarah Scott's *Millennium Hall* and George Giss-
ing's *Odd Women* establish a continuum between disability and femininity so that forms of self-evident biological differences contest rigid
patriarchal norms.[10] Disabled people emerge as spectacles in popular
and high-art dramas; for example, myriad short-statured people perform in works that perpetuate comic traditions in miniatures as cute or
perverse (like *The Wizard of Oz,* Werner Herzog's *Even Dwarves Started
Small,* Federico Fellini's *Satyricon,* Ingmar Bergman's *The Silence,* Salman
Rushdie's *Shame,* and John Irving's *Son of the Circus*). Disabled people
serve as the recipients of poetic gifts, such as the boy to whom Robert
Browning dedicates his "Pied Piper of Hamelin," as well as the rebuked
"crippled" character in the poem who ironically regrets his inability to
keep pace with the forever lost children of Hamelin (fig. 6).

Western painting traditions often depict cripples being healed by
Christ and the saints. In fact, these repeated depictions of miraculous

Figure 6

From Robert Browning's *The Pied Piper*. Illustrated by Kate Greenaway. London:
Warne, 1888. 44. Courtesy of Indiana University Libraries

healings serve to solidify the authority of Christ's claims to his status as a prophet. One could speculate that the primary shift in emphasis from the Old to the New Testament circulates around the treatment of disability figures. Whereas Leviticus devotes most of its narrative to the designation of an array of bodily blemishes that bar one from participation in temple rituals, the Gospels document numerous episodes of "cripples" returned to the temple after their infirmities are cured. Yet ironically both testaments promote a form of erasure: the old banishes cripples from religious visibility through segregation, while the new manages to erase disability through the promise of a miraculous cure (fig. 7). In either case,

Figure 7

Masaccio. *Saint Peter Healing a Cripple with His Shadow.* Fresco, 1426-27. Cappella Brancacci, Santa Maria del Carmine, Florence. Alinari / Art Resource, NY

Figure 8

Raphael (with Giulio Romano and Giovan Francesco Penni). *The Fire of Borgo*. Fresco, 1514-17. Vatican Museum, Rome. Alinari / Art Resource, NY

any risk of a sustained intimacy with disabled people is alleviated by their effective ouster from public view. Commerce with cripples may prove so distasteful that scenes featuring a healing touch can include episodes such as that of Saint Peter healing the halt and lame with nothing more corporeal than his passing shadow.

In an opposing vein, Raphael's acclaimed painting *The Fire of Borgo* reminds us of Vergil's story about the founder of Rome who refuses to leave his blind and lame father, Anchises, behind in Troy (*Aen.* 2.857–984; figs. 8 and 9). In the foreground, Aeneas gazes downward, concentrating on his task, his father's limp body draped over his back. Disability here provides the celebrated effort of the more able son, but it also designates that which is most worthy of salvation, because the father could easily have been left behind in the violent razing of the city. Anchises's legacy could have been sacrificed in the press to flee and begin again in the midst of a youthful ahistoricism, but Raphael highlights the fact that Rome begins with a devotion to infirmity as value rather than with its exorcism.

Figure 9

Detail of Aeneas carrying his father, Anchises. From
Raphael's *The Fire of Borgo*. Alinari / Art Resource, NY

Disability perspectives emerge through the review of centuries of
formal appraisal concerning works such as Raphael's last masterpiece,
The Transfiguration (fig. 10). Critics have commented on the balanced
mirroring of the painting's two spheres, on the painter's perfecting of
the classical ideal, on the blinding of the onlookers who witness Jesus's
resurrection, on the allegorical rendering of human doubt and loss of
faith, et cetera. Nearly every aspect of the painting has been interpreted
and reinterpreted, but through each generation of scholarship the
young boy's "lunatic" body (as it is commonly called) remains resistant
to a more dynamic interpretation. Still, the incurable disabled figure remains undeniable in a viewer's field of vision.

Figure 10

Raphael (completed by Giulio Romano and Giovan
Francesco Penni). *The Transfiguration*. Oil on panel, 1518-
20. Pinacoteca, Vatican. Alinari / Art Resource, NY

Whereas the myriad bodies of the painting seem to echo one another's classical definition, the boy's twisting body marks him as too in-
dividuated—a breech in the classical ideal of bodily symmetry (fig. 11).
While his outstanding features can be represented in the rigid tension of
the muscles of his legs and arms and in the "unnatural" contortion of his
body, the locus of his difference is also to be found in the fact that his out-
stretched arm (like that of the one apostle near him) and his straining
gaze effectively break the division of realms between earth and heaven.

Figure 11

Detail of the "lunatic boy." From Raphael's *The Transfigura-tion*. Alinari / Art Resource, NY

His body, not Christ's more ethereally perfected presentation, directs us away from and therefore toward the reality of human difference. In a portrait of remarkably classical bodies, the ideal threatens to be lost in its repetitious display. Without the "lunatic" body's contortions the paint-ing's aesthetic effect would be lessened or obscured in the mass produc-tion of nonblemished bodily forms. The ideal of the classical body depends on this marked contrast for its realization. The aberrant body must be conjured up if its perfected bodily antithesis is to take shape and enact transubstantiation in Christian hagiography.

The unexpected manifestation of corporeal difference anchors the otherworldly portrayal of fabulous and science fiction locations. A pointed example occurs in the figure of the "lame balloonman" in section 1 of E. E. Cummings's "Chansons Innocentes":

In Just—
spring   when the world is mud-
luscious the little
lame balloonman

whistles   far   and wee

and eddieandbill come
running from marbles and
piracies and it's
spring

when the world is puddle-wonderful

the queer
old balloonman whistles
far   and   wee
and bettyandisbel come dancing

from hop-scotch and jump-rope and

it's
spring
and

    the

        goat-footed

balloonMan   whistles
far
and
wee   (24)

While the world opens up into the "puddle-wonderful" and mud-lusciousness of a postwinter thaw, children race in undifferentiated couples while being contrasted with the singular "lame" and "goat-footed" balloon man who surreptitiously "whistles / far / and / wee." The "queer" figure threatens to destroy the idyllic revery of the scene, until the last stanza, when he is finally catapulted into the mythic figure of Pan, who presides over the seasonal transformation of the natural world. The poem has to make three separate runs at the disabled figure before his differences can be drawn up into the romance of the scene.

This momentary recalcitrance to the poet's aesthetic landscape comments on a difficulty of the imagination to transfigure disability in its fantastical project.

The poem evokes childhood, and similarly many children's stories, such as *The Marvelous Journey through the Night*, use disability to provide bold evidence of an alien, surreal geography and of the power of imagination: "When you see a pirate with a wooden leg walking across the ocean, and there's a blind man beside him, who's showing him the way—then you're in paradise" (Heine 15). These reassurances made to childhood fears, which often circulate around encounters with disabled people, appear alongside scores of Mother Goose rhymes from British folk traditions that openly mock disabled people and beggars: "As I was going to sell my eggs / I met a man with bandy legs, / Bandy legs and crooked toes; / I tripped up his heels, and he fell on his nose" (*Real Mother Goose* 109).[11] "Bandy Legs" invokes the rhetorical construct of fierce natural survival, in the playground location of "Blind Man's Bluff" and even "Three Blind Mice" as taunts, where children are represented as more honest in their mocking of "cripples" and "misfits." (Note typical playground scenes in United States public health films such as *Are You Fit to Marry?* [1927]; also, note the character Piggy in *Lord of the Flies*.) Cummings's poem traces out a process of poetical effort by transforming the interfering lame man into a goat-footed satyr myth. At the same time, the arrival at a pure fantasy is secured by an unexpected inversion of cultural values, where disability suddenly becomes a desirable and valued mode of being. Instances are the venerable insights of the power-chair driving leader of X-Men comics; the bold stump arms of the Powerpuff Girls cartoon series (who brag that their lack of fingers means they can avoid employment in the traditional feminine roles of stenographer and typist); even the compensatory powers of Norse myth leaders, including one-eyed Odin and the amputee Tyr. Ultimately, the power of many fantastic inversions may hinge on the unlikelihood that readers will find such an alternative value system in ordinary life.

Most often, the suppression of disability in salons and religious locations historically claimed for their civilizing functions provides the contrast against which fantasied inversions gain their powerful allure. Distorted sufferers abound in religious renditions of hellish landscapes and punctuate nightmarish depictions of demons dragging off the condemned (fig. 12). Many representations go for blatant equations between earthly offense and physical anomaly. In Andreas Mantegna's 1502 painting *The Triumph of Virtue*, the aesthetically appealing goddess

Figure 12

Andreas Mantegna. *The Triumph of Virtue*. 1497. Louvre, Paris. Giraudon / Art Resource, NY

directs a consortium of contorted, one-armed, lame, and racialized figures out of the garden of virtue and into the muck (fig. 13). This parallel between bodily anomalies and personal malignancy reverberates as the commonsensical antithesis to the equation in classicism, "a sound mind in a sound body." The goddess's violent expulsion of aesthetic misfits is corroborated by the visible bodily aberrancies sported by those banished to the underworld. The otherness of their figures serves as proof that the appropriate culprits have been identified and properly sentenced.

The ability of art to mobilize representations of disability in so many antithetic directions serves as a wellspring of disability studies scholarship. Do art and literature flatly participate in the ideological prescription of attitudes? Or do they offer self-reflexive commentaries on cultural beliefs about disability? These questions are difficult if not impossible to answer once and for all. Artistic and narrative discourses deploy the ambiguity of visual and print signifiers in order to manifest

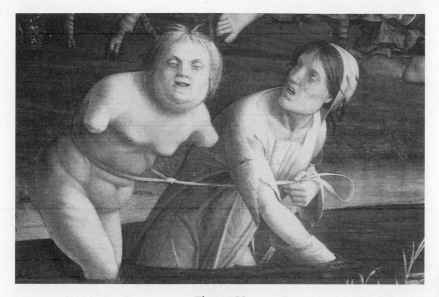

Figure 13

Detail of the vices from Mantegna's *Triumph of Virtue*. Giraudon / Art Resource, NY

(but not resolve) the unacknowledged conflicts of a period. Writers and artists give expression to that which troubles the ideals of their cultures (and themselves). As historical scapegoats, charitable objects, non-working or noncompensated classes, and deviations from perceived population averages, people with disabilities become topical objects, if not narrative agents, in every tradition.

In contrast with classicism, grotesque art may caricature depictions of disabilities and multiply anomalies until a veritable democracy of corporeal excesses seems to emerge. The celebrated eighteenth-century essayist and scholar Georg Christoph Lichtenberg analyzes this aspect of William Hogarth's engravings.[12] Lichtenberg points out that Hogarth, instead of reproducing the romance of the drawing room like the rest of his contemporaries, created social satires of rich and poor alike through his generous visualizations of their bodies. In the world of Hogarth's caricatures, no class of social elites is allowed the luxury of escape from his liberal grotesqueries. Lichtenberg's commentaries on these engravings emphasize the innovation of corporeal anomaly, and his own small stature and curved physique help explain the source for his famous disability-centered appraisal that garnered Hogarth's work trans-European acclaim in Hogarth's own time.

Another striking example of political undercurrents in the representation of disability can be found in the first English translation of the profusely illustrated 1671 edition of *A Brief Prospect of the Life of Aesop* (fig. 14). The instructive lesson that accompanies each engraving seeks to correct the presumption that a "Transcript of so Stupendous a Deformity" would be incapable of contributing to a social order.

> For [Aesop] was of a sharp Head, flat Nos'd, his Back roll'd up in a Bunch or Excrescence, his Lips tumerous and pendant, his Complexion black, from which dark Tincture he contracted his Name

Figure 14

Aesop. Frontispiece of *The Fables* (Harris). Woodcut, 1634.

(Aesopus being the same as Aethiops), Large Belly, Crooked Bow-
Legs, Thersites in Homer was but an imperfect Transcript of so Stupendous a Deformity.   (Harris i)

The racial allusion to "Aethiops" draws parallels between physical
anomalies and concepts of race in seventeenth-century Britain. This biographical commentary emphasizes the terms of disability's otherness
across a field of socially constructed differences that encompasses race,
class, nationality, gender, sexuality, and normative aging. In this popular account Aesop's storytelling wizardry, despite his physical shape, instructs readers to look beyond his figure to his accomplishments. *Brief
Prospect* works to shock readers in its provision of a visual accompani-
ment to horror-laden description; then it lays further claim of Aesop's
storytelling powers by taking us on his journey of insult and embrace at
royal courts. In a twist, the widely read Story of Sop vehemently insists
that only wrong-headed and unreasonable audience members continue
to discount Aesop for his anomalies.

In querying disability figuration, segregation, cure, celebration, no-
toriety in and erasure from textual records, further research mysteries
emerge. How does the apparent absence of so many disability histories
help us review medieval wheeled vehicles in the acclaimed Florentine
Gothic painting *The Thebaid* (c. 1410) (fig. 15)? In this detailed rendering of a fantastic monastic community where nearly every walker carries a staff, a viewer is hard pressed to separate cripples from converts.
Methods for transversing the mountainside multiply across the otherworldly painting. We can note the many ramped pathways and the absence of stairs that function as a portrait of early architectural access,
which can be discerned in ancient Greek towns ranging from Delphi to
Meteora. We can begin to think about how the implantation of stairs
comes attached with historical expectations of ambulatory norms—
decisions about who will be included and excluded from public forums.
We can even find the ramped, multiply mobilized monastic communities alluring for their alternative to the asylum shuffles and socially
enforced impoverishment of disabled populations in our current climate
of postdeinstitutionalization and nursing home confinement.

And I would suggest that these figures lead us to a key inversion of
disability studies: Rather than query, What are societies to do with disabled populations?, we ask, "How can we truly understand a culture
until we know how its disabled members see it, read it, understand it,
and critique it?"[13] Disability studies offers a platform and an interdisciplinary arena for the analysis of social meanings ascribed to variations

Figure 15
_____

The Thebaid, attributed to Paolo Ucello. Detail. Tempera on wood, c. 1420.

across bodily and cognitive forms; it also supplies a generative ground from which to question the centrality of disability to representational meaning itself.

NOTES

1. My title is drawn from Michel de Montaigne's essay "Of a Monstrous Child" ("D'un enfant monstreux"). Montaigne argues that disabilities are merely further manifestations of "the immensity of God's works composed of an infinity of forms" ("l'immensité de son ouvrage l'infinites des formes qu'il y a comprinses") (bk. 2, essay 87; fig. 16). Montaigne would counter sixteenth-century folk discourse that takes disabilities as messages from a supernatural being.
2. In *Enforcing Normalcy,* Lennard Davis emphasizes that success and celebrity often override artists' disabilities as a defining feature of their work (9).
3. For a synthesis of scholarly work on James, see Yeazell (689).
4. In her essay "Last Words," Joan Didion discusses the importance of Hemingway's depression and multiple disabilities to his conception of himself as a writer. Interestingly, Didion's insightful attention to Hemingway's physical and cognitive vulnerability might be attributed to the experiences with disability and misdiagnosis that Didion describes in "The White Album."

Figure 16

Double-bodied man. From Antoine Pare, *Monstres et prodiges*. Paris: Le Club Français du Livre, 1573. Editions Droz

5. Byron believed that *The Deformed Transformed* would prove to be his magnum opus. Yet when Shelley read an early draft and told him that he thought the work derivative of Goethe, Byron threw the entire manuscript into the fire. Despite the melodramatic gesture of disgust with Shelley's response, Byron had secretly kept another copy of the manuscript hidden. The drama was never finished, and act 3 exists only in an incomplete, albeit evocative, state. The notes and dialogue available suggest that Byron planned to end the play with the irony of the physically perfect Arnold being thrown over for the now deformed dark man.

6. Further interpretations of disability contexts for Byron's drama can be found in Mitchell and Snyder, "Re-engaging" and "Transforming."

7. See Helen Deutsch's important study of the relation of Pope's disability to his poetical method in *Resemblance and Disgrace: Alexander Pope and the Deformation of Culture*. For further research into the navigation of denigrating social definitions by disability scholars and artists, see Mitchell and Snyder, "Representation."

8. See also O'Connor's point that excessive sentiment perpetuates oblivion about genocidal practices toward handicapped children: "Sentimental attitudes toward handicapped children, which encourage the habit of hiding their pain from human eyes, are of a piece with the kind of thinking that sent smoke billowing from the chimneys of Auschwitz. I would venture to guess, in fact, that many parents of handicapped children would hesitate to dismiss this comparison as a grotesque exaggeration" (qtd. in Oe 94).

9. This ordinance was introduced to me by Vicki Ann Lewis, who included it in her play *P*H*Reaks* (see Baizley and Lewis).

10. See F. Nussbaum's discussion of Scott's novel in "Feminotopias." In the introduction to *"Defects"*: *Engendering the Modern Body,* Deutsch and Nussbaum theorize disability issues in eighteenth-century literature and culture.

11. See also other disability nursery rhymes such as "The Crooked Sixpence": "There was a crooked man, and he went a crooked mile, / He found a crooked sixpence beside a crooked stile; / He bought a crooked cat, which caught a crooked mouse, / And they all lived together in a little crooked house" (102).

12. Barbara Maria Stafford briefly assesses the relation of Lichtenberg's disabilities to his reading of Hogarth's prints: "Pluralism made Lichtenberg an astute observer of urban life. He remains the still unsurpassed interpreter of Hogarth's city satires. As a dwarfish hunchback, he resembled those 'remarkable' perambulating characters populating the *Harlot's Progress* (1732) and *Rake's Progress* (1735) and the *Marriage a la Mode* (1743–1745)" (128).

13. This wonderful paraphrase, condensed from key passages in Oe's *A Healing Family,* was fashioned by Louise DeSalvo for the University of Michigan Press book series Corporealities: Discourses of Disability.

HELEN DEUTSCH

Exemplary Aberration: Samuel Johnson and the English Canon

Viewed in itself [. . .] a disabled body seems somehow *too much* a body, *too real*, too corporeal: it is a body that, so to speak, stands in its own way. From another angle [. . .] a disabled body appears to lack something essential, something that would make it identifiable and something to identify with; it seems *too little* a body: a body that is deficiently itself, not quite a body in the full sense of the word, *not real enough*.

—James I. Porter

Disability Studies and the Limits of the Individual

James I. Porter pinpoints the dilemma facing the scholar of disability as one of the limits of perception, of identification with the corporeal itself: the disabled body in its physical excess "stands in its own way," blocking the transparency necessary to render it a medium in which viewers can recognize themselves. From another angle, as the critic shifts his gaze, such a body is not excessive, not *"too real"* but rather lacking "something that would make it identifiable and something to identify with": it is *"not real enough"* (xiii). At once too much itself and not enough to be a self, disability in Porter's passage is articulated as a paradox that delimits the intelligibility of individuality. How different is it possible for a body to be before its difference becomes unrecognizable? At what point—a point that varies over time—does corporeal particularity erase or obscure the marks that render bodies legible, "real" objects of communal identification and sympathy?

What forms of embodiment at given historical moments, in other words, set the limits for the definition of the individual case—and by *case* I refer to both body and example—itself? How might a disabled body both negate and exemplify individuality? This paradox can be conceived as a problem of style, since style, both in its literary and corporeal manifestations, functions both as a mode of individual self-creation and as a cultural inheritance that delimits individuality.[1] I focus here on a case that challenges the legibility and exemplarity of corporeal difference in Britain at the end of the eighteenth century, that of the professional author, in particular the man termed by his contemporaries both "Great Cham" (i.e., Tartar monarch [Boswell, *Life* 1: 348–49]) and "Caliban" (Boswell, *Life* 2: 129) of letters, Samuel Johnson.

What becomes possible when we think of disability not only as lack, not only as stigma, but also as excess, as a form of idealization? What facets of bodily difference emerge when we focus on the early modern construction of some sorts of disability as forms of genius? A number of scholars have described the eighteenth century as a transitional moment in the history of representations of disability, a period suspended between religious wonder at monstrous forms and unawed scientific classification of natural difference (surveyed at length in Deutsch and Nussbaum).[2] The very corporeality of the disabled body in the eighteenth century, redefining the limits of the natural, "impinged on present reality" (Curran and Graille 7).

If a newly naturalized disability caused the eighteenth century to doubt its own eyes, it also challenged the accepted hierarchy and presumed mutual resemblance of mind and body, unmooring fixed conceptions of agency and intention. Suspended between two narrative constructions of the disabled individual, eighteenth-century paradigms of disability existed in formative relation to the concept of individuality. The earlier paradigm viewed disability as a largely visual sign of deserved divine punishment for moral failings, while the modern paradigm conceived of disability as ineffable identity in the familiar narrative terms we now recognize: a vehicle to a proof of inner worth, an obstacle to be heroically conquered by a randomly afflicted individual (Davis, "Dr. Johnson"). The eighteenth century, then, was torn in its representations of disability between two ideas of agency—one divine and insurmountable, one human and exceptional. In one model the body is a sign for God to write on, in the other the body is rendered significant by individual attempts to overcome it. Contemporary responses to Johnson's multiple disabilities, in particular to his ambiguously motivated movements, mutterings, and rituals, which contemporaries dubbed "convulsive starts and odd gesticulations" (Boswell, *Life* 1: 95), provide a perfect example of this indeterminacy of agency that rendered Johnson at once a representative and monstrous figure in his time.

"I have seen no more evident monstrosity and miracle in the world than myself. We become habituated to anything strange by use and time; but the more I frequent myself and know myself, the more my deformity astonishes me, and the less I understand myself" (Montaigne 787). The greatest monster, Michel de Montaigne thus observes in his essay "Of Cripples," is not the other's physical difference but rather the inner difference of one's own individuality. My research considers the history of the authorial body in eighteenth-century Britain, beginning with the visible deformity of Alexander Pope's curved spine (*Resemblance*) and closing with the indecipherable inwardness figured by Samuel Johnson's unruly body, a history that constitutes a chapter in the eighteenth century's reconception of bodily particularity in relation to new forms of social distinction.[3] The figure of the professional author, often a self-made man (or, the subject of another essay, a self-made woman), threatened preexistent social differences in a burgeoning capitalist society with the spectacle of corporeal uniqueness threatening to unseat a distinctive mind.[4]

Deidre Lynch has portrayed the history of the concept of character in the eighteenth century as a lengthy battle with bodily particularity. The first part of the century, she argues, delineated a socially and corporeally legible code of character based on the fixed impressions of print culture, a code that veered toward deformity as it approached individuality. That "insensible more or less" that rendered a character a caricature thus became the subject of heated debate (23–79). As eighteenth-century thinkers contemplated and resisted the idea of character as bodily peculiarity, they vacillated between two senses of *nondescript:* that of the indistinguishable gentleman-observer whose business, on the grand tour and in the novels of midcentury, was to view and appropriate the characters of others (80–119) and that of "real characters" in the colloquial sense, people so unusual, so odd, that they beggared description (77–78).

Character, for eighteenth-century public men, thus came to entail a rejection of individual bodily display for the uniform of indistinguishability, a uniform that lent itself to interiority, to the possibilities of individual depth and to the viewer's identification.[5] By the end of the eighteenth century, character's mark had become its opposite: visible bodily excess was replaced by the invisible sign of true character, of the discerning and indiscernible individual, who needs careful reading, who can read properly, and whose exterior is unremarkable, a "body of blank surfaces" (Lynch 161). In his spectacular physical singularity, and in what some contemporaries considered the monstrous embodiment of his literary style, Johnson from this perspective seems an uncanny figure who haunted contemporary ideas of selfhood with the image of past models of monstrosity and identity, at once signifying and occluding individuality and agency.

The singularity of the man of letters at the end of the eighteenth century became both a cultural metonymy—and a cultural other—for a new form of individuality. This idea of the author draws on a long tradition of corporeal representation that reads disability as the result of great mental agency sometimes overcoming and sometimes overcome by the body's force. Disability has in fact distinguished the English literary canon—itself a product of the eighteenth century—as a catalog of authorial monsters and paradoxically representative oddities. (One of Johnson's many sobriquets was "Oddity" [Boswell, *Life* 3: 209].) By the late eighteenth century, the exceptional man of feeling and letters had rewritten the standard equation of sound mind in sound body along the new diseased lines of the culture of sensibility.[6] This pathologization of genius endures in a twentieth-century medical literature that puzzles over the remains of authorial corpses and asks the question that the neurologist (neurology being the scientific heir to sensibility) and Johnsonian Russell Brain put succinctly, "since the genius is by definition abnormal, and is so by virtue of an abnormal nervous system, what is the relationship between the nervous abnormality we call genius and those more familiar abnormalities we call disease" (10).

At once monument and monster, printed voice of unmistakably fixed distinction and aberrant spectacle in seemingly constant motion, Johnson enacted the mind-body problem of his time in ongoing performance. The contemporary William Cadogan's marginalia to his copy of Boswell's *Life of Johnson* are typical in his contempt for the man Cadogan sarcastically considered "a very amiable Monster & as rational as his Cat or Dog." Equally typical is Cadogan's conflation of Johnson's embodied bestiality with his literary style: "His Brutality and thy Folly, Bozzy, were ever, I believe, very prominent and *con*spicuous &·his Style ie. the construction and form of his sentences was easy and *per*spicuous—they were without difficulty analyzed, but without his Dictionary not to be understood" (Payne 12). The satirist Cuthbert Shaw described the face of a monster-breeding Johnson that frightened the Muses though "stamp'd" with "rigid morals" (16), and Soame Jenyns echoed this moral doubleness with his epitaph of Johnson: "A scholar and a Christian—yet a brute" (qtd. in Kelley and Brack 10). Called "bear" (Boswell, *Life* 2: 269, 5: 384 and 575), "great unlick'd Cub" (A. Campbell xxxix), "savage" (Richard Cumberland, qtd. in Page 61), an effeminate Polyphemus (Hawkins 147), "madman" (Ozias Humphrey, qtd. in Page 30); branded "Irish chairman, London porter, or one of Swift's Brobdingnaggians" (William Temple, qtd. in Page 23); mistaken for an inspired idiot (Boswell, *Life* 1: 146–47), a robber (Northcote 73); possessed of a body considered at once super- and subhuman, of "*heroic* stature" though "slovenly put together" (William Cook, qtd. in Brack and Kelley 125; Ingrams 47, 68); and marked by a variety of excesses and lacks, including partial blindness, deafness, and other "corporeal defects" (Frances Reynolds, qtd. in Hill 2: 276, 299), Johnson exemplified the simultaneous "too real" and "not real enough" of the limits of the individual case, in the flesh.

Samuel Johnson; or, Exemplary Aberration

Johnson, indeed, stands as one of England's greatest characters, as well as one of her greatest caricatures.

—Lawrence C. McHenry, Jr.

In describing his first encounter with Johnson, the Reverend Thomas Campbell, writing in his personal journal, is prompted to address him directly:

Johnson, you are the very man Lord Chesterfield describes:—a Hottentot indeed, and tho' your abilities are respectable, you never can be respected yourself. He has the aspect of an Idiot, without the faintest ray of sense gleaming from any one feature—with the most awkward garb, and unpowdered grey wig, on one side only of his head—he is for ever dancing the devil's jig, and sometimes he makes the most driveling effort to whistle some thought in his absent paroxisms.   (qtd. in Hill 2: 41)

Campbell describes the ultimate monstrosity, a man who is at once a character and a caricature (McHenry 168), an original and a parody. Just as his prose persona shifts, so Campbell cannot fix his perspective on the paradoxical spectacle of respectable abilities housed in an "Idiot's" form. Moving from Johnson himself to Lord Chesterfield's famous portrait of a type, the "respectable Hottentot," Campbell abandons physical description in his account of Johnson's senseless face, moving away from the body itself to its various manifestations: the unfashionable clothing, the ungovernable motions (nervous tics here described as "devil's jig"), the inharmonious "absent paroxisms."

The oxymoron of "respectable Hottentot" (a passage from Chesterfield's letters that was immediately assumed to describe Johnson, though this was not Chesterfield's intention) [7] rewrites the mind-body paradox as a violation of proper social and civilized hierarchies. The case of Johnson transforms a centuries-old imagination of the deformity of genius into a parodic body, a body in motion, whose shape and gestures challenge the limits of social intelligibility:

> There is a man, whose moral character, deep learning, and superior parts, I acknowledge, admire, and respect; but whom it is so impossible for me to love, that I am almost in a fever whenever I am in his company. His figure (without being deformed) seems made to disgrace or ridicule the common structure of the human body. His legs and arms are never in the position which, according to the situation of his body, they ought to be in, but constantly employed in committing acts of hostility upon the Graces. He throws any where, but down his throat, whatever he means to drink; and only mangles what he means to carve. Inattentive to all the regards of social life, he mistimes or misplaces every thing. He disputes with heat and indiscriminately, mindless of the rank, character, and situation of those with whom he disputes; absolutely ignorant of the several gradations of familiarity and respect, he is exactly the same to his superiors, his equals, and his inferiors; and therefore, by a necessary consequence, absurd to two of the three. Is it possible to love such a man? No. The utmost I can do for him is, to consider him a respectable Hottentot.
>
> (letter 212, qtd. in Hill 1: 384)

Johnson is a monster, then, at once corporeal and social. If his figure seems designed to "disgrace or ridicule" the human body, the movements of that body, while not clearly intentional, actively deform social ritual and destroy proper social distinctions.

Johnson appears in similar circumstances as a potential exception to Johan Caspar Lavater's popular theory of physiognomy, that is, "that the resemblance of forms implies always that of minds" (1: 192). "Look at Samuel Johnson:" an imagined interlocutor demands, "he has the air of a porter; neither the look, nor a single trait about the mouth, announce a penetrating mind, a man versant in the Sciences." Lavater defends himself obdurately: "I have often [. . .] ascribed sense and genius to persons who were entirely destitute of them; but never, as far as I know, did I take a man of sense for an idiot. So true it is, that the signs of ge- nius are striking and infallible [. . .]." Deformed by class, Johnson may appear to have "the air of a porter," but a closer examination of his face, as depicted by two portrait engravings and (added in the first English translation in 1789) an engraving of Johnson's death mask, reveals to Lavater's discerning eye "signs of sagacity and meditation. [. . .] Though nothing were seen of that face but the forehead, or the eye, or the chin, in each of these features, taken separately, might be traced the expression of exquisite sense:—how much more is this discoverable in the combination of the whole!"(1: 194).

What Lavater characterized as "those half-opened eyes, that air of reflection" (193), others stigmatized as a squint.[8] If we turn to the work of Johnson's most well-known portraitist, Sir Joshua Reynolds, we can see how a corporeal sign in the author's case can indicate both common defect and exceptional subjectivity. Johnson was displeased when Reynolds depicted his chronic nearsightedness in a portrait (fig. 1) in which the author scrutinizes a book held close to his face; he declared that "he would not be known by posterity for his *defects* only, let Sir Joshua do his worst. [. . .] I will not be *blinking Sam.*" (Hill 1: 313). Yet such defects are also the subject of the portrait in figure 2, said to have been modeled after the figure of Socrates in Raphael's *School of Athens* (Yung). Reynolds's apprentice and biographer James Northcote de- scribes the painting thus: "Sir Joshua had given to Dr. Johnson a copy of that portrait now at Knowle, the seat of the late Duke of Dorset, in which the Doctor is represented with his hands held up, and in his own short hair; it is nearly a profile [. . .]" (Northcote 1: 234–35).

In Reynolds's hands, as these two images show, the squint becomes a mobile sign that can convey either disability or sensibility, visible lack or inner excess. In the second portrait, Johnson's eyes are narrowed into a squint, but the context removes his expression from the iconography of defect and into a realm of indeterminacy that is very much of his his- torical moment.

Figure 1

Sir Joshua Reynolds, *Samuel Johnson*. Painted c. 1775. Engraved by John Hall. Frontispiece to volume 1 of *The Works
of Samuel Johnson*, ed. Hawkins, London, 1787-88. Reproduced by permission of the Huntington Library, San
Marino, California

   The pose of Johnson's hands here heightens this ambiguity. Are his
togalike garment and bare head meant to aid the viewer in recognizing
an expressive, stylized movement of classical oratory? Or is Reynolds instead capturing a more personal sense of his subject's interiority?[9] Or is
this pose an accurate depiction of one of Johnson's strange "motions or
tricks," which Sir Joshua himself believed often accompanied guilty
thoughts (Boswell, *Life* 1: 144) and which his sister, Frances Reynolds,

Figure 2

Samuel Johnson. Mezzotint engraved by James Watson after a 1769 portrait by Reynolds, 1770. Reproduced by permission of the Huntington Library, San Marino, California

described as follows: "[A]s for his gestures with his hands, they were
equally as strange; sometimes he would hold them up with some of his
fingers bent, as if he had been seized with the cramp, and sometimes at
his Breast in motion like those of a jockey on full speed" (qtd. in Hill
2:274).

For the twentieth-century doctor, medical historian, and Johnsonian Lawrence C. McHenry, Jr., this image is evidence for a successful diagnosis, in a 1967 medical article, of Johnson with Tourette's syndrome.

For the art historian Duncan Robinson in 1992, by contrast, the portrait's "stark realism can only be explained in terms of the profound respect both artist and sitter had for mind over matter" (91). This "extraordinary image" depicts "the eighteenth-century's greatest master of the English language poised on the boundaries of definition." Perhaps unintentionally, and despite his certainty that mind has prevailed over matter in this image, Robinson fails to identify what remains undefined: is it the thought of the "enlightened state of mind" that we sense is invisibly "poised on the boundaries of definition" (93), or do the indecipherable gestures of the body convey the indefinable power of Johnson's subjectivity?

Yet Johnson himself, along with Northcote and other contemporary commentators and viewers who "much admired" the portrait (Northcote 1: 235), took no special notice of the gestures.[10] With its indeterminate relation to intention, Johnson's pose evokes the paradoxical figure of the author, at the limits of bodily intelligibility for his contemporary audience. From different historical perspectives this image is, like the eighteenth-century construction of genius as disability, at once excessive and lacking, classically idealized and clinically realistic.

For Thomas Carlyle, and for the Victorians more generally, the man of letters functioned no longer as a monster but as a hero. Carlyle distinguished Johnson as "one of our great English souls," a man of untapped potential whose struggle with exceptional hardship made him great:

> Nature, in return for his nobleness, had said to him, Live in an element of diseased sorrow. Nay, perhaps the sorrow and the nobleness were intimately and even inseparably connected with each other. At all events, poor Johnson had to go about girt with a continual hypochondria, physical and spiritual pain. Like a Hercules with the burning Nessus'-shirt on him, which shoots-in on him dull incurable misery: the Nessus'-shirt not to be stript-off, which is his own natural skin! In this manner *he* had to live.   (178)

Johnson had compared himself and had been compared by others (somewhat ironically) to Hercules, with whom he shared his large stature and his melancholy (Thrale, qtd. in Hill 1: 180). But Carlyle transforms the author's physical monstrosity into a heroically interior, indeed spiritual, battle.[11]

More apt for the historical moment that this essay ponders is figure 3, from Daniel Lysons's 1796 illustrated guide to London: John Opie's portrait of Johnson in the year of his death placed atop a pedestal. Engraved

Figure 3

John Opie, *Samuel Johnson*. 1783-84. Engraved by Daven-
port. From Daniel Lysons, *Historical Account of the Environs of
London*, London, 1796. Reproduced by permission of the
Huntington Library, San Marino, California

on the pedestal is an image of Hercules slaying the Hydra. Such an image makes us wonder about differences that Carlyle has successfully collapsed into the sentimentalized figure of Johnson the great soul. At the
turn of the eighteenth century Johnson was envisioned as both monster
slayer and monster, both Hercules and Hydra. Epitomizing both excess
and lack, he figured for his time an irresolvable paradox of mind and
body that today haunts our constructions of individuality and its bodily
limits.

Imagining Other People

In its most familiar manifestations, Johnson's ghost has functioned as heroic icon for an idea of eighteenth-century England. The bodily difference that informs the cultural myth of English literary authority personified in Age of Johnson classrooms and Johnson societies around the world is largely disavowed today in an affirmation of scholarly community and mass identification. The archaeological work that this essay has tried, however briefly, to exemplify attempts to restore to cultural memory that bodily difference in all its social and ideological ambiguity. I thus intend to reopen the end of Johnson's story—that most disembodied of universal genres, the English literary canon itself—to new consideration. I hope to reveal in the process the changing historical limits of both individuality and sympathy (or what the opening of this essay calls recognizability), limits that it is our mission as scholars of disability to continue to question and redefine in the present moment.

In writing *Life As We Know It: A Father, a Family, and an Exceptional Child,* Michael Bérubé says of his son, James, "'Value' may be something that can only be determined socially, by collective and chaotic human deliberation; but individual humans like James are compelling us daily to determine what *kind* of 'individuality' we will value, on what terms, and why" (xix). Like Johnson in his time, James, who has Down syndrome, is exceptional. The fullness and complexity of his being puts into question the ways in which we define bodily difference and mark the limits of decipherable, valuable, indeed "exceptional" individuality. Recent research on the genetic bases of human difference, Bérubé argues, suggests that the genetic differences among individuals are far greater than those among nations, races, or genders. The result demands a rethinking of the notions of individuality and relation: "Either we humans are hopelessly atomized, each sealed within the biochemical prison of the self, or we're more closely related to each other than we can bear to think" (24). Rewritten on the chromosomes is the eighteenth-century terror of the twin excesses of individual difference and sympathetic community; limits defended against in Johnson's case by constructing him as monster or, equally problematically, as sentimental hero.

"It is part of my purpose," Bérubé states, "in writing this book, to represent Jamie as best I can—just as it is part of my purpose, in representing Jamie, to ask about our obligations to each other, individually and socially, and about our capacity to imagine other people" (xix). My project joins with Bérubé's in this challenge to the limits of sympathy, delineating an earlier chapter in the history of "our capacity to imagine other people." This capacity is at once historical, ethical, and aesthetic. It demands moral acts of imagination, interpretation, and communication that provide literature classrooms with purpose, and it puts disability studies at the center of literary studies today.

NOTES

1. On this ambiguity in literary style, see Stewart, "Lyric Possession." On styles of corporeality, see Elias; Bremmer and Roodenburg.

2. In an important counterargument, Pender claims that wonder coexisted with scientific progress in seventeenth- and eighteenth-century British culture.

3. What Garland-Thomson argues about the American nineteenth-century freak show can be applied to the eighteenth-century author: "the domesticated freak simultaneously embodied exceptionality as marvel and exceptionality as anomaly, thus posing to the spectator the implicit political question of how to interpret differences within an egalitarian social order" (*Extraordinary Bodies* 17).

4. For the author as representative figure of the self-made individual in eighteenth-century England, see McKeon.

5. C. Gallagher bases her account of the rise of the novel at midcentury on the political, social, and emotional benefits of identifying with nobody in particular (145–203).

6. Boswell, in his periodical paper *The Hypochondriack*, characterizes his and Johnson's common malady, melancholy's eighteenth-century heir, hypochondria, as an unhealthy mind in a healthy body, proud indiscernible mark of the excessive sensibility of the man of feeling (2: 236–38). For hypochondria as mark of male lettered community, see Deutsch, "Symptomatic Correspondences."

7. While Boswell and many contemporaries identified Johnson as Chesterfield's subject, Hill argues in his note to this passage that Chesterfield indisputably was referring to Lord Lyttleton.

8. For a fascinating discussion of eighteenth-century conceptions of the squint and its iconography in political caricature, see S. West.

9. Graves and Cronin are the first commentators on the portrait I have found to describe it definitively as depicting Johnson "standing arguing, with his two hands half clutched, in one of his most characteristic attitudes" (2: 519). L. F. Powell observes that the portrait must be "idealized," since "Johnson is represented as wearing a loose robe-like garment, which he is otherwise not known to have worn; he is enforcing argument by gesticulation, a practice which he is known to have condemned [. . .]; and he is shown in the prime of life, between 40 and 50, whereas at the time of the painting he was actually 60" (Boswell, *Life* 4: 448). Johnson's aversion to rhetorical gesticulation is often commented on (see, e.g., Boswell, *Life* 1: 334; 4: 322–23), but this portrait foregrounds the ambiguous relation of purposeful gesture accompanying public speech to the perhaps unintentional movements of private reverie. Yung argues, "by its commonly known title *Dr. Johnson Arguing* it is in fact misleading since Johnson is not in argument with anyone but is mentally wrestling with himself," while also noting the mimetic accuracy of the "strange gesture" (103).

10. A nineteenth-century viewer describes the image as of Johnson "with his arms raised and his hands bent" (Timbs 109–10). Reyde quotes a late-nineteenth-century description from the *Gentleman's Magazine* of "Sir Joshua Reynolds's best portrait of Dr. Johnson, at perhaps not above 45 years old, in an attitude of deep thought, hands lifted breast high, and the fingers half-spread in a particular manner, and uncloathed neck" (1: 17).

11. For the beginnings of this metaphor in Boswell, see his description of Johnson's mind as "Colisaeum" (*Life* 2: 106).

JENNIFER L. NELSON

Bulwer's Speaking Hands: Deafness and Rhetoric

Reason and the sayings of the learned ancients [. . .] prove these cosmetic gestures of the hand to be things of great moment and the very palm and crown of eloquence.
                                          —John Bulwer, *Chironomia*

Gesture and eloquence, mind and body: for John Bulwer, rhetorician, these things are intertwined through physical, manual bodily movements. Bulwer's preoccupation with the body and its movements has caused a modern critic to humorously dub him a seventeenth-century muscle man (Greenblatt, "Universal Language"). Muscles and their motions do abound in Bulwer's works; his 1644 *Chirologia* and *Chironomia* deal with the many expressive gestures that may be used in public speaking and that can be sculpted to an art. As can be seen in the title page (fig. 1), *Chirologia* focuses on the various natural expressions of the hands and their meanings—"pronunciation"—and *Chironomia* focuses on the art of rhetoric, where carefully controlled bodily movements strongly figure. His *Pathomyotomia* deals with the facial muscles, movements, and expressions, and his *Philocophus; or, The Deafe and Dumbe Mans Friend* deals with deaf people, their sign language, and a proposed school for the deaf. For Bulwer, motion is what makes man a perfect creature (Greenblatt 26–27), whether it be expression through the motions of the hands, fingers, face, larynx, or lips. Bulwer

211

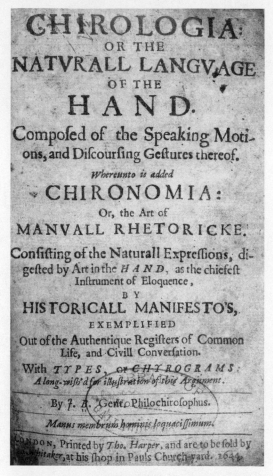

Figure 1

Title page of *Chirologia; or, The Naturall Language of the Hand*. Reproduced by permission of Gallaudet University Archives

notes that speech and "Words are nothing else but Motion" (*Philocophus* 19); this is the moment where speech and manual signs share a common ground for him. He indicates, many times over in his works, that motion in whatever form is the universal thing binding all people. Rhetoric is composed of motions and consequently so are the sign languages of the deaf. Gestures, as the "universall language of Humane nature," are what the deaf have in common with hearing people (a3v–a4r), and Bulwer appropriates this knowledge to anticipate the elocutionary movement in rhetoric.

Bulwer changed the face of rhetoric by turning it back to the some-what lost classical canon of delivery; by rescuing it bodily from a mostly mental, postclassical emphasis on invention and style; and by ushering in a renewed consideration of performance as persuasion that would unfold even more fully in another hundred years, with the elocutionary movement's emphasis on the role that the body plays in public speak-ing. Where did Bulwer's rhetorical precociousness come from? And how exactly does deafness fit in with his ideas on rhetoric? After all, people do naturally gesture when they speak, to punctuate, enhance, or forcibly draw attention to their words; such gesturing is what *Chirologia* and *Chironomia* are about, with only slight notice given to deaf people. However, I argue that Bulwer's manual rhetoric is largely underpinned by the presence of deaf people and their sign language in his life; they had a much greater influence on this rhetorical enterprise than is gen-erally thought or known. That influence is indicated by Bulwer's 1648 *Philocophus,* where he praises deaf people, their sign language, and their intellectual capacities; he also acknowledges his debt to deaf people in this book. That Bulwerian elocution and rhetoric have been influenced by the sign language of the deaf is clearly stated in *Philocophus:*

> This language you [the deaf Gostwicke brothers] speak so purely, that I who was the first that made it my Darling study to interpret the naturall richnesse of our discoursing gestures, not onely to the distinguishing of all the Corporall and Nationall Dialects thereof, and regulating the naturall as Accessories and Adjuncts of Rhetori-call Elocution; but to the following of them downe to their spring heads and originall, even to the finding out their Radicall Deriva-tions and Muscular Etymologies [. . .].   (a3v–a4r)

That he applied his "Darling study" of "our discoursing gestures" to the "Accessories and Adjuncts of Rhetoricall Elocution" is manifestly stated here. His notice of specific deaf people and their already existing sign language had an effect on his "regulating" and furthering of rhetorical speech through gestures.

In addition to writing *Philocophus,* Bulwer personally knew a number of deaf people in his time, such as Mr. Crisp, brother of Sir Nicholas Crisp, and he was apparently related by blood to the deaf Gostwicke brothers (Dekesel 41); these brothers are in the dedication of *Philocophus,* which also lists a fair number of deaf people in the seventeenth-century deaf community in England. Evidence gleaned from his will indicates that he adopted and provided for a deaf child named Chirothea—literally, one who uses sign language (12). These interactions with deaf people indicate a greater influence on Bulwer's rhetoric—and therefore on the rhetorical tradition—than might be supposed from his *Chirologia* and *Chironomia*, which cite the Greek and Roman orators, philosophers, politicians, and teachers, as well as other great names, in support of his enterprise rather than deaf people. It is *Philocophus* that truly indicates his use of sign language in behalf of eloquence. Kristiaan Dekesel hints at this influence as well: he notes that the Gostwicke brothers and Chirothea were likely the "motivation behind these two treatises [*Chirologia* and *Chironomia*]" (13).

In deafness, Bulwer found a space where gestures and speech intersect, and in this space deafness ironically is used to support eloquence. In his conflation of gestures and speech onto the plane of bodily motions, Bulwer embodies the elocutionary movement's focus on the issue of delivery through the controlling of the various parts of the body and its motions, as well as voice modulation, matters that arise from nature and its "imprints." He writes that nature

> imprints upon the body the active hints of her most generous conceits, darting her rays into the body, as light has its emanation from the sun; which eloquent impressions, a kind of speech most consonant to the mind, are in the moving of the hand so neatly wrought and emphatically produced that the hand many times seems to have conceived the thought. He, therefore, that would purchase the repute of an accomplished rhetorician must pursue the knowledge of this art which consists in understanding the lawful garb and ordered motions of the hand, the most puissant agent of the soul, and which hath by some been called mens corporis, or the mind of the body; [thus, we have] the voice of philosophy [. . .].   (Chirologia 170–71; *Chironomia*)

Bulwer is very taken with the idea that the art of public speaking depends on the natural connection between the mind and the body, which is epitomized in gesture as a "substitute and vicegerent [sic] of the tongue" (15). Gestures are as valid as the tongue, and they are "the mind of the body."

A knowledge of the attitudes and background of the time preceding Bulwer helps us appreciate his insistence on the importance of gesture and the body in the art of persuasion. Early modern England generally believed that eloquence was speech and that to be a true human being one had to hear and therefore speak.[1] An account written roughly ninety years before Bulwer wrote his works makes even more clear the speech-and-hearing bias that permeated society. Thomas Wilson, in the *Arte of Rhetorique*, says that God

[s]till tendering his own workmanship, stirred up his faithful and elect, to persuade with reason, all men to society. And gave his appointed ministers knowledge both to see the natures of men, and also granted them the gift of utterance, that they might with ease win folk at their will, and frame them by reason to all good order.

And therefore, whereas men lived Brutishly in open fields, having neither house to shroud them in, nor attire to clothe their backs, nor yet any regard to seek their best avail: these appointed of God called them together by utterance of speech, and persuaded them what was good, what was bad, and what was gainful for mankind. And although at first, the rude could hardly learne, and either for strangeness of the thing, would not gladly receive the offer, or else for lack of knowledge could not perceive the goodness: yet being somewhat drawn and delighted with the pleasantness of reason, and the sweetness of utterance: after a certain space, they became through nurture and good advisement, of wild, sober: of cruel, gentle: of fools, wise: and of beasts, men. Such force hath the tongue, and such is the power of eloquence and reason, that most men are forced even to yield in that, which most standeth against their will.   (18–19)

With Wilson as a predecessor, Bulwer is attempting to write gestures and corporeality against a historically established religious and rhetorical body of work where the tongue is the "power of eloquence and reason," since only through utterance does God's appointed call those who lived "Brutishly" and convert them to reason and civilization.

In contrast to Wilson's insistence on vocal utterance, Bulwer sees manual signs in a valid light, in that hands are capable of a sort of speech: *Chirologia* is "Composed of the Speaking Motions, and Discoursing Gestures thereof." He notes that the use of manual signs is the "naturall language of the Hand" (1). He points out here that there is no compelling reason that people should talk: " 'Tis apparent, that there's no native law, or absolute necessity, that those thoughts which arise in our pregnant mind must by mediation of our tongue flow out in a vocal stream of words" (17). This statement is a prelude to the idea that deaf people can sign as hearing people can talk:

A notable argument we have of this discoursing faculty of the hand in our common jesters who without their voice, speaking only by gestures, can counterfeit their manners, fashions and significant actions of men; which [argument] may be more confirmed

by that wonder of necessity which nature worketh in men that are
born deaf and dumb who can argue and dispute rhetorically by
signs, and with a kind of mute and logistic eloquence overcome
their amazed opponents; wherein some are so ready and excellent,
they seem to want nothing to have their meanings perfectly understood.   (17)

Bulwer here assigns eloquence and rhetorical power directly to the signs
of the deaf and in so doing recognizes the deaf and their use of sign language. He further appears to privilege gestures by saying that the number of gestures exceeds the "numerical store of words"; he proceeds to
give a long list of the things that can be expressed through gestures (20).
A section titled "Dactylogia" in *Chirologia* discourses on the capabilities
of the hands in elocution: "And as we can translate a thought into discoursing signs, so the conceptions of our mind are seen to abound in
several dialects while the articulated fingers supply the office of a voice"
(120). Voice is provided as much by the fingers as by the mouth.

Beyond the eloquence inherent in gestures, Bulwer further invokes
religion to support his argument that they are valid as carriers of meaning. In religion, he notes that the body is superior to the tongue, because
"the general language of the body, is more vocal and effectual than the
explications of the tongue, and more religiously true to the soul" (31).
He also writes that "the hands and blessing seem to be conjugates in the
school both of nature and grace" and that benediction is "a natural right
near allied unto the hand and of spiritual affinity with prayer" (110).

Not only does Bulwer invest gestures with heavy rhetorical eloquence and religious significance but also his method of analyzing gestures emphasizes his devotion to the belief that manual signs are of
paramount importance in public speaking. From *Chirologia*'s detailed explications of various significant gestures ("I reprove," "I extol," etc.), one
can see that he is remarkably sensitized to gestural visual effects and
their physical production, a very deaf quality, one that may have arisen
from his experience with the deaf and their sign language. He is also visually attuned in his constant use of chirograms throughout his books.
His works stress the importance of gestures as the "crown of eloquence"
in a concrete, almost bodily way through the rare visual presentation of
many chirogrammatic plates, which portray drawings of hands and
their proper shapes. For example, the illustration for "invito" ("I invite")
shows a hand upturned and curved gracefully inward, toward the
speaker's body (51, 115). To extend the middle finger is "a natural expression of scorn and contempt" (132, 143). Bulwer's rhetorical order-

ings of manual movements are clear when he says these tables of gestures, "besides their typicall significations, are so ordered to serve for
privy cyphers for any secret intimation" (142). Figure 2 serves as "a
corollary of the speaking motions" (note such visual expressions as
"adoro" and "castigo"). Not only do gestures have a typical, clear meaning for many, but also they can serve as abstract "privy cyphers" of
meaning, much as words and sign language signs do.

From *Chirologia*, Bulwer moves to *Chironomia* and its chirograms,
which he calls "the Art of Manuall Rhetorique"

> with the Canons, Laws, Rites, Ordinances, and Institutes of
> RHETORICIANS, both Ancient and Moderne, Touching the Artificiall
> managing of the HAND in Speaking. Whereby the Naturall
> GESTURES of the HAND, are made the Regulated Accessories or
> faire-spoke adjuncts of RHETORICAL utterances. With TYPES, or
> CHIROGRAMS: A new illustration of this Argument.
>
> (Chirologia 145)

In *Chironomia* he continues the vein of thought he started in *Chirologia*,
that the hand is fully capable of eloquence in its own right. In fact, gestures win out over the mouth hands down, since they can function by
themselves, whereas speech cannot function properly without gestures:

> Whereas man by a happy endowment of nature is allowed two in-
> struments, speech and a hand, to bring his concealed thoughts
> unto light; the tongue, without the hand, can utter nothing but
> what will come forth lame and impotent, whereas the hand, with-
> out the discourse of the tongue, is of admirable and energetical ef-
> ficacy, and hath achieved many notable things.   (156–57)

He eloquently insults further the impotent, gestureless mouth and says
that gestures enhance speech greatly, as there is a lack in speech that
gestures fill:

> Speech divided from the hand is unsound, and, brought into a
> poor and low condition, [it] flags and creeps upon the ground. The
> babbling tongue (indeed) may have a long and spacious walk, and
> the full mouth may prate and run o'er with large and loud imper-
> tinencies; but without the concurrence of the hand, the mouth is
> but a running sore and hollow fistula of the mind [. . .].
>
> (157)

He praises the hand in conjunction with the mouth. More, he clearly
idealizes the hand and universalizes gestures, as when he says that not
only

Figure 2

Bulwer's "corollary of the speaking motions." From *Chirologia*. Reproduced by permission of Gallaudet University Archives

doth the hand in one speech or kind of language serve to intimate and express our mind: it speaks all languages, and as an universal character of reason, is generally understood and known by all nations among the formal differences of their tongue. And being the only speech that is natural to man, it may well be called the tongue and general language of human nature which, without teaching, men in all regions of the habitable world do at the first sight most easily understand.   (16)

Bulwer has been accused by Stephen Greenblatt and others of being overly utopian and idealistic in praising gestures so highly and proffering them as the perfect universal language of human beings. Bulwer does seem to overstate the potential of gestures, for his utopian impulse notwithstanding, signs made by the hands are just as referential as words issuing from the mouth. It can be argued, however, that he is talking about motion as a universal impulse, since he says that if people didn't move in one way or another, they would be like plants. Does Bulwer really subscribe to the myth that sign language is universal? Dekesel thinks he simply "meant that gestures are a universal phenomenon, that they are in use all over the world" (39).

As in *Chirologia* and *Chironomia*, Bulwer in *Philocophus* opines that speech has more "life and efficacy" (a3v) when joined with gestures. He continues his belief in the universality of motion: "To speak, is nothing else but by certain motiuncles of the Tongue and Lips, to intimate and signifie certaine things, as it is agreed between those that speak together" (29). He also notes that speech doesn't require a "voyce," but it requires motion; it can "produce mute and inaudible articles of Elocution" (49). Again we have an elocution that results from lip motions and not specifically from the sound of the voice itself. As a result of his motion-based philosophy of universality, Bulwer stresses the idea that the use of the voice over hands is arbitrary: if speech were wholly natural, we'd speak without teaching, and speech is "compacted or performed by use and custome" (133, 136). This observation opens the gateway to the idea of the deaf as being able to communicate in a way that is not automatically speech, an idea that would have been a radical concept for the general public of that time:

What though you cannot expresse your mindes in those verball contrivances of mans invention; yet you want not speech, who have your whole Body, for a Tongue, having a language more naturall and significant, which is common to you with us, to wit

gesture, the generall and universall language of Humane nature
[. . .].   (a3r–a3v)

In his motional philosophy, Bulwer creates a viable, equal—even arguably exalted—space for gestures and sign languages, a space where
the deaf and their sign language have changed the face of rhetoric. Not
only does he use his familiarity with deaf people and sign language to
extend the field of rhetoric but also he validates sign language and encourages the development of the intellect of deaf people. He writes at
length in *Philocophus* about the legal and intellectual indignities visited
on deaf people and proposes a school for the deaf. He insists that sign
language can be used as the pathway to learning to read and write—and
perhaps even to speech. Strangely enough, though Bulwer sees gestures
as being able to function alone without speech, even he ends up with a
speech bias, in that he theorizes the ultimate goal of the learning of
speech through sign language. However, anything else would have been
too radical for his audience.

The influence exerted on Bulwer's rhetoric by the presence of the
deaf and their sign language in his life brings up a number of issues and
implications that beg discussion, such as whether or not this influence
helps validate the sign language of the deaf and what the nature of this
influence is. For Bulwer, deafness and the deaf body in language are the
grounds on which his rhetorical arguments are built, ironic as that may
sound. His rhetoric depends on a metaphor, that of the silent deaf body,
for the deaf and their sign language are still largely absent from his art of
speech even as he uses his familiarity with deafness and deaf people to
apply gestures as a supplement to or replacement for oratory. Bulwer's
art of rhetoric may be seen to be erected on an Irigarayan "silent
ground" of deafness—Irigaray argues that the patriarchal thinker builds
his discourse on the silent ground of woman (Moi 131)—and in that
way Bulwer is appropriative and reconstitutive of the facts of deafness,
although his intentions are good, considering that he thought highly of
gestures in the face of a long speech-based rhetorical tradition. Though
he sees universality in motion and therefore validates the sign language
of the deaf as he knows it through people like Chirothea, the Gost-
wickes, and Mr. Crisp, in actual practice gestures function as the "bearer
of cultural information" and participate in the production of meanings
(Foster 14), which are artificial and restricted by society. The deaf aren't
ultimately equalized through their use of gestures, since for society gestures must ultimately be a means to prop up the mouth rather than
function alone. Bulwer moves from a recognition of sign language to a

discussion of how it can be used as a gateway to speech. Bulwer both validates and appropriates deafness, and in his doing so deafness functions as an insight for hearing people. Disability presented as insight, metaphor, or helpmate is a common although not always politically appropriate approach to disability studies, since it contributes something to an abled population.

In the end, however, Bulwer's idea of educating the deaf was a relatively new notion in his time; it predated institutionalized deaf education by a hundred years. It was in the mid-1700s when Abbé de l'Epée of France pioneered deaf education, through sign language, on a mass scale. According to Dekesel, "Before [Abbé de l'Epée's] time, educating a deaf person was hardly thought of as possible, but by the time he was finished, general opinion had started to imagine it feasible" (45). Bulwer's knowledge and use of deafness contribute significantly to his writings on elocution, and this knowledge also makes him probably the first British person to write empathetically about deafness and sign language in any depth. Dekesel dubs him the "founding father of British sign language research" (11). Gestures therefore serve as a two-way street between deaf and hearing people, even though speech on both sides is the ultimate goal.

NOTE

1. This speech bias is borne out by the literal absence of the deaf as real people from the literature of the time, except for occasional, brief, usually allegorical mentions of them, such as of Abessa in Spenser's *Faerie Queene:* "But the rude wench her answer'd naught at all, / She could not hear, nor speak, nor understand" (1.3.11). Here, deafness for Abessa means that she is allegorically "outside the sphere of divine salvation" (Nelson and Berens 61). Deafness is also often used as a metaphor or as an exercise in power. Shakespeare has numerous references to deafness and dumbness, as when the Prince tells Romeo he will be "deaf to pleading and excuses" (*Rom.* 3.1.192). To play deaf is to engage in an exercise in power, but this exercise works only if one can hear and is a member of an aural society. See Nelson and Berens for a long discussion of deafness and its various functions in early modern literature.

The Twin Structure: Disabled Women in Victorian Courtship Plots

At the opening of the immensely popular Victorian melodrama *Les deux orphelines* (*The Two Orphans* [Cormon and D'Ennery]), two pretty, identically dressed sisters named Henriette and Louise set out together for Paris.[1] Within minutes of their arrival in the city, loutish aristocrats separate the sisters. Henriette is abducted and her virtue endangered; Louise is dragged to the docks and abandoned. Henriette is saved by an honorable aristocrat who wants to marry her; Louise is taken in by streetwise beggars who taunt her, beat her, and force her to sing in the streets for alms. Henriette gets married. Louise has a happy ending, too—not as a wife but as a daughter. Through a remarkable series of coincidences, she recovers the mother who had abandoned her on the steps of Notre Dame fourteen years earlier. The curtain closes on the happy tableau of Henriette in the arms of her lover and Louise in the arms of her mother.

What comes between the two young women's shared beginning and their very separate endings? The plot offers only one clear reason: Henriette can see, and Louise is blind.

Les deux orphelines is a particularly legible example of what I term the twin structure, a pervasive trope in Victorian literature in which two women characters, one disabled and one nondisabled, are paired in a courtship plot that assigns them two very different physical, emotional, and sexual roles.[2] One women is courted and married; the other suffers, feels unsatisfied longings, and expresses her emotions in a public and pro-

222

Figure 1

Lillian and Dorothy Gish played Henriette and Louise in
Orphans of the Storm, D. W. Griffith's 1921 film version of *Les
deux orphelines*. Photo courtesy of Museum of Modern Art
Film Stills Archive, New York, NY

longed fashion before she is assigned a role outside the world of courtship
and marriage. The unfolding of the two women's divergent fates elaborates
a complex of messages about ability and disability, femininity and sexuality, the dangers of emotional expression, and the range of social roles available to Victorian women. Ironically, the narratives do not emphasize what
these twins share; rather, they reiterate the idea of their essential and ir-
revocable difference. A nondisabled woman, most of these stories tell us,
will develop her identity in the social world of courtship and marriage,
which (however problematically) represented a woman's only access route
to financial security and social status; a disabled woman must develop outside it.

While critics have paid attention to disabled characters in Victorian
literature, they have almost always read them as emotional props, plot

stimulants whose ontological status is closer to scenery than character; or else such characters are read as metaphors for the situation of some other group within Victorian culture (e.g., women or the poor). Similarly, while critics assiduously examine Victorian characters marked by gender difference or ethnicity as representations of groups with historically particular social and political identities, disabled characters are rarely accorded any historicity.[3]

My analysis of Charles Dickens's *The Cricket on the Hearth*, in contrast, reads the "Blind Girl," Bertha Plummer, as a character whose emotionalism, deployed as it is in the context of a courtship plot to which she is emphatically and painfully denied access, evokes the culturally traumatic points of contact among Victorian discourses of femininity, disability, and sexuality.

Bertha Plummer's plot trajectory does reference that of many Victorian women whose social identity was defined by their failure to marry. The narrative's ultimate reinforcement of the status quo of marriage, coinciding as it does with her removal from the plot, suggests that one of the functions of the disabled woman character is to shore up the institution of marriage—and the idea of a married woman's happiness—by embodying the miseries of the woman who must live outside it. The disabled woman is thus cast as a particular version of surplus or odd woman, alluding to the never-married Victorian women who kept house with parents or siblings or managed an uncertain existence in professions that rarely ensured them social or financial status.

More startling, given the pervasive stereotyping of disabled women as nonsexual subjects in nineteenth- and twentieth-century culture, the disabled woman character is often implicitly linked through her emotional volatility to the dangerous concept of female sexuality and thus to the fallen Victorian woman.

Because disabled women characters' emotional responses inevitably evoked the sexuality of disabled as well as of nondisabled women, however, the ritual excision of these characters at the end of so many courtship plots serves not only to purify the plot of the specter of the fallen nondisabled woman but also to remove the equally potent threat of the sexual and potentially reproductive disabled woman, a figure whose dangers were amply suggested by contemporary social science and medical texts.

The repetition and popularity of the twin structure make it a significant site of analysis in the cultural history of disability. The works in which this narrative pattern is transgressed, however, are equally important. My conclusion briefly addresses those stories in which disabled women not only marry but also become mothers and the contexts that enable this outcome.

The conflict, crisis, and resolution of *The Cricket on the Hearth* hinge on people's failure to see the truth about those they love. The main plot involves the laborer John Peerybingle's fear that his young wife, Dot, loves another man. Dot unwittingly arouses John's suspicions through her secret plans to reunite her friend May Fielding with May's long-absent lover, Edward Plummer, before May makes an unhappy marriage to the rich manufacturer Tackleton. Love, courtship, and happy marriages are the significant goals to which the plot progresses.

Given the structure and emphasis of the plot, Dot Peerybingle's logical twin is May Fielding. Instead, Dickens creates a third young woman with her own dreams of courtship and marriage and makes her more central to the plot than the virtually absent, silent May. Blind Girl Bertha Plummer, Edward's sister, lives with her father in a tumbledown cottage where they make toys for Tackleton. As the narrator describes it, however,

> Caleb lived here, and his poor Blind Daughter somewhere else—in an enchanted home of Caleb's furnishing, where scarcity and shabbiness were not, and trouble never entered. [. . .] The Blind Girl never knew that iron was rusting, wood rotting, paper peeling off; the size, and the shape, and true proportion of the dwelling, withering away. The Blind Girl never knew that ugly shapes of delf and earthenware were on the board; that sorrow and faintheartedness were in the house; that Caleb's scanty hairs were turning greyer and more grey, before her sightless face. The Blind Girl never knew they had a master, cold, exacting, and uninterested—never knew that Tackleton was Tackleton in short; but lived in the belief of an eccentric humourist who loved to have his jest with them, and who, while he was the Guardian Angel of their lives, disdained to hear one word of thankfulness. And all was Caleb's doing [. . .].   (182–83)

Deceived by her father about all the significant realities of their lives, Bertha falls in love with Tackleton. Her distress on learning of May's engagement to Tackleton and her even greater distress when Caleb decides to unburden himself of all the loving lies he has told her form two of the story's significant moments of crisis and emotional overflow.

As conventionally effective as she is in eliciting other characters' true feelings, Bertha becomes a problem for the story when she expresses her own, in floods of language and tears. What makes Bertha's emotionality so errant a force is not its intensity, which is, like her picturesquely gesturing hands and "blank sightless face" turned up as the tears flow down it, conventional to representations of blindness in Victorian culture. But when Bertha cries, "Oh father, father! [. . .] Oh my hard, hard fate!" and sinks to the floor before May Fielding, "clasp[ing] her garments in an attitude of mingled supplication and love" and hiding her face in May's dress, this conventional behavior paralyzes the story and most of the other characters when Bertha's friends realize that her agony is not that of an afflicted, childlike blind girl but that of an unrequited lover (201).

When the rupture of Bertha's romantic dreams is compounded by her father's confession that he has deceived her, she unburdens herself again, bitterly reproaching Caleb in a "passion of regret" that leaves him "afflicted": "'Oh why,' cried the Blind Girl, tortured, it seemed, almost beyond endurance, 'why did you ever do this? Why did you ever fill my heart so full, and then come in like Death, and tear away the objects of my love? O Heaven how blind I am! How helpless and alone!'" (222). Bertha's announcement of her blindness at this particular point in the narrative emphasizes the nature of her suffering: she had imagined herself a heroine with the same potential for love and marriage as Dot or May. Now, however, she realizes that her embodiment has arbitrarily precluded those outcomes.

When Dot makes Bertha realize the extent of Caleb's sacrifice for her, a second, appropriate supplication results, this time before Caleb. Holding her father's head to her breast, Bertha cries, "It is my sight restored. It is my sight! [. . .] To think I might have died, and never truly seen the father who has been so loving to me" (223). The narrative specifically tries to solve the problem of her desire by shifting it to the appropriate context of parent and child, and she actually describes the renewed bond as encompassing the return of her lost lover: "Nothing is gone. [. . .] Everything is here—in you. The father that I loved so well; the father that I never loved enough, and never knew; the benefactor whom I first began to reverence and love, because he had such sympathy for me; All are here in you. Nothing is dead to me. [. . .] And I am NOT blind, father, any longer!" (224). This declaration hastily restores the intimacy between her and her father. Their reunion, however, has little of the simple relief of Louise's reunion with her mother at the end of *Les deux orphelines*; Bertha's thwarted desire for Tackleton makes a smooth return to her father's hearth impossible.

When a wild and rollicking wedding dance produces what we would now call a Dickensian close, Bertha's joy is moved to the edge of that noisy room. She plays her liveliest harp tune but does not join in the dance, a throng so democratic that it includes the reformed ogre Tackleton, cranky Mrs. Fielding, and even, according to one set of illustrations, the cat and the dog.

Whereas Louise's happy reunion with her mother is what makes the last scene of *Les deux orphelines* heartwarming, the time of Bertha's significance is past by the close of this melodramatic story. At the same time, the resolution of her part of the plot is an unquiet one. When the narrative threads have finally been sorted out, Bertha lingers on the melancholy outskirts of the world of courtship and marriage. For all that *The Cricket on the Hearth* inscribes visual impairment as a metaphoric condition, the story's benign repression of Bertha's desire, anger, and importance as a character attaches a dangerous emotional excess to the one case of blindness that is physical, not metaphoric.[4]

I now want to explore why Bertha and other disabled characters are cast as emotional centers in courtship plots, and what is the function of ultimately marking that emotion as excessive and casting it out. The concept of a feeling body was central to both Victorian ideologies of disability and Victorian ideologies of womanhood. Medical, educational, and charitable writing positioned disabled people in an emotional economy in which their significance derived from their supposed capacity to express their misery and stimulate the sorrow of those who saw them. Women's identification with feeling received even more extensive treatment in the nineteenth century; a wide range of Victorian writers attributed an essential emotionality to women, a "greater affectionateness" and "greater range and depth of emotional experience" (Lewes 131).

This construction of woman as a deeply feeling body took two forms; either she "transcend[ed] both nature and rationality by means of her spirituality and intuitive powers," becoming a moral guide through her "marvellous faculty of sympathy and intuition," or she was "a prelogical being, existing outside of rationality in a state of nature" (Pykett 164–65). Without a moral framework to control it, the emotionalism of prelogical woman was considered volatile enough to be a moral disability or even deformity.

Victorian melodramas reiterated this construction of women and disabled people as creatures of feeling by casting them as the emotional centers of the plot; they both expressed their feelings and, by displaying their suffering and joy, stimulated the feelings of the other characters and of the audience. In this context, a character both female and disabled could generate a phenomenal emotional charge.

Representations of disability were also shaped by theater censorship. When strict limits were placed on the dialogue in plays performed in unlicensed theaters, characters that could be made to convey ideas through their bodies were particularly expedient.[5]

Partly as a result of this history, literary critics have frequently interpreted visibly disabled characters as vestigial figures from the melodramatic stage, positioning them as ontologically somewhere between scenery and character and useful as expressions of extreme emotion and abstract states. Peter Brooks, for example, writes that their "very physical presence evokes the extremism and hyperbole of ethical conflict and manichaeistic struggle" (57). Tony Tanner, similarly, sets up his reading of the blind beggar with the statement that "a blind person is almost literally a presence and an absence combined" (302).

Further, while representations of women, or of people of a particular social class or ethnicity, are usually historicized in late-twentieth-century criticism in a web of social and political identities and power relationships, disabled characters are most often treated as if they have no historical referents and often used as critical narrative null sets, convenient containers for the essential human emotions required by the nondisabled characters around them.

When these highly charged bodies in the courtship plots of Victorian literature are read as more than engines of pathos, they are still interpreted primarily for what they express about the nondisabled. Helena Michie, for example, has read disabled women characters and women's experiences of disability in Dickens's fiction as a vehicle through which nondisabled women's sexuality can be articulated. She asserts that in *Our Mutual Friend* "by making [the dolls' dressmaker] Jenny [Wren] a child and a cripple, Dickens outlines a safe space for the articulation of female sexuality" (212). Following this model, the exclusion of blind women characters at the end of courtship plots may simply be an example of the sighted woman picking up the burden of feeling after the blind one has carried it to the safe space of married relations. Or, if we look at it in a more sinister light, the blind girl is a whipping girl for expressed female sexuality, and her exclusion is a reminder that the emotionally restrained woman is the one who wins status in Victorian novels (and in the material world outside them).

Either way, disabled women characters may present the engaging possibility of anchoring emotionality to a few distinctive female bodies and thus injecting a form of organization and clarity into the disturbing concept of womanly feeling. Such characters make it possible to locate all a woman's disturbing otherness not only in her body but also in a specific location that can be seen, discussed, medicalized, and sometimes cured, in reasonably polite literature.[6]

I agree that disabled women characters in courtship plots are suggestive figures for all women and their dangerous capacity for feeling. But we need to go beyond that interpretation and assume that the emotional charge the blind woman carries also accrues to herself and alludes to contemporary concerns about the actual blind women who were increasingly visible figures in Victorian culture.

Social and charitable reformers, journalists, and even some blind writers mostly confirm the final message of *The Cricket on the Hearth*: while blind men arouse suspicions of malingering and debauchery, blind women are spiritual, childlike, and in need of fatherly care—but not through marriage, and especially not through marriage to blind men. The Charity Organisation Society Special Committee on the Blind even advocated blind school sanctions against all graduates who intermarried. While blind women certainly did and do marry, the force of these cultural messages was powerful, as exemplified by the situation of Elizabeth Gilbert, one of the earliest activists for the blind. Gilbert accepted as a fact that "she had to renounce [. . .] her [own] ideal of marriage," yet she "warmly approved of marriage for the blind, and was sometimes charged with promoting it injudiciously" (Martin 74, 282).

An examination of several decades of the *Lancet* and a preliminary study of the history of medicine offer more of the context behind the problematization of blind women and marriage. In the extended commentaries on eye ailments that fill the pages of the *Lancet*, a recurrent connection is made between ophthalmias and venereal disease. Ophthalmia neonatorum, or babies' sore eyes, a gonorrheal infection, was by 1875 the cause of 25% of all childhood blindness in England (Farrell 227). Because Victorian scientists' understanding of what bodily conditions could be passed on to others and of how that transmission might occur was still very much in an early stage, however, diseases like ophthalmia generated substantial debate and decades of uncertainty. An anticontagionist or miasmist might argue that the disease was produced by the first contact with harsh light, with cold air, or with some other environmental factor. A contagionist would argue that the cause was contact with "morbid secretions" in the birth canal but might also concede that the environmental factors provided an essential predisposing cause, a necessary catalyst for the disease (Lawrence 628). Because any physical condition had the potential to be perceived as transmissible by contact, by miasmatic air, or by a combination of contact and environment, figures associated with disease were inevitably subject to free-floating suspicion.[7]

The possibility of hereditary transmission only added to the dangerous resonances of blindness in Victorian culture. Midcentury principles of heredity were remarkably fluid. Most physicians and the general public "assumed that heredity was a dynamic process beginning with conception and extending through weaning" (C. Rosenberg, "Bitter Fruit" 191). Not only physical traits like hair color and height but also diseases like syphilis and addictions like alcoholism were considered truly hereditary in the nineteenth century; an ill parent would produce a "vitiated sperm or ovum" and finally offspring with "defective" constitutions, if not the parent's particular illness (Lomax 24). Even the theory of maternal impressions, which posits that a pregnant woman who sees a disabled person will bear a child with that disability, though it may stretch our credibility far beyond its limits, is still referenced by physicians writing in the *Lancet* in the 1820s and by journalists as late as the 1840s.

One woman's blindness, then, was constructed in a web of associations that read blindness backward, as the product of contagious sexuality, and forward, as the harbinger of dysgenic human production. The fabric of uncertainty and anxiety about bodily conditions and their potential to circulate suggests the excitement of representing blind women as desiring and the necessity of thwarting that desire before it resulted in reproduction. Going back to Michie, if disabled women characters promised a safe space for articulating nondisabled women's desire, that safety was provisional only. Because the sexuality—and reproductive potential—of these real women was a source of as much cultural anxiety as that of the fallen woman, disabled women characters had distinct limitations as safe spaces for figuring and exploring the sexuality of nondisabled women. Similarly, while disabled women may serve both as scapegoats whose ritual removal purifies and stabilizes the marriage plot and as emotional prostheses,[8] playing the music for others to dance to, disabled women characters tend to become the narrative focus because of their compelling instability as figures for cultural trauma regarding impairment and the uncertain pathways by which it was produced and reproduced.

To bring a blind woman of reproductive age into a courtship plot, then—to have her fulfill her role of emotional center but fulfill it in terms of heterosexual longing—is neither to raise a random figure of pathos and irony nor to evoke an essential truth about disability. Whatever else stories like *Cricket* may do, they raise the specter of a historically terrifying figure, not an image of a timeless disabled woman barred from marriage through the essence of her impairment.

As much as the twin structure was reiterated and preserved, it is important to note the contexts in which writers moved away from it in significant ways. In Dickens's "Doctor Marigold," for example, the deaf and abused child Sophy Marigold grows up to marry a deaf man she meets in school and to have her own child. In Charlotte Mary Yonge's *The Clever Woman of the Family,* a fascinating novel for its extension of the twin structure to an ensemble piece in which almost everyone in a group of men and women friends has some kind of impairment, the "cripple" Ermine Williams is a model wife and (adoptive) mother. Similarly, in Dinah Craik's *Olive,* the "deformed" Olive not only marries her nondisabled friend's widower but also proves herself superior, as a wife and mother, to her dead friend.[9]

Among the significant qualities of these works is that in none of them is the disabled woman the center of pathos in the overt way that she is in *Cricket* or in *Les deux orphelines.* While her situation and suffering generate sympathy in the plot, someone else in the plot is the center of emotional expression. The marriageable disabled woman in these narratives, while she may evoke the conventional suffering of representations of disability in melodrama and in charity discourse, does not evoke the discourse of woman as emotional and sexual danger. Her marriage derives, in fact, from her ability to display the "passionlessness" that Nancy Cott argues was a strategic emotional mode for Victorian women.

Along the same lines, when disabled women in Victorian narratives marry and become mothers, they almost always build their families through adoption rather than biology. Sophy Marigold is an interesting exception. Her marriage to another deaf person could be read as a comforting assurance to the nondisabled reader that the different would marry the different, and that therefore the problem of surplus women would not be significantly affected by the existence of young women with disabilities. Alternatively, Sophy's marriage might be read as an alarming development, given the strenuous objections of social reformers to intermarriage, based on the assumption that disabled offspring might result and that these children would represent "one more of the minor streams which ultimately swell the great torrent of pauperism"

(Great Britain xii). In either case, the question of whether Sophy's baby will hear or be deaf forms the plot's climax, and its tearful resolution combines the reunion of Sophy with her hearing father and the comforting (in the cultural context of Victorian social reform) news that the child can hear.

None of these wives and mothers is blind, which makes Wilkie Collins's *Poor Miss Finch* (1872) one of the most interesting narratives of physical disability the century produced. While some of Collins's novels use the twin structure, in *Hide and Seek* and *Poor Miss Finch* his only heroines are disabled, and in *Poor Miss Finch* he creates the only novel I have ever encountered in which a blind woman flirts, falls in love, is courted by two men, marries, has biological children, and lives happily ever after in financial and emotional security. The fact that the work has only recently come back into print suggests that Victorians were not the only ones who were uncomfortable with its plot.

NOTES

1. Eugène Cormon and Adolphe Philippe D'Ennery 's *Les deux orphelines* (1874) generated English translations and versions on both sides of the Atlantic. After its stage success, seven silent film adaptations kept the melodrama alive, notably D. W. Griffith's *Orphans of the Storm* (1921), which stars the Gish sisters. Most recently, the play loosely informed Jean Rollins's 1995 film *Les deux orphelines vampires*. See Norden 35–37, 59–65, for a rich discussion of the play's film history from a disability studies perspective.

2. Male versions of this twin trope occur in the courtship plots of *Nicholas Nickleby, The Mill on the Floss,* and Dinah Mariah Mulock Craik's novel *John Halifax, Gentleman.* As well as in stage melodramas like *Les deux orphelines,* twins abound in the sensational works of Charles Dickens, Wilkie Collins, Mary Elizabeth Braddon; in the domestic melodramas of the religious lady novelists Charlotte Mary Yonge and Craik; in the political romances of George Meredith and Anthony Trollope; in the neopsychological novels of George Eliot and Thomas Hardy; and in the late-Victorian Gothic works of Robert Louis Stevenson and Bram Stoker, to name only a few. The twin plot is a favorite device of the television soap opera, itself a descendant of Victorian serial fiction. The use of twin characters to thematize and demarcate human relationships of identity and difference extends, of course, throughout the history of literature.

3. The significant exceptions to this trend continue to emerge with the growth and development of disability studies as a distinct field of critical inquiry. See, for example, Garland-Thomson's *Extraordinary Bodies;* Herndl's *Invalid Women;* Klages's *Woeful Afflictions;* Mitchell and Snyder's *Narrative Prosthesis;* Gitter's essays ("Blind Daughter," "Deaf-Mutes"); and the essays in edited collections by Davis (*Disability Studies Reader*), Deutsch and Nussbaum, and Mitchell and Snyder (*Body*), all of which enact strong examples of literary criticism with a disability studies perspective.

4. See Gitter, "Blind Daughter," for a brilliant discussion of the compulsive referencing of fictions about blindness and recovered sight in Dickens's *Cricket on the*

Hearth. Gitter argues that these references mark, with special sadism, Bertha's blindness as literal and incurable.

5. See Gledhill for a discussion of this history.

6. Garland-Thomson discusses a similar mechanism in nineteenth-century American literature, in which "maternal benefactresses" and their physically disabled recipients are divided into "corporeal and incorporeal figures" ("Benevolent Maternalism" 576). This "splitting" allows the transfer of dangerous cultural material to disabled figures and opens up a "narrative safe space where the maternal benefactress can generate a moral society and a feminine liberal self," concepts Garland-Thomson anchors to evolving nineteenth-century ideologies and debates (577).

7. See Hamlin; Ackerknecht, for discussions of contagionism and anticontagionism.

8. For a discussion of disability as narrative prosthesis, see Mitchell and Snyder, this volume, as well as their book *Narrative Prosthesis.*

9. See LaCom for a disability studies interpretation of this novel.

CHRISTOPHER KRENTZ

Exploring the "Hearing Line": Deafness, Laughter, and Mark Twain

In his autobiography, Mark Twain recalls a childhood friend, Tom Nash, who suddenly became deaf at the age of fifteen. "He couldn't hear himself talk," Twain says. "When he supposed he was talking low and confidentially, you could hear him in Illinois" (37). Twain's whimsical exaggeration turns Nash's loud voice into caricature and illustrates a larger trend in Twain's writing: that of making deafness into a source of laughter.

From Nash's shouting to the duke's pretending to be deaf in *Adventures of Huckleberry Finn* (1885), Twain repeatedly presents comical send-ups of deaf and hearing people interacting with or mimicking each other. Yet this aspect of his oeuvre has received little scholarly attention. While critics have explored his treatment of race, gender, the South, and a host of other topics, they have seemed curiously content to leave his portrayal of deafness alone. This essay argues that, far from being obvious or peripheral, Twain's deaf-related comedy goes to the heart of how he and other nineteenth-century Americans grappled with difference. Eric Lott (*Love* and "Mr. Clemens"), Shelley Fisher Fishkin, and others have recently elucidated Twain's complicated relation to blackface minstrelsy, African American vernacular, and other racial issues. Using their work as a starting point, I investigate Twain's conflicting attitudes toward deafness. Through his deaf-related humor, Twain explores what we, following W. E. B. Du Bois's concept of the color line, might term the hearing line, that invisible boundary that separates deaf and hearing

234

human beings. In the process, he expresses both fear and sympathetic understanding, simultaneously challenging and reinforcing stereotypes about deaf people.

As a concept, the hearing line contains not only striking similarities to Du Bois's color line but also some important differences. While the color line is typically written on the skin, the hearing line is invisible; deaf and hearing people look alike, after all. Deafness becomes apparent only through behavior, when a person does not respond to sound, uses sign language, or perhaps speaks in an unusual manner. Moreover, the hearing line is somewhat more permeable than the color line, since one's hearing status can—and often does—change during one's life. That most deaf people have some residual hearing complicates things further. Like the color line, the hearing line reveals an intricate relation among physical difference, social construction, and identity. If, as Samira Kawash has argued, racial passing plays on the color line, "exposing racial difference as a continually emerging distinction" (63) we can say something similar about the hearing line. By transgressing its boundaries and testing its borders, people name and define auditory status.

When Twain interrogated the hearing line in his writing, he was building on a small but distinct tradition in Western literature of using deafness for comic purposes.[1] He follows this custom of slapstick deaf comedy, but expands on it, making it somewhat more complex. Here, he was no doubt influenced by his own experience with deaf people; he met and associated with the deaf throughout his life. As noted above, a childhood friend became deaf at age fifteen. Moreover, a pilot Twain worked with on a Mississippi steamboat, Brown, was deaf. While Twain lived in Washington, DC, following the Civil War, he likely encountered deaf students from the National Deaf-Mute College. When he moved to Hartford in 1871, he settled not far from the American Asylum for the Deaf, which had several hundred deaf pupils and teachers. He could well have seen them around town.[2] Finally, he met Helen Keller in the mid-1890s and became friends with her.[3] These personal interactions may have enabled him to see through some of the stereotypes that surrounded deaf people and to write about them more realistically.

Yet if these encounters with deafness made Twain more knowledgeable and sympathetic, they may also have made him fearful of becoming deaf himself. As Lennard J. Davis reminds us, people commonly feel apprehension at the prospect of disability (*Enforcing* 12–13). For Twain, one could imagine that the fear of deafness was especially acute, since he had a close brush with becoming deaf as a boy. In his autobiography, he recounts how he and Nash went ice skating on the Mississippi River one night. The ice began to break, Nash fell into the frigid water, and as a result he caught a fever that left him completely deaf. "Within a year or two speech departed, of course," Twain says. "But some years later he was taught to talk, after a fashion—one couldn't always make out what it was he was trying to say" (37). Twain probably realized how easily it could have been he, and not Nash, who plunged through the ice. For the man who achieved so much through speech and sound—by listening to frontier tales, by becoming famous as a public speaker, conversationalist, and writer in the oral vernacular—such a possibility must have been disturbing. Through his portrayals of deafness, Twain implicitly confronts this fear and attempts to convert it into mirth.

Twain's encounters with deaf people may have prompted yet another reaction: fascination and envy. If, in his interactions with Nash and Brown, Twain saw isolated deaf people who were trying—and largely failing—to fit into a hearing world, in Washington and Hartford he found a different sort of deaf person. The schools there helped to produce vibrant communities based not on sound, but on vision: the students, teachers, and staff members at these schools all communicated through sign language. Observers of signing deaf people often noticed what seemed an astonishing thing: far from appearing dejected or pitiable, deaf people who signed frequently radiated happiness. For example, when the American Asylum in Hartford had its first alumni reunion in 1850, one hearing teacher noted, "A more happy assemblage it was never our good fortune to behold. It was most pleasant to see the joy that beamed from all their faces, and gave new vigor and animation to their expressive language of signs" (Barnard 201). Such deaf people did not fit the public's construction of deafness. They did not look like victims of social isolation, and their cheerfulness caught people off guard. As an anonymous author put it in 1835, "There is usually more animation (*eagerness,* perhaps, would better express what is meant) in the countenance of [a deaf person]. There is, too, a hilarity in the smile of the deaf that seems to ask amusement, not sympathy" (Mann 276–77). The unexpected "smile of the deaf" invites levity; it prompts fascination and even a discernible envy among hearing observers. Such deaf people function almost as jesters. To hearing spectators, their apparent happiness must have sometimes seemed so surprising, so different from the presumed calamity of their situation, that it appeared the stuff of comedy.

Although Twain probably observed such groups of signing deaf people and they likely affected his thinking about deafness, he does not represent them directly in his work. His deaf characters are always isolated, trying to fit into a hearing society of speech and sound. The comedy invariably revolves around individuals who attempt to cross the hearing line: he shows deaf people trying to act hearing and hearing people trying to act deaf. They never quite succeed in their attempts at passing. The result is a sometimes hilarious, sometimes pathetic game of identity shifting, where characters struggle to be what they are not and constantly bumble and parody one another and themselves. In the process, Twain explores what it means to be deaf or hearing. He considers all the complex reactions to deafness in nineteenth-century America: as ridiculous, terrifying, touching, fascinating, and amusing. He probes these apparent contradictions, this tension between fear and empathy, and tries to come to terms with the elusive hearing line.

Shouting across the Hearing Line

Twain's representations of deaf people often involve shouting, whether by the deaf themselves or by the hearing people trying to communicate with them. The shouter figure tests and reveals the boundary that separates the deaf and the hearing. Tom Nash is one such screamer. As we have seen, Twain pokes fun at his boyhood friend's loud voice. He draws out the humorous gap between Nash's intention to speak softly and his yelling; part of the joke is that Nash does not realize what he is doing. The episode points to the comedy implicit in a deaf person speaking at all. In talking, Nash is essentially trying to cross the hearing line and to act hearing. He somewhat resembles James Weldon Johnson's ex-colored man, William Faulkner's Joe Christmas, or other examples of racial passing in literature. Just as the ex-colored man and Christmas look white, so Nash appears to be a "normal" hearing person; he can pass as hearing until his shouting voice reveals that he is on the opposing side of the hearing line. His situation is made more complex by the fact that he was once hearing. Becoming deaf at age fifteen, he was what in the nineteenth century would have been called "semi-deaf," the equivalent of what we call late-deafened today. His shouting voice is a testament not just to his current deafness but also to the fact that he once was on the other side of the line.

If Nash has a complex relation to the hearing line, so does Brown, the crusty steamboat pilot in *Life on the Mississippi*. Twain tells us that Brown "was deaf (although he always pretended he wasn't)" (350). However, Brown appears to have a good deal of hearing. He seems to

have no trouble understanding face-to-face conversation; he successfully passes as hearing until a faraway shouter reveals his deafness.
Here, the screamer is Twain's brother Henry, who yells to Brown an order from the captain to stop at a landing. "I very much doubted if he had
heard the order," Twain says. "If I had had two heads, I would have spoken; but as I had only one, it seemed judicious to take care of it; so I kept
still" (350). Sure enough, Brown sails by the landing and later denies
that Henry had said anything. Young Twain stands up for his brother,
and he and Brown wind up fighting as the steamboat plunges ahead
with no one at the wheel. The comedy stems not so much from Brown's
deafness as from his foolish denial of it. The episode has a certain pathos,
for Brown is ashamed of his deafness; he would rather fight than admit
he is deaf. Does he try to pass as hearing to keep his job? We cannot tell,
although prejudice against deaf people was certainly common. At any
rate, Henry's shouting explodes his charade, and the captain, who does
not like Brown, laughingly excuses Twain for his crime of fighting with
a pilot. When Brown demands that either he or Twain go ashore, the
captain tells him to leave the ship. Brown, the belligerent deaf grouch,
is vanquished, and the chapter ends with Twain relishing his own ability to hear. "I listened to George Ealer's flute; or to his reading from his
two bibles, that is to say, Goldsmith and Shakespeare," he says (353).
The account does not express sympathy for Brown. Twain chooses not
to help him when he suspects he has not heard, and gets pleasure out of
casting the surly pilot from his position of power. It is a victory of youth
over age, truth over falsehood, laughter over bitterness, and hearing
over deafness.

In *Huckleberry Finn,* we find a more sympathetic treatment of a deaf
character as Twain takes us into the realm of sentimental literature. The
shouter now is the fugitive slave, Jim. He tells Huck about his daughter,
'Lizabeth, who caught scarlet fever at age four. Soon after she recovers,
he asks her to shut the door. She does not respond and "jis' stood dah,
kiner' smilin' up at me" (136). Jim yells and, when 'Lizabeth still does
not obey, strikes her. Moments later, the wind bangs the door shut and
Jim notices that his daughter does not react to the noise. He says:

> De chile never move'! My breff mos' hop outer me; en I feel so—
> so—I doan' know *how* I feel. I crope out, all a-tremblin', en crope
> aroun' en open de do' easy en slow, en poke my head in behine de
> child, sof' en still, en all uv a sudden, I says *pow!* jus' as loud as I
> could yell. *She never budge!* Oh, Huck, I bust out a-cryin' en grab

her up in my arms, en say, 'Oh, de po' little thing! [. . .] Oh, she
was plumb deef en dumb, Huck, plum deef en dumb—en I'd ben
a-treat'n her so!   (156)

Once again, the shouter reveals deafness. The episode serves further to
humanize Jim for Huck; earlier, Huck is surprised to learn that a
"nigger" like Jim even cares about his family. Moreover, the scene sets
up the duke's acting deaf in the following chapter, as I discuss below.
The episode presents the deaf girl sympathetically and seems more
poignant than comical. 'Lizabeth has more in common with Charles
Dickens's sentimental heroines than with Twain's other deaf characters
(perhaps because she is Twain's only female deaf character). Unlike
Brown, she is a helpless, angelic victim. Her innocent smile contrasts
with Brown's bitterness, much as her passivity differs from his actively
trying to manage his fate. Some aspects of the account seem a bit far-
fetched. She probably would not have lost her ability to speak so soon
after losing her hearing. It is also difficult to believe that she could not
feel the vibrations of the door slamming shut just a few feet away from
her. Such elements reveal the limits of Twain's knowledge and show
how he presents a somewhat narrow account of the deaf experience.
'Lizabeth's muteness and obliviousness add to her vulnerability; they
underscore the helpless deaf girl's dependence on her hearing father.
Most significant, the incident makes Huck and Jim's differences recede
more. Against the startling void of 'Lisabeth's deafness, they are united
as hearing people.

   With these and other shouter episodes, Twain illustrates the immensity of the hearing line.[4] Yet if he humanizes deaf people somewhat, he
also reinforces stereotypes about them. The shouter episodes reveal
Twain's own firm stance on the hearing side of the line. We do not see
any congenitally deaf people—or "deaf-mutes," as they were called—in
these scenes. The deaf person is "semi-deaf": newly deafened, like Jim's
daughter; late-deafened, like Tom Nash; or hard-of-hearing, like Brown.
Such people have a more complex relation to sound and their deafness,
since they often seem stuck between the hearing and deaf worlds,
perched uncomfortably on the hearing line. It would be as if, in treating
the color line, Twain wrote solely about light-skinned African Americans. No deaf characters use sign language (although when Twain's
hearing characters act deaf, they pretend to sign). Speech and sound are
the norm. In this oral world, deaf people are isolated, different. The deaf
person tries but inevitably fails to negotiate the world of sound, and the

gap, while often humorous, frequently buttresses the view of hearing people as superior and the deaf as pitiable, self-deluded, bitter, or just ridiculous.

Perhaps we can best see these audist assumptions by comparing Twain's shouter episodes with written anecdotes by deaf Americans, who also found the hearing line funny. Their journals and newspapers frequently contain humorous observations about deaf-hearing interaction. For example, William B. Swett, a deaf workman, reported the following encounter with a hearing man in the late 1860s:

> My signs and gestures and my little slate, of which I made free use in talking with my companions, soon attracted the attention of the company, to most of whom a deaf-mute was evidently a new thing. One man in particular, an Irishman [. . .] after eyeing me intently for some time, approached me, laid a hand on my shoulder, looked me in the face, and then, making the sign of the cross, he nodded, went back to his seat and resumed his pipe, apparently satisfied that it was all right. I could not help smiling at his behavior. (5)

Here, the tables are reversed. The hearing person's actions are comical and unexpected, while Swett inhabits the role of the amused observer. The man responds to Swett's signs with a sign of his own, but his sign of the cross is rather absurd in its portentousness and pity, as out of place as Nash's yelling voice may have seemed to Twain. The perspective is from the deaf side of the hearing line, where visual communication is the norm. Swett, a deaf man from a deaf family, is secure and comfortable with his deaf identity. He does not try to hide it, like Brown, or to speak, like Nash.

Deaf writers also poke fun at semideaf trickster figures who flirt with both sides of the hearing line, but again the underlying paradigm is different. *The American Annals of the Deaf and Dumb* contains an account of William Chamberlain, a "semi-mute" who tried to pass as hearing to serve in the Civil War. He enlists in the Union army and "was never detected until I attempted to pass the guard line one day, when my inability to hear the sentinel led to the discovery of my deafness" ("A Deaf Soldier" 54). Once again, a shouter reveals a person's deafness. But the comedy here lies not in his detection so much as in his temporary success at duping the hearing. He manages to reenlist and pass an exam by a doctor, "whose questions I readily comprehended from his lips, and who never suspected that I could not hear a sound." He is eventually caught and cast out: "I was very much annoyed, as I really desired to serve my country" (54).[5] The comedy primarily resides in just how close Chamberlain comes to pulling off the act. His temporary passing is empowering, a source of amusement and fascination to his deaf friends. Even his eventual failure is humorous rather than pathetic, since it serves as a reassuring confirmation of his membership in the deaf community. Chamberlain, like most deaf people, faces discrimination by the hearing world. Such stories served to reinforce the group's identity, to pull deaf people together through shared experiences. The power balance—and the humor—has shifted, based solely on the identity of the narrator and the audience. If Twain's shouter episodes ultimately confirm hearing values, Swett's and Chamberlain's narratives reinforce deaf people's identity and their secure place on the deaf side of the line.

Playing "Deef and Dumb"

In *Roughing It* (1871), when Twain breaks the silence and says something to a woman sitting near him, she responds with surprise. "Danged if I didn't begin to think you fellers was deef and dumb," she says (27). Twain was not pretending to be deaf, but sometimes his characters do. Ironically, when his hearing characters try to pass as deaf, they appear more deaf than his deaf characters. They do not speak and sometimes even pretend to use sign language, whereas none of Twain's deaf characters signs. He includes deaf impostors in two of his best works, *The Adventures of Tom Sawyer* (1876) and *Huckleberry Finn*, both of which he wrote while residing primarily in Hartford. In creating such episodes, he may well have been affected by the strong deaf community in that city. Not only did the deaf people there sign with one another, but hearing teachers and friends often signed with them, as well. A hearing person who signs proficiently can look deaf; to an outsider, there is often an implicit comedy in a hearing person using sign and gesture. Such silent communication has been associated with humor at least since Rocius, the great Roman pantomime comedian (Baynton 86).

Acting deaf for personal gain was not uncommon in nineteenth-century America. When Kentucky opened its school for the deaf in 1823, its first teacher proved to be a hearing person who faked deafness; he was fired as incompetent (Gannon, *Deaf Heritage* 2). During the Civil War, some people acted deaf to avoid conscription. In 1862, *The Charleston Mercury* wryly noted that "some of the ablest-bodied men in town [. . .] have suddenly gone deaf" ("Richmond News"). P. T. Barnum once asked an employee to act deaf as a publicity stunt (Benton

119), while panhandlers and confidence men sometimes pretended to be deaf to win the pity—and money—of a gullible public.

People acted deaf for the pleasure of it. While some of the enjoyment often came from fooling others, some came from the pretending to be deaf (so long as it was temporary) itself. In an 1886 novel by Kate Douglas Wiggin, *The Birds' Christmas Carol,* the children "play 'Deaf and Dumb School' all afternoon" (30). To act deaf, to enter a silent world where talking is forbidden and all communication must come visually, through gestures and facial expressions, is an exciting game. We can discern similar pleasure in a blackface minstrel routine, *Not As Deaf As He Seems,* which was performed in San Francisco in 1865. Orpheus, a young man pretending to be deaf, goes to Plato for music lessons.

> *Plato.*   Well, can you sing?
>
> *(Orpheus looking vacantly before him.)*
>
> *Plato. (Impatiently, nearly knocks Orpheus over with a shove.)* I ask you, can you—oh, put up that trumpet ag'in! *(Orpheus takes horn from bag, and applies it to his ear.)* Can you sing?
>
> *Orpheus.*   Yes.
>
> *Plato.*   Ah, that's better. Where's your voice, high or low?
>
> *Orpheus.*   Yes, I've brought my banjo.   (2)

The farcial exchange is more ridiculous than any of Twain's shouter episodes, for both characters are hearing. The audience knows that Orpheus is a fraud, and can laugh at both his burlesque of deaf people and his duping of the hapless music teacher. The sketch blurs the color line (through blackface) and the hearing line (by featuring deaf impostors), yet it remains the product of white hearing fantasies and fears. Performing in blackface and acting deaf parallel each other in many ways. In both, the white hearing performers assume the role of dreaded, fascinating others and simultaneously ridicule and pay tribute to them. If, as Lott has argued, blackface was underwritten by fear and attraction, so was acting deaf. The engagement with the color and hearing lines both reinforced differences and provided the opportunity to erase them. The popularity of the *Not As Deaf As He Seems* skit—it was republished at least once—demonstrates the pleasure many nineteenth-century Americans felt at vicariously transgressing the hearing line.

These lessons must not have been lost on Twain, an admirer of blackface minstrelsy and American burlesque humor. He experiments with a deaf impostor in *Tom Sawyer* and then in *Huckleberry Finn* produces one of the most sophisticated treatments of deaf frauds in American literature. The people who act deaf in Twain's work are villains. Their attempts to cross the hearing line are often quite comical, but such routines also contain an implicit threat: they almost allow unscrupulous characters to take advantage of innocent people. In *Tom Sawyer,* Injun Joe pretends to be an "old deaf and dumb Spaniard" after Tom identifies him as a murderer (140). To appear like an old Spaniard, he dons a clownish outfit, including cape and goggles. To act deaf, he presumably does not talk or respond to sound, although Twain never shows this directly. The disguise allows Injun Joe to elude capture despite a massive search. Apparently no one thinks a deaf person could be of any significance, although the deaf Spaniard shows up in town shortly after Injun Joe disappears.[6] The fugitive uses his deaf role to spy and plot his revenge. We learn his true identity when Huck and Tom overhear him speak:

> "Dangerous!" grunted the "deaf and dumb" Spaniard, to the vast surprise of the boys. "Milksop!"
> The voice made the boys gasp and quake. It was Injun Joe's!
> (140)

Once again, a voice points to which side of the hearing line a person belongs. While Nash's shouting reveals his deafness, here Injun Joe's normal-sounding voice demonstrates he is hearing. This unexpected regularity, for all its humor, is frightening. The boys "gasp and quake," for if Injun Joe detects them, he could well kill them too. Yet the menace is never severe, for in this boy's adventure story we know Tom and Huck will prevail. The comic threat of Injun Joe's charade vanishes when the townspeople discover his corpse.

In *Huckleberry Finn*, Twain provides his longest and most ingenious treatment of the hearing line. Like Injun Joe, the duke acts deaf to try to take advantage of other people. When he and the king learn of Peter Wilks's death, they pretend to be his brothers from England to claim the estate. Since one brother, William, is deaf, the duke becomes a deaf impostor, which he says will be easy since he "had played a deaf and dumb person on the histrionic boards" (160). *Histrionic* is the proper term here, for the duke's rendition of deafness is highly theatrical, a burlesque of the deaf people that Twain may have seen around Hartford. "The duke [. . .] made all sorts of signs with his hands and said 'Goo-goo—goo-goo-goo,' all the time, like a baby that can't talk," Huck tells us (163). The duke's inane goos parody some deaf people's attempts at speech. Huck's colorful similes heighten the comedy; he likens the duke's voice not only to a baby's but also to "a jug that's googling out buttermilk" (187). We see the nonsense of the duke's goos even more clearly when he skips back and forth over the hearing line; he talks normally to the king in private, and at one point he even sends the king a note correcting his speech. It is a brilliant twist, the deaf person correcting the hearing person's speaking ability, and one of several masterful touches in the whole exaggerated episode. In addition to spoofing deaf people's voices, the duke travesties sign language, concocting meaningless signs as he goes along. The king participates in this signplay as well, for he often acts like the duke's interpreter. When they arrive, he makes "a lot of idiotic signs to the duke on his hands" (161). The two frauds treat this mock signing seriously, for it is the key to their performance. At one point, when the king makes his ludicrous signs, the duke watches him "stupid and leather-headed for a while, then all of a sudden he seems to catch his meaning, and jumps for the king, goo-gooing with all his might for joy" (165). The duke's hyperbolic reactions are a caricature of deaf people who communicate effectively through sign; his antics are as grotesque a representation as that of white men in blackface, singing outlandish versions of what they claim are Negro songs.

Perhaps the most striking aspect of the Wilks episode is that no one questions the duke's deafness. While the doctor and townspeople suspect the two are impostors, they never shout at the duke to test his hearing, as happens in so many other Twain scenes. They do not eavesdrop outside the king and duke's room and overhear them talking, as Huck and Jim do with Injun Joe. They do not even think to wonder about the duke's signing ability, although the doctor immediately doubts the king's British accent. These oversights become especially visible when the second set of would-be brothers arrives. The new deaf William has his arm in a sling, which means, his ostensible brother explains, that he "can't even make signs to amount to much, not 't he's only got one hand to work them with" (188). Anyone who has been around signing deaf people knows this statement is ridiculous; deaf people are perfectly capable of holding whole conversations with one hand, whether they are carrying a baby or have a broken arm. If Twain was unaware of this fact, it would be another example of the limitations of his representations of deaf people. Yet the sling could mean that the second Wilks brothers are impostors as well. The king points out that the sling is "very convenient, too, for a fraud that's got to make signs, and hain't learnt how" (188). One might wish that Twain had pushed the sign language aspect further and had the townspeople, in their inquisition in the tavern, test the two deaf Williams' ability to understand signs from their brothers. One somehow wants the duke's charade to be exploded, just as Nash's and Brown's efforts to pass as hearing are inevitably exposed.

While we are at it, we could add the wish that Twain, to complete his exploration of the hearing line, had written about a strong deaf person like Swett: someone who was confident in his position on the deaf side of the hearing line, in his ability to communicate through sign language and writing, and in avoiding the pitfalls of speech. We do get a caricature of someone like Swett in the duke's comical charade, but we never get the real thing. Twain does not satisfy these desires, just as he never quite provides a strong black character who is free of what Ralph Ellison calls the minstrel mask (50). For all the suggestiveness of his deaf episodes, Twain finally keeps his portrayals in the relatively harmless realm of comedy. Just as he had a profoundly ambivalent attitude toward African Americans, so he seems to have been simultaneously convinced of deaf people's humanity and disturbed by their difference. Perhaps we can take this ambivalence as another reminder of how Twain was a product of his times and constrained by contemporary assumptions about deafness.

Although Twain did not push his treatment of the hearing line as far as he might have, he nevertheless produced some of the most illuminating—and humorous—literary treatments of deafness in his day. By including deaf people in his work, he made his writing more democratic; he represented marginalized people in the tradition of Walt Whitman and Herman Melville. His deaf-related comedy helped nineteenth-century Americans to negotiate the arrival of deaf people in society. His humor allowed readers to vent their fears and, at the same time, underscored deaf people's humanity even as it ridiculed the differences brought out by the hearing line. Perhaps most important, by writing about deafness Twain began to make it more familiar to the reading public.

Fittingly, one of his last recorded encounters with deafness was with the first deaf person in his life, Tom Nash. In his autobiography, Twain recounts how he returned to Hannibal fifty-five years after their skating misadventure and met Nash again. One can imagine that it was a powerful moment: Twain, the famous author and speaker, returning in his white suit to his hometown and encountering a boyhood friend whose deafness could easily have been his own. To Twain, Nash may have resembled something of a doppelgänger, a "there but for the grace of God go I" figure. He says he saw his old friend approaching "across a vacant space," which perhaps is a fitting metaphor for the gap that separates deaf and hearing people. He went to meet him, which we might read as an indication of how hearing people need to be flexible and willing to meet deaf people halfway in communicating. Twain concludes, "He came up to me, made a trumpet of his hands at my ear, nodded his head toward the citizens and said confidentially—in a yell like a fog horn—'Same damned fools, Sam'" (37). It is a perfectly told anecdote. Once again, Nash's shouting voice, made more comical by his confidential manner and the foghorn simile, becomes a source of mirth. However, Twain humanizes his friend even as he ridicules him. Nash appears not obtuse but genial and sarcastic, calling the citizens (and perhaps also himself and Twain) "damn fools." The presentation gently mocks and empathizes at the same time, as much of Twain's most effective humor does, inviting readers to laugh and realize anew how full of human foibles we all are. Twain manages to bridge the "vacant space" that separates him and Nash and to bring deaf and hearing people closer together through comedy. In confronting the formidable hearing line that so often separates the deaf and hearing, he seems to say, the best way to try to achieve connection is with empathy and laughter.

NOTES

1. For example, Aristophanes, in his play *Knights*, has one character call another deaf, apparently to emphasize the latter's clownish nature; Chaucer, in *The Canterbury Tales*, makes his exuberant, playful Wife of Bath somewhat deaf; and Shakespeare has one of his most popular comic characters, Falstaff, briefly act deaf in *Henry IV, Part Two*. However, actual deafness has a minor role in these works, and profoundly deaf characters are almost entirely absent in them.

2. Although there is no record of Twain visiting the American Asylum for the Deaf, he knew Edward Miner Gallaudet, the president of the National Deaf-Mute College and a leader in deaf education during the late nineteenth century. When Gallaudet resided in Hartford during the years 1887–89, he lived near Twain, and they sometimes interacted. See Boatner 117–19.

3. Keller includes a loving chapter on Twain in her autobiography *Midstream: My Later Life* (1929). She says that Twain "knew with keen and sure intuition many things about me [. . .] things that others learned slowly or not at all" (48).

4. In essays such as "How the Author was Sold in Newark" (1893) and "A Little Note to M. Paul Bourget" (1897), Twain returns to the slapstick comedy of deafness. In both, the deaf characters are more generalized types than individual people. Although hearing characters shout to the deaf ones, communication fails hilariously, serving to reify the hearing line and to demonstrate anew the gap that separates deaf and hearing people.

5. While Chamberlain was not allowed to serve, several deaf and hard-of-hearing Americans did fight in the Civil War. William Simpson, a hard-of-hearing man from Saint Louis, went to New York, pretended to be hearing, and enlisted there. Another account tells of a deaf Confederate prisoner whose guard was also deaf; they supposedly carried on lively conversations in sign language. Two other deaf men, Hartwell Chamberlayne and William M. Berkeley, served in the Confederate army, which may have been more willing to let deaf men fight because of its pressing need for soldiers. See Gannon, *Deaf Heritage* 10.

6. Although the people in *Tom Sawyer* do not suspect Injun Joe's masquerade, in nineteenth-century America deaf people were sometimes accused of being frauds with evil intentions. When Edmund Booth, a deaf teacher and writer, was traveling in the Midwest in 1839, he was stopped by citizens who thought he resembled a murderer on a handbill. They believed he pretended to be deaf, and only after inspecting his luggage did they let him go (Booth 2). Similarly, during the Civil War, Union soldiers refused to believe that an eighteen-year-old southern boy, Joshua Davis, was deaf, thinking him a spy instead. Finally an officer who knew the manual alphabet finger-spelled to him, "Are you deaf?" Joshua responded in signs, and the officer ordered him to be released (Gannon, *Deaf Heritage* 9).

ROBERT J. SCHOLNICK

"How Dare a Sick Man or an Obedient Man Write Poems?" Whitman and the Dis-ease of the Perfect Body

In 1856 Walt Whitman completed two works intended for publication as separate volumes, the second edition of *Leaves of Grass,* which appeared in September, and a prose jeremiad, *The Eighteenth Presidency!,* which, although it was set in type, never was published (Allen 170–71). Both works voice Whitman's anguish over the prospects for American democracy in that fateful presidential election year, in which the Democratic candidate, James Buchanan, running on a platform of noninterference with slavery, defeated John C. Fremont, a Republican, and the former Whig president, Millard Fillmore, now of the American Party. Whitman feared that, as reflected in the civil warfare of Bleeding Kansas, the American nation had begun the process of destroying itself. Expressing his belief that a healthy body is a metonym for a healthy nation and, the converse, that an enfeebled body reflects a failure within the body politic, he deployed a rhetoric of health, disease, and disability to address the national crisis. Describing the supposedly enfeebled political class as "blind men, deaf men, pimpled men scarred inside with the vile disorder, gaudy outside with gold chains made from the people's money," in *The Eighteenth Presidency!* he summoned what he imagined as a generation of vigorous young men to take charge (1337–38). "Poem of the Road" (later titled "Song of the Open Road") warned that "None may come to the trial till he or she bring courage and health" (Leaves 232).

248

Whitman's urgent summons to his fellow citizens to adopt the practices of healthy living constituted a significant portion of his agenda for America. "All comes by the body—only health puts you rapport with the universe," he wrote in "Poem of Many in One" (later titled "By Blue Ontario's Shore"). "Produce great persons, the rest follows," he affirmed (181). "Poem of the Road" stated flatly, "He travelling with me needs the best blood, thews, endurance" and warned that only the healthy are eligible to join him in the great American procession:

> Come not here if you have already spent the best of yourself!
> Only those may come who come in sweet and determined bodies,
> No diseased person—no rum-drinker or venereal taint is permitted
>   here [. . .].   (232–33)

In promoting physical health as a means of fostering national stability, control, and improvement, Whitman excluded those lacking the best blood. This exclusion raises the question of just how he and his contemporaries understood the etiology of sickness and disability. To what extent are people responsible for their personal health and that of their offspring? What is the connection between Whitman's metaphoric use of the language of health as applied to the nation and his actual treatment of the figure of the disabled?

My purpose is to explore Whitman's complex, sometimes contradictory, and shifting treatments of the concepts of health, disease, and disability. After considering the poet's own and his family's involvement with disease and disability, I analyze his efforts as a journalist to inculcate achieving vigorous physical health and production of offspring as a means of promoting the progress of the American nation. I then examine the role of the compassionate healer that he developed in the 1855 edition of *Leaves of Grass;* much of the power of the volume's lead poem, later "Song of Myself," is due to its joyful enactment of practices of vigorous health, even as it gives voice to "the diseased and despairing" and articulates "the rights of them the others are down upon, / Of the trivial and flat and foolish and despised" (*Poetry* 50). Implicit in Whitman's first volume is the assumption that national progress and acceptance of the disabled are not opposed concepts, that diversity contributes to the national fabric. Next I focus on the 1856 *Leaves of Grass,* for it is there that, in reacting to the threat of national dissolution, the speaker deploys a prescriptive and exclusionary rhetoric of health and disability. I then look at Whitman's role as compassionate healer in the Civil War hospitals, as reflected in the prose collection *Specimen Days* and the *Drum-Taps* poems. At a time when hospitals became a source of meaning for poet and nation, Whitman no longer could state that "only health puts you rapport with the universe." Confrontation with death, illness, and disability forced the poet to face a conflict at the heart of his poetic project: his urgent push for national health and progress collided with his central commitment to democratic inclusion of the disabled. Finally, I consider the continuing tension in Whitman's work between his cult of vigorous personal and national health and his compassionate treatment of the disabled and exploration of the experience of disability.

From Disabled Family to Healthy Nation: The Therapeutics of Poetry

The poet who alternately embraced and rejected the disabled was all too familiar with various forms of disability and illness in his own family. When Whitman was only six, an unnamed younger brother died in infancy, and in 1864 the poet was forced to commit his older brother, Jesse, whom he had helped care for, to the King's County Lunatic Asylum, where Jesse died six years later. Another younger brother, Eddie, in the words of Harold Aspiz, "seems to have been feeble-minded, epileptic, and emotionally disturbed, his crippled left hand and paralyzed left leg indicating that the poet's paralysis, like his dizzy spells and his appearance of being prematurely old, had a complex family history." That paralysis was caused by a stroke in 1873. His brother Andrew died "aged thirty-six, apparently of tuberculosis of the throat" (Aspiz 18). Whitman himself was hardly the exemplum of the "perfect health" that he would claim for himself in "Song of Myself" (*Poetry* 188).

As a journalist in the 1840s Whitman formulated what Aspiz termed a "gospel of physical improvability," which he planned to direct "to the favorite target of his reformistic age, the young men and boys of America" (49). He considered using lectures, magazine articles, and a manual of instructions to promote his evolving gospel of healthy living, which he based on such commonsense measures as plentiful fresh air, exercise, and frequent bathing as well as avoiding overeating, drunkenness, and other abuses of the body, including masturbation. As a newspaper editor, Whitman promoted public health as offering the best chance of realizing improvements in urban living in the face of rising mortality rates from diseases such as cholera. On 12 May 1846, he wrote an editorial in the *Brooklyn Eagle* supporting a bill to construct a state facility for the humane care of the mentally ill and retarded, who were housed in "the wretchedest of our wretched county poor houses" (*Journalism* 360).

Like many Americans in antebellum America, Whitman criticized the dominant modes of contemporary medicine, those practiced by the regular physicians, who still resorted to such heroic treatments as bleeding and the use of strong purgatives and emetics to cure the patient. His 16 April 1846 essay in the *Eagle* entitled "Is Not Medicine Itself a Frequent Cause of Sickness?" charged that

> the violent stimulants and narcotics which are favorites with a majority of the physicians, cannot be used without the most serious and permanent effects on the system. [. . .] How much of the fevers, aches, rheumatisms, chronic and acute complaints [. . .] come to us through the physic vial. [. . .] There is much humbug in the pompous pretensions of the medical art. There are very few real *specifics* for disease in the whole catalogue of the pharmaceupist. Doctors and apothecaries pretend to know altogether too much. It will go down among those who understand very little of physiology and anatomy [. . .] but to all others, much of the loftiest pretensions of either the "regular doctor," or "quack" doctor, is but a matter of sounding brass and a tinkling cymbal.
>
> (*Journalism* 332–32)

In his therapeutic nihilism, Whitman articulated the suspicions of many ordinary Americans and also the judgment of a small group of elite physicians, many of whom were Bostonians who had studied in Paris. Notably, in his 1835 address to the Massachusetts Medical Society, "Self-Limited Diseases," Jacob Bigelow of the Harvard Medical School stated that it was "the unbiased opinion of most medical men of sound judgment and long experience" that "the amount of death and disaster in the world would be less, if all disease were left to itself" (55).

Despite his admiration for certain physicians whom he observed closely in the New York hospitals, Whitman looked elsewhere for healing strategies. Although he refrained from advocating any one of the numerous alternative therapies, including Thomsonianism, homeopathy, and Grahamism, he preferred them to standard practice, as he wrote in the *Brooklyn Eagle* on 1 June 1846: "Their excellence is nearly altogether of a negative kind.—They may not cure, but neither do they kill—which is more than can be said of the old systems. They aid nature in carrying off the disease slowly—and do not grapple with it fiercely, and fight it, to the detriment of the patient's poor frame, which is left, even in victory, prostrate and almost annihilated" (*Journalism* 392–93). Much better, he wrote, would it be to inspire the patient to draw from the healing powers of nature itself, a task that he as poet would take up.

Whitman was writing at a time when, as the medical historian Charles E. Rosenberg observed, disease was understood not as a "discrete entity—or even a well-defined physiological process with a peculiar natural history" but rather as "the sum of one's transactions with the environment—the resultant of a total physiological process. Hereditary constitutional endowment was one given, the peculiar pattern of life through which that original endowment passed, another" (*No Other Gods* 29). As Whitman put it, disease "is the result either of hereditary causes or a long train of circumstances acting, perhaps slowly and silently, long and long before the disease itself breaks out" (*Journalism* 393). There was a perception, as Rosenberg explained, that certain chronic and constitutional categories of illness, including "cancer, gout, mental illness, tuberculosis, and heart disease [. . .] seemed to be inherited in patterns of general, though not inevitable constitutional weakness. They appeared to be progressive, largely idopathic, and related to individual idiosyncrasies of temperament and resistance." What could be done? Even in cases of inherited tendency toward illness, "judicious prophylactic counsel might make the difference between being a merely potential and actual victim" (29, 32). Accordingly, the properly motivated and informed citizen could do much to resist illness and promote health. This effort became especially important in view of the widespread "assumption that acquired characteristics, even patterns of behavior, could be inherited. At the moment of conception the particular biological identities of both parents were resultants of the cumulative interaction of all those habits, accidents, illnesses—and original constitutional endowments—which had intersected since their own conception" (27). Revealing his involvement in phrenology, which, as Rosenberg remarked, was "widely accepted and diffused in ante-bellum American society" (42), Whitman adopted what Aspiz called the "vulgar Lamarckian faith that everyone, from prostitute to poet, may better herself or himself, up to a limit imposed by nature, and that *in time* America will evolve a race of heroes by interbreeding her best specimens and breeding out her unwholesome biological strains" (Aspiz 194). Conversely, abuse of the body could result in serious harm to the individual and to future generations. If, then, health could be achieved by following established practices for healthy living and successful procreation, and the most effective way to combat illness and to improve health came from harnessing the body's innate powers, then the poet might well play an integral role in promoting the health of the body politic.

In "Song of Myself" the Whitman persona, himself a paragon of health, takes up the role of heroic healer, rushing to the bedside where, after telling the "physician and priest [to] go home,"

> I seize the descending man. . . . I raise him with resistless will
> [. . . . .]
>
> I dilate you with tremendous breath. . . . I buoy you up;
> Every room of the house do I fill with an armed force. . . . lovers of
>   me, bafflers of graves:
>
> Sleep! I and they keep guard all night;
> Not doubt, not decease shall dare to lay finger upon you,
> I have embraced you, and henceforth possess you to myself,
> And when you rise in the morning you will find what I tell you is
>   so.
>
> I am he bringing help for the sick as they pant on their backs,
> And for strong upright men I bring yet more needed help.
>
> *(Poetry* 73)

The poet also boasts of creating health in another way: "On women fit for conception I start bigger and nimbler babes, / This day I am jetting the stuff of far more arrogant republics" (73).

The speaker in "Song of Myself" refuses to countenance any divisions in the body politic, affirming, "Whoever degrades another degrades me." He will "accept nothing which all cannot have their counterpart of on the same terms" (50). Everyone, he insists, is welcome to participate:

> I will not have a single person slighted or left away,
> The keptwoman and sponger and thief are hereby invited. . . . the
>   heavy-lipped slave is invited. . . . the venerealee is invited,
> There shall be no difference between them and the rest.   (44)

The "venerealee," who in 1856 will be excluded from the procession on the "Open Road," finds a place among all those whose lives enrich the nation. Through his catalogs, the speaker identifies with "whatever is commonest and cheapest and nearest":

> The farmer stops by the bars of a Sunday and looks at the oats and
>   rye,
> The lunatic is carried at last to the asylum a confirmed case,

> He will never sleep any more as he did in the cot in his mother's
>   bedroom;
> The jour printer with gray head and gaunt jaws works at his case,
> He turns his quid of tobacco, his eyes get blurred with the
>   manuscript;
> The malformed limbs are tied to the anatomist's table,
> What is removed drops horribly in a pail; [. . .]   (39)

In another 1855 poem, "The Sleepers," the healing power of the poet is grounded in his powers of identification with one and all, his willingness to "dream in my dream the dreams of all the other dreamers" (108). Whitman concludes with a vision of healing that comes through the agency of the night and the poet's transforming presence:

> The stammerer, the sick, the perfectformed, the homely,
> The criminal that stood in the box, the judge that sat and sentenced
>   him, the fluent lawyers, the jury, the audience,
> The laugher and weeper, the dancer, the midnight widow, the red
>   squaw,
> The consumptive, the erysipalite, the idiot, he that is wronged,
> The antipodes, and every one between this and them in the dark,
> I swear they are averaged now. . . . one is no better than the other,
> The night and sleep have likened them and restored them.   (114)

Whitman, Phrenology, and the Trial of 1856

Whitman added twenty new poems to the 1856 edition of *Leaves of Grass,* which now contained thirty-two in all. Several of the new poems, including "Sun-Down Poem" (later "Crossing Brooklyn Ferry"), "Poem of the Sayers of the Words of the Earth" (later "Song of the Rolling Earth"), and "Poem of Wonder at the Resurrection of the Wheat" (later "This Compost") do not treat explicit political subjects. Yet most take on the role of inculcating the cult of vigorous health and those other qualities that are necessary if the nation is to survive its time of trial. As Gay Wilson Allen remarked, the 1856 edition combined a "robust-health motif" with an "excessive nationalism." Allen also noted that the volume was Whitman's first "experiment in working out a dramatic-allegorical sequence" (127, 83–84).

The phrenological publishers Fowler and Wells released the book, although the firm's name does not appear on the title page. However, as Aspiz recognized, the firm's phrenological principles and its method of constructing books served as the key structural principle:

Like many of their publications, [the 1856 edition] may be read as a guidebook to the secrets of health, social justice, and spiritual advancement. It resembles one of their octavo handbooks: its table of contents seemingly offers thirty-two prescriptive poems about the attainment of physical, spiritual, and national greatness. [. . .] Its poems *could*, in fact, serve a perceptive reader as a manual of physical-moral self-discovery.   (117)

The Whitman persona now assumed the role of saving the nation. "By great bards only can series of peoples and States be fused into the compact organism of one nation," he wrote in "Poem of Many in One." The poet becomes "the equalizer of his age and land, / He supplies what wants supplying—he checks what wants checking" (Leaves 188–89). Through the poet the many are integrated into one, thereby bringing health to the nation. Above all, what is needed is health, as Whitman stated in a stanza cited above: "All comes by the body—only health puts you rapport with the universe." Then, after asserting, "Produce great persons, the rest follows," the speaker silences the diseased: "How dare a sick man, or an obedient man, write poems? / Which is the theory or book that is not diseased?" (181). If the nation is to "be better than all that has ever been before," it must heed the poet's directives:

Fear grace! Fear delicatesse!
Fear the mellow sweet, the sucking of honey-juice!
Beware the advancing mortal ripening of nature!
Beware what precedes the decay of the ruggedness of states and
          men!   (182)

He raises the stakes by identifying America's global role: "Any period, one nation must lead, / One land must be the promise and reliance of the future" (183).

Reflecting on the responsibility of parents, the speaker as eugenicist connects the health of citizens at the moment of procreation with their success in producing healthy future citizens:

Bravas to states whose semitic impulses send wholesome children
          to the next age!
But damn that which spends itself on flaunters and dallyers, with
          no thought of the stains, pains, dismay, feebleness, it is
          bequeathing!   (188)

Precisely to avoid such "stains" and "feebleness," the persona articulates what he calls the "idea of perfect individuals," with the "bards" walking "in advance, leaders of leaders" (190). Through such works as "Poem of Women" (later "Unfolded out of the Folds"), "Poem of Remembrance for a Girl or a Boy of These States" (later dropped from *Leaves*), and "Poem of Procreation" (later "A Woman Waits for Me"), the speaker, who assures his readers that he has not abused his body, warns of the dire consequences of ignoring the established principles of health and breeding.

In "Poem of Salutation" (later "Salut au Monde"), the poet seeks again to ward off the internal threats to the nation by reminding readers of America's global responsibility as carrier of the democratic vision: "Each of us limitless—each of us with his or her right upon the earth, / Each of us here as divinely as any is here." But after affirming universal divinity, the persona introduces the discourse of racial superiority, which, not surprisingly, includes that of disability.

> You Hottentot with clicking palate!
> You wooly-haired hordes! you white or black owners of slaves!
> You owned persons dropping sweat-drops or blood-drops!
> You felons, deformed persons, idiots!
> You human forms with the fathomless ever-impressive countenances
>   of brutes!
> You poor koboo whom the meanest of the rest look down upon,
>   for all your glimmering language and spirituality!
> You low expiring aborigines of the hills of Utah, Oregon, California!
> You dwarfed Kamskatkan, Greenlander, Lapp!
> You Austral negro, naked, red, sooty, with protrusive lip, grovelling,
>   seeking your food!
> [. . . . .]
>
> I do not refuse you my hand, or prefer others before you,
> I do not say one word against you.   (119–20)

The work reflected widespread contemporary notions of racial hierarchy as well as the myth of an America that is destined to absorb all into itself. From our immediate concern with the cultural position of the disabled, it is significant that the list of inferior races also includes deformed persons, who are linked with criminals and the mentally disabled:

> I see the menials of the earth, laboring,
> I see the prisoners in the prisons,
> I see the defective human bodies of the earth,
> I see the blind, the deaf and dumb, idiots, hunchbacks, lunatics,

I see the pirates, thieves, betrayers, murderers, slave-makers of the
    earth,
I see the helpless infants, and the helpless old men and women.

(116)

From today's perspective, the poem embodies what Lennard Davis, in
Enforcing Normalcy, has called the "loose association between what we
would now call disability and criminal activity, mental incompetence,
sexual license." That association, Davis wrote, "established a legacy that
people with disabilities are still having trouble living down" (37). It is
revealing that the edition of 1856, which most strongly expressed its author's perception of threat to the body politic, also contained poems that
deal most explicitly with the place of the disabled.

In applying what Allen called Whitman's "robust health motif" to
the ills of society, Whitman directly addresses America's youth, as in
"Poem of Remembrances for a Girl or a Boy of These States," where he
urges them to avoid "decay, consumption, rum-drinking, dropsy, fever,
mortal cancer [and] inflammation." Even so, he concludes by reminding readers, "Recall the sages, poets, saviours, inventors, lawgivers, of
the earth, / Recall Christ, brother of rejected persons—brother of slaves,
felons, idiots, and of insane and diseased persons" (Leaves 276–77).

The Wound Dresser: The Terror of Civil War

In *Specimen Days* Whitman reported that, "startled by news" that his
brother George was "seriously wounded" at Fredericksburg in 1862, he
went down "to the field of war in Virginia" (*Poetry* 730). He remained in
Washington, where he worked part-time in the army paymaster's office
and devoted himself to visiting the sick and dying in the vast hospitals.
The poet who had bragged about his own vigorous health and celebrated that of his fellow citizens now had to confront death, dismem-
berment, cruelty, and courage on a scale never before seen. He would in
fact blame his later illnesses on the strain of his nursing rounds during
the war. The poet who in "Song of Myself" was able to "seize the descending man. . . . I raise him with resistless will" (73) came to confess
in "The Wound-Dresser" that "my fingers fail'd me, face droop'd and I
resign'd myself, / To sit by the wounded and soothe them, or silently
watch the dead" (443). In attempting to sum up his Civil War writings
and the nation's war experience, he discovered that only one word
would do:

As I have look'd over the proof-sheets of the preceding pages, I
have once or twice fear'd that my diary would prove, at best, but
a batch of convulsively written reminiscences. Well, be it so.
They are but parts of the actual distraction, heat, smoke and excitement of those times. The war itself, with the temper of society preceding it, can indeed best be described by the very word
convulsiveness.   (799)

So deeply scarred were Union prisoners of war in Confederate prisons
that he wrote, "The dead there are not to be pitied so much as some of
the living that come from there—if they can be call'd living—many of
them are mentally imbecile, and will never recuperate" (789–90). All
that the healer of 1855 could do is "soothe and relieve particular cases,"
he wrote in "Patent-Office Hospital," where he graphically described
"very bad cases, wounds and amputations" (741).

Whitman reported on acts of generous healing, as in the story he
heard from a wounded Pennsylvanian who told him of a middle-aged
southerner who moved among "the dead and wounded" Union soldiers
"for benevolent purposes [. . .] treated our soldier kindly, bound up his
wounds, cheer'd him, gave him a couple of biscuits and a drink of
whiskey and water" (739). Calling his wartime experiences, "with all
their feverish excitements and physical deprivations and lamentable
sights," the "most profound lesson of my life," Whitman sought to create a new national identity, one forged not on the principles of robust
health but in the hospitals: "I can say that in my ministerings I comprehended all, whoever came in my way, northern or southern, and
slighted none. It arous'd and brought out and decided undream'd-of
depths of emotion. It has given me my most fervent views of the true
ensemble and extent of the States" (800).

Whitman blamed the stress and strain of his wartime hospital experiences for the paralytic stroke that he suffered in 1873. In a poem written in its aftermath, "Prayer of Columbus," published in *Harper's
Magazine* in March, 1874, he identified with Columbus at the end of his
life, calling himself "A batter'd, wreck'd old man [. . .] / Sore, stiff with
many toils, sicken'd nigh to death" (540). Even so, he refused to surrender the notion of perfect health. On the contrary, in revising "Song
of Myself" in 1881, he added the following four lines to the second
stanza of the poem's first section, tying his entire poetic achievement to
what he now called "perfect health":

My tongue, every atom of my blood, form'd from this soil, this air,
Born here of parents born here from parents the same, and their
      parents the same,
I, now thirty-seven years old in perfect health begin,
Hoping to cease not till death.   (188)

These lines raise once again the question of the position of the disabled in Whitman's poetry. If, as the persona here implies, the possession of perfect health is a precondition for writing poetry, then all those
whose health is less than perfect are denied a voice. There is also a na-
tivist cast to the assertion that the fact that Whitman was "born here of
parents born here" is responsible for his perfect health. Inescapably, his
use of the notion of perfect health brings with it the establishment of its
opposite, the disabled, as a cultural category.

Yet even as he was unable to surrender physical perfection as an
ideal, Whitman wrote movingly of the disabilities and compensations of
illness and old age in such poems as "You Lingering Sparse Leaves of
Me" (633) and "An Evening Lull" (635). His work is driven by a tension
between the search for physical vigor, for perfect health, and his compassionate embrace of all forms of human limitation. Both as journalist
and as poet, he deployed a discourse of national perfectibility, which
carried with it distinct eugenicist implications about the value of different races and individuals. But he also drew from a discourse of democratic inclusiveness in which all people are valued on their own terms.
The tension between these two languages lies at the heart not only of
Whitman's life work but also of the America whose song Whitman sang.

CAROL POORE

"No Friend of the Third Reich": Disability as the Basis for Antifascist Resistance in Arnold Zweig's *Das Beil von Wandsbek*

In a recent issue of the *Disability Studies Quarterly*, Lennard Davis outlined what he termed the three phases of cultural analysis that usually accompany emergent social movements for liberation, and he referred specifically to the development of disability studies in the humanities ("Enabling").[1] In the first phase, critics expose negative stereotypes and point to the inaccuracies in traditional representations of previously oppressed groups. In the second, they seek to unearth positive or subversive representations of these groups in earlier texts. Accompanying this archival approach, new texts may be created from within the groups in question, texts that hold up more positive or realistic role models. Finally, the third is a "theoretical phase which seeks to recast the whole way the culture has conceived of the emergent category" (249). In the case of disability, this phase means probing into all the ways concepts of normalcy function as a hegemonic force throughout culture.

If we view these phases as overlapping and augmenting one another, this schema provides a useful tool for defining the tasks of disability studies in the humanities and also for understanding the significance of depictions of disability in particular texts. In a discussion at the 1998 meeting of the Society for Disability Studies about images of disability in European art, for example, the historian Paul Longmore noted what he termed the "relentless negativity" of such images. Along these lines, literary scholars are eloquently spelling out the ways in which disabled characters have almost always served as metaphors for some variety of evil or weakness. Such figures have usually been excluded from any normalizing contexts that would allow them to appear simply as ordinary human beings whose existence is not permeated with symbolic meaning (see Garland-Thomson, *Extraordinary Bodies* 10–11; see also Mitchell and Snyder, *Body* 12). On the one hand, from William Shakespeare's *Richard III* to Stanley Kubrick's *Dr. Strangelove,* associations of disability with power have generally conjured up evil, danger, and the uncanny. On the other, disability has also functioned as a ubiquitous metaphor for all types of weakness and impotence, with Charles Dickens's Tiny Tim the quintessential example. Accordingly, one task of the cultural analysis that accompanies today's civil rights movement of people with disabilities is to expose and critique the omnipresent stereotypes and negative metaphors of disability in our cultural heritage. This project is necessary because of the grave consequences these widely accepted negative images had and still have for the lives of people with disabilities.

Another essential focus of disability studies is the search for images of disability that are more positive or realistic and that have been forgotten or suppressed. Such representations would have to show at least some tendency toward lessening the metaphoric significance of disability in favor of portraying disabled characters who are defined not solely by stigmatized bodily difference or whose social exclusion is realistically portrayed, that is, as caused by oppressive environments rather than by inherent individual flaws. Due to the relentlessly negative tradition of discourse about disability, we know as yet of very few such alternative representations of disability from earlier times. Furthermore, because of the long history of neglect, institutionalized control, and violence directed against people with disabilities and because we have often been isolated from one another, it has been perhaps more difficult for us than for some other minority groups to come together in supportive subcultures.[2] We have rarely lived in situations that sustained efforts to create our own images of ourselves—images that would challenge negative stereotypes. However, in the last twenty years or so, the disability rights movement has created environments that enable just such cultural experiments in self-definition. New kinds of images are being created by writers, artists, film directors, dancers, actors, and cultural critics who are conscious of the socially constructed nature of disability (e.g., see

Snyder and Mitchell). And these representations call into question many of the fundamental assumptions about normalcy that seem to be such a natural part of much of our cultural heritage. Therefore, if we think that cultural representations are a significant factor in shaping perceptions of reality, it is central to our liberatory project to find or create images of disability that either show disabled people as ordinary or conceive of disability in entirely new, avant-garde ways.

One of the very few early literary representations that go beyond using disability as a negative metaphor is to be found in a most unexpected place: a German exile novel published in 1943, Arnold Zweig's *Das Beil von Wandsbek* (*The Axe of Wandsbek*). This text furnishes a unique example of what an alternative portrayal of a disabled character could entail at a time when the most intense repression was being directed at groups of people with disabilities—the Nazis' sterilization and "euthanasia" campaigns. What makes this novel even more interesting as a case study in disability imagery is that Zweig, according to his own statements, intended to use his character's disability as a metaphor in a traditional way. But, as it happens so often with truly great writers, the text knew more than the author, and this character turned out to be a genuine utopian figure, more than a mere metaphor.

Arnold Zweig (1887–1968) is one of Germany's best-known twentieth-century novelists of the realist tradition.[3] After the mid-1920s, his increasingly serious vision impairment made it necessary for him to dictate almost all his novels and other works to a secretary. Having become internationally famous for his antiwar novel *Der Streit um den Sergeanten Grischa* (The Case of Sergeant Grischa) in 1927, Zweig was intensely engaged in speaking out against fascism in the last years of the Weimar Republic. Immediately after the Nazis came to power in 1933, he and his family went into exile, settling in Palestine. They remained there until 1948, when Zweig was invited to return to the Soviet Occupation Zone. Until his death twenty years later, he remained an active and much honored writer in the German Democratic Republic, while he was more or less ignored in the former Federal Republic of Germany due to his leftist politics (see Hermand, *Engagement* 173–91).

Das Beil von Wandsbek, first published in 1943 in Hebrew translation and then in 1947 in German, has been called "the most convincing depiction of German fascism in the exile novel" (Hermand, *Arnold Zweig* 96). The setting is Hamburg in the years 1937 and 1938, a time when national socialism appeared to be invincible. Yet Zweig noted that he had found a plot that enabled him to portray the "rising Third Reich as containing its own downfall" (*Beil* 600; all translations from German in this essay are mine). The butcher Albert Teetjen is a small shopkeeper, war veteran, and SS man who is gradually being squeezed out of business by larger grocery stores. When a prison in Hamburg searches for an executioner to decapitate four communists, Albert takes the job because of the pay and because he believes in the Nazis' political mission. For a time afterward, things seem to go well for Albert and his wife, Stine. However, although Albert carried out the execution wearing a mask, rumors surface among his Wandsbek neighbors that he killed the four prisoners with his butcher's ax. For a variety of reasons, they boycott his shop, and in the end he and Stine commit suicide. Zweig interwove a number of subplots into this basic narrative, thereby creating a highly differentiated picture of fascism as it was manifested among all social classes in Hamburg.

In this novel, which probes deeply into psychic entanglements between humane and cruel impulses, the only major character who remains untainted and who points positively toward a better future is the young "cripple" Tom Barfey, the son of a washerwoman. It is Tom who, as a committed antifascist, unleashes the boycott that finally destroys Albert. In an epilogue to the 1951 edition of his novel, Zweig described what he intended with this character: "It was one of the underlying thoughts in my novel that the German resistance to Nazism was crippled like my Tom Barfey, and was just as brave as he was" (*Beil* 598). In other words, Zweig meant this disabled character to serve as a metaphor for the courageous effort to overcome weakness, a stereotypical attribute often employed in well-intentioned depictions of disability. However, closer scrutiny shows that Zweig actually created an unusual and much more interesting portrayal—one so unusual, in fact, that critics have hardly known what to say about Tom Barfey because he confounds their assumptions about disability.[4]

It is possible to ascertain the functions of this disabled character by exploring the nature and significance of Tom's antifascism: specifically, how it is linked to Albert the executioner. Such a focus brings out two main ways in which the portrayal of Tom's disability is central to Zweig's far-reaching critique of national socialism in the novel. These are a depiction of the hostility and cruelty directed against Tom because of his extraordinary body,[5] which Zweig used to expose the violent underpinnings of the Nazis' *Volksgemeinschaft* (national racial community), and an affirmative portrayal of Tom as an ordinary young man who desires to lead an active, full life. This focus offers an alternative not only to Nazi policies, which sought to exclude and eliminate people like Tom, but also to the overbearing cultural tradition of defining people with disabilities solely in terms of their "defects."

Albert's downfall is caused mainly by his desire to belong to what is shown in the novel as the wrong kind of community, the Nazi *Volksgemeinschaft*. As a small shopkeeper, Albert fears he will sink to the level of factory workers dependent on wages, and so he is ready to do anything to maintain his status. At numerous points when things appear to be going well for them, both Albert and Stine remark on how wonderful it is "to belong" (*Beil* 39),[6] to be secure among people just like themselves. Albert feels that he fits in, because he has carried out the execution as the higher-ups wanted and also because his well-functioning body enables him to be accepted into this type of community. As Zweig wrote in a note about his novel in 1955, "Health [was] the precondition for becoming a tool of the ruling class" (604).

When Tom Barfey first appears in the novel, it is in close conjunction with Albert and Stine: they desire to belong to, and Tom is excluded from, the *Volksgemeinschaft*. Tom and his mother live in a dilapidated roof-gable room across from Albert and Stine's apartment in the working-class neighborhood of Wandsbek. When the couple looks up in his direction, they can see him moving around in front of the stars, a small, almost otherworldly figure. Throughout the novel, Albert's relationship to Tom is one of benevolent distance, while Stine's is more complex. The narrator introduces Tom as a boy who came into the world "crippled," with legs that were much too small and weak, and immediately sets up a contrast between how he was treated during the relatively progressive Weimar Republic and after 1933. Having learned to propel himself through the streets on a low, wheeled platform like a small war veteran, he attended school, had enlightened teachers, and delighted his neighborhood when he did well.

After 1933, however, this atmosphere of protectiveness and kindness toward Tom gradually changes as the Nazis begin to proclaim a "cult of youth, beauty, and health" and to inveigh against "coddling the sick and disadvantaged" (48). Soon Tom hardly dares to go out on the street anymore, let alone to school, for fear of being attacked by storm-trooper toughs; he withdraws to the world of the rooftops. The narrator describes what Tom has lost in the Nazis' exclusionary *Volksgemeinschaft*:

> With the disappearance of the Republic and its government, its humanitarian and democratic institutions, he had been robbed of his youth, and indeed, of life itself. He was young; he saw things

clearly; since he couldn't use his legs, he used his mind. Albert
Teetjen was right enough when he suspected that Tom Barfey was
no friend of the Third Reich.   (48)

From the outset, then, Tom is depicted as a young man with much potential whose opportunities have been drastically curtailed by the cruel
propaganda and policies of the Nazis.[7] In contrast to stereotypical portrayals of disability, this novel shows Tom's growing isolation as caused
by an oppressive system rather than by his own supposed physical or
moral "defects."

Tom's antifascism is motivated by his well-founded fear of violent
physical harm and, more generally, by the growing atmosphere of hostility directed against him because of his conspicuously nonconforming
body. In the first scene where Tom appears, the sympathetic physician
Käte Neumeier is explaining to his mother what to do if the authorities
want to "castrate" him—that is, how to prevent him from being steril-
ized under the Nazis' eugenic laws. Her advice is to claim that Tom's
disability resulted from his mother's overwork rather than from a
hereditary defect and that sterilizing him would destroy the genetic heritage of his father, a brave soldier who died in the First World War. The
Nazis' plans to eradicate people like him make Tom into their implaca-
ble enemy. The narrator states: "This explained the deadly hatred with
which Tom followed every move of the new state. [. . .] Anyone associated with this state or anyone who acted enthusiastically on its behalf
was in his eyes damned. On the day of reckoning that person must be
removed" (50).[8] That the topic of eugenic sterilization hardly appears
elsewhere in German exile literature[9] is another clear indication of how
well Zweig understood the extent of fascism's thrust toward homoge-
nization and threat to individually unique modes of being.

Tom has to stop school and is threatened with sterilization, but the
violence directed against him is shown as having a further dimension.
With rare insight, Zweig captured one of the more intense, yet indirect
ways in which exclusion of people with disabilities was and is practiced.
A consciousness of types of vision pervades the novel: appreciative looks
between the handsome husband Albert and the pretty wife Stine; ad-
miring or envious glances directed at the couple by their neighbors and
acquaintances; and a scene where Dr. Neumeier and a friend observe
Albert's execution of the four communists through a telescope, guiltily
feeling that the executed men are looking directly back at them. Tom is
shown as sensing that there is a growing danger behind the way people
look at him on the street. Their staring at his conspicuous body is a first

step toward objectification and indicates the propensity to violence against him that is lurking just below the surface.

Under national socialism, with its insistence on conformity of body and mind, all deviation became increasingly dangerous. Indeed, Nazi ideologues repeatedly conjured up images of disability as one way of attacking their opponents—witness Hitler's fulminations in 1937 against "degenerate" art for its depictions of what he termed "cripples and cretins."[10] This thematic complex is made particularly explicit in a scene in Zweig's novel where Dr. Neumeier offers to take Tom along on a trip to the Hamburg zoo. The prospect overjoys Tom, since he has never been there before: "Earlier he had been too small to propel himself out there, and now he didn't dare to attract people's attention." Tom even feels that he has to exercise caution and avoid his formerly friendly neighbors; he says to his mother and Dr. Neumeier, "I won't put them to the test and lead them into temptation, but I'll deliver them from the evil of my appearance, unless they care to visit me themselves." Having been forced to withdraw into isolation, Tom experiences his excursion to the zoo as a liberation from his "voluntary-involuntary citadel" (166, 168). The gatekeepers put up some argument when they see Tom approaching on his wheeled platform, but Dr. Neumeier persuades them to admit him. They finally agree, because "there weren't so many visitors on this Sunday afternoon, visitors who would have made the appearance of the cripple into a sensation by staring and turning around to gape at him" (169–70). In the novel's depiction of Nazi Germany, Tom is surrounded by people with acceptably functioning bodies whose self-preservation depends increasingly on being able to fit smoothly into the social organism. Therefore, he is constantly being seen as a disturbance in the synchronized visual field of the national racial community.

The ways in which Tom is shown as directly and indirectly excluded from the *Volksgemeinschaft* are obvious motivations for his antifascism. But the antifascist significance of this character also comes out in a more unusual way—paradoxically, because he is depicted as a rather ordinary young man. In spite of Zweig's expressed intention to use his character as a metaphor for the brave will to overcome adversity, such bravery is not the ultimate message of his novel. Surprisingly, the narrative more or less takes for granted that Tom wants to lead an active life through work and to express love and sexuality. Since the Nazis and their sympathizers want to prevent him from doing these things, his very existence appears as a challenge to national socialist perspectives and policies.

Tom's desire to develop himself as much as possible is thwarted when he has to stop going to school. Confined to his room, he earns a little money to help his mother through secretarial work—copying letters, leaflets, and advertisements. While most contemporary readers would have seen this occupation as more than adequate for a disabled person, Zweig shows the job as far below Tom's capabilities. Of more significance for the plot is the portrayal of Tom's political commitment, specifically, his involvement in the neighborhood boycott of Albert. It is Dr. Neumeier who conceives of the boycott plan after she realizes that Albert was the executioner. Wondering how many Germans are ready to carry out unhesitatingly such orders from above, she decides that it is her duty to render this one "willing executioner" (Goldhagen) harmless. Accordingly, she hits on the idea of asking Tom to start spreading the rumor that Albert decapitated the four communists and that he did it with the butcher's ax that he is still using to cut up meat.

Despite his involuntary confinement to his rooftop room, Tom is still entwined in the novel's working-class milieu through his mother and through other visitors. He is not characterized as a communist, but he has read Marx and sees the effects of wage labor on his mother and most of the people around him. Therefore, both his solidarity with the four executed communists and his own oppressive situation make him eager to bring the truth to light by unleashing the boycott against Albert. He tells his mother the rumor and instructs her to gossip about it in the households where she goes to wash clothes. Once the story starts to spread, Albert gradually loses customers. Some boycott him because of their antifascist sympathies; others because of reservations about the hygiene in his shop; and still others, his SS comrades, because he did not share his executioner's pay with them. Albert becomes furious and then desperate, feeling that he, a "real man," is powerless against the "invisible dwarfs" weaving their net around him (359).

Several aspects make this portrayal of a disabled character extremely unusual for its time. First, instead of drawing on stereotypes of passivity, the narrative invests Tom with subjective agency, showing that his political commitment and his embeddedness in the working-class milieu enable him to become the antifascist catalyst for the executioner's downfall. Second, the narrative does not highlight Tom's bravery in taking on an active, oppositional stance. Rather, it strikes the reader as self-evident that Tom acts according to his life experiences and interests. And finally, although of course his options are severely circumscribed due to the oppressiveness of Nazism, he is described as an "opponent to be reckoned with" (544). That is, instead of using the stereotypical technique that associates disability with power to represent evil or danger, this novel portrays a disabled character whose resisting actions in the world are directed toward a positive end—the overthrow of an oppressive system.

A similar approach is at work in the passages where Tom expresses feelings of love and begins to live out his sexuality. In the European cultural heritage people with disabilities have almost always been represented either as sexless (and therefore either angelic or embittered) or as weirdly perverse. Tom is neither. Zweig not only depicted his disabled character as capable of intense desires and emotions but also imagined Tom as inspiring similar feelings in women. Such interpersonal relationships are absolutely ordinary, furnishing as they do the clichéd material for romance novels. However, because Tom is disabled, they take on a utopian quality.

First, as most young working-class men would have done, Tom has trysts with some of the young women in his neighborhood. They seem to enjoy meeting him in his rooftop hideaway, although they are faced with the typical problem of having to avoid his mother (322). The trysts are only diversions, however, compared to Tom's real love, which is for Stine, Albert's wife. Zweig constructed this strand of the plot in such a way that Stine is placed between her husband, whom she cares for deeply, and Tom, to whom she is increasingly drawn as the boycott against Albert progresses. In this sense, the novel is a story of a typical love triangle.

Stine visits Tom and his mother frequently to bring them leftover cuts of meat and to plan her washing day. In the first passage where Tom appears, she asks Albert whether she should put up her hair before going up to the roof, and he replies that no one is going to fall in love with her on the stairs. It does not occur to Albert that someone like Tom could possibly be his rival in love. However, when Stine's head emerges through the roof's trapdoor, Tom takes advantage of the opportunity to kiss her and bury his face in her loose hair. She pushes him away, saying that she could really like him if he weren't so impertinent. The most striking thing about this passage is that Zweig has Stine respond to Tom in a very natural way, neither patronizing nor repulsed; she responds as a married woman might to any other likable but fresh young man. His disability is shown as a fact, but it is not presented as the defining factor that overshadows all his other qualities.

In the context of her unease about the execution and the couple's growing awareness that they are being boycotted by their neighbors, Stine's feelings gradually turn more toward Tom: "Stine did not tell [Albert] that Tom had been becoming more demanding recently, and that she had great difficulty 'putting him in his place,' as people say" (344). After experiencing economic ruin, Stine's ultimate decision to commit suicide is intertwined with her thoughts about Tom and her last visits to him. When Stine goes up to see Tom for the last time, she finally allows herself to think of him as a lover who has displaced Albert: "She realized with pleasure what strong arms he had, and that now she had a lover whose mustache felt very different from Albert's familiar one" (524). Thinking of her impending death, Stine regrets that she will not be alive to see what will become of Tom, musing to herself, "A lad with such a bright mind and with so much love to give—and instead of normal legs, the legs of a child, pitiful sausages. When he got older and had children, would their limbs be straight and would they be all right? The Nazis didn't think so, but what did *they* know!" (506). Stine simply assumes that Tom will find a partner and father children someday and that there is no reason to prevent him from doing this. The reader sees Tom here from Stine's perspective, which is not one of cold curiosity or medicalized brutality but that of a loving woman. Thus Tom appears not as a dehumanized object of Nazi eugenic policies but as a desiring and desirable man. The positive portrayal of his ability to love is a direct challenge to all fascist efforts to exclude and eliminate people like him from the *Volksgemeinschaft.*

How was it possible for Zweig to create such an unusual disabled character, one who is unique in literature from this period? Perhaps his own disability, a serious vision impairment, gave him an understanding of some of the complexities of living as a disabled man in Germany at this time.[11] Another factor can be deduced from the novel itself: the depth of Zweig's approach to realist narrative, which sought to create both psychologically believable characters as well as social types. Zweig did not rely on facile stereotypes—in this instance, outworn metaphoric representations of disability. Rather, even though he knew well the dangers of being an outsider, he also saw that affirming such a position could entail the possibility of representing a more profound liberation. Therefore, Zweig not only explored how an ordinary man like Albert could become an executioner under the extreme, murderous conditions of Nazism.[12] He also created in his Tom Barfey a great utopian image: a character whose antifascism is rooted in his extraordinary body and who is simultaneously, in the best sense of the word, an ordinary man.

NOTES

This article is dedicated to my colleagues in the Department of German at Brown University who hired me as an assistant professor in 1982: Dagmar Barnouw, Bill Crossgrove, Kay Goodman, Fred Love, Albert Schmitt, Duncan Smith, and Robert Warnock—a unique group of genuine intellectuals.

1. The schema Davis develops is loosely based on Frantz Fanon's discussion of the development of a national culture in *The Wretched of the Earth* (1961).

2. Much archival work remains to be done in these areas. For example, institutions and residential schools, though strictly controlled environments, may have provided opportunities for contact among people with disabilities that led to various kinds of resistance and activism.

3. Biographical information on Zweig is taken from Hermand, *Arnold Zweig*. For an analysis of several other portrayals of disability in German literature, see Hamilton. For a discussion of more positive images of disabled women in contemporary literature, see Garland-Thomson, *Extraordinary Bodies* 103–35 (ch. "Disabled Women as Powerful Women in Petry, Morrison, and Lorde").

4. For misunderstandings of Tom Barfey, see Vormweg; Walter.

5. I take the term "extraordinary body" from Garland-Thomson, *Extraordinary Bodies*.

6. There is an English translation of the novel by Eric Sutton, *The Axe of Wandsbek*, but it is full of inaccuracies and omissions.

7. We know very little about how people with different kinds of disabilities experienced daily life during the Third Reich. This is an important field for future research.

8. See Reiter. Reiter's article describes the case of an infant with birth defects similar to Zweig's Tom Barfey who was killed in one of the Nazis' "euthanasia" centers in Lüneburg. See also Ebbinghaus et al.; Projektgruppe.

9. The only other German exile novel I know which takes up the theme of involuntary eugenic sterilization is Maria Leitner's *Elisabeth, ein Hitlermädchen* (1937), which was reissued in 1985 by the Aufbau-Verlag in Berlin.

10. See the facsimile of the *Entartete Kunst* exhibition brochure in Barron 16.

11. Birgit Lönne explains that Zweig planned to write a novel entitled *Die Hemmung* (The Inhibition/Hindrance) that he said would "tell the story of my eyes" (642).

12. Christopher Browning draws on archival sources to trace the steps by which a group of ordinary men from Hamburg became mass murderers.

SANDER L. GILMAN

The Fat Detective:
Obesity and Disability

The definition of a disability seems to be rather clear. The World Health Organization, in its 1980 *International Classification of Impairments, Disabilities, and Handicaps*, distinguishes among impairment, disability, and handicap. Impairment is an abnormality of structure or function at the organ level, while disability is the functional consequence of such impairment. A handicap is the social consequences of an impairment and its resultant disability. Thus cognitive or hearing impairments may lead to communication problems, which in turn result in isolation or dependency. Such a functional approach (and this approach is echoed in American common and legal usage) seems to be beyond any ideological bias.

When, however, we substitute "obesity" for "cognitive impairment," there is suddenly an evident and real set of implied ethical questions in thinking about disability. What is obesity? While there is a set of contemporary medical definitions of obesity, it is also clear that the notion of who is obese changes from culture to culture over time. Is obesity the end product of an impairment, or is it the impairment itself? If obesity must begin with an impairment, what organ is impaired? Is it the whole body? Is it the digestive system? the circulatory system? Or is it that most stigmatizing of illnesses, mental illness? Is obesity the result of an addictive personality (where food is the addiction)? Is addiction a sign of a lack of will? Or is addiction a genetically preprogrammed error in the human body, which expresses itself in psychological desire for food or the mere

271

inability to know when one is no longer hungry? Is the impairment of obesity like lung cancer in that it is the result of the voluntary consumption of a dangerous substance? Is food addictive like nicotine, or is it merely an interchangeable sign in society for those things we all desire but most of us can limit? Surely it is not possible to go without food as one could go without cigarettes. Is the obese person mentally or physically disabled? Can you be both obese and mentally stable? Is the social consequence of obesity isolation or a central place in the society? Are you in the end treated like a social pariah or Santa Claus?

The study of obesity in its cultural and social contexts provides a wide range of interlocking questions about the cultural construction of disability. The role that gender plays is one further variable in the study of the cultural representation of the obese body. Recently, Steven Shapin wrote a striking essay on the eating habits of skinny philosopher-scientists. His argument is that, at least in the West, there is a powerful myth about the need for such men to have a lean and hungry look. That his examples are all men is not incidental. Our collective fantasy of the appropriate body of the male thinker stands at the center of Shapin's work. In this essay I ask the corollary question, What happens to the image of the thinking male when that male body is fat, even obese? Shapin's point, of course, is that Sir Isaac Newton, that proverbial thinker who is reputed to have forgotten whether he ate his chicken or not, actually died hugely bloated. There is a great disparity between the way we imagine that bodies should look and function and our mythmaking about them. In complicated ways, as Irving Kenneth Zola has indicated, detective fiction is a complex mirror of late-nineteenth- and early-twentieth-century popular culture (see "Portrayal" and "Any Distinguishing Features?"; Harrowitz). And the fat detective is the antithesis of the lean philosopher.

The fat detective reflects in complex ways how general as well as medical culture shifted its image of the thinking body in the late nineteenth and early twentieth century. What is there about the representation of a fat, thinking body that makes a fat detective a different category than a thin philosopher? This tale is rooted in a certain notion of the body and its relation to thought. The image of the fat detective can be found well before the nineteenth century and continues today—for example, as many of us have seen, in the overweight title character in the recent BBC detective series *Cracker*, Dr. Eddie "Cracker" Fitzgerald (played by Robbie Coltrane). Dr. Fitzgerald is an out-of-work forensic psychologist who occasionally helps the Manchester police crack hard-to-solve cases by interrogating (or "cracking") suspects and witnesses.

But the central quality of this character is his nervousness, his sense of himself as a misfit, his marginal status as a professional. His oversized body seems to symbolize this sense of emotional fragility. But it also determines his mode of inquiry. His approach is empathetic rather than analytic; he feels with and for the victims, and even with the criminals, instead of being a pure intellect uncovering the crime. One can note, however, that when ABC unsuccessfully remade *Cracker* for American television and moved its setting to diet-conscious Los Angeles, the svelte Robert Pastorelli was called in to play the protagonist, now called Gerry Fitzgerald. The character was the same; only the body was different. The viewers' response was equally different.

The fat detective's body is a different sort of male body from that of the skinny philosopher. Huge, ungainly, sedentary, it houses the brain of a different sort of detective from the strong hard-boiled or the thin ratiocinating one. It is a body out of all moderation. It is not a modern body, if by modern we imagine the body as trained, lithesome, strong, active, and thus supremely masculine. Such an obese body seems more feminine but certainly not female; it is expressive of the nature of the way that the detective seems to think. His thought processes strike us as intuitive and emotional rather than analytic and objective—in other words, feminine. The ratiocinating detective, such as Edgar Allan Poe's C. Auguste Dupin, thinks with his brain. The hard-boiled detective, such as Dashiell Hammett's Sam Spade (at least in Humphrey Bogart's rail-thin depiction), thinks with his fists. Our fat detective seems to think with his gut. For it is the visible body fat that marks his body. He is no Sherlock Holmes, whose "kingdom is his study and his weapons are intellectual—logic, memory, concentration. He traps criminals in the corridors of his own mind rather than in a back alley at midnight. He is a cultivated gentleman, whose recreation is the library" (D. Anderson 113). The fat detective is a countertype to this intellectual detective. He thinks but is primarily intuitive and empathetic; he needs his fat as a shield from the world. His physical immoderation becomes a means of showing both his vulnerability and his strength. He is sedentary rather than active; his intellectual gifts feed his intuition.

Of all the central figures in the shaping of our collective fantasy about what the detective's body looks like, the most important is Holmes (Rauber). Created in 1887 by Arthur Conan Doyle, whip-thin, addicted to cocaine rather than food, always ready to head off on a chase at the drop of a clue, he remains the exemplary rational detective (Smead). His regular feats of observation stun his rather dull-witted companion Dr. John Watson, but they all rely on the ability to link facts causally, following the model of analytic thinking Doyle learned in medical school from Dr. Joseph Bell (R. Thomas). Again it is the scientist, but here the scientist as activist, who makes the perfect intellectual detective. He often sinks into a stupor, aided by his tobacco and cocaine. But this detective also goes out into the world gathering facts. Holmes roams the length of Europe—all the way to Tibet—for knowledge. His is the explorer's body, Sir Henry Morton Stanley's body, as well as that of the detective.

But there is another Holmes in these tales. Holmes's older and wiser brother, Mycroft, who is introduced in 1892 in the *Strand Magazine*'s publication of "The Case of the Greek Interpreter" (Sobottke; Pasley; Beaman; Propp). He is huge and sedentary. "Mycroft Holmes was a much larger and stouter man than Sherlock. His body was absolutely corpulent, but his face, though massive, had preserved something of the sharpness of expression which was so remarkable in that of his brother" (Doyle 294). Mycroft's intelligence glimmering in his eyes (the mirrors of the soul) seems overburdened by his primitive body. There is something quite archaic about it; he has "a broad fat hand, like the flipper of a seal" (295). He is not quite a sloth but close enough.

Mycroft is the better brother, as his younger sibling grudgingly admits. Holmes states that "he was my superior in observation and deduction. If the art of the detective began and ended in the reasoning from an arm-chair, my brother would be the greatest criminal agent that ever lived" (293). What makes Holmes better is that he is willing to use his powers in the world. Mycroft in the end is merely an amateur sleuth, not a really consulting detective. The amateur nature of his undertaking is seemingly tied to his lack of desire to pursue truth to its bitter end: "What is to me a means of livelihood [says Holmes] is to him the merest hobby of a dilettante" (294). Here the quality of the amateur is central. Such a detective is not professional, one whose world is the world of action, but an amateur whose interest includes other models of the world besides that of rational detection. Mycroft is the model that eventually evolves into the string of fat detectives that culminates in *Cracker*. Fat detectives of the 1890s and the turn of the century are imagined as thinking differently. They are related to Sherlock Holmes, but they appear to think, instead, through their bodies. This impression is deceptive: their bodies provide an image of obesity that masks their sharp powers of observation and deduction.

The primitive body that thinks in an intuitive way becomes one of the models for the detective in the course of the twentieth century.

Other versions of the fat sleuth followed Mycroft. In 1911 G. K. Chesterton began the publication of his Father Brown tales.[1] The personality and the body of the fat amateur detective are again linked. The priest's body is represented as chubby; his response to the murders he investigates is intuitive rather than rational. Chesterton saw the Father Brown stories as a means of furthering his Anglo-Catholicism, which was seen in England, even after Cardinal Newman, as a form of the irrational. The squat body of Father Brown represents the innate seeking for truth beyond logic. He is the embodiment of the idea of thought and faith being aspects of one truth. It is a truth to be found by those who are able to see it, not necessarily by those ordained by the state to seek it.

By 1934 and the publication of Rex Stout's first Nero Wolfe mystery, the tradition of the fat detective as a countertype had been well established (Isaac; see also Gerhardt). In 1929 there was Duddington Pell Chalmers, the obese detective hero of John T. McIntyre's *The Museum Murder*, as well as Gerald Verner's Superintendent Budd, "the stout detective, who is fat, lazy, graceful on his feet," "prone to shut his eyes while thinking," and "not susceptible to feminine beauty" (McAleer 552). Like Father Brown, celibate by definition, Nero Wolfe has a body that is not sexualized—any more than is that of Mycroft Holmes. Yet this feminizing quality of the male body masks a life of passion. In the course of the Nero Wolfe mysteries we learn of his earlier romantic attachments, which all took place before the detective's present bulk both inhibited and freed him from the power of physical passion.

In Rex Stout's first novel, *Fer-de-Lance* (1934), the hard-boiled associate of Wolfe, Archie Goodwin, notes the almost primordial in the shape of Wolfe's body, like the early twentieth-century fantasies of Neolithic man: "Wolfe lifted his head. I mention that, because his head was so big that lifting it struck you as being quite a job. It was probably really bigger than it looked, for the rest of him was so huge that any head on top of it but his own would have escaped your notice entirely" (2). Wolfe's body is not only fat, it is huge and primordial in its form.

Wolfe's fat is the fat that protects:

> I said to him something I had said before more than once, that beer slowed up a man's head and with him running like a brook, six quarts a day, I never would understand how he could make his brain work so fast and deep that no other men in the country could touch him. He replied, also as he had before, that it wasn't his brain that worked, it was his lower nerve centers [. . .].   (2)

Wolfe, unlike Archie, thinks with his guts: "I am too sensitive to strangers, that is why I keep these layers over my nerves" (164). His fat isolates his nerves: "I carry this fat to insulate my feelings. They got too strong for me once or twice and I had that idea. If I had stayed lean and kept moving around I would have been dead long ago" (*Dead Body* 119). One of the best commentators on the Wolfe novels observed:

> Upholders of order are our romantic heroes, and Wolfe qualifies under that category. His daily schedule is as much an insistence on order as a tribute to it: similarly, Wolfe's fat, his gruffness, and his seclusion betray his struggle to insulate himself from emotions, to harness them, to grant them a place, but a smaller one than they claim. Reason then is a goal; it is also a process, a struggle. The Wolfe novels value it as both.   (D. Anderson 23)

The primordial body struggles with its basic emotional nature. Fat is the weapon that enables Wolfe to succeed as a detective.

But one must note that for Wolfe thinking is an act done with the body:

> Wolfe looked up again, and his big thick lips pushed out a little, tight together, just a small movement, and back again, and then out and back again. How I loved to watch him doing that! That was about the only time I ever got excited, when Wolfe's lips were moving like that. [. . .] I knew what was going on, something was happening so fast inside of him and so much ground was being covered.   (*Fer-de-Lance* 4–5)

The pursed lips are the organ of eating but also the organ of thought. Here the parallel to the rest of the lineage of fat detectives is clear. The body has its own life and its own rules. It complements or contradicts the rational mind and provides the means by which fat detectives set themselves off from all other scientific observers.

The popularity of Nero Wolfe began a rather long series of spin-offs of fat detectives in the mass media, beginning with Dashiell Hammett's Brad Runyon from 1946 to 1950 on ABC radio. The announcer opened the show with the following observation: "He's walking into that drug-store . . . he's stepping onto the scales . . . (SNICK! CLICK!) Weight: 237 pounds . . . Fortune: Danger! Whoooo is it? The . . . Fat Man!" (*Brad Runyon*). The oversized actor J. Scott Smart, who actually outweighed his character by over thirty pounds, played him on radio. World-weary, Runyon was a cross between Wolfe and Sam Spade. The first episode was *The Black Angel,* broadcast 26 November 1946. The body of the fat detective on the radio could be evoked only by the image in the listener's mind. As such the Fat Man's bulk became part of the fantasy of the obese body as heard rather than seen. Rex Stout's Nero Wolfe himself joined the invisible world of the fat detective on the radio. In 1982, the Canadian Broadcasting Corporation tried its hand at bringing back old-time radio with thirteen one-hour episodes of Nero Wolfe, all based on novellas or short stories written by Stout. The svelte Mavor Moore played the bulky Nero Wolfe, but all the listener heard was the voice of the fat detective.

A more visible world of the fat detective played itself out on television. In 1981, NBC had a TV series based on novellas and short stories by Rex Stout, which starred William Conrad as Nero Wolfe. Conrad, whose voice was well-known from his role as the lanky sheriff on radio's version of *Gunsmoke*, had gone on to play Frank Cannon, a tough, expensive, overweight private detective, a sort of hybrid between Sam Spade and Nero Wolfe (Gunning). Directed by George McCowan, the Cannon series began a highly successful run in 1971, which concluded only in 1976. The key to Cannon's character lies in the fact that his wife and infant son died in an automobile accident; after that he placed all his energy and considerable weight into his new profession of private detective. In 1987 Conrad continued a version of the Nero Wolfe character in *Jake and the Fatman*, produced by Ron Satlof and Fred McKnight, in which his role as J. L. "Fatman" McCabe was much more sedentary. He was transformed into a slovenly former Hawai'ian cop turned Honolulu district attorney. From Fatman to Cracker, the space of the fat detective is again filled with the emotional, elemental, intuitive, empathetic.

Certainly the key figure in today's representation of the fat detective is to be found on ABC-TV's *NYPD Blue*. He is Detective Andy Sipowicz, played by Dennis Franz. Since premiering in 1993, the show has come to center itself about this character. The cocreators Steven Bochco and David Milch, along with the executive producers Mark Tinker and Michael Robin, continued Franz's character from one who had appeared in Bochco and Milch's earlier success, *Hill Street Blues*. Franz had played Lieutenant Norman Buntz from 1985 to 1987. But Buntz was merely a tough cop. The darkness and complexity of Sipowicz are clearly related to his sense of self as a detective. He is a recovered alcoholic, the father of a son he neglected (and who is killed in the course of the show), a man of open emotions and clear prejudices. He is a muscular man gone to fat. It is because of rather than despite these flaws that he is able to empathize with his colleagues and generally have insight into his own character. The flaws make him into a better detective. Franz had played in two short-lived detective series (*Beverly Hills Buntz* [1987] and *NYPD Mounted* [1991]) in which the complexity of the fat character was lacking. It was in *NYPD Blue* that he was able to develop his role as a detective, using his fat body as an image for his flawed character. Bochco and Milch used this quite self-consciously in the series. The body size of the character was literally exposed in a nude scene, one of the first on commercial television, in which Franz was photographed from the rear. His body became the icon for the figure of the fat detective. His mode of approach is that of the hard-boiled detective, the muscular detective gone to seed, but his fat body is also seen as an external sign of an empathetic nature.

The image of the giant, hulking, primitive body, which responds to stimuli seemingly intuitively, in a way more basic than rational thought, remains a powerful cultural commonplace. The fat leads us to assume a primitive state. In a cartoon drawn by Scott Adams, the creator of *Dilbert,* a baby dinosaur comments to Dogbert, "My dad says that good is what you know in your heart. He says evil is a bad gut feeling." Dogbert replies, "Well, of course, your dad's brain is so tiny that his other organs have to pitch in like that." The baby dinosaur replies, "Maybe I shouldn't learn about life from a guy who counts with his toes." And Dogbert concludes, "And thinks with his guts" (82). With their guts is the way that fat detectives seem to think—but, of course, we know better.

Michel Foucault, in *The Uses of Pleasure,* wrote that there has always been a contrast between pleasure and the rational in the West:

> The relationship of the logos to the practice of pleasures was described by Greek philosophy of the fourth century. [. . .] Moderation implied that the logos be placed in a position of supremacy in the human being and that it be able to subdue the desires and regulate behavior. Whereas in the immoderate individual, the force that desires usurps the highest place and rules tyrannically, in the individual who is *sophron*, it is reason that commands and prescribes.   (86–87)

What happens when desire becomes a means of thinking, an alternative mode of intelligence? The immoderate, according to the Greeks, could never rationally think. Our fat detectives seem to do well in this department, for their job, always well done, is to solve the case. And that they do with elegance and grace—not despite but because of their bulk. Their bodies, however, also represent their mental state. Their masculinity seems both compromised and expanded by their bulk. Are they the ultimate new man in their sensitivity and their seemingly intuitive intelligence? For the fat detective, the question is not whether he is physically or emotionally impaired or whether he has a social handicap because of this impairment. The functional consequences of his impairment, his obesity, is clearly not a disability but an advantage. Being fat is what frames his ability to function as a thinking machine. The texts of fat detectives provide complexities for any study of disability and its social reading in modern culture.

NOTES

This essay is dedicated to my friend and colleague Laura Otis.
  1. On Father Brown and Sherlock Holmes, see Edwards; Raubicheck.

Enabling Pedagogy

JIM SWAN

Disabilities, Bodies, Voices

I speak as a crippled woman. At the same time, in the utterance
I redeem both "cripple" and "woman" from the shameful
silences by which I have often felt surrounded, contained, set
apart; I give myself permission to live openly among others, to
reach out to them, stroke them with fingers and sighs. No body,
no voice; no voice, no body. That's what I know in my bones.
                                            —Nancy Mairs, "Carnal Acts"

I f we ask what's new about the new field of disability
studies, there's a clear answer: it is people with disabilities making themselves heard politically, socially, culturally. They were
heard in 1988, when students, faculty, and alumni at Gallaudet
University went on strike rather than accept, once again, the appointment
of a hearing president for the only Deaf liberal arts campus in the United
States (Gannon, *Week*). They are heard every day in the language and enforcement of the Americans with Disabilities Act, from the local street corner, where a bus accommodates (or fails to accommodate) a wheelchair
passenger, to the United States Supreme Court and its recent ruling that a
woman infected with HIV has the protection of the ADA and must prevail
in court against the dentist who refuses to treat her (*Bragdon v. Abbott*).
They are heard, too, in autobiography, criticism, poetry, fiction, and drama
in a wave of new publications (e.g., Davis, *Enforcing*; Finger, *Bone Truth*;

Garland-Thomson, *Extraordinary Bodies*; Fries, *Staring*; Linton; Mairs, *Waist-High*; Mitchell and Snyder, *Body*; B. Shaw).

But how is this new? How is it any different from the emergence of African American or Irish or Jewish writers, or Chicana or Asian American filmmakers? How does it stand apart from other instances of historically silenced groups making themselves heard? The answer, I think, is the particular viewpoint that disability studies brings to an understanding of the body—an understanding that writing is not only *about* the body but *of* and *from* the body too. As Nancy Mairs puts it—in words that should be stitched permanently into the memory of every writer, disabled or not: "No body, no voice; no voice, no body" ("Carnal Acts" 61).

The voice of the writer is, first and foremost, an embodied voice—embodied even beyond Larry Eigner's canny definition of the self as "some head you can't go around" (129), to include the whole body, head and all.[1] But also, conversely, the body must be a voiced body, for the unvoiced body—unacknowledged, disowned, hidden by "shameful silences" (Mairs, "Carnal Acts" 61)—is a body lost to the self and to the self that writes. This connection of voice and body has a lot to do with what Simi Linton calls the borders of disability studies, the policing of what kind of writing counts as disability studies and what kind counts as not disability studies (133). In question for Linton is the embodied perspective of people with disabilities and its role in literary theory and research:

> Yet to be fully explored [. . .] is the kinesthetic, proprioceptive, sensory, and cognitive experiences of people with an array of disabilities. For instance, because I use a wheelchair, I utilize my upper body for mobility and rock back and forth as I propel myself forward. My height when I am vertical differs from my measured height horizontally, and my impairment influences my height relative to objects in the world and to other people. [. . .] Given that my experience or the experience of someone who is blind or deaf, or of someone who has mental retardation has been underrepresented across the disciplines, we are missing the constructs and theoretical material needed to articulate the ways impairment shapes disabled people's version of the world.   (140)

The embodied perspective of disabled persons that Linton calls for is the necessary ground for realizing the agency of the disabled subject, and it must be a fundamental part of any curriculum in disability studies. Otherwise, the pervasive cultural studies model, with its strong Foucauldian commitment, its tendency to view the body as no more than the site of contested cultural discourses, renders the question of the disabled subject unapproachable. For there is a contradiction, often overlooked, in the concept of discourse, a contradiction observable across disciplines, in linguistics and literary-cultural studies. To oversimplify: discourse in cultural studies is synonymous with ideology and the Saussurean linguistic system (langue); while, in linguistics, discourse is language in use (Saussure's parole), the domain of situated utterances and speech acts by speakers continuously and actively negotiating meanings in context and among themselves. Consequently, the notion of a subject of discourse can have two contradictory meanings. It is either one who is *subject to* the hegemony of a cultural ideology that is internalized and therefore inaccessible and nonnegotiable; or it is one who acts as agent and *subject of* cultural meanings that are understood to be contingent, negotiable, and revisable.

This contradiction in the concept of discourse is a problem already recognized in cultural studies itself (see, e.g., Montgomery and Allan), but it needs to be considered specifically in the context of disability studies. A good example is the introduction by Lennard Davis to the recent anthology he edited, *The Disability Studies Reader* (1997). Davis makes a case for disability studies as a new discipline "that places disability in a political, social, cultural, context, that theorizes and historicizes deafness or blindness or disability in similarly complex ways to the way race, class, and gender have been theorized" (3). That is, he seeks to theorize disability studies on the model of cultural studies. In doing so, he wishes to exclude the kind of disability writing that appears to be addressed to people without disabilities in order to inform or "sensitize" them about what it is like to be disabled (5). Such an exclusion—or policing of the borders—is understandable: the writing in question seems to assume that the nondisabled represent a standard of judgment to which the disabled must appeal for approval, a notion that is entirely unacceptable. However, excluding this kind of writing runs the risk of excluding the writing that Linton calls for, the writing of the embodied subject.

Thus a basic issue for disability studies is the question of categories: not just what counts as disability studies but what counts as disability itself. Even the terms I have been using bear out this issue. For instance, pairing *disabled* and *nondisabled* avoids the troubling implications of *disabled* and *normal* (see Davis, *Enforcing*), but it still projects an all-or-nothing, binary division between disability and its opposite, while in fact the relation that people actually experience is a continuum and a mixture of impairments and abilities, which is probably why we have so much trouble naming the opposite of *disabled.* Nondisabled? Temporarily enabled? Normate? (But *ableist* by analogy to *sexist* and *racist* seems apt.) Even the widely accepted phrase "persons with disabilities" still invokes a set of binary opposites.

One benefit of the kind of writing that Linton calls for is that the accumulated stories of embodied subjects and voiced bodies cannot fail to problematize such categories and motivate a search for better ways to conceptualize disability. In pursuing this question, I have found that, side by side with cultural difference, the study of cognitive difference has great potential for opening up new ways of thinking about culture, language, and the body. Much of my own work has been focused on blind and deaf-blind writing and what it tells us about different ways of conceptualizing experience ("Touching Words"). Blindness, in particular, raises fundamental questions about the ordinary experience of the visual and its importance for a theory of disability and for the curriculum coming out of that theory.

The importance of the visual is readily apparent in the way that information today is pervasively channeled into visual media and displayed on the surfaces of printed pages, television screens, and computer monitors (to say nothing of billboards, the sides of blimps and buildings, the rumps of designer jeans). In such an environment, the body is easily absorbed into the category of visual information, where it can be conceptualized as a site of convergence for competing social discourses—such as fashion, gender, class, and race, as well as disability. What is easily lost in this way of thinking is the nonverbal action of the body and its capacity to slip past the categories and codes of social discourse or to infiltrate and transform them. *Nonverbal,* however, does not mean unvoiced. To speak of the body at all is to bring it into language, to voice it. But, as body, as a biology of hungers and pleasures, energy and fatigue, metabolic routine, disruption and repair, the body is mute. To speak, the body requires mastery of a language, a mastery that belongs routinely and unremarkably to any member of a culture. (It does not require a theory and an academic degree.) For example, at a summer camp recently, where kids with disabilities get to live together away from home for a week or two, there were four girls in wheelchairs with spina bifida, a condition that often leaves the lower body paralyzed and requires the use of a catheter. Three to four times a day, the girls wheeled down to the infirmary to change their catheters. These were girls just entering puberty. They dressed and presented themselves as if conscious of their emerging sexuality. And they playfully identified themselves as the Cath Club, thus sidestepping the potential stigma of their disability by flaunting its hidden and conventionally shameful tokens.[2] So, the body—here a voiced and sexualized body—simply overruns the categories of an ableist, stigmatizing discourse to find its own expression.

This action of the voiced body is what is new about the new field of disability studies. Disability compels us to consider bodies as such—just as, for Barbara Rosenblum, chemotherapy for cancer disrupts the link between body and voice that is otherwise transparently routine, leaving her with the puzzle of a body turned alien and incomprehensible:

> When you have cancer, you are bombarded by sensations from within that are not anchored in meaning. They float in a world without words, without meanings. You don't know from moment to moment whether to call a particular sensation a "symptom" or a "side effect" or a "sign." [. . .] Words and their referents are uncoupled, uncongealed, no longer connected.   (103)

Thus the impaired body calls into question the nature of the unimpaired body and the ordinary, taken-for-granted features of its enabling and sustaining presence in thought, perception, and language. Many of these features are already understood in recent work in philosophical and cognitive semantics. Horst Ruthrof, for example, calls for a "somatic turn" to answer the "linguistic turn" of thirty or forty years ago. He insists that "any semantics which is to give a satisfactory explanation of how we grasp our world by means of language must find a niche for corporeality" and that "without the non-verbal, language is empty" (3, 238). Similarly, George Lakoff argues systematically against the Cartesian tradition of a mind/body split and shows how the cognitive models with which we form basic categories of perception "are directly *embodied* with respect to their content, or else they are systematically linked to directly embodied models" (13).

This tie between disability studies and an embodied semantics will be tested most immediately in the classroom, where it may be useful sometimes to offer students an opportunity to experience what it is like to be physically or perceptually impaired. Ear stoppers for a day, or a blindfold, wheelchair, or crutches do convey something like the experience. But there are limits to what these simulations of disability can tell us.

In August and September 1998, several members of the Internet discussion list Disability Studies in the Humanities (DS-HUM) joined in a penetrating discussion of whether classroom simulations of disability serve as effective teaching tools or just confirm stereotypes and preju-dices.[3] A repeated criticism was that simply trying on a disability (e.g., spending a day in a wheelchair) cannot convey the continuous, no-time-out experience of being impaired. Worse, it focuses too much at-tention on the impairment and too little on the social construction that turns impairment into disability. The risk is that a simulation will simply confirm nondisabled persons in their belief that they are normal and therefore superior to anyone who is disabled—though, of course, with the added belief that they are now sensitized with feelings of guilt and pity for the plight of the disabled. A suggested alternative is to consider how the technological culture, the materially constructed environment, which is the result of specific design and policy decisions, acts to enable even those who think of themselves as already enabled on their own. In this view, culture and technology, the telephone and the paved high-way, the public school and the home mortgage function as prostheses to overcome the limitations and extend the capabilities of—in principle—all members of society. However, the prosthetic function of these facili-ties and institutions tends to be invisible and unacknowledged, making it possible to exclude certain groups from being considered worthy of the same prosthetic consideration as that given to others—without the exclusion appearing to be an exclusion at all.

In my classroom I avoid doing simulations, but I do use exercises that quickly raise basic issues about embodied perception and experi-ence. Drawing on Lakoff's analysis of prototypes and category struc-tures, I ask students to jot down the first thing they can think of that is a member of a particular category. The choices are usually pre-dictable: bird (sparrow, robin, pigeon, but rarely ostrich or penguin), flower (rose, carnation, tulip, but rarely asphodel or foxglove), and so on. Unlike the classical model, which imposes an all-or-nothing set of criteria for category membership, where all members belong equally and completely to the category, in this model some are "better" mem-bers than others and are perceived as prototypes, while others are mar-ginal but still qualify as members. So, the category person with a disability, the most frequent response by far is "someone in a wheel-chair," confirming the visual semiotic that structures the category. Lin-ton in her wheelchair is a "better" member of the category than Rosenblum in chemotherapy.

For another exercise, when reading a blind or deaf-blind writer with a class, I have asked students to do something very simple. First, they are to stand up and find some clear space where they won't bump into one other. Next, I ask them to stand on one leg. That's easy enough. Then I ask them to close their eyes. Immediately, most of them find that they must open their eyes or they will fall over. This exercise provides a good opportunity to start thinking about eyesight as an orienting, balancing, sustaining phenomenon. If people think about sight at all, they tend to think of it as the experience of an independent ego actively directing its gaze to pick out features of interest. But the experience of standing on one leg and almost falling over when we shut our eyes tells a different story. It's not the same as becoming disoriented in a darkened room, because there we are presumably standing on both legs. But on one leg, we experience directly how exposure to the structure of the visual field, its up-and-down alignment with the pull of gravity and light, directly affects our trust in the groundedness of the body and its orientation in space. Its opposite is proprioception, the nonvisual sixth sense that, if Descartes had recognized it, we might have been spared a lot of trouble about the mind/body split—our ongoing, barely conscious awareness of the position, orientation, and movement of our bodies and limbs in space. Some people lose their proprioception to disease, and the effect can be devastating. For they lose much of the sense of their existential selves and must deliberately watch their arms and legs in order to move and act effectively.[4] In the exercise, ideally, students who lose their balance with their eyes closed discover how visual perception shapes and sustains their experience, even in so trivial a matter as standing in a room. Perhaps they also discover their proprioception, which usually functions unnoticed under the dominance of the visual. There are always a few students who do not lose their balance, and they often turn out to be dancers or similarly trained athletes, or people who do yoga, tai chi, and the like.

These exercises provide a glimpse of the role of visuality in how we categorize the world and orient ourselves within it. What they do not do is attempt to simulate a disability or impairment, and it is important to see why such an attempt will most likely fail. David Goode, an ethnomethodologist, did a field study of two young teenage girls who, as victims of rubella syndrome, were almost completely deaf and blind and had never developed language.[5] The perceptual lack, and the lack of language in particular, put into question their status as experiencing subjects. Could Goode, or anyone, have access to their subjectivity? With one of them, Christina (or Chris), Goode came to see that her subjectivity was constructed in ways that depended on who was observing her: medical professionals, primary-care staff, family, or Goode himself.

It appeared that only those who worked closely with Chris reported that she showed rationality and purpose in her activities. The higher up the chain of professionalization, the more negative and pessimistic was the assessment. According to physicians and specialists, she was severely retarded, uncommunicative, autistic, and unlikely to respond to (re)habilitation. Goode doubted such reports. Seeking to bracket out his own physical and perceptual biases as much as possible, he spent time wearing a blindfold and ear stoppers. But, very quickly, he understood that his self-imposed deaf-blindness could not match even the most elementary features of Chris's experience:

> When I tried to eat my meal while "deaf-blind," I realized that what I was trying to do while eating was to produce that course of events that I already understood to be "mealtime" through my participation in the hearing, seeing, and speaking culture. The "meal" was already in my head, so to speak, and the deaf-blindness only posed technical problems to me in trying to produce it deaf-blindly.
>
> This was not at all the kind of deaf-blindness that the children experienced, since their "meal" was not in their heads at all. Thus, while they ate, they would finger and feel their food, sniff the food, examine it carefully with their residual vision—things that I did not do and for which I had no particular motivation while experiencing my temporary deaf-blind meal.   (25)

Chris's congenital deaf-blindness was impossible for Goode to match—impossible even if, all of a sudden, he were to become really deaf-blind. To be deaf-blind as she was, he would have to have been born that way. Moreover, like her, he would have to lack language, to have never produced or comprehended a linguistic utterance of any kind.[6] Such a lack would mean that he would have no way to form the question, "What is it like to be deaf-blind and have no language?" Or even to know that there was such a question to be asked.

Still, Goode does learn something from his simulated deaf-blindness, "such as the relative danger of a world that is unpredictable or unanticipatable. Relying primarily on the kinesthetic sense and sense of smell makes the experiential world relatively 'thin,' immediate, unpredictable, and therefore dangerous. [. . .] In a sense, one's world is collapsed to one's immediate bodily space" (25).

This understanding of the close relation between visuality and one's existence as a subject of perceptible space is a fundamental theme of blind writing. One of the best accounts of blindness anywhere is John

Hull's *Touching the Rock*. It is organized as a journal of closely observed moments when, after years of surgery and declining eyesight, Hull must finally accept that he is blind. He understands acutely the effect of no longer being able to visualize space or visualize himself in space, and he looks forward to moments when the wind is blowing or when it rains. In wind and rain, sound performs the role of light in shaping a three-dimensional space where usually there is no space. Without sound, the space around him feels empty, and the occasional bit of noise seems to come from nowhere and then disappear. There is no shape or continuity of space, no sense of things existing before or after they happen to announce themselves as sound. Opening the door one evening, he hears the rain in the garden, and in its multiplicity of sounds he can make out various features in the otherwise invisible scene, even the contours of the lawn, as the rain "shapes out the curvature" for him (30). It is "an experience of great beauty," he says. "I feel as if the world, which is veiled until I touch it, has suddenly disclosed itself to me. [. . .] I am no longer isolated, preoccupied with my thoughts [. . .] I am presented with a totality, a world that speaks to me" (31).

At another time, in early morning rain, he listens for what the rain tells him of the many textures, layers and shapes of the world in earshot. Thinking of the common opinion that the blind live in their bodies and not in the world, he compares his sense of his body to his sense of the rain. The body too is multilayered and multitextured, and he apprehends it not as an image but as multiple "arrangements of sensitivities, a conscious space comparable to the patterns of the falling rain. [. . .] My body and the rain intermingle, and become one audio-tactile, three-dimensional universe, within which and throughout the whole of which lies my awareness." Hull underscores the sharp contrast between the simultaneity and totality of perception in a moment like this, its pleasure heightened by a feeling of recovered loss, and the very different experience of "the single-track line of consecutive speech which makes up [his] thoughts." He imagines the rain stopping and his sense of the world suddenly shrinking to the surface of his body. Then he goes a step further and imagines himself paralyzed from the neck down, deprived even of his body sense, and he wonders at what point he becomes "only a line of thought-speech" (133). His narrative returns again and again to this difference between the three-dimensional totality of perception in rare moments of fully realized acoustic space and the linearity of discursive thought.

A remarkable outcome of Hull's reflection on his experience is the possibility of imagining the body in a manner unaffected by the visual.

Such imagining is not easy to do in a culture saturated by the technology of the camera. But, in Hull's account, instead of the sighted experience of a strongly outlined figure with prominent features and symmetries, the blind body is felt to be distributed casually and pleasurably in space, as so many floating "arrangements of sensitivities." In effect, Hull takes Goode's discovery of a space that is dangerously unpredictable for the deaf-blind and his own blind perception of space as isolating and empty, and he reframes them as something beautiful. In doing so, he complicates the idea of disability, as indeed he does later in the book, when he questions whether blindness may not actually be a "dark paradoxical gift" (205). He also complicates the usual understanding of the way bodies are located in an environment, describing the relation as an intermingling of self and space evoked by sound and suggesting a special ecology of existence in a landscape. Moreover, Hull's experience is not so entirely different as to be incommensurable with sighted experience. Like students in a classroom exercise who learn by losing their balance with their eyes closed, Hull can be understood as exploring versions of perception and relatedness available to sighted experience but usually hidden under the dominance of the visual. It may be from this vantage that he begins to think of blindness not as a lack or an absence but as a new existence, a gift.

So much of what Hull reveals is the awkwardness of the terminology with which we approach describing impairments and disabilities. Even these words—*impairment* and *disability*—cause uneasiness. For instance, Mairs deliberately chooses to call herself crippled, because, she says, "it lets you know what my condition is," in contrast to euphemisms like "mobility impaired" or (laughably) "handi-capable" that might soften her reality—even though, at the same time, she acknowledges how deeply offensive the word *crippled* is to many people with disabilities (*Waist-High* 12). In contrast, the Deaf reject being categorized as disabled and assert their status as members of a unique culture, with its own history and community, and as speakers (signers) of a fully developed natural language—even though, at the same time, they must often invoke the Americans with Disabilities Act in order to gain basic services, like adequate sign-language interpretation for business, legal, and professional activities.[7]

This uneasiness with terminology is being addressed now by the World Health Organization (WHO) in a revision of its *International Classification of Impairments, Disabilities, and Handicaps* (*ICIDH*), first published in 1980. WHO has proposed a new scheme that substitutes the deliberately neutral terms *activities* and *participation* for the older terms *disability* and *handicap,* as in the title: *International Classification of Impairments, Activities and Participation (ICIDH-2).* These new terms avoid many negative implications in the old ones, which tended to focus on the individual and to encourage seeing the relation among terms as a one-way progression from impairment to disability to handicap, as if paralleling the development of an illness or injury toward deeper levels of incapacity. In the earlier scheme, *disability* described the degree to which one was restricted in performing an activity; *handicap* described the degree to which one could no longer fulfill a social or economic role. With the new proposal, *activity* describes the nature and extent of one's functioning at a personal level, and *participation* does the same for one's social involvement. In both instances, the focus is on the situated, contextual nature of impairment, with more emphasis on the effects of the physical and social environment. The new scheme distinguishes firmly between a medical model and a social one, but without turning them into binary opposites. For the medical model, health care policy is the basic issue, and it is understood to be a political issue: How good is the care? Who has access to it? For how long? Do they have choices? Who pays for it? For the social model, the issue again is political, and WHO argues that "it is the collective responsibility of society to make the environmental modifications necessary for the full participation of people with disabilities into all areas of social life" (6). For both models, it's a question of nothing less than human rights.

The new classification proposed by WHO echoes Victor Finkelstein's distinction between a medical model that focuses on the physically impaired individual and a social model that focuses on "the nature of society which disables physically impaired people" (qtd. in Fries, Introduction 7). But for WHO, both models, medical and social, are political in nature. And both are informed by a concept of disablement that defines complex relations among impaired body, social environment, and public policy. The concept is universal in its application and not just a label to mark one group or person off from another. Of course, it does not mean that "we are all disabled" (a platitude that Mairs dismisses as mealymouthed). What it does mean is that terms like *disabled* and *nondisabled* are not binary opposites but, instead, describe variable positions on a multidimensional gradient.[8]

Categorization, then, is a basic question raised by the new field of disability studies, and it is the writing of disability, the writing of embodied voices and voiced bodies, that makes this question basic. Speaking of her experience in a wheelchair, Linton reflects on how the form of that experience "has an impact on my sense of my body in space and affects the information I am exposed to and the way I process sensory information" (140). This is the voice of cognitive difference, a voice heard in Hull's celebration of his body as not an image but multiple "arrangements and sensitivities," in Eigner's version of the self as "some head you can't go around," in Rosenblum's distress over living under chemotherapy in "a world of random body events" (103), in young campers flaunting the tokens of their condition as members of the Cath Club. The voiced body is the body made present in language, and it is the version of discourse that poses the speaker as an agent of negotiable meanings that needs emphasis here in addition to the version that poses the speaker as a subject of ideology.

In his memoir *Body, Remember,* Kenny Fries tells of living with stunted and deformed legs and one day finding himself standing in the Holocaust Memorial Museum in Washington, DC, noting which of his roles would have marked him for death first: he would have been killed not as a Jew, not as a homosexual, but as a disabled man (208). It is a powerful narrative moment, of a man stunned by the thought of a discourse so violently irrational that it would have killed him three times over. But in Fries's writing there is another mode, another discourse, that voices the body as a site of negotiable meanings. His poem "Excavation" reaches past the name-calling (*"Freak, midget, three-toed / bastard"*), past the limiting categories (*"Disabled, crippled, deformed"*), past the social discourse that disables impaired people, but it does not reach past the body itself. On the contrary, in the imagined violence of tearing deeper into the skin, to find "the bones at birth I wasn't given," the poem renders the body as it is, illuminates it, the twisted feet, the rough skin, the scars and holes where steel pins had fastened reconfigured bones (*Anesthesia* 4, *Staring* 146). All this is registered in careful, exact detail, without sentimentality but at the same time animated by a feeling that only this body, this voice, can communicate in this time and place.

NOTES

For their contributions to an ongoing dialogue on disability, I owe thanks to members of my graduate seminar Writing and the Body: Ann Keefer, Susan Mann-Dolce, Susannah Maritime, and Mark Peters.
  1. Larry Eigner (1927–96) was born with cerebral palsy, the result of a forceps accident at the time of delivery. He published his first book of poems in 1953 and became a leading figure for poets during the last several decades, from Black Mountain poets in the 1950s to L=A=N=G=U=A=G=E poets today. A few of his poems appear in Fries, *Staring Back*.

2. I owe this anecdote to Susan Mann-Dolce and her student, Doreen Coyne, who have both worked at the camp. Mann-Dolce, trained as an occupational therapist, is working toward a cross-disciplinary PhD with the aim of bringing to her profession (and the summer camp) the opportunity provided by writing workshops for people with disabilities to write their way out from under a medical discourse and reclaim their lives from its limiting categories. The first writer-in-residence at the camp was Anne Finger.

3. Participants included Brenda Brueggemann, Johnson Cheu, Tom Connors, Beth Ferri, Martha Stoddard Holmes, Mark Jeffreys, Linda Kornasky, Sat Bir Kaur Khalsa, Vivian May, Jennifer Sutton, Carolyn Tyjewski, and Lynda Webb.

4. See "The Disembodied Lady" in Sacks, *"Man"* 42–52.

5. Depending on when a pregnant woman is exposed to the disease, rubella syndrome (or German measles) affects the fetus with varying severity. The two girls observed by Goode were profoundly disabled, with mental retardation, heart deformity, and other developmental impairments, in addition to being deaf-blind and alingual. Other outcomes might be just deafness or blindness. For instance, Stevie Wonder's blindness is the result of rubella syndrome.

6. Two concepts that are often confused are language and communication. People communicate with one another all the time with gestures and grunts, laughs and sobs, hugs, caresses, and blows. But none of this is linguistic, none of it is language. We commonly use metaphors, like "body language" or "the language of music" or "the language of mathematics," but these are still only metaphors. They do not describe the unique kind of communication, whether spoken or signed, that has both a semantics and a grammar and that enables users to produce and comprehend propositions. All language use is propositional, a fact underscored by Dadaist and other deliberate efforts to produce nonsense—for example, Hugo Ball's 1916 sound poem "gadji beri bimba" (Stewart, "Letter" 31–32). And all language use is situated and contextualized between speakers, whose meanings are contingent, negotiable, and revisable on the fly. No other form of communication is both propositional and contingently situated the way language is. Goode records all sorts of communication with Chris, but the two never exchange a linguistic utterance. Consequently, a fundamental question for Goode is whether he or Chris can enter into the other's world, or, even more fundamental, whether she can be said to be aware of existing in a world at all. For to conceptualize a world means being capable of using both metaphor and irony, both the capacity to say what something is by saying what it is like, and the understanding that such a description is unlike its referent ("My mistress' eyes are nothing like the sun" [Shakespeare's sonnet 130]), that it is contingent and never more than an approximation. It is this dual capacity that gives language its power and flexibility, that makes it something one can use, and only language makes this capacity available.

7. Interpreting has been a thorny issue at the MLA Annual Convention in recent years, where interpreters provided by the MLA, either for individual Deaf members or for sessions with Deaf presenters, are rarely trained to deal with the language of literary and cultural discourse.

8. The concept of social or cultural difference tends to get overworked. Paradoxically, it is not perceived difference that arouses people to oppose one another so much as a disquieting recognition of sameness. A Muslim woman in Bosnia confirmed this in 1996 when she said, "It's not because we are different that they want to kill us, it's because we are so much alike."

JAMES C. WILSON AND
CYNTHIA LEWIECKI-WILSON

Constructing a Third Space: Disability Studies, the Teaching of English, and Institutional Transformation

Contestation and renegotiation of the meaning of spaces is also always possible.
—Alison Blunt and Gillian Rose, "Women's Colonial and Postcolonial Geographies"

We come to disability studies as parents of a child with disabilities and as teachers of writing and literature interested in applying feminist, postcolonial, and disability theory to issues of literacy. When our son was born twenty-one years ago with hydrocephalus and a range of disabilities, he was immediately inserted into a complex array of institutions and inscribed by their medical, legal, social, and educational discourses. We have seen firsthand how institutions and discourse systems can both empower and disempower the disabled. Our experiences led us to a deeper understanding of how difference challenges traditional assumptions and epistemologies and reinforced our commitment to addressing these implications in the classroom. As the knowledge from our personal and professional lives converged in disability studies, our teaching continued to evolve as did our understanding of disciplinarity and our thinking about the relations and boundaries between the academy and the community.

While institutional encounters tend to reinforce the unequal power relations inherent in any interaction between individual and institution, they do not have to: negotiations between individuals and institutions can sometimes be mutually transforming. In her study of how literacy functions in encounters between disabled children and their parents and institutions, Ellen L. Barton concludes that both parties in such encounters "collaborate in the enactment of the power and authority of that institution" (414). It is our hope that as disabled people enter the university in greater numbers, they and those they encounter will not simply reenact existing relations but will collaborate in remaking this institutional space.

If one thinks of space, using the cultural geographer Peter Jackson's words, "as a social construction or a 'way of seeing'" with "reciprocal links between social relations and spatial structures" (181), then it is clear that even now the university as a social space can be read as an environment intended for nondisabled persons. Often such intentions are built into the literal landscape of a university's inaccessible buildings and classrooms, but such intentions are no less a part of the cultural and mental landscape of its faculty and administration, revealed in pragmatic arguments about cost as well as deeply embedded in traditional humanist concepts such as universality. In this essay we discuss the usual ways of seeing that disability challenges, present some ideas for incorporating disability issues into language and literature classes, and reflect on the questions involved in transforming teaching and curriculum. We urge others to think about how disabled and nondisabled people might reimagine the spatial, cultural, and intellectual landscape of the academy through an encounter with disability and how this academic transformation might contribute to the remaking of other social spaces.

The Law and the Body

What is at stake is the relation between the law and the body–a body is itself defined, delimited, and articulated by what writes it.
—Michel de Certeau, *The Practice of Everyday Life*

Disability law has produced an increased demand for higher education, a growing population of publicly educated students with disabilities who seek postsecondary education. The Americans with Disabilities Act of 1990 and earlier laws of the 1970s not only have increased the expectations–and frustrations–of disabled persons for access to and accommodations in higher education but also have produced the need for

greater critical literacy for students with disabilities, so that they can negotiate the maze of potentially enabling as well as potentially resistant
institutions and laws. According to the National Clearinghouse on Postsecondary Education for Individuals with Disabilities, "administrators
sometimes react to requests by interpreting the laws arbitrarily and by
setting contradictory or inequitable policies" ("Higher Education"
1). Ironically, even when administrators implement clear procedures
and guidelines in response to disability law, "some faculty refuse to comply with the laws" (2). Conflicts between students and institutions over
policies and accommodations do occur, and in these conflicts disabled
students, advocates, and faculty members need to take active roles in
making the case not only for supporting the disabled with necessary
services but also for making inclusion an opportunity for transforming
teaching and knowledge making.

Disability law has also produced a student (disabled) body marked,
delimited, and articulated by the law. The letter of the law requires institutions to make reasonable accommodations and to set up uniform
and equitable policies. That is, the law writes on particular disabled bodies, no two of whom have the same needs, a generalized grid or map labeled "disabled student." The inevitable clash between this generalizing
language of the law and the particularity of human bodies, and between
dominant ways of thinking and new challenges to that thinking, can be
grasped when one asks what reasonable accommodations are and what
equity means in specific cases.

To give one example, a graduate student with severe crippling arthritis of the hips requests that the English seminar room be changed because the only elevator serving that floor is distant and often broken.
She cannot climb the stairs to the third floor. In the chaos of reschedul-
ing, another inaccessible classroom is assigned. After three changes, a
suitable meeting place is found. The nondisabled students grumble because the first four classes have met in different rooms. The elevator has
not been repaired or relocated. Next semester, another graduate student
recovering from radical cancer surgery must rely on this same distant
and unreliable elevator in order to get to classes and to her office to meet
with her own first-year writing students for conferences.

The university might claim to have accommodated these students
reasonably, even though in no way did it change its spatial landscape in
its encounter with disability. In the words of Rod Michalko and Tanya
Titchkosky, social theorists of disability, the intentions of this environment would still have to be "understood as [. . .] strictly for those who

are able-bodied" (221–22). Though "the confrontation between disability and an environment often seduces members of a community (able-bodied and disabled alike) into conceiving of pragmatism as the only way of reading the interactions that occur," Michalko and Titchkosky state, "it is, after all, people who produce such intentionality" (224), people who reproduce it, and people who can construct different relations.

And what of the cultural landscape inside college classrooms? Conflicts in beliefs about equity become an important classroom dynamic, as this second example shows. A first-year student in a composition class has cerebral palsy. She uses a wheelchair and requires an instructional aide for keyboarding and note taking. Another student in the same class needs extra time for the final essay exam because of his dyslexia, but he enters the essay himself directly on the computer. He relies heavily, however, on its spell-checking and grammar programs to edit his final copy. All semester their instructor worries about equivalences, remaining skeptical that the student with an aide is doing her own work, worrying that the dyslexic student's need for extra time and editing help may cause his failure in other classes. But the instructor is reluctant to discuss these worries or to work individually with the two disabled students, fearful of calling attention to them as different and of making them objects to the rest of the students. The instructor also feels that giving them extra attention would be unfair to the other students.

These examples are presented not as cautionary tales of good or bad teaching but to depict the complex ways that including the disabled challenges customary assumptions. For instance, the particular accommodations needed by the students in the second example conflict with traditional beliefs in the academy about individual work, standardization of skills, and fairness (conceptualized as sameness). Indeed, we recognize the classroom teacher's worry about calling attention to a disabled student. Discussing disability does introduce the risk of reducing the student to the student's disability or of making the disabled student a spectacle, a body to be gazed at as "other." But silence, however tactful it might at first seem, is not helpful either. It furthers the invisibility of disabled students and reproduces fairly widespread assumptions about the norm. One assumption we frequently encounter is the claim often made by nondisabled students, but sometimes by the disabled as well, that disabled persons just want to be treated like everyone else, therefore one should overlook and not mention their disability. We know from our own experiences as parents of a disabled child that silence about disability most often works to preserve exclusion, requiring the disabled to assimilate to physical and social environments that remain unchanged and unchallenged, environments intended for others, not them.

While there is no single answer to this dilemma, teachers need to reflect on ways they might acknowledge and creatively accommodate differences without turning a disabled student into an object, a token representative, or a victim. Such acknowledgment requires flexibility on the part of instructors, who need to learn to be comfortable speaking about issues of difference and to understand that disabled students themselves hold a range of views and levels of comfort in identifying themselves as disabled. Ideally, instructors should be willing to assist each (disabled) student to coconstruct the best individualized learning relationship.

Perhaps the deepest conflict experienced in the academy arises from the usual and familiar way that our society measures equity. Carl Gutierrez-Jones argues in "Injury by Design" that Americans traditionally employ "injury rhetoric" to contest equity. He notes that such rhetoric "model[s] as it does a balance of moral equivalences, legitimat[ing] notions of harm and remedy that only make sense in reference to the norm itself—to injure may thereby be equated with displacement from the norm" (88). Concepts of universality and the norm are deeply embedded in academic culture, and inclusion can very quickly trigger cries of reverse discrimination, exclusion, or injury from the seemingly displaced group that identifies itself as the norm. In the first example, the able-bodied seminar students who felt displaced because they had to change rooms several times identified themselves as the norm; in the second example, the teacher's worry that she wouldn't be fair to other students if she gave extra attention to the disabled ones came from that same identification.

A sympathetic reader might well ask at this point, What can I do about the condition or location of elevators and classrooms? or, How can I coconstruct an individualized teaching plan with each student, given my large class sizes? In the short run, of course, teachers cannot change the physical landscape. They can, however, adapt their teaching practices, as their local situation allows, to be more accommodating. We offer here a list of adaptations we have made. Some of these might work for others, some may not. Certainly what a teacher and students feel comfortable with will vary according to the circumstances and the class. Overall, our recommendations focus on three areas: making creative adaptations in teaching, enhancing access, and representing disability in the classroom.

Although we teach in different kinds of institutions and at different levels, we both teach writing, and we have found that many of the routine practices of writing pedagogy (student-teacher conferencing, small-group workshops, etc.) are effective or adaptable in accommodating the individual needs of disabled students. We talk to our classes at the beginning of each term or semester about learning differences, and we indicate that we are willing to accommodate different needs—for example, by providing large-print lecture notes, sending notes by e-mail, or allowing students to audiotape classes. We go further and convey that we are willing to adapt or codesign assignments with students to fit their particular learning strengths as well as to address particular learning needs. We let students know we are willing to codevelop with them strategies for success, and we stress that they have much to teach us and other students.

An important aspect of accommodation is access. By being flexible, teachers can compensate for less than ideal campus spaces and make learning more accessible. For example, if elevators are distant or unreliable, we offer to meet with students in alternate and more accessible (or just more comfortable) locations—the library, a computer lab, a student commons room, and so on. Access also means that a teacher be willing to conference by phone or e-mail.

Above all, we recommend openness in talking about disability. Because we have a disabled son, we often bring our experiences into the class as a way of representing the subject of disability without connecting it to any particular student present, thus introducing disability from the start. We mention that disabled students may, if they wish, identify themselves, and we offer opportunities for all students to conference privately with the professor, in person or by e-mail. We also incorporate the subject of disability into our curriculum in many of the composition, literature, and interdisciplinary classes we teach and encourage a variety of approaches, ranging from memoir writing and other forms of self-representation to critical and research projects connected to disabilities. However, we do not require personal topics or self-disclosure. Some students feel uncomfortable with the personal, while others welcome the opportunity to do serious work on a subject connected to their lives. Rather than approach disability as an identity, we integrate it into the curriculum as a social construction, a critical modality, and a community issue. We encourage nondisabled students as well to investigate disability issues and to reflect on the critical perspective gained from their investigations. For example, a hearing student did a memorable project in a composition-and-literature class, making a video presentation of herself reading a story aloud while signing it. She played her video to the class and then discussed the intricacies of making an American Sign Language presentation. For her paper project, she wrote about the literary and communicative considerations involved in re-presenting the story in different forms of literacy—print, oral storytelling, and signing.

Inclusion of disabled students, anchored in disability law, brings into the academy a legal discourse that emphasizes equity, accommodation, and reasonableness. As we hope the above examples demonstrate, however, when teachers begin to meet these challenges and make accommodations, they are likely to experience contradictions in these legal concepts and conflicts with customary thinking. Faced with such conflicts (say, between equity as sameness and the particular needs of a disabled student), many teachers retreat to business as usual. Clearly, in cases of conflict, the limits of the terms *reasonable* and *equitable* are likely to return—like a compass needle to the north—to the dominant lines of power and the already inscribed attitudes. Sustaining inclusion, then, will ultimately require more than merely assimilating the disabled into classrooms. It means inquiring into the social processes of encoding and decoding, and this fact makes English studies classrooms not only appropriate but central sites for addressing disability issues, involved as they are with the reading, articulation, and reinterpretation of meaning in language and culture.

Transforming the Classroom into a Third Space

[The] Third Space [. . .] constitutes the discursive conditions of enunciation that ensure that the meaning and symbols of culture have no primordial unity or fixity; that even the same signs can be appropriated, translated, rehistoricized, and read anew. [. . . It is] the precondition for the articulation of cultural difference. [. . .] It is in this space that we will find those words with which we can speak of Ourselves and Others.
—Homi K. Bhabha, "Cultural Diversity and Cultural Differences"

We borrow the concept of third space from postcolonial studies. From our work in critical literacy, feminist, and postcolonial studies, we would like to challenge educators to think beyond accommodation, to make their classrooms a third space, one in which teacher, students, and knowledge making are transformed by encounters with disability. Imagining a third space means thinking beyond center versus margin or dominant versus subordinate groups (which reinscribe the rhetoric of norm and injury). It means rethinking pedagogy as an engagement with disability itself. And this rethinking would include learning not only from encounters with particular students who are disabled but also from encounters with disability studies theory.

In describing a third-space pedagogy, we borrow from and rewrite the critical educator Paulo Freire's notion of the dialogic point of encounter. We retain from Freire the importance of openness to otherness but would unsettle the concept of dialogue, implying as it does exchange between two speakers in opposite positions. The concept of a transformative third-space classroom, in contrast, starts from the understanding that all of us move in and out of multiple subject positions that may be interconnected, overlapping, and conflicting. For example, all human beings at any time can become members of the disabilities community, and all disabled people are also affected by their race, class, and gender locations, and by their location in a particular nation. All these ways of being situated interact with being disabled in significant and different ways. Moreover, as members of the same broad cultural community, we are also called into identification and disidentification with groups by many shared cultural and political forces. Instead of engaging in an exchange between two positions, then—for example, between disabled and nondisabled—the transformative classroom creates the conditions for all participants to enunciate and examine these multiple locations and social encodings.

Freire writes that the point of encounter requires "faith, that one believes in other[s . . .] even before [she or] he meets them face to face" (79). However, as we have argued—by encouraging assimilation and largely maintaining environments and attitudes intended for the norm—familiar thinking rooted in disability law renders those (disabled) others mostly invisible in academic spaces. Disability studies can provide the critical perspective necessary for the disabled to become visible. Subjects are already interpellated by language, law, experiences, and attitudes, as Judith Butler explains in *Excitable Speech*. Therefore, before creative and transformative encounters can even take place, students and teachers need disability studies theory to see both themselves and others. Such seeing involves understanding how everyday assumptions constitute an ableist point of view as well as a recognition of how nonableist points of view complicate and might transform social practices.

Where should disability studies appear in the curriculum? We believe, as Rosemarie Garland-Thomson argues in "Integrating Disability Studies," that "it should be an integrated part of all the courses we design, just as many of us have begun to consider race, gender, and class issues as fundamental aspects of all disciplines and subjects of inquiry"

(16).[1] In a number of the classes we teach (e.g., composition, women's studies, and graduate professional writing), we integrate readings from disability studies, memoirs by disabled writers, and videos made by disability activists. Assignments, depending on the particular course, might ask students to analyze cultural images of the disabled, explore new ways of representing the disabled in their writing, or reflect on the critical issues of difference in our culture. The students' reflective responses can be openings to discuss the ways that disability is familiarly encoded in language and social practices.

It has been our experience that when students encounter voices from disability culture, they tend to hear those voices in the common social scripts of individualism and individual rights based on a mythic norm: that is, they hear the rhetoric of victimhood, bias, and injury, and they place disability in the familiar mainstream-versus-minority construction. Consider these reflections written by seniors and graduate students in a medicine-and-science writing class after watching Sharon Snyder and David T. Mitchell's video *Vital Signs: Crip Culture Talks Back.*

> "After seeing the film, I got the impression that persons with disabilities are offended by nondisabled persons who try to be pleasant, because they feel these pleasantries translate to pity. [. . .] To look at a person's disability and try to understand it through asking questions or entering into some sort of discourse with the disabled individual seems to me to be the only way to break the barriers, clarify the stereotypes, clear up the myths, and ease the discomfort of interactions between disabled and nondisabled individuals."

> "[This video] pointed out some of the underground currents of discrimination against people with disabilities. I use the terms 'underground' because I think many of the grievances discussed in the video are often swept under the carpet of mainstream culture, as a way for able-bodied people to ignore the pertinent issues and discriminatory acts encountered by our neighbors who happen to be on crutches, in wheelchairs, or disabled in some other way."

> "I liked the way the film was about the people, and got into their lives, childhoods, and feelings about being disabled and about how they are treated. Most films on the topic do objectify the [disabled], as many said, and turn them into something other than humans."

> "Until I watched the movie I did not picture disabled people as a different culture."

"As probably intended, some of the interviews were harder to watch than others, but I got the distinct idea that [the producers] did not intend the audience to feel comfortable. [. . .] It also seemed appropriate that these people were speaking for themselves instead of having a celebrity (Jerry Lewis, for example) or a medical or political expert speaking for them or about them. [. . .] For me, it was very eye-opening [. . .] the fact that these people are so much more than their disabilities also jumps out. [. . .] The tendency for me especially is to not talk about the obvious, not to talk about the disability. [. . .] One thing I am wondering now that I'm thinking more about it is what exactly did the directors hope to achieve: awareness, attitude change, or some more concrete societal change? Who is the intended audience?"

"I'm always a bit skeptical when I watch a documentary about a politically charged issue. I have to say that [this one] wasn't much of an exception. I found it interesting that when presenting a culture in which 60 percent (I think it was said) are unemployed, the filmmakers chose to speak with individuals who were clearly educated and articulate. [. . .] So I wonder if the images presented aren't a little bit skewed and I wonder what the film would have been like if the makers had talked with some of the [unemployed majority]."

We arranged these responses in an order that may suggest a movement from thinking about disability as a matter of individuals who suffer deficit or loss to seeing the disabled as a culture and disability as a social construction to be politically reclaimed, to use the disability studies theorist Simi Linton's term in *Claiming Disability*. Although such a movement would mirror the lines of argument of most disability studies theorists, our teaching goal is not to have students "reconstruct" their thinking about disability according to a "correct" theory. Rather, our goal is to encourage them to examine and conceptualize their encounters with disability. While we readily acknowledge that the work of engaging with and reseeing disability is indeed political, as the last student argues, we strive to keep class discussions reflective and reflexive—that is, in the form of thoughtful, open-ended conversations that include a critique of our enterprise. As students articulate the range of views inscribed in culture and reflect on these, their discourse can be vehicles for discussion and analysis and a starting point for the production of new thinking. As Kris Gutierrez, Betsy Rymes, and Joanne Larson argue in "Script, Counterscript, and Underlife in the Classroom: James Brown

versus Brown v. Board of Education," the third-space classroom
"requires more than simply 'adding-on' the student script; it requires
jointly constructing a new sociocultural terrain in the classroom" (468).

As we are conceptualizing it, a third-space classroom is performative,
to use Butler's term (*Excitable Speech*), calling into being new modes of
address and inquiring into the uses and effects of language and cultural
images. She writes:

> The performative is not a singular act used by an already estab-
> lished subject, but one of the powerful and insidious ways in
> which subjects are called into social being from diffuse social quar-
> ters, inaugurated into sociality by a variety of diffuse and powerful
> interpellations. In this sense the social performative is a crucial part
> not only of subject formation, but of the ongoing political contes-
> tation and reformulation of the subject as well.   (160)

As Butler's word "insidious" makes clear, such remaking is not innocent.
However, it is important to remember that all classrooms participate in
subject formation and reproduce a social order that, as human agents,
we may change. How we might (or might not) change it, why, and to
what ends are all possibilities open to debate.

A third-space classroom is thus admittedly a political contestation
and a remaking of subjectivity, but it must preserve a process that is
dynamic and open, encouraging the transformation of knowledges including those of the teacher and the academy as well as those of the students. We turn to feminist theory for a model. In theorizing new
"imagined geographies," the feminists Alison Blunt and Gillian Rose
posit "a fluid space that tries to acknowledge difference," one that shares
the characteristics of feminist epistemology, "fragmented, multidimensional, contradictory, and provisional" (5, 7). In our teaching, we encourage students to examine the rhetorical constructions of difference
and the dominant cultural narratives that both teachers and students
employ. We do not offer answers but pose questions that turn a critical
lens back on us and our projects, challenging students to think about the
boundaries among academic disciplines, community, and discursive
spaces.

The questions we put to students are ones we ask ourselves: How
does disability studies change the boundaries of disciplinary knowledge?
How should our society, our communities, and our universities take up
diversity issues? In particular, how does disability help us think critically
about the rhetoric and practices of pluralistic inclusion and consider

new ways in which difference can really speak to, challenge, and transform institutions, communities, and people? How can disability studies address the material needs of the disabled, about 70% of whom are presently unemployed according to the 1998 National Organization on Disability–Harris Survey of Americans with Disabilities (Taylor)? Will access to the academy provide access to employment and economic space?

These questions cannot yet be answered definitively. However, we believe that by incorporating disability issues into the curriculum as widely as possible, by engaging with disability studies theory, and by rethinking disciplinary knowledge as a result of this encounter, teachers and students, the disabled and nondisabled can indeed participate in remaking the social and physical landscapes of the university. For this remaking to happen, teachers need to take the first steps in transforming their teaching in a way that allows them to engage with issues of disability and with the disabled. Then the question will become, Can the transformative process engendered by the third-space classroom extend beyond the university to other, larger, social spaces?

NOTE

1. See Linton, Mello, and O'Neill for a general discussion of incorporating disability into curricula; see Garland-Thomson ("Integrating") for ideas about incorporating disability specifically into literature classes.

GEORGINA KLEEGE

Disabled Students Come Out: Questions without Answers

Once, in an undergraduate fiction-writing workshop, a student wrote a story about a Deaf woman. The woman was married to a hearing man and had two hearing children. In the central scene, the couple was discussing having a third child, and the woman announced that she hoped the child would be Deaf. A distinctive feature of the story was the way the author handled the characters' dialogue. The characters were using American Sign Language, and the author had, in effect, transcribed their conversation without translating it. She was trying to capture the flavor of ASL while making the language comprehensible to an English-speaking reader.

The story generated a lot of discussion. It turned out there was another student in the class who knew ASL because her mother was deaf. The story's author had learned ASL in high school so she could interpret at assemblies and theatrical events. Together they introduced the class to basic elements of the language and did an impromptu performance of some of the story's dialogue as a demonstration. As we discussed this dialogue, I reminded the class of discussions we had previously about how such authors as William Faulkner and D. H. Lawrence rendered dialect. Was this the same or different?

A student said that he found the story convincing because he'd heard on a segment of *Sixty Minutes* that all Deaf people want to have Deaf children so they can all speak the same language. The generalization made me uneasy, so I asked, "Can we say *all* Deaf people?" This question sparked some discussion about deafness, the physical condition, versus Deafness, the linguistic and cultural minority.

I was pleased that the class wanted to talk about these issues but felt compelled to guide the discussion back to the student's story. This was a fiction-writing workshop after all, not a class in disability studies. I kept asking questions about elements of fiction we'd discussed all term. We talked about the sequence of scenes (Did that flashback work?), about narration (Could she have written the story in the first person?), about characterization (Was there a need for more background information and, if so, how much and where?).

As the discussion was beginning to wane, a student, who had been uncharacteristically quiet so far, began a sentence with the phrase "Speaking as a disabled person" and raised the question of whether a hearing person could or should write from the perspective of a Deaf person. We'd talked about similar issues before: Could a male author write from a female point of view? Could an African American represent an Asian American's experience? Was this the same situation or different?

Naturally class ended before we could answer all the questions we'd raised. Still, I felt the story's author had received some useful feedback. I left the classroom making a mental list of additional points I wished to bring up at our next meeting. Distracted by these thoughts, I was a little surprised when the student with the disability followed me back to my office. He seemed agitated, a little out of breath. Before we even sat down, he said, "That's the first time I ever did that."

"Did what?" I asked, because I genuinely did not know.

"You know," he said. "The first time I ever said it in front of people like that. The first time I ever called myself *disabled*."

Many people might have been startled by his statement. His disability was readily apparent to everyone in the class. Everyone but me, that is, because I am legally blind. Still, I knew he was disabled. He rocked from side to side when he walked, and he dragged one foot. I could not tell if he used a cane or wore leg braces and would not hazard to put a name to his condition. Even if I had been unaware of these traits, however, I knew he was disabled because we'd talked about it. He'd explained to me that sometimes he used a wheelchair, in museums or the grocery store, but generally he did not. He'd also referred to operations he'd undergone and mentioned that he'd been a poster child and appeared on a telethon. On these occasions we'd also talked about my disability: When did my condition develop? How did I handle all the reading I had to do? And we talked about the differences between having a visible disability like his and an invisible one like mine, which is apparent only when I use a white cane or read braille.

These conversations were always comfortable—matter-of-fact exchanges of information. Furthermore, I knew he'd talked about his disability with other instructors. So why was it such a big deal for him to identify himself as disabled on this occasion? The question I asked was "Why haven't you ever said it before?"

"I don't know," he said. "I guess I didn't want to be one of those whiny wheelies."

His reluctance reminded me of the reluctance of some women to identify themselves as feminists even though they have beliefs and expectations that could be defined as feminist, for fear they would seem strident and unfeminine. Was he worried that calling himself disabled would make him appear abrasive and militant? In fact, he had a chip on his shoulder and could be rather edgy, argumentative, defensive. He was also smart, quick-witted, prone to make ironic asides. These were all traits that conform to a stereotypical disabled personality—the cranky cripple rather than the cheerfully stoic kind. These facets of his personality may well have evolved as ways to counter playground taunts or to repel patronizing pity. But he might have turned out this way because he'd grown up without a father or for some other reason I didn't know.

In any case, he did not seem like someone who worried about offending people. Before I could ask another question, he said, "You should have seen the way they looked when I said it."

I almost cautioned him against being oversensitive, but I stopped myself. I had noticed a pause after he spoke, but since I can't make eye contact or read people's expressions, I had no idea what sort of nonverbal communication might have occurred. Still, I told him that I didn't think his classmates' response to his word came from hostility or prejudice. Rather, they had been brought up not to stare at people with disabilities, not to call them names, not to ask rude questions. For him to bring it up forced them to violate all those parental admonitions, to look at his disabled body and give it a name.

Of course they should have been used to this simply because they had a professor with a disability. From the first day of class my presence challenged many of their assumptions. In my class, they were obliged to break the cardinal rule of classroom decorum and speak without raising their hands, since I cannot see this gesture. Also, since I read tape-recorded versions of their written work, they were obliged to think about how their writing would sound out loud. Eventually they'd got used to what's different about my classes; they even learned to tease me about it. When I asked, "Who's not here today?," someone was bound to say, "Please raise your hand if you're absent."

Although my students had a greater awareness of disability issues than the general nondisabled public, when the student with the disability "came out" in my class, it was still startling, subversive, perhaps even revolutionary. For many, a disabled person is a unique individual with a specific physical, perceptual, or cognitive problem marked by a distinct set of characteristics or behaviors. Thus, a person with a mobility impairment seems to have little in common with someone who is visually impaired. The student in my class was not merely identifying an obvious physical fact about himself. He was claiming identity with the Deaf woman in the story; with me, his blind professor; and with numerous other people who had various deficits, impairments, and anomalies. He was saying, "I speak for all these."

Did he have the right to do this? Is there really such a thing as a disabled perspective? Did this student and I share common beliefs and values that transcended all other identity categories? I admit these questions make me uneasy. Every female is not a feminist. Similarly, every disabled person is not a disability rights activist or an expert in disability studies. I write and think about disability issues, but I write and think about a lot of other things too. Of all the adjectives I can use to describe myself, *disabled* is only one of many and not always the first I mention. When I encounter such phrases as "blind lust" or "lame response" in a student's writing, I will probably mark it as a cliché. When I encounter a disabled character in a work of literature, I may analyze the cultural attitudes connected to that representation. A nondisabled instructor could do the same. Do my students find it more memorable when I do it, because they perceive me as speaking from personal experience? Did this student feel comfortable coming out in my class because I have a disability, or would he have done it anywhere? Did the student who wrote the story about the Deaf woman feel I would be more receptive to it than a nondisabled teacher?

I don't have all the answers. I do resent any inference that the mere fact of my disability augments my teaching qualifications or that there is a pedagogical value in exposing my disability to nondisabled students.

This practice smacks too much of the freak show and casts me in the role of goodwill ambassador sharing the quaint beliefs and customs of my alien world.

While I resist displaying myself as an exotic species, I am also a reluctant role model for students with disabilities. I'm unconvinced that the ways I deal with my disability are worthy of emulation. Furthermore, I am not always as sensitive and sympathetic as I could be. I have a chip on my shoulder too. Like many disabled people who went through school before IDEA (Individuals with Disabilities Education Act) and ADA (Americans with Disabilities Act), I must quell the urge to say, "You kids today have it so easy." While they may enjoy the advantages of legally mandated access and new assistive technologies, the world continues to be far from perfect.

Still, my disabled students and I have much in common. We do not, for instance, take for granted that the university environment and practices were designed with us in mind. This can make us cranky, but it can also make us resilient and adaptable. These are qualities we need, since legally mandated access does not eliminate all barriers. The student who came out in my class had told me on a previous occasion that another professor once asked him, "What's wrong with you?"

"I didn't know what he meant at first," he said. "I thought maybe my nose was bleeding or something."

"What did you tell him?" I asked.

"I told him what he wanted to know," he said. "I should have told him it was none of his business. I mean, if I was blind or deaf, I would have had to explain things to him. What's 'wrong' with me makes no difference to how I read or write or talk."

I asked him if he wanted me to do something, to speak to the professor or take some other action. He said he did not. Perhaps he sensed that my anger with my colleague would have made me an ineffective advocate. Instead, we talked about what we found wrong with the question, articulating a response for the next time it was asked. What was wrong with the question was not the way it violated contemporary codes of political correctness, not to mention older codes of common courtesy. What was wrong with the question was the way it assumed that we people with disabilities perceive ourselves to be defective, deficient, substandard, that we long for the abilities we lack, experiencing eye envy, leg envy, ear envy. A better though more challenging answer to the question would be to say, "There is nothing wrong with being disabled." Disability is a fact of life for some of us. It demands our attention and effort in certain situations. If we long for anything, it is better assistive technologies, better architecture, better attitudes among the nondisabled.

When this student came out in my class, it was unclear how the event would affect his future life. Had he now appointed himself official spokesperson for disability issues? Would his spin on things be the same as mine? We disagreed about many things. I told him that a lot of Deaf people reject the disability label, preferring to be identified as a linguistic or cultural minority. Then we argued about identity politics. I said, "I don't think it's a question of whether a nondisabled person has the right to write about a disabled person. It's a matter of whether or not the writing seems genuine and doesn't conform to stereotypes."

"I hate the way they always want us to be inspirational," he said.

I wanted to caution him against divisive generalizations and thought of asking, "Can we really say *always*?" But in this instance I found myself on his side of the divide, so I said, "I hate it, too."

Sometimes, the consequences of coming out as disabled are more practical than philosophical. In a sophomore-level literature class, a student stayed after the first session to ask a question. From the way she let other students go before her, I sensed that she wanted to speak to me privately. When everyone else was gone, she pointed to a line in my syllabus and said, "It says here that this is available in large print."

I noticed that she was making a statement, not a request. I also noticed that she made no mention of herself, as if she were asking for a friend who wasn't there. I gave her the large-print syllabus and explained that I could produce all the course materials—handouts, quizzes, exams—in this or other formats.

I had already explained to the class about my disability. Now I told her that to the extent that I can read print at all, it must be very large. I showed her some pages of notes I had and some other materials, naming the different font sizes. She seemed a little overwhelmed by the range of options. Although we were still not talking about her or her disability, I finally asked, "Which one would you prefer?"

"Whatever's easiest," she blurted, as if it required extra effort to produce a text in 18- rather than 14-point type. I surmised she was new at this, perhaps newly disabled. She was uncertain how to ask for what she needed, uncertain how much was permitted. But the ice was broken now, and she volunteered that she was in her forties, a returning student. She'd dropped out of college when she was twenty to get married and raise her children, and now she was back. Then finally, she told me that she was deaf in one ear and blind in one eye, which was why she was asking about the large print. She could read standard print, but it was a slow and difficult process. So for my course she'd bought the textbooks as soon as they showed up in the campus bookstore and had been reading ahead during the term break.

I asked her if she'd ever been to the university's Office of Disability Services. Perhaps they could offer some additional assistance.

"But I'm not disabled," she said.

I guessed it was the word *disabled* that made her balk. Yes, she had "something wrong" with her, but she was not disabled. She was normal, a normal person with a problem.

Though "deaf in one ear and blind in one eye" sounded like a disability to me, I wasn't going to argue with her. Instead, I gave her some basic information about what an office of disability services does. I said it was a resource, a place to ask questions, to try out technologies and techniques. I also said that it could be helpful to make contact with other students with disabilities, who might offer additional advice, even if they had different disabilities. I have learned a lot about reading audio books from a dyslexic and about crossing streets from a paraplegic. I sensed the phrase "other students with disabilities" was presumptuous on my part. It forced her to picture herself as part of a group she'd always perceived as alien—people in wheelchairs, people with garbled speech, people with missing limbs. So I hastened to add that many people with disabilities develop their own adaptive strategies without others' advice, such as buying the textbook early in order to give themselves extra reading time.

"Or like sitting in the front row," she said. "And I always sit on this side, so I can use my good ear to hear."

I was pleased that I hadn't offended her, but I sent her to Disability Services with some trepidation. At their worst, such offices exist merely to protect the institution from lawsuits. In other cases they may offer only those accommodations experts deem appropriate for a particular disability without fully assessing the student's individual needs. A student who fails to benefit from the prescribed accommodation or asks for something else can be labeled a malingerer or troublemaker. I didn't tell her all this, however. She was an adult and could decide for herself. I didn't want to poison her with my paranoia. My own bad experiences with the Evil Custodial Oppressor might scare her away from possibly valuable services.

Two weeks later she was back, breathless with gratitude. "Disability Services was so helpful," she told me. They had calibrated and certified her impairments and offered all sorts of visual and audio aids. She was going to try a hearing aid, magnification devices, audio books. I offered to share the taped versions of my texts and gave her a few tips about aural reading.

"It's such a relief," she told me. "I've been this way all my life, but I never really talked about it before." Because she had always thought of herself as an individual with a unique problem, it was a revelation to discover not only that there were other people with similar conditions but also that there were others who had thought up ways of dealing with them. She was learning to shift her attention from what was wrong with her to what was wrong with the educational environment that barred her access to it. I was glad for her, glad that coming out was a positive experience, glad that her transition from "normal person with something wrong" to "person with a disability" was going smoothly.

But by the end of the term she was angry. There was trouble with Disability Services. They refused to order recorded books for the next term until all the other students had turned in their requests. I gave her a phone number and told her she could order the books on her own, warning that if she did this, she might be viewed as subversive.

She took this advice without comment. Was she developing a chip on her shoulder? She was still angry, about something else. "When I dropped out of college, I thought there was something wrong with me," she said. "If I'd known all this before, I never would have dropped out of school. Why did I have to wait so long for this help? Why did everybody think it was better to say I was 'not college material' than to say I was disabled?"

I had no answer to this question. I offered some personal history, telling her that though I was diagnosed as legally blind when I was eleven, I didn't really talk about it until I was well into adulthood and first started teaching. We talked about the nature of an invisible disability, about stoicism, about the temptations and risks of passing. I did not presume to advise her about dealing with her past, but I wanted her to know that my own disabled identity has evolved over many years and continues to evolve.

I was reminded that I had only one disabled professor during my entire college career, though he did not identify himself as such. His disability affected his use of one arm, and, as far as I could tell, he was able to write, type, and carry things with the other, so he did not need to speak about his disability to his classes as I do. He was not the sort of person who invited personal disclosures, and though I must have had a conversation with him about my disability, I cannot imagine the possibility of any discussion of our shared experiences as disabled people. I had "something wrong" with my eyes, he had "something wrong" with his arm; we had nothing in common. For me to claim otherwise would have been as shocking to him as it was unthinkable to me.

The world has changed a lot since then, and the change manifests itself in university classrooms. As more and more students with disabilities pursue higher education, disability becomes a central topic for scholars not only in the social sciences, medicine, and law but also in history, literature, even creative writing. Social evolution seldom follows a smoothly linear path. It can create discomfort and discord. It can raise more questions than it answers. And while I have few answers, I believe that as long as disability remains a taboo topic, progress is impossible. When disabled students come out, they assert that there is nothing wrong with being disabled. We have a right to a place in the classroom, as students and teachers. As we come out, we demonstrate that there is more than one way to move through space, to access a text, to process information, to communicate—more than one way to be a human being.

"It's better now than it used to be," I told my student. "Now at least there are more of us around."

"Us" was presumptuous, pushing her to the other side of the us/them divide. But I sensed she was moving in that direction anyway. Then she said, "I guess sooner or later they'll have to get used to us."

BRENDA JO BRUEGGEMANN

An Enabling Pedagogy

Standing in front of a new class, each and every time, I feel the burden of representation.[1] Somewhere in the briefing over course policies, the obligatory run through the syllabus, the remarks on key texts and assignments, and the stumble over reading a roster of names I might struggle to pronounce and will struggle even more to hear correctly if I don't get them right the first time—somewhere in there I need to tell them I'm deaf. Only I won't use that word. I'll opt for "hard-of-hearing."[2] And then I'll wince some, because I'm sure they're figuring, "Gee, I guess she's a lot older than she looks." So I'll quickly add that it's a genetic condition I've had from birth and begin rambling fast and nervously about how I have no hearing whatsoever in the three highest pure-tone frequencies they use in audiological exams; that I possess about moderate hearing in the three lower frequencies; that I am therefore very hard to fit for hearing aids (which I do sometimes now wear thanks to the wonders of digital technologies, which can enhance some of the pure-tone frequencies without also amplifying others); how I have never heard a bird or bell or the top three keys on the piano; how I can't hear whispers or even soft-spoken folks; why I tune to lower-pitched male voices easier than female ones; how I worried so much over whether I would be able to hear my own children once they were born; why I struggle most with consonants; how I patch together the sense of what my students are saying in class by maximizing body language and other contextual clues around what they say and

317

by lipreading (explaining, too, that most deaf people aren't in fact very adept at this skill, so please don't take me as representative); that I have a tendency to move in on their space—to go toward them—when they are talking so that I can maximize those clues all the more (which I illustrate even as I am explaining it); how they'll be able to contact me by phone (preferably not) and why e-mail is the best bet; how they'll often have to repeat what they say in class and maybe too what someone else has said ("So, hey," I joke, "you gotta pay attention in this class!"). They are definitely paying attention now.

At this point, for all they might or might not know about disability in general or deafness in particular, about disabled persons generally or d/Deaf people specifically, they are at a loss for words or responses. Their silence facing my presence, their muteness alongside my apparent mutability, brings both them and me to the center of disability and its key paradoxes as I've found those paradoxes encountered, time and again, in the language and literature courses I've taught where disability figures strongly.[3]

First and perhaps foremost, we face dealing with the erasure of disabled subjects from the public sphere. The apparent invisibility of disabled subjects in places like the academy confronts us. My representation, standing before this class, makes visible an anomaly that is hard to fit. (Even doubly disconcerting perhaps, when the disabled subject sits at the teacher's desk rather than in the student's seat.) We'll have to encounter, too, the way disabled subjects are often used, then erased, from the literature we'll read, the popular culture that surrounds us. And all this time, I'll be standing there, quite unerased, in the front of the classroom, gravitating toward whoever is speaking.

Second, and tied to the first, we'll encounter the economic argument used to deny access; we'll have to consider the cost of accommodating single disabled persons (because the economic argument always begins by singling out, dividing and conquering) in these hallowed halls where many can't pass (let alone get in the door, both figuratively and literally) because accessibility costs (as does excellence). I represent those costs—my "specials" not necessarily hanging out all over the place but evident enough if you go looking: the cost of my hearing aids; the price of an interpreter or real-time captioning from time to time; the TDD and special volume-control handset hooked to my phone; the office alarm light for door knocks, phone rings, fire alarms; and even my specially requested, acoustically favorable, room—University Hall 114—for my classes and an enrollment cap (so I can hear them all) of twenty-six students for my courses. We'll all have to ask ourselves at some point, implicitly or explicitly, consciously or not (and yes, I'm included in this we, since I do a lot of this asking, especially in a hard quarter, of myself), Is it worth it?

Most of the time it is (and I like to think that my students come away thinking the same). But even the asking of the question poses the third representational paradox of disability we'll encounter—the very instability of the category. Disability stabilizes most in its instability. The definition of disability always begins (and probably ends, too) in its ambiguity, in its indeterminate boundaries. Just ask the doctors who are often asked to certify disability.[4] Just ask the public school teachers and administrators floating, often unanchored, in the flotsam and jetsam of mainstreaming. Just ask the literature we'll be reading, where disabled characters often come and go, bobbing to the surface and then being swept away in the current of the theme they serve. Just ask the people sitting next to you in class, who may or may not be disabled (for disability is as invisible as it is visible); who may be disabled but are only recently coming to know that, to (self-)identify as disabled (this happens a lot in the classes I teach); who may identify with disability through some close relationship they have with a disabled person; or who may not have any concept or familiarity (yet) with disability. Just ask me. There's a lot of instability shaking up any classroom like this, in terms of disability, before I even enter the room. But when I come in, claiming disability but markedly invisible in that claim, things really start rattling—they don't see the hearing aids unless they get real close and look, my accent can easily be attributed to other sources, I pass at lipreading and contextualizing pretty well most of the time.

What also begins to rattle students in these classrooms where I teach language and literature from, around, or with a disability perspective is, fourth, the way disability is represented in literature and film. Particularly palpable distinctions arise when we read disability autobiography or memoir—the experience rendered firsthand—against or alongside literature, canonical or not, that has disabled characters in it. Incongruity appears when we watch major films centered on a disabled life (and here, the able-bodied actors who portray disabled characters win Oscars with notable frequency) and then view some key documentaries done by disabled people about disabled people. We've been taught to love literature in part because of the way it so represents life, the ways in which we can see and know ourselves even better through the characters on the page. But when first-person disability narratives or documentaries stand next to our classic (and even mainstream) literature and film, those classic and mainstream representations lie. Thus, what we've been taught now seems a lie, and then we also risk not liking the picture we've come to see of ourselves.

That we don't know how to represent ourselves is the fifth problem handed to us by disability. Faced with the incomplete and now obviously unstable face of disability, we're not sure what to draw in there. We're even less sure about how what we draw will reflect back on our face. Should we be nice? Patently patronizing? Innocently curious? Confess our culpability? Look away? Hold the door open for that wheelchair? Greet the blind person or just slip silently by? Feel bad that disabled people are cheaply used and even blatantly abused in so much of our literature? Vow never to watch another film that features a disabled character? Police parking lots, reporting those who abuse the handicapped parking spaces? Write a story with a real disabled character now that we've met some in memoir and documentaries? Volunteer at an assisted living center or sign up to read for blind recordings? Promise never to think about race, class, sexuality, or gender again without also thinking about disability?

Or should we resist? Proclaim our innocence, our too-easy victimization in being labeled as evil able-bodied oppressor? Not let lies be countered with more lies (especially when we feel they are about us)? Get rowdy back? Question privilege in general (as the thing that divides disabled from able-bodied no matter which side you are on)? Suddenly that old school playground chant rings all too real in our ears: "I'm rubber, and you're glue. Whatever you say bounces off of me and sticks to you." What we say and do and believe about disability suddenly begins to be what we say and do and believe about ourselves. These representations are getting sticky—tricky too.

We can try, as we often do in our teaching and scholarly lives (as both students and teachers), to turn to theory. But in a classroom where disability sits, either peripherally or centrally, we'll have a hard time representing a theory too. This difficulty is yet another problem that comes when disability enters a literature-and-language classroom—the sixth and final one, which I highlight in the scenes that follow. For disability, as both a lived experience and a developing field of study, struggles with its critical apparatus, searches for the right theoretical frame to fit its face(s). Disability theory can complement—by both teaching to and learning from—our already existing work in gender, sexuality, race, and class. It intersects well with and can even enhance our study of genre. It can both shadow and eclipse—take from and give back to—feminist theory, queer theory, Marxism, literary criticism, historicism, social constructionism, to name but a few. It spans literary periods and languages. It serves and is served by, as Sharon Snyder argued earlier in this volume, "infinities of forms."

Most of all, I argue throughout this essay, disability enables insight— critical, experiential, cognitive, and sensory. It is this enabling, this insight, that I am after in all my classrooms, whether disability is the subject or not. My (fairly recent) entry into disability studies; my use of disability memoir and documentary alongside representations of disability in literature, film, and popular culture in many of my courses now; and my self-identification as disabled (only in the last ten years of my life) have led to what I call an enabling pedagogy, a theory and practice of teaching that posits disability as insight.[5] My use of *we* throughout this first section has been far more than a stylistic nuance aimed at feigning inclusiveness. I'm honest here: this place is not one I thought I belonged to either for a long time. Disability has only recently come as insight into my life, enabling me both professionally and personally.

Centering the Subject: Representations of (Dis)Ability in Literature and Film

The first entirely disability-centered course I taught was a junior-senior English major course, Representations of (Dis)Ability in Literature and Film, under my department's grab-bag number, English 575, Themes in Literature. The course was indeed a grab bag, representing texts across multiple genres (drama, film, documentary, novels, poetry, and autobiography) and approaching disability from multiple—sometimes complementary, sometimes competing—perspectives. I had wanted to mix so much together quite deliberately and for several reasons. First, my intuition told me that I couldn't introduce disability as insight in reading literature and studying film to a group of junior-senior English majors unless I got them into the class in the first place. I sensed that a multiple-genre approach with texts and authors who were both familiar and strange as well as plenty of visual, nonreading (i.e., film) material thrown in would help reel in enrollment. I needed to make the course accessible at the outset, interesting to our undergraduate body, regardless of the status of their own individual bodies.

Second, I ranged widely across genres and paired, sometimes tripled, texts in order to shake up norms surrounding notions of disability and disabled people. By setting texts in conversation, harmonious or discordant, with one another, I thought we might best be able to explore literary representations—in their plurality—about bodies, minds, abilities, and disabilities. I wanted to make a web of meaning for the way (dis)ability is employed in literature and film and, in so doing, to position disability as insight into reading literary and cultural representations of what bodies and minds can do and be. I opened with a preliminary lecture outlining some of the authors and characters luminous in the canon (ones my students might already be familiar with) who also happened to be disabled: Homer, Tiresias, Captain Ahab, Alexander Pope, Samuel Johnson, Quasimodo, Benjy Compson, Flannery O'Connor, Richard III, et cetera.

I led the first couple of classes into territory I was most familiar with so that I might model some approaches to issues, discussion, and critical analysis when disability figures a text and our reading of it. I opened with a contemporary eighty-minute performance—a kind of disability documentary—by Neil Marcus and Access Theater titled *Storm Reading*. From the opening shot of this videotaped performance, Marcus shakes sensibilities. Stuttering profoundly in the first excruciatingly long two minutes of the performance, he mounts incredible tension in his audience (both the live performance and his video-viewing audience here on a Wednesday afternoon in January in an Ohio State University classroom). We all leaned forward to listen harder, our brows furrowed, our emotions racing between an outwardly directed sort of captive anger (and fear) at possibly having to listen to this incomprehensible voice for eighty long minutes and an inwardly focused, fidgeting embarrassment over Marcus's condition—general dystonia (an allover spasticity that makes this body stormy). We were caught in his storm—a bit frightened, uncomfortable, seeking escape. Then, just in time, as the tension mounts highest and the thunder almost breaks in us, both a sign language and voice interpreter appear and smooth things out for us, accommodating us. They say and sign together, echoing Marcus, "People are always watching me . . . they're watching to see how well I do this thing . . . this thing called 'human.' "

Later, we had a powerful, honest, and stormy discussion about our overwhelming physical and emotional discomfort in that opening two minutes of *Storm Reading*—our sense of discomfort at Marcus's struggling to speak and then our equal sense of discomfort for having been so impatient and uncomfortable in the first place. One student, speaking bravely, related it further to the power that infuses speaking:

> It brought up all these bad memories of times in grade school when certain teachers would force certain students to stand and speak before the class and they just couldn't do it. The students called on would hate it. Those of us listening would hate it. We

would all hate the teacher for making us all so uncomfortable. Speaking up and speaking well is always hard to do.[6]

From there I lead them into a reading of Mark Medoff's *Children of a Lesser God,* an award-winning play, where deaf Sarah Norman (the play on *normal* obvious here) challenges the high cultural premium placed on speaking up and speaking well that is enforced on her. We pair that play with a viewing of the film that follows it—starring William Hurt and Oscar-winning deaf actress Marlee Maitlin—and we find that some representations around disability and speaking remain the same, but some significantly differ between the original play (where Medoff did careful research on oral/sign issues in Deaf communities and worked with d/Deaf actors) and the more mass-marketed Hollywood film. Then I add another corner, triangulating the representations of speech and hearing issues in culture and literature by showing the award-winning 1994 French documentary by Nicholas Philibert, *In the Land of the Deaf.* Philibert's documentary, filmed in French Sign Language and some spoken French, subtitled in English, investigates an area far broader than speech, taking on representations of language per se. Beyond this set of three texts, whose issues and elements I am personally and professionally familiar with, I step back from such a definitive lead on discussion and analysis. While I still offer some background into the texts and authors and key issues that compose the rest of the course, I let groups of three to four students take turns helping design and lead discussions for any one reading or class period. I do this not because I am a proponent of the (now old-fashioned) student-centered classroom (although I am that too) but because I am convinced that my students won't get to disability as insight if I put in the batteries, turn it on, and shine the light for them. I can enable. But they will have to enable themselves too.

In this fashion, we roll through Hugo's *The Hunchback of Notre Dame* (and wonder, to begin with, why the hunchback, Quasimodo, became the center of the Anglicized title), and then we take in three different film versions—all deemed classics—of the novel. Disney's newest version of the *Hunchback* has just come out on video, and so our discussion of children and disability, the infantilizing of people with disabilities, and the patronizing of people with disabilities that springs from viewing this film leads us, the straight and the crooked, into a series of texts about parent-child relationships with disability factored in: Paul West's now published-as-a-pair texts about his deaf and brain-damaged daughter—his long epistolary essay *Words for a Deaf Daughter* (1970) and the following "wish-fulfillment" (as West himself called it [Preface xi]) novel *Gala* (1975); the Nobel

Prize–winning author Kenzaburo Oe's recent meditation on life with his brain-damaged son, *A Healing Family;* and Anne Finger's gutsy parent-with-a-disability-encounters-potential-child-with-a-disability autobiographical work, *Past Due: A Story of Pregnancy, Birth, and Disability.*[7]

Just as parents (and children) complicate life in our culture with their disability and with their views about disability, so too does war—and disabled veterans of war in particular—further mess up the story, further fracture our representations. We spent some time in this fragmented place reading Dalton Trumbo's manifesto classic *Johnny Got His Gun* and viewing Jon Voight and Jane Fonda's poignant, award-winning, post-Vietnam film *Coming Home.* My students had far less trouble conflating and cross-reading disability and war-veteran issues than I thought they would. They came, on their own, to interrogate the subtle but strong us/them splitting at work between official forms and less official ways of thinking that might separate "veteran, disabled" from just "disabled." This recognition of categories within categories among the disabled—a phenomenon I label crip-casteing—occupied their imagination for some time as they pondered the inherent hierarchies in the category of disability itself.

Thus, we came to talk about representations of those born disabled as opposed to representations of those who became disabled. And even among the became disabled, my students noted how certain ways of becoming were more acceptable or fashionable or exalted than others and that it mattered too, what caste you belonged to before you became disabled—so that Christopher Reeve's grand fall during an equestrian jumping competition and Jim Brady's being gunned down rank far above Joe Citizen's spilling across the roadway on his Harley after a three-beer pub stop. We could then begin to locate—in the literature we were reading, the films we were viewing, the culture we were living in—the distinctions within distinctions, representations within representations, categories within categories, and even easy conflations within easy conflations laid out between: disability as a convenient metaphor and the disability one really lives with and experiences; "They deserve to be disabled" and "Pity them for their disability"; a disability you stare at and one you look away from; freaks and the disabled; physical disability and mental disability; congenital and acquired disabilities; "veteran, disabled" and just disabled; temporary and permanent disabilities; disfigurement and disability; and normal and not.

Suddenly, disability didn't look so strange or so rarely encountered. For their final projects, the class pushed and probed these distinctions further, peeling back layers upon interesting layers of representations about bodies, exploring the depth and range of human "(dis)(abilities)"—as one student came to rewrite the operative word in the course title—that have decorated and littered our literature and culture for centuries upon centuries. One student, for example, compared Bernard Pomerance's play *The Elephant Man* to several "scientific" accounts of the real Elephant Man, John Merrick. Another was spurred on by Cheryl Marie Wade's "sassy-girl" poetry and performances and investigated both the poster-child and Jerry Lewis–inspired telethon scenes surrounding many disabilities. Intrigued by the performance approach to disability that disabled people often use to repaint the portrait of disability in fiction and poetry, another student did a study of disabled actors and disability theater groups across the country. Hopefully headed for a Hollywood career himself, one young man carried out a careful and quite comprehensive analysis of how and why actors have often won Oscars for their performances of disabled characters.

New texts like Lucy Grealy's *Autobiography of a Face* caught the eye and imagination of another student, who found herself most interested in disability's complication of beauty as a concept that so controls our culture. Current literature and cultural constructions of disability also caught imaginations: one student did a kind of cultural studies analysis of the Vietnam Veterans Memorial (including a weekend trip to DC to visit the memorial firsthand) from a disabled perspective; another spliced together a film-scene collage of key disability moments from box-office-hit movies over the past decade and wrote an explanatory essay of the project and its critical findings; one creative writer wrote a short story with a central character based on her grandmother, recently disabled through a stroke. Also in a creative vein, three students performed their disabled coming out—one with a self-made documentary of his lifelong learning disability in which, among other things, he demonstrated, close up, the remarkable way he must tie his shoes and remember a phone number; a second—inspired by poets like Kenny Fries, Mary Duffy, and Cheryl Marie Wade—wrote and then gave a reading of her poetry that stitched in her hidden disability; and the third wrote a creative nonfiction meditation on the medical data she had uncovered about her own and others' asthma. A student whose part-time job had her logging in hours as an assistant manager at Barnes and Noble quantified and qualified the disability memoirs that stacked the current nonfiction shelves during the last month of our class. Another student reread a book she had read in a team-taught women's studies and

African American studies class the quarter before—Audre Lorde's *The Cancer Journals*—in order to lend disability as insight to Lorde's slim volume this time around.

We shared all our projects during the final-exam period of the course, and I have to admit that the most powerful moment for me, as the instructor, in that entirely powerful closing event was when the three students who had outed their disabilities under the guise of this final class project stayed behind, engrossed in conversations with one another, as the rest of us filed out. Through the literature we had read and the discussions we had had, these three (and more, I hope) found individual identity, personal strength, creative capabilities, representative power, and community.

Composing Disability

"My mother doesn't think it's right that my English teacher is deaf." I don't even have to go back and read that one again. It sinks in well enough the first time. Dropped in the middle of an otherwise quite pleasant, seemingly benign paper from one of my recent freshman honors composition students, the exclusion of me as a human being (let alone as a competent English professor and, mind you, the grader of this very paper) in this line leaves me little space for meaningful response. I give the paper a B, making doubly sure that this grade stands fair against the assessment criteria I've dutifully handed out and discussed with my students (thank God) way back in week 1 of the quarter. I rub my temples a little, pick up a stray rubber band on the desk and twist it tight, unmercifully and nervously, in my hands for a minute. I go downstairs to make a cup of tea.

With civility, and red rubber-band marks making my hands itch a little, I go to the next paper.

I have made Abilities in America the title of an otherwise subjectless freshman composition course (an honors one at that) this quarter, because I think we can read race, class, gender, sexuality, and a whole host of other American-as-apple-pie cultural-academic concerns well through the lens of disability (and therein, satisfy the required diversity component my university names for both the first- and second-year writing courses) and also because in the middle of this quarter a three-day national colloquium, "Enabling the Humanities: Disability Studies in Higher Education," will take place on my campus. I am coordinating this event at the Wexner Center for the Arts, and I've arranged to have my students personally meet many of the authors they will read in this course. It seemed like a good idea at the time.

But John's mother, for one, isn't buying it.

I won't lie about it: a number of dangerous, demeaning, disturbingly uncivil actions and reactions have occurred in the courses I've taught (six of them now) where disability has been the focal point. We lash out when we feel threatened. And when something goes wrong with our body or mind, or with the bodies and minds of those we know and love well, that tends to be threatening. After all, if they—no, make that we— can legally, morally, easily abort fetuses for chromosomal aberrations like Down syndrome after early detection, compliments of an amnio- centesis (or other similar tests performed rather routinely on newly pregnant women these days), what's to stop us from getting rid of us— or Grandpa, or Aunt Sally, or brother Mike—when chromosomes or other conditions happen to create some aberration in our, or their, form or function? We may as well all, both disabled and able-bodied, get un- civil now—while we still have the chance.

On the first day of Honors Freshman Composition, after I've handed out the syllabus and course information sheet, given my spiel about my hearing loss, given a brief speech about why Abilities in America is my chosen title for this course, and then gushed about how lucky they are to have a chance to meet personally with authors and scholars and film directors and performers at the upcoming EH (Enabling the Humanities) colloquium whose material they will also cover in class, and they've mostly just stared blankly at me (truly, who could blame them?)—I fi- nally ask them to brainstorm hot issues in America. Civilly, dutifully they rattle off many, gaining speed as they go, until we have a whole boardful. I ask someone to pick one, just one. "Date rape," suggests a girl, giggling.

I don't think it's funny. But I don't start down that road. "Okay," I say. "Date rape and disability—how are they related?" Their stares are not so much blank now as saying, "What?! You are one crazy woman. What kind of question is *that*?" Full of meaning.

"Well, they are," I plunge on, crazy woman with an answer. Forking two ways, I talk briefly first about how statistics on sexual abuse record alarmingly high numbers among disabled, institutionalized persons, both young and old (often at the hands of their caregivers but some-times, too, among each other) and, second, about how disabled people are more often than not perceived as either asexual or abnormally sex-ual. The potential for abuses—sexual and otherwise—is great when hu-man beings are disregarded as somehow less than human. I tick off examples through history, recent and long past.

They still look a little spooked but not quite so suspicious of me now. "Your turn," I say. "Go ahead, pick one item here on this list. Grab a few classmates close by. Spend the next five minutes seeing if you can figure out a relation to disability." Some are stretching it, but they can pretty much all do it. Euthanasia, they find, is easy; they are very aware of who Dr. Kevorkian's clients have primarily been. Abortion too is easy. Interestingly, though, they focus mostly on how a disabled woman would most likely want an abortion. (You can be sure I'm taking notes on this for our discussion on the intersections between feminist studies and disability studies that will occur later in the quarter.) "And now," one of them offers hesitantly, "I think you can get an abortion if you know you will have a Down syndrome baby." But I can tell they don't want much to talk about that. I let it go, too. We'll come back to it, ready or not, when we get to Finger's riveting and treacherously, ethically complex personal narrative.

"Body piercing," offers one young man, chosen spokesperson for a group of unpierced bodies in the corner by the door. He shrugs. "We couldn't really find much connection . . . except maybe . . . ," and here his voice lowers enough that I see the other students lean forward to catch it, though my lipreading skills come to my rescue, "well, that those who do it have sick minds. Or . . . "—he smirks a little now—"that body piercing is a way of disabling yourself." The air crackles, some metal flashing and hot around the room. I jot a quick note to my-self, "What bodies can/can't do to themselves; crippling one's self; cf. Goffman's *Stigma*." (And although I don't tell them about it, I think of the sadomasochist Bob Flanagan, a performance artist with cystic fi-brosis, and his profound, transgressive film, *Sick*.) Then I turn the con-versation quickly away from this exercise, trying to cool the air and create a safe place here on the first day where we can share our writing and have civil albeit free-speaking discussions later. I begin the peda-gogue's drone about the next class assignment and gearing up for the first paper. But inside, in my disabled soul, I'm singing, truly delighted: it's only the first day and they've already taught me something new. Body piercing and disability. I hadn't thought of that. Surely, Erving

Goffman, famed sociologist of the 1950s and 1960s who studied "the presentation of self in everyday life" (*Presentation*) and how stigma works in our culture as well as how institutions form their own frames—surely Goffman would get it: the visible stigma of piercing, the management of a spoiled identity when metal marks flesh, flashes a self (*Stigma*).

I've taught freshman composition enough times to know all too well that most of the time most of the students will resist most any subject you put before them in this required class. (Honestly, even instructors usually come to resist the subject they place on the syllabus themselves.) I was worried, to be sure, about putting a subject I cared so passionately about in the middle of this obligatory, knee-jerk but kicking-damn-hard-back kind of resistance. "But hey, this won't be so bad after all," I told myself, a little skip in my step, as I walked back to my office.

In Honors Freshman Composition that spring quarter they kicked so hard and so often that it was hard not to fold into a fetal position, protecting my head, praying for my ribs, when I entered the classroom each day. I also had a graduate student in there doing her teaching apprenticeship with me that quarter, so I tried not to look scared, feel wounded, run away. I was passing as brave. Barely, barely passing.

Most hated the disability documentaries I showed—films I had laughed, cried, and cheered over with graduate students in my disability seminar the year before and with my colleagues in disability studies at national conferences. Marcus, the playwright and actor who could barely speak, wound up angering them in a scene from his *Storm Reading*, when he dared, humorously but seriously, to portray himself as a waiter. "What gives him a right to think he can hold a job like that in the first place?" one student shot out, and half a dozen others nodded vehemently.

Deep breath. Chant "civility" to myself. "I don't know. What *does* give him the right? Can we talk about that?" I prompted back, teeth grinding behind the bravery, my feigned pleasantness nearly poisoning me. "What kind of job is waitressing?" I asked further. "Who makes a living at it? Who *wants* to make a living at it? Why do people wait tables in the first place?" We had opened a complicated discussion on economics and access here—a can of worms squirming with the right to work, the ability to work, the desire to work, the necessity of work, the accommodation of work. Even I was afraid to stick my hand in.

Another day, after we watch Billy Golfus's award-winning *When Billy Broke His Head*, a disability documentary undeniably with attitude, another kick-back comment lands in the middle of the classroom. Golfus has documented some of the protests at the Colorado State House by disabled citizens seeking equal access with dignity. These citizens wanted to be able to get a wheelchair, not just a foot, in both the statehouse doors and the Denver bus systems. They'd gone to the statehouse and barricaded the entry escalators that take employees and visitors up one floor from the street-level entry to the offices. "They can't do that!" yells one of my students. "They can't obstruct and prevent someone from entering that building. Those people have rights!" He's really riled.

"And hey, you're right!" I cheer him on. He beams, righteous. Then I pick up that comment and lob it back to him, heavy and hard. "'Those people'—the ones in the wheelchairs—they have rights, too! Those escalators prevent them from entering the building, from being citizens in their own state's government. *That's* the point!"

But the moment I've said it, while I'm a little refreshed that I've countered logic for logic, rights for rights, I'm also sorry. While a good handful of the other students witnessing this exchange get those little "Oh wow! I see what you mean!" lightbulbs over their heads and I know then that I've gained a little disability awareness with them, I've also lost this student forever. Alienated him, silenced him, pinned him to the mat. The only way he'll be back is to try pinning me in another match. I've forfeited teaching for wrestling.

I try not to worry about it. I'm passing as brave again.

They got pretty mean about handicapped parking spaces too. One student in particular brought it up almost every class period, until I finally (privately, not publicly this time) invited him to do his research paper assignment on this topic, to find out just who, how, and how many got those parking spaces. My plan was that once he found out how complicated it was to get a handicapped parking permit and also how many nondisabled people abused the system, his anger would be appeased and he'd be out there, in parking lots across America, leaping to help anyone who rightfully parked in that blue-symboled, front-row space and shaking his angry fist at those who slipped illegally into those spots.

Well, he did his research. He found out that it was fairly complicated to get a special little blue-symboled tag for your car—but not nearly complicated enough, he argued. He found out that yes indeed there were quite an astonishing number of Americans who used and claimed they needed these permits either permanently or temporarily. But this is the problem, he argued: the system is soft; anyone can get a permit, all you have to be is smart, sneaky, or persistent; there are too many cripples out there who probably shouldn't be driving in the first place. (His next paper, in an assignment that asked the students to extend an idea from one of the previous assignments, was on the national shame of and danger in senior citizens driving—and how our disability-sensitive attitudes had only added to this shame and danger.) And he counted. Kept track of how many handicapped spots on central campus weren't used over a week's time and compared that to how many cars were turned away from several Ohio State University parking garages each day when the Full sign came on, how many student cars in a given hour circled some of the prime surface lots. He had an e-mail chat with the OSU director of traffic and parking, who claimed that, sure, too many good spaces on campus were given up to handicapped spots. "What a shame," my student wrote. He took note of how empty the handicapped spots were at his favorite mall one weekend. (Some were taken, some weren't. Case in point: "This privilege is a massive waste of taxpayer's money," he wrote.) Oh well, I sighed and bravely surmised, at least he learned how to do good research. I was learning some things too. When Nancy Mairs came to read and do a workshop at the "Enabling the Humanities" colloquium in midquarter, most of my students chose her from among the five available attend-an-author-reading options. We'd read half her essays in *Waist-High in the World* by that point in the class, and although they didn't always like her directness, they liked that she wrote fairly short essays and not those "novels that go on too long." Most of my students did actually like what she had to say. They liked her simple style, and they also wrote unabashedly of how amazed they were that she "wore really nice clothes, makeup, and fixed herself up." They learned, as one girl put it, that "disabled people care what they look like, too. They are just like the rest of us." Visibility mattered. And although I can't say this was the picture I most wanted them to get of or from Mairs, some other frames were becoming clearer to me.

For what happens here, in the tale of my student's resistance, makes even me suspicious. I become framed as the heroine. Brave, insightful, enlightened, ever-so-kind. Bad able-bodied young students. Good disabled me. The plot looks a little too simple, the characters definitely flat, the story too stable. I'm not telling the truth. I'm fictionalizing the nonfictional, creating for my convenience.

Okay, so I'm not all that bad either.

It took another six months, into the fall of the next year, when the leaves began falling and I had my students' evaluations back, both the discursive and the university standardized bubble-form evaluations—and my students hadn't, in fact, trashed me—that I started to see it another way, hear a different tune, walk a bit in their shoes. In a culture where cars aren't just tools to get you from here to there but extensions of psyches, identities writ large, no wonder the idea of privileged parking matters, really matters. Even more threatening when you are probably just settling into your first car, claiming your first parking spots. It's a Porsche-eat-Porsche world out there.

Likewise, in bodies hard, young, and generally able—yet still not likely to have been meaningfully employed in a rewarding career—my students are acutely aware of the place waitressing occupies on the totem pole of "things I want to be when I grow up and that Mom and Dad will be proud they paid for my college education for." No wonder then that Marcus and Golfus weren't funny, threatening as they were in not only their unemployment but also their flauting and parodic portrayals of it (never mind that both Marcus and Golfus are employed—self-employed—and have obviously talented careers as writers, performers, filmmakers). These parodies and the (non)possibilities for a man who can't even work at McDonald's jars and kicks at their freshly freshman bootstrap views of "You can do anything if you just work hard enough at it or pay enough money for it." No wonder they wanted often to strike back or just curl up and roll away, protecting their heads at all costs.

I wanted them to understand me, to get *in* disability, and to see themselves there. But I wasn't willing to understand them, to get *in* their abilities, to see myself there. I hadn't yet got to disability as insight, to understanding that the us/them sword (as I myself had placed it in the middle of this classroom) cuts both ways. I was stuck, like Dr. Seuss's famous (star-bellied) Sneetches, in enforcing and capitalizing on a direct desire to be other. I had forgotten just how unstable and unstabilizing (dis)(ability) can be.

———————

I also wasn't paying much attention to one of the major lessons I've learned from my own and others' disabled lives and even more from the way their lives are constructed socially by people around them: adaptability. It takes most of us a little time to adapt. Paradigms have to shift.

Paradigm shifts are often revolutionary, and, according to the scientific philosopher Thomas Kuhn, it takes some time and distance for the full impact of a revolution to be known. One day, nearly hyperventilating and hysterical (I'd just read the paper on handicapped parking), I lurched into a colleague's office two doors down. She has long taught courses in twentieth-century American literature; in recent years she has gone on to emphasize, in both her undergraduate and graduate courses, gender and sexuality in those texts, to turn to homo- and hetero-ideologies as they run through, sometimes conflicting and sometimes intricately interwoven with each other in the canonical and non-canonical literature of our culture and century. I needed to know that I was going to be all right, that I would survive the final three weeks of the course, that I wouldn't be some bizarre university newspaper headline in the very near future. "They'll remember this, Brenda," she assured me. "Years from now—maybe forty years, for some of them—they'll get it." I wobbled out, dabbed some concealer around my red-rimmed eyes, and went off to teach that class again.

In the end, and happy endings are always best, she was right. Two students did powerful final projects investigating the medical, emotional, familial, financial, and social impacts of a parent's recent entry into a disabled life. Not only did they find out reams about the parent's condition that the doctors weren't telling them but they also interviewed the parent and others around the parent to offer a multiply framed view of the disability. One student even concluded with the curious way she and others were still bracketing off the disability from the person (her parent). Another student, who was impressed with Susan Nussbaum's play *Mishuginismo* and Cheryl Marie Wade's performance piece "Zeus," did a twin analysis of medical and social treatments of adolescent disabled women, particularly in relation to their sexuality. All along, the student kept comparing those treatments to the medical and social treatments of her own sexuality—which wound up not looking so good in the end either. For a group presentation, three young women interviewed two very smart deaf/hard-of-hearing girls in their dorm. The three confessed to "watching them [the deaf girls] from a distance" for all the months before they took this class, never daring to approach them as friends, peers, human beings. In the video interview they showed in class, my three students and these two others are getting along pretty well. Two of these girls—one deaf, one not (from my composition class)—went on to share leadership positions in my department's undergraduate English organization. They became good friends.

A young man wrote a response to Mary Duffy's performance in *Vital Signs* (Snyder and Mitchell). In that piece Duffy stands behind a velvet backdrop—beautiful, nude, statuesque, and armless too—reciting her poems. He spent a long time looking through books of art, studying Greek statues, reading about them, in order to reflect for a mere two pages on why arms can seem of little sexual significance ("I never say to my buddies at the bar, you know, 'Hey, look at the arms on that babe'") . . . until they aren't there. Another male student, also fascinated with bodies and physique—a bodybuilder and Gold's Gym employee himself—had a grand time digging through various sources, from physical education journals to Rosemarie Garland-Thomson's edited collection *Freakery*, then layering that study with two interviews he was granted with disabled members of his gym. Finally, a young woman who had always been drawn to Frida Kahlo's work (she was intending to be a double major in art history and women's studies) discovered—thanks to the cover of Garland-Thomson's other book, *Extraordinary Bodies*—that Kahlo was disabled later in life. That disability was the subject of the student's final paper and project. When I saw her just last quarter, she said that she had worked even more on the project, expanding it even further, for an art history class and had been asked to make a presentation about Kahlo at a conference with her mentor-professor.

My point in this litany of successful papers and projects is, I hope, more than just bragging, more than just washing out some of the bad taste that kept getting in my mouth that quarter. It's not about what I did or didn't do in putting disability, full throttle, in a course like freshman composition. It's about what we did. How it opened up an astonishing array of topics to research and write on, how many students (no, not all of them) found meaningful personal and passionate ways to connect to the material, social, and individual world of disability, and how I moved closer to an enabling pedagogy. Even my seemingly failed effort to convert Mr. Parking Spaces, I'd have to admit, led to research and writing done carefully, with passion.

I've spent a lot of time in this essay on only one of the six courses I've taught with disability at its center. I suppose this focus is due to the weight a course like freshman composition carries in a huge land-grant university like my own. Every student who comes to Ohio State, save for a handful of very remarkable few, must take the course. That's a lot of students. Year after year. It's a contentless course for the most part.

Any and every composition instructor can—and often does—insert nearly any and every possible topic for readings to fill in the spaces between small and large writing assignments, for diving boards to spring, foundations to ground, and kites to fly ideas for writing.

This course comes guaranteed with student resistance at the outset. To put disability there was truly the greatest challenge of my eighteen years of teaching students from ages twelve to sixty-eight. Teaching writing was always what I had done best. Being disabled was always what I had done—not best, but just done. But in that doing I had also been very careful to pass at my doing, to look as if I were not doing the disability thing. Ever and always a keen observer of contextual cues (my way of hearing), I have noted well the stigma and fear and loathing and curiosity and staring and general perplexity that hazes over a room when a disabled person visibly enters. So I had been careful about when and where and how I wore my star.

But here, in the spring of 1998, directing the three-day colloquium "Disability Studies in Higher Education" and walking into Honors Freshman Composition with a syllabus entitled "Abilities in America," I was letting it all hang out. And you know, it wasn't so discrediting after all. It was enabling.

One student wrote to me nine months later, when she was seeking a letter of reference from me for various honors and summer positions: "I always think about Disability 101. I see things in terms of disability now. I question representations of the disabled in media, in language. I question myself and my own ideas about the disabled. I try to imagine myself into a disabled experience [. . .]." Her imagining, her move toward disability as insight, marks the enabling pedagogy I am seeking to enact. It is my belief that the range and depth of the pieces collected in this volume will offer disability as insight into language and literature and that, when used in both graduate and undergraduate humanities courses in particular, they will enable us all to enact an enabling pedagogy.

NOTES

1. Fortunately, I never stand alone. Particular colleagues and friends, some disability-identified and some not, often stand with me when I teach (even if it's not about disability) and certainly when I write. They have all had an active role in the writing of this essay: Georgina Kleege, who has taught me much about writing, about living strongly but gracefully with disability, and about teaching, too; Johnson Cheu, who always challenges and always enables my thinking about both disability and teaching; Rosemarie Garland-Thomson and Sharon

Snyder, my coeditors, who have copiloted much of my career in disability studies and whose scholarship I first learned from; Maureen Stanton and Melissa Goldthwaite, members of my essay writers' workshop group who asked all the hardest—and best—questions in reading this essay's first draft and whose writing I am always seeking to emulate.

2. My choice of the label "hard-of-hearing" is best explained in two other essays I've written, "On (Almost) Passing" and "Are You Deaf or Hearing?" Both are in my book, *Lend Me Your Ear: Rhetorical Constructions of Deafness*. Although my audiogram might well certify me as severely to profoundly deaf, my predominantly mainstreamed education (in a time before there was mainstreaming as we know it today), my skills at lipreading (sometimes a source of pride, sometimes of shame), my late arrival to sign language (at age 29), and some late involvement in and awareness of the Deaf community (at age 31) preclude me from using or choosing either of the full-fledged designations—*deaf* (denoting an audiological condition of severe hearing loss) or *Deaf* (denoting a cultural and linguistic allegiance).

3. To date, I have taught six courses that I would claim as primarily disability-centered and have significantly intersected disability issues into at least four others. For syllabi and other material pertaining to these courses, see my Web site: http://people.english.ohio-state.edu/brueggemann.1/. Additional disability-in-the-humanities course descriptions and syllabi are available at the Disability in the Humanities (DS-HUM) Web site: www.georgetown.edu/crossroads/interests/ds-hum/.

4. Deborah Stone recounts in *The Disabled State* how physicians repeatedly testified before congressional committees in the 1940s, as the social welfare system was being reformed principally around the category of disability, that they would more often than not be unable to adequately certify the unbounded, highly contextualized designation of *disabled* for any of their patients.

5. I cannot thank Lennard Davis enough for the insight that led to my ideas about disability as insight. In *Enforcing Normalcy: Disability, Deafness, and the Body*, he posits it in his crucial fifth chapter. I also acknowledge a debt to Jennifer Nelson, who has made me think hard about the uncomfortable and often unwanted position that disability as insight can still leave disabled people in—as they are called on to educate, yet again, their nondisabled acquaintances, students, colleagues about what disability is and isn't.

6. The fear of speaking in public is, coincidentally, the number one fear cited by most Americans in a recent survey, according to *The Everyday Writer* (Lunsford 274).

7. The next time I teach the course, I will be sure to include Michael Bérubé's personally essayistic *Life As We Know It: A Father, a Family, and an Exceptional Child*.

MICHAEL BERUBE

Afterword:
If I Should Live So Long

In recent years I have often wondered whether my approach to disability studies has been a normal one. By this I mean, on the one hand, that I have a more or less predictable set of anxieties for someone more or less "in the field" who does not identify as disabled—or, as many people would say, does not *yet* identify as disabled. As a result I am watchful for those aspects of my life and work in which my attitude toward disability remains that of a person who grew up thinking unreflectively about human beings in precisely the terms that have been called into question by disability studies, that is, where the default position is to see people without disabilities as normal and to see that category of the normal, like the category of whiteness, as unmarked. In those terms, certainly, it would be a thoroughly undesirable thing to have a normal (or normalizing) approach to disability. On the other hand, there is also a sense in which my introduction to the subject of disability was normal in that it was entirely unremarkable and widely generalizable, specific neither to me nor to any of the various group identities and subject positions I might plausibly claim to occupy. And in that sense my entry into disability studies is normal insofar as it may eventually serve as one of the vehicles by which other nondisabled scholars can imagine a productive relation to the field. For my relation to disability was made visible (or, to use a less loaded and more compelling term, became *inescapable*) to me only when I was thirty years old, and my relation to disability ever since has been both voluntary and involuntary. My point in opening with the odd term *normal*, then, is simply that there is nothing especially idiosyncratic about my relation to disability; any number of people could say pretty much the same thing for pretty much the same reasons, including millions of people with disabilities whose disabilities did not exist or manifest themselves until later in life, or millions of people with disabilities who figure their own relation to disability as both voluntary and involuntary.

"Disability stabilizes most in its instability," writes Brenda Jo Brueggemann in this volume ("An Enabling Pedagogy"). "The definition of disability always begins (and probably ends, too) in its ambiguity, in its indeterminate boundaries." That's one crucial reason why some people with disabilities do not identify as disabled, and why the question of self-identification in disability studies is so complex; but it's also one reason why people with and without disabilities might find in disability studies new forms of knowledge and understanding that can transform every aspect of the humanities. To put this another way: it is by now a truism, marked by the phrase "temporarily able-bodied" and by numerous essays in this collection, that disability can affect any one of us. But the contributors to this volume are collectively saying something quite different and perhaps even more destabilizing—namely, that disability *studies* can affect any one of us. Surely it's time for scholars in the humanities to begin pondering the implications of this possibility.

The publication of this volume is, of course, one important index of the disciplinary maturity of disability studies in the humanities; *Disability Studies* will serve countless scholars, students, and general readers as an introduction to what has been done and what can be done when we read literature, criticism, and theory through the many matrices of disability. But this book is also an index of—or, at the very least, a hopeful gesture toward—the potential universalization of disability studies across the fields of the human sciences. And it does not seem coincidental that the potential universalization of the field of study should be accompanied by fresh emphases on the potential universalization of disability. Let me put this another way: although the field self-consciously likens its category of identity to the other categories of identity interrogated by the social and cultural movements of the past thirty years (as in Rosemarie Garland-Thomson's claim that disability "is a culturally fabricated narrative of the body, similar to what we understand as the fictions of race and gender"), disability studies theorists' every invocation of race, gender, class, and sexuality serves at once to liken disability to other forms of identity and differentiate disability from other forms of identity. For in one sense disability remains a minoritized identity, and, as *Disability Studies* shows, disability studies is energetically examining its points of confluence with feminism and queer theory, its points of convergence with the history of theories about race, its points of coincidence with accounts of the rise of industrial capitalism. But in another sense disability is a curious kind of minoritized identity, which, if we take due account of temporality in our theories of identity, a vast majority of our fellow human beings will occupy at one point or another in their lives. The medicalized understanding of disability is gone, replaced by a minority model that seems, oddly enough, applicable not only to minoritized identities but also to the problematic of identity as such. And applicable also to all the sociohistorical determinants of identity: although you can't think about disability without thinking about individual persons (what else would we be talking about?), you can't think about disability without thinking about environments (natural and built), laws, institutions, public policies, biomedical discourses, and a whole host of phenomena not reducible or specific to individual persons.

Disability Studies makes its claim on universalism in the opening paragraphs of its introduction. "Disability," write Sharon Snyder, Brueggemann, and Garland-Thomson, "names the naturally occurring or acquired bodily variations that accrue as we move through history and across cultures. [. . . D]isability as both a bodily condition and a social category either now or later will touch us all. The fact that many of us will become disabled if we live long enough is perhaps the fundamental aspect of human embodiment." Disability studies, accordingly, can address an essential component (I use *essential* advisedly) of what it means to be human, to have a human body. But there's a specific danger on the road to universal access, a danger that the function of disability studies in the academy will be understood not to enable but to humanize the rest of the humanities. Georgina Kleege, for instance, writes in part to refuse "any inference that the mere fact of my disability augments my teaching qualifications or that there is a pedagogical value in exposing my disability to nondisabled students. This practice smacks too much of the freak show and casts me in the role of goodwill ambassador sharing the quaint beliefs and customs of my alien world." Kleege is writing about classroom politics, about the perils of coming out as disabled to students with and without disabilities; but her remarks also pertain more generally to the intellectual position of disability studies in the humanities. For many reasons, disability scholars will refuse, as Kleege does, the role of the native informant. Not only because it smacks of the freak show but also because the politics of bodily representation are so very complicated: no one form of disability can possibly represent every other imaginable form, and no one scholar of disability, regardless of whether the scholar identifies as disabled, can possibly represent the field. To assume otherwise is to ask scholars with disabilities to bear what Brueggemann calls an undue and often paradoxical "burden of representation." Most of all, however, no one wants to represent the field as a goodwill ambassador to the normal humanities; that's not what the *enabling* invoked in this volume's subtitle will involve, and that's not what the universalization of disability studies will entail.

What then might universalization entail? Every essay in this collection affords an answer; some open out onto new modes of pedagogy and scholarship, and some imagine—or begin—conversations between disability studies and the theoretical inquiries of the past thirty years, as in Martha Stoddard Holmes's link between the disabled woman character in nineteenth-century British literature and the fallen Victorian woman or Robert McRuer's deft elaboration of Adrienne Rich and Judith Butler en route to a conjunctural analysis of heteronormativity and "the system of compulsory able-bodiedness." Perhaps most provocative at the moment, though, are the various ways in which disability studies participates in the ongoing construction of the cluster of ideas that go under the general name of social constructionism. Indeed, in contemporary debates over the status of social constructionism, the study of disability sits at a crucial juncture. On the one hand, disability is quite obviously constructed (a "culturally fabricated narrative," in Garland-Thomson's phrase), insofar as there are any number of social contexts in which deafness is not disabling or as wheelchairs would signify (and get around) very differently in a world without stairs. On the other hand, disability is often quite immediately physical, material, and substantial (the Žižekian "hard kernel" of reality, in David Mitchell's phrase), regardless of what any academic social theorist or any proponent of so-called common sense might think or say about it. That disability is at once a question of the body and a question of the built environment makes it a central subject for the humanities—and for the social and natural sciences, and thus for new forms of cross-disciplinary study.

Take for instance Mark Jeffreys's account of his brother Jim and his family's insistence on appearing normal in group photographs. "What strikes me now as awful about all this," Jeffreys writes, was not that culture constructed us. Culture could take my brother's healthy, nimble leglessness and make it into a dark comedy of monstrosity, a nearly immobilized boy cyborg, one half flesh, one half mechanism. But if culture was as omnipotent as constructivist theory would have it, and the body was entirely culture's fiction, then culture could have also succeeded in erasing the difference it could not tolerate. Instead, Jim's body, and Jim, resisted. Well enough to talk about making our culture accommodate physical difference; but only in acknowledging that there is some physical reality beyond culture can that accommodation be reached.

I don't happen to agree with this entirely: social constructionism doesn't necessarily propose or enable the erasing of bodily difference, for one thing, and for another, it may be possible to accommodate physical difference by acknowledging a physical reality within culture rather than beyond it. Nonetheless, the passage is an important one for two reasons. First, because Jeffreys is basically right: whenever we get too blithe about the possibility that social constructions can be constructed otherwise, too complacent in our belief that we can change a socially constructed world by the end of next week, we need to remember (*body, remember,* to steal a phrase from the title of Kenny Fries's memoir) that there's a *there* there, that the biological materiality of the body is susceptible to a finite (and sometimes severely delimited) number of constructions. It's also worth remembering that most of our culture is socially constructed along the medical model to begin with. Which leads me to the second reason I focus on this passage, namely, its varied constructions of social constructionism. What precisely counts as social constructionism here or, for that matter, in disability studies in general? Jim's prosthesis is a social construction, in a literal sense. But the stigma attached to the monstrous legless body is also a social construction. And so is the Jeffreys family's desire not to be stigmatized, to write instead its own fabricated narrative of normality: the pressure to conform is woven into the very texture of the social fabric. Family portrait photographs, action figures, grooms taller than their brides—all these are social constructions as well. But as Jeffreys points out, they are all constructions *of something*—in this case, constructions of bodies, human bodies that are themselves constructed by something other than (and in addition to) cultural forces.

Not least among the things disability studies brings to the humanities is this salutary and perhaps overdue respect for the variety of human bodies and the varieties of social constructionism. Again and again in these essays readers will remark on (and, I think, learn from) disability studies' dual focus on the body as material artifact and the body as social construction; again and again in these essays readers will be struck by the necessary oscillation between understanding disability in terms of individual human bodies and understanding disability as a means by which societies have categorized and deindividualized human bodies.

Why a *necessary* oscillation between hard kernels and social constructions, between bodies that matter and the locations of culture? Because, I think, there lurk in this volume and in disability studies profound questions of social and cultural justice. Disability studies knows full well that the location of human bodies in human cultures is not merely an academic question. As Tobin Siebers writes, marking one of many links between psychoanalysis and politics, "The same arguments that demonstrate that people with disabilities make bad patients and analysts suggest that they make bad citizens." Carol Poore introduces her essay on Arnold Zweig's remarkable novel *Das Beil von Wandsbek* in still broader terms:

> One task of the cultural analysis that accompanies today's civil rights movement of people with disabilities is to expose and critique the omnipresent stereotypes and negative metaphors of disability in our cultural heritage. This project is necessary because of the grave consequences these widely accepted negative images had and still have for the lives of people with disabilities.

Poore goes on, of course, not simply to critique negative images but also to analyze a powerful counterexample, a novel in which disability does not serve merely as what Mitchell calls "narrative prothesis." But the question of justice is worth pursuing in these terms all the same. The stereotypes, metaphors, and images of disability have been primary means by which human cultures have constructed disability in systems of compulsory able-bodiedness. The representation of disability (in both the aesthetic and the political sense of representation) has also been the construction of disability—and needs to be reexamined by scholars in the humanities precisely for its effects on, or its productions of, the actual bodies of actual persons. At stake here is a question of justice for people with disabilities: *this project is necessary because of the grave consequences these widely accepted negative images had and still have for the lives of people with disabilities.*

But what if there were no such consequences? Counterintuitive and counterfactual though the question may be, what if those images had no impact whatsoever on people with disabilities? The project of disability studies, I believe, would be altogether necessary nonetheless, as would its oscillations between social constructionism and critical realism, because there is still another question of justice here, a question of how to understand human variety and mutability in the most fluid, capacious, and adequate manner possible. *Adequate,* because the question of the representation of human beings to human beings—in public policy; in social theory; in art, literature, and academic collections of essays—is very much a question of adequacy, of inventing modes of understanding that will be adequate to the staggering complexity of the subject, adequate to the ancient imperative of the humanist to perceive nothing human as alien. In this volume alone readers can begin to work toward an adequate understanding, of Teresa de Cartagena's fifteenth-century *Arboleda de los enfermos*; Audre Lorde's twentieth-century *The Cancer Journals*; Charlotte Mary Yonge's *The Clever Woman of the Family*; Lord Byron's *The Deformed Transformed*; Flying Words Project's ASL poetry; Sophocles's Oedipus; Sigmund Freud's account of narcissism; Mark Twain's sense of hearing; Walt Whitman's body politics; Oliver Sacks's case studies; Samuel Johnson's idiosyncrasies; Montaigne's cripples; John Bulwer's speaking hands; sex, death, difference, life writing, and the emerging possibility of a critically queer and severely disabled cultural politics. It is a question of doing justice to the subject, and it is a project to last many lifetimes. Yet someday soon, perhaps, disability studies will be widely understood as one of the normal—but not normalizing—aspects of study in the humanities, central to any adequate understanding of the human record. And perhaps I will see that day myself. If I should live so long.

NOTES ON CONTRIBUTORS

MICHAEL BERUBE is Paterno Family Professor of Literature and the Liberal Arts at Pennsylvania State University and author of *Life As We Know It: A Father, a Family, and an Exceptional Child* (Vintage, 1998).

BRENDA JO BRUEGGEMANN is associate professor of English at Ohio State University. She is the author of *Lend Me Your Ear: Rhetorical Constructions of Deafness* (Gallaudet UP, 1999) and numerous articles on deafness, literacy, disability studies, and qualitative research intersections in other collections and journals. She has served on the MLA's Committee on Disability Issues in the Profession and as a special interest delegate for disability on the MLA Delegate Assembly. In 2001, she received her university's Distinguished Diversity Enhancement Award for her work on campus related to disability issues.

LEONARD CASSUTO is associate professor of English at Fordham University. He is the author of *The Inhuman Race: The Racial Grotesque in American Literature and Culture* (Columbia UP, 1997). His work on Oliver Sacks has also appeared in *American Quarterly*.

G. THOMAS COUSER is professor of English at Hofstra University. He is the author of *American Autobiography: The Prophetic Mode* (U of Massachusetts P, 1979), *Altered Egos: Authority in American Autobiography* (Oxford UP, 1989), and *Recovering Bodies: Illness, Disability, and Life Writing* (U of Wisconsin P, 1997). His current work focuses on the ethics of life writing.

MICHAEL DAVIDSON is professor of literature at the University of California, San Diego. He is the author of *The San Francisco Renaissance: Poetics and Community at Mid-Century* (Cambridge UP, 1991) and *Ghostlier Demarcations: Modern Poetry and the Material Word* (U of California P, 1997). He has published eight books of poetry, the most recent of which are *Post Hoc* (Avenue B, 1990) and *The Arcades* (O Books, 1999).

LENNARD J. DAVIS is professor and head of the English department and professor of disability studies in the College of Health and Human Development at the University of Illinois, Chicago. He is the author of *Factual Fictions: The Origins of the English Novel* (1983, U of Pennsylvania P, 2001) and coeditor of *Left Politics and the Literary Profession*. His works on disability include *Enforcing Normalcy: Disability, Deafness, and the Body* (Verso, 1995), which won the 1996 Gustavus Myers Center for the Study of Human Rights annual award for the best scholarship on the subject of intolerance in North America, and *The Disability Studies Reader* (Routledge, 1996). He has also written a memoir, *My Sense of Silence* (U of Illinois P, 2000), about growing up in a Deaf family and edited his parents' correspondence, *Shall I Say a Kiss: The Courtship Letters of a Deaf Couple, 1936–38* (Gallaudet UP, 1999). He was a founding member of the MLA Committee on Disability Issues in the Profession and is an active member of Children of Deaf Adults (CODA).

HELEN DEUTSCH is associate professor of English at the University of California, Los Angeles. She is the author of *Resemblance and Disgrace: Alexander Pope and the Deformation of Culture* (Harvard UP, 1996) and coeditor (with Felicity Nussbaum) of *Defects: Engendering the Modern Body* (U of Michigan P, 2000). Her current book project, "The Case of Doctor Johnson," investigates the relation of Samuel Johnson's singular body to his monumental body of work and exemplary literary authority.

ROSEMARIE GARLAND-THOMSON is associate professor of Women's Studies at Emory University. Her scholarly publications and professional activities are devoted to developing the field of disability studies in the humanities. She is the author of *Extraordinary Bodies: Figuring Physical Disability in American Literature and Culture* (Columbia UP, 1997) and editor of *Freakery: Cultural Spectacles of the Extraordinary Body* (New York UP, 1996). She is currently writing a book on staring and a book on the cultural logic of euthanasia.

SANDER L. GILMAN is Distinguished Professor of the Liberal Arts and Medicine at the University of Illinois, Chicago, and director of the Humanities Laboratory. The author or editor of over sixty books, he wrote *Seeing the Insane* (1982), about visual stereotyping of the mentally ill, and *The Fortunes of the Humanities* (Stanford UP, 2000). He is special guest editor of *Patterns of Prejudice: The New Genetics and the Old Eugenics: The Ghost in the Machine* (Sage, 2002). At Cornell University he held the Godwin Smith Professorship of Humane Studies, and at the University of Chicago he was Henry R. Luce Distinguished Service Professor of the Liberal Arts in Human Biology.

DIANE PRICE HERNDL is associate professor of English at Iowa State University and the coeditor of *Feminisms: An Anthology of Literary Theory and Criticism* (Rutgers UP, 1997). She is the author of *Invalid Women: Figuring Feminine Illness in American Fiction and Culture, 1840–1940* (U of North Carolina P, 1993) as well as articles on feminist theory and American fiction. She is at work on two projects on biotechnology and feminist ethics, including "Thinking through Breast Cancer."

MARTHA STODDARD HOLMES teaches British literature and cultural studies at California State University, San Marcos, where she is assistant professor of literature and writing studies. Her book *Fictions of Affliction: Physical Disability in Victorian Culture* is forthcoming in the University of Michigan Press's series Corporealities. She is currently working on a book-length manuscript on Charles Dickens, Wilkie Collins, and the melodramatization of disability in Victorian culture.

MARK JEFFREYS is associate professor of English at the University of Alabama, Birmingham. He has published several essays on modernist poetry and on genre theory of the lyric in journals such as *PMLA, Criticism, Texas Studies in Language and Literature,* and *Journal of Modern Literature.* He is the coauthor of *Teacher's Guide to the Norton Anthology of Poetry* and the editor of *New Definitions of Lyric: Theoretical and Critical Essays* (Garland, 1998). He has recently turned to research on metaphors of genetics and cultural evolution.

ENCARNACION JUAREZ is assistant professor of Spanish literature at the University of Notre Dame. She has published *Italia en la vida y obra de Quevedo* (1990) and articles on Quevedo, Lope de Vega, la monja Alferez, Alonso de Contreras, *Guzmán de Alfarache,* and autobiographies written by women during the medieval and Golden Age periods. She is presently writing a book-length project on the role of clothing and body ornaments in the formation of identity in the autobiographical writings of the Golden Age.

GEORGINA KLEEGE is the author of a novel, *Home for the Summer* (Post-Apollo, 1989), and a collection of personal essays, *Sight Unseen* (Yale UP, 1999). She has recently completed a new book called "Writing Helen Keller."

CHRISTOPHER KRENTZ teaches English and American Sign Language at the University of Virginia, where he also directs the ASL Program. He is the editor of *A Mighty Change: An Anthology of Deaf American Writing, 1816–1864* (Gallaudet UP, 2000).

CYNTHIA LEWIECKI-WILSON, associate professor of English and affiliate of the Women's Studies Program at Miami University, teaches composition, literature, and women's studies at Miami's Middletown campus. She is the author of *Writing against the Family: Gender in Lawrence and Joyce* (Southern Illinois UP, 1994), coauthor of *From Community to Col-*

lege: Reading and Writing across Diverse Contexts (St. Martin's, 1996), and has written articles on teaching writing and literature. With James C. Wilson she coedited *Embodied Rhetorics: Disability in Language and Culture* (Southern Illinois UP, 2001).

NANCY MAIRS was awarded the 1984 Western States Book Award in Poetry for *In All the Rooms of the Yellow House* (Confluence) and a National Endowment for the Arts Fellowship in 1991. Her works of nonfiction are *Plaintext* (U of Arizona P), *Remembering the Bone House, Ordinary Time, Carnal Acts, Voice Lessons, Waist-High in the World,* and *A Troubled Guest* (Beacon). Living in Tucson, she is a research associate with the Southwest Institute for Research on Women.

ROBERT McRUER is assistant professor in the Department of English and associate director of the Human Science Program at George Washington University. He is the author of *The Queer Renaissance: Contemporary American Literature and the Reinvention of Lesbian and Gay Identities* (New York UP, 1997). His current book project, "De-Composing Bodies: Cultural Signs of Queerness and Disability," is about the intersections of queer theory and disability studies. His articles have appeared in such journals as *Genders, Children's Literature Association Quarterly,* and *Journal of Homosexuality.*

DAVID T. MITCHELL is director of the doctoral program in disability studies at the University of Illinois, Chicago, and associate professor in the Department of Disability and Human Development. He is a former president of the Society for Disability Studies and a founding member of the MLA Committee on Disability Issues. He is the coauthor, with Sharon Snyder, of *Narrative Prosthesis: Disability and the Dependencies of Discourse* (U of Michigan P, 2001); coeditor of *The Body and Physical Difference: Discourses of Disability* (U of Michigan P, 1997); producer and codirector of *Vital Signs: Crip Culture Talks Back* (Fanlight Distributing, Boston), which won documentary awards including an Apple and the Grand Prize at Rehabilitation International 1996; coeditor of the special issue on disability studies in the humanities for *Disability Studies Quarterly;* and series editor of Corporealities: Discourses of Disability for the University of Michigan Press. He is currently working on a new book, "American Physiognomies: Toward a Theory of a National Body."

JENNIFER L. NELSON received her PhD from the University of California, Berkeley, and teaches at Gallaudet University, the only university in the world for the deaf. She has published on Deafness-related issues in traditional literature, works in the field of American Sign Language literature, and is coediting an anthology on that subject. She is also a freelance illustrator.

CAROL POORE is professor of German studies at Brown University and engaged in introducing disability studies into the Brown curriculum. She has published numerous articles on literary and cultural representations of disability in Germany and the United States. Her most recent book is *The Bonds of Labor: German Journeys to the Working World, 1890–1990* (Wayne State UP, 2000).

ROBERT J. SCHOLNICK is professor of English and American studies at the College of William and Mary. He has published numerous essays on nineteenth-century American literature and culture in such journals as *American Literature, Journal of American Studies,* and *American Studies.* His *Edmund Clarence Stedman* appeared in 1977 and an edited collection, *American Literature and Science,* in 1994.

TOBIN SIEBERS is professor of English language and literature and director of the Comparative Literature Program at the University of Michigan. He has been selected for fellowships by the Michigan Society of Fellows, the Guggenheim Foundation, the Mellon Foundation, and the Institute for the Humanities. In 1999 he was nominated for a Pushcart Prize for "My Withered Limb," an account of growing up with polio. His principal contributions to literary and cultural criticism have been in ethics. Other areas include aesthetics and politics of identity, literary criticism of the cold war era, disability studies, psychoanalysis, literature and anthropology, and creative nonfiction. Siebers's major publications are *The Ethics of Criticism* (Cornell UP, 1988), *Morals and Stories* (Columbia UP, 1992), and *The Subject and Other Subjects: On Ethical, Aesthetic, and Political Identity* (U of Michigan P, 1998). He is also the editor of *Heterotopia: Postmodern Utopia and the Body Politics* (U of Michigan P, 1993) and *The Body Aesthetic: From Art to Body Modification* (U of Michigan P, 2000). His most recent work on the personal world of men is *Among Men* (U of Nebraska P, 1999).

SHARON L. SNYDER is coeditor of *The Body and Physical Difference* (1997), coauthor of *Narrative Prosthesis* (2000), and editor of Corporealities, the first book series on disability studies in the humanities—all these at the University of Michigan Press. She has directed two documentaries: *Vital Signs: Crip Culture Talks Back* (1996), winner of the Grand Prize at Rehabilitation International, and *A World without Bodies* (2002), a video on the Nazi euthanasia program. She is at work on "The Cultural Locations of Disability," an analysis of the historical constructions of disability in the United States. A founding member of the MLA Committee on Disability Issues in the Profession, she is assistant professor in the Department of Disability and Human Development at the University of Illinois, Chicago.

JIM SWAN is associate professor of English at the State University of New York, Buffalo, where he regularly teaches a seminar on writing and the body. He was program chair for the 2001 conference of the Society for Literature and Science. He is at work on a book titled "Body Language: Essays on Discourse and Embodiment."

JAMES C. WILSON is the author of several disability-related articles, including "Making Disability Visible: How Disability Studies Might Transform the Medical and Science Writing Classroom" in *Technical Communication Quarterly,* and coeditor, with Cynthia Lewiecki-Wilson, of *Embodied Rhetorics: Disability in Language and Culture.* He teaches professional writing and editing at the University of Cincinnati, where he is associate professor.

WORKS CITED

Ackerknecht, Erwin. "Anticontagionism between 1821 and 1867." *Bulletin of the History of Medicine* 22 (1948): 569–93.

Adams, Scott. *Bring Me the Head of Willy the Mailboy!* Kansas City: Andrews, 1995.

Allen, Gay Wilson. *The New Walt Whitman Handbook.* New York: New York UP, 1975.

Altick, Richard. *The Shows of London.* Cambridge: Belknap–Harvard UP, 1978.

Anderson, Benedict. *Imagined Communities: Reflections on the Origins and Spread of Nationalism.* London: Verso, 1983.

Anderson, David R. *Rex Stout.* New York: Ungar, 1984.

Anderson, Laurie. "Monkey's Paw." *Strange Angels.* CD. Warner Brothers, 1990.

Are You Fit to Marry? 1927. Orig. *The Black Stork* (1917). Videocassette. John E. Allen.

Art. Rage. Us: Art and Writing by Women with Breast Cancer. Introd. Jill Eikenberry. San Francisco: Chronicle, 1998.

Asch, Adrienne, and Harilyn Rousso. "Therapists with Disabilities: Theoretical and Clinical Issues." *Psychiatry* 48 (1985): 1–12.

As Good As It Gets. Dir. James L. Brooks. Perf. Jack Nicholson, Helen Hunt, and Greg Kinnear. TriStar, 1997.

Aspiz, Harold. *Walt Whitman and the Body Beautiful.* Urbana: U of Illinois P, 1980.

Baizley, Doris, and Victoria Ann Lewis. "Selected Scenes from *P*H*Reaks: The Hidden History of People with Disabilities.*" Fries, *Staring* 303–32.

Barnard, Henry. *Tribute to Gallaudet: A Discourse in Commemoration of the Life, Character, and Services of the Rev. Thomas H. Gallaudet, with an Appendix.* 2nd ed. Hartford: Brockett, 1859.

Barron, Stephanie. *"Degenerate Art": The Fate of the Avant-Garde in Nazi Germany.* New York: Abrams, 1991.

Barthes, Roland. *Camera Lucida: Reflections on Photography.* Trans. Richard Howard. New York: Hill, 1981.

Barton, Ellen L. "Literacy in (Inter)Action." *College English* 59 (1997): 408–37.

Bauby, Jean-Dominique. *The Diving Bell and the Butterfly.* Trans. Jeremy Leggatt. New York: Knopf, 1997.

Bauman, H. Dirksen L. "Toward a Poetics of Vision, Space, and the Body: Sign Language and Literary Theory." Davis, *Reader* 315–31.

Baynton, Douglas C. *Forbidden Signs: American Culture and the Campaign against Sign Language.* Chicago: U of Chicago P, 1996.

Beaman, Bruce R. "Mycroft Holmes, Agoraphobe." *Baker Street Journal* 26 (1976): 91–93.

Bennet, William J. *To Reclaim a Legacy: A Report on the Humanities in Higher Education.* Washington: NEH, 1984.

Benton, Joel. *Life of Hon. Phineas T. Barnum.* Philadelphia: Edgewood, 1891.

Bérubé, Michael. *Life As We Know It: A Father, a Family, and an Exceptional Child.* 1996. New York: Vintage, 1998.

Bickford, Susan. "Anti-anti-identity Politics: Feminism, Democracy, and the Complexities of Citizenship." *Hypatia* 12.4 (1997): 111–31.

Bigelow, Jacob. "On Self-Limiting Diseases." Starr 55–56.

Bloom, Allan. *The Closing of the American Mind: How Higher Education Has Failed Democracy and Impoverished the Souls of Today's Students.* New York: Simon, 1987.

Blunt, Alison, and Gillian Rose. "Introduction: Women's Colonial and Postcolonial Geographies." *Writing Women and Space: Colonial and Postcolonial Geographies.* Ed. Blunt and Rose. New York: Guilford, 1994. 1–25.

Boatner, Maxine Tull. *Voice of the Deaf: A Biography of Edward Miner Gallaudet.* Washington: Public Affairs, 1959.

Bogdan, Robert. *Freak Show: Presenting Human Oddities for Amusement and Profit.* Chicago: U of Chicago P, 1988.

Booth, Edmund. *Edmund Booth, Forty-Niner: The Life Story of a Deaf Pioneer.* Stockton: San Joaquin Pioneer and Historical Soc., 1953.

Bordo, Susan. *Unbearable Weight: Feminism, Western Culture, and the Body.* Berkeley: U of California P, 1993.

Bornstein, Melvin. "Analysis of a Congenitally Blind Musician." *Psychoanalytic Quarterly* 46 (1977): 23–77.

Boswell, James. *The Hypochondriack.* Ed. Margery Bailey. 2 vols. Stanford: Stanford UP, 1928.

———. *The Life of Samuel Johnson, LL.D.* Ed. George Birkbeck Hill. Rev. L. F. Powell. 6 vols. Oxford: Clarendon, 1934–50.

Brack, O M, Jr., and Robert E. Kelley, eds. *The Early Biographies of Samuel Johnson.* Iowa City: U of Iowa P, 1974.

Brad Runyon. The Thrilling Detective Web Site. Ed. Kevin Burton Smith. 27 Aug. 2001 <http://www.thrillingdetective.com/runyon_brad.html>.

Bragdon v. Abbott. 118 S. Ct. 2196. US Supr. Ct. 1998.

Bragg, Bernard. *Lessons in Laughter: The Autobiography of a Deaf Actor: As Signed to Eugene Bergman.* Washington: Gallaudet UP, 1989.

Bragg, Lois. "From the Mute God to the Lesser God: Disability in Medieval Celtic and Old Norse Mythology." *Disability and Society* 12.2 (1997): 165–77.

———. "Oedipus Borealis: The Aberrant Body in Barbarian Europe." *Disability Studies Quarterly* 17.4 (1997): 258–62.

Brain, Russell. *"Some Reflections on Genius" and Other Essays.* London: Pitman, 1960.

Bremmer, Jan, and Herman Roodenburg, eds. *A Cultural History of Gesture.* Cambridge: Polity, 1991; Ithaca: Cornell UP, 1992.

Brooks, Peter. *The Melodramatic Imagination.* New Haven: Yale UP, 1976.

Brown, Eleanor Gertrude. *Milton's Blindness.* 1934. New York: Columbia UP, 1968.

Browning, Christopher. *Ordinary Men: Reserve Police Battalion 101 and the Final Solution in Poland.* New York: Asher, 1992.

Browning, Tod, dir. *Freaks.* MGM, 1932.

Brueggemann, Brenda Jo. *Lend Me Your Ear: Rhetorical Constructions of Deafness.* Washington: Gallaudet UP, 1999.

———. "On (Almost) Passing." *College English* 59 (1997): 647–60.

Bulwer, John. Chirologia; or, The Natural Language of the Hand *and* Chironomia; or, The Art of Manual Rhetoric. 1644. Landmarks in Rhetoric and Public Address. Ed. James W. Cleary. Carbondale: Southern Illinois UP, 1974.

———. *Pathomyotomia; or, A Dissection of the Significative Muscles of the Affections of the Minde.* London: W.W., 1649.

———. *Philocophus; or, The Deafe and Dumbe Mans Friend.* London: Moseley, 1648.

Burgan, Mary. *Illness, Gender, and Writing: The Case of Katherine Mansfield.* Baltimore: Johns Hopkins UP, 1994.

Burlingham, Dorothy. "Some Notes on the Development of the Blind." *Psychoanalytic Study of the Child* 16 (1961): 121–45.

Butler, Judith. "Critically Queer." *GLQ: A Journal of Lesbian and Gay Studies* 1.1 (1993): 17–32.

———. *Excitable Speech: A Politics of the Performative.* New York: Routledge, 1997.

———. *Gender Trouble: Feminism and the Subversion of Identity.* New York: Routledge, 1990.

────. "Imitation and Gender Insubordination." *Inside/Out: Lesbian Theories, Gay Theories.* Ed. Diana Fuss. New York: Routledge, 1991. 13–31.

Bynum Walker, Caroline, ed. *Fragmentation and Redemption: Essays on Gender and the Human Body in Medieval Religion.* New York: Zone, 1991.

────. "Why All the Fuss about the Body? A Medievalist's Perspective." *Critical Inquiry* 22.1 (1995): 1–33.

Byron, Lord George. *The Deformed Transformed.* Byron, *Poetry* 467–534.

────. *Poetry.* Ed. E. H. Coleridge. New York: Scribner's, 1901. Vol. 5 of *The Works of Lord Byron.*

Campbell, Archibald. *Lexiphanes: A Dialogue.* London, 1767.

Campbell, Katie. *The Steadfast Tin Soldier.* Parsippany: Unicorn, 1990.

Campbell, Mary B. *The Witness and the Other World: Exotic European Travel Writing, 400–1600.* Ithaca: Cornell UP, 1988.

Canguilhem, Georges. *The Normal and Pathological.* Introd. Michel Foucault. Trans. Carolyn R. Fawcett and Robert S. Cohen. New York: Zone, 1991.

Carlyle, Thomas. *On Heroes, Hero-Worship, and the Heroic in History.* Ed. H. D. Traill. New York: Scribner's, 1903.

Cassuto, Leonard. "Oliver Sacks: The P. T. Barnum of the Postmodern World?" *American Quarterly* 52.2 (2000) : 326–33.

Certeau, Michel de. "Montaigne's 'Of Cannibals': The Savage 'I.'" *Heterologies: Discourse on the Other.* Trans. Brian Massumi. Manchester, Eng.: Manchester UP, 1986. 67–79. Vol. 17 of *Theory and History of Literature.*

────. *The Practice of Everyday Life.* Trans. Steven Rendall. Berkeley: U of California P, 1984.

Cheney, Lynne V. "Scholars and Society." *ACLS Newsletter* 1.3 (1988): 5–7.

Children of a Lesser God. Dir. Randa Haines. Perf. William Hurt, Marlee Matlin. Paramount, 1986.

Chiten, Laurel, dir. *Twitch and Shout: A Documentary about Tourette Syndrome.* New Day Films, 1994.

Christiansen, John B., and Sharon N. Barnartt. *Deaf President Now! The 1988 Revolution at Gallaudet University.* Washington: Gallaudet UP, 1995.

Coleman, Richard L., and James W. Croake. "Organ Inferiority and Measured Overcompensation." *Individual Psychology* 43.3 (1987): 364–69.

Collins, Wilkie. *Hide and Seek.* 1854. New York: Dover, 1981.

────. *Poor Miss Finch.* New York: Collier, n.d. Vol. 15 of *The Works of Wilkie Collins.*

Cormon, Eugène, and Adolphe Philippe D'Ennery. *The Two Orphans; or, In the Hands of Heaven.* Trans. N. Hart Jackson. *Melodrama Classics.* Ed. Dorothy Mackin. New York: Sterling, 1982. 121–74.

Cott, Nancy. "Passionlessness: An Interpretation of Victorian Sexual Ideology, 1790–1850." *Women and Health in America.* Ed. Judith Walzer Leavitt. Madison: U of Wisconsin P, 1984. 57–69.

Couser, G. Thomas. "Autopathography: Women, Illness, and Lifewriting." *A/B: Auto/Biography Studies* 6 (1991): 65–75.

———. "Conflicting Paradigms: The Rhetorics of Disability Memoir." Wilson and Lewiecki-Wilson. 78–91.

———. *Recovering Bodies: Illness, Disability, and Life Writing.* Madison: U of Wisconsin P, 1997.

Craik, Dinah Maria Mulock. *Olive.* 1850. New York: Garland, 1975.

Crary, Jonathan. *Techniques of the Observer: On Vision and Modernity in the Nineteenth Century.* Cambridge: MIT P, 1990.

Crimp, Douglas, and Adam Rolston. *AIDS DemoGraphics.* Seattle: Bay, 1990.

Cubbage, Maxwell E., and Kenneth R. Thomas. "Freud and Disability." *Rehabilitation Psychology* 34.3 (1989): 161–73.

Cummings, E. E. *Complete Poems, 1913–1962.* New York: Harcourt, 1980.

Curran, Andrew, and Patrick Graille. "The Faces of Eighteenth-Century Monstrosity." *Eighteenth-Century Life* 21 (1997): 1–15.

Daniels, A. M. "Sick Notes." Rev. of *Recovering Bodies: Illness, Disability, and Life Writing,* by G. Thomas Couser. *Times Literary Supplement* 24 Apr. 1998: 31.

Davidson, Michael. "Strange Blood: Hemophobia and the Unexplored Boundaries of Queer Nation." *Beyond the Binary: Reconstructing Cultural Identity in a Multicultural Context.* Ed. Timothy Powell. New Brunswick: Rutgers UP, 1999. 39–60.

Davis, Lennard J. "Constructing Normalcy: The Bell Curve, the Novel, and the Invention of the Disabled Body in the Nineteenth Century." Davis, *Reader* 1–28.

———, ed. *The Disability Studies Reader.* New York: Routledge, 1997.

———. "Dr. Johnson, Amelia, and the Discourse of Disability in the Eighteenth Century." Deutsch and Nussbaum 54–74.

———. "Enabling Texts." *Disability Studies Quarterly* 17.4 (1997 [pub. 1998]): 248–50.

———. *Enforcing Normalcy: Disability, Deafness, and the Body.* New York: Verso, 1995.

———. *My Sense of Silence: Memoirs of a Childhood with Deafness.* Champaign: U of Illinois P, 2000.

"A Deaf Soldier." *American Annals of the Deaf and Dumb* 20 (1875): 54.

de Baecque, Antoine. *The Body Politic: Corporeal Metaphor in Revolutionary France, 1770–1800.* Trans. Charlotte Mandell. Mestizo Spaces / Espaces Métissés. Stanford: Stanford UP, 1997.

Debord, Guy. *The Society of the Spectacle.* Detroit: Black, 1983.

Deitch, Jeffrey. *Post Human.* New York: Distributed Art, 1992.

Dekesel, Kristiaan. "John Bulwer: The Founding Father of BSL Research." *Signpost: The Newsletter of the International Sign Linguistics Association* (Winter 1992): 11–14; (Spring 1993): 36–43.

Dennett, Andrea Stulman. *Weird and Wonderful: The Dime Museum in America.* New York: New York UP, 1997.

Derrida, Jacques. *Of Grammatology.* Trans. Gayatri Chakravorty Spivak. Baltimore: Johns Hopkins UP, 1976.

———. *Writing and Difference.* Trans. Alan Bass. Chicago: U of Chicago P, 1978.

Deutsch, Helen. *Resemblance and Disgrace: Alexander Pope and the Deformation of Culture.* Cambridge: Harvard UP, 1996.

———. "Symptomatic Correspondences: Engendering the Author in Eighteenth-Century Britain." *Cultural Critique* 42 (1999): 35–80.

Deutsch, Helen, and Felicity Nussbaum, eds. *"Defects": Engendering the Modern Body.* Ann Arbor: U of Michigan P, 2000.

Deyermond, Alan. "Las autoras medievales castellanas a la luz de las últimas investigaciones." *Medioevo y literatura: Actas del V Congreso de la Asociación Hispánica de Literatura Medieval.* Ed. Juan Paredes. Granada: U de Granada, 1995. 31–52.

———. "'El convento de dolençias': The Works of Teresa de Cartagena." *Journal of Hispanic Philology* 1(1976): 19–29.

———. "Spain's First Women Writers." *Women in Hispanic Literature: Icons and Fallen Idols.* Ed. Beth Miller. Berkeley: U of California P, 1983. 27–52.

Dickens, Charles. *The Cricket on the Hearth. Christmas Books.* 1852. Oxford: Oxford UP, 1954. 155–234.

———. "Doctor Marigold." *Christmas Stories.* 1871. Oxford: Oxford UP, 1956. 433–72.

Didion, Joan. "Last Words." *The Best American Essays, 1999.* Ed. Edward Hoagland. Boston: Houghton, 1999. 63–73.

———. "The White Album." *The White Album.* New York: Simon, 1970. 11–48.

Dorris, Michael. *The Broken Cord.* New York: Harper, 1989.

Doyle, Arthur Conan. *The Original Illustrated Sherlock Holmes.* Facsim. ed. New York: Castle, n.d.

Du Bois, W. E. B. *The Souls of Black Folk.* 1903. New York: Norton, 1999.

Ebbinghaus, Angelika, et al., eds. *Heilen und Vernichten im Mustergau Hamburg: Bevölkerungs- und Gesundheitspolitik im Dritten Reich.* Hamburg: Konkret, 1984.

Edwards, Owen Dudley. "The Immortality of Father Brown." *Chesterton Review* 15 (1989): 295–325.

Eigner, Larry. *Areas Lights Heights: Writings, 1954–1989.* Ed. Benjamin Friedlander. New York: Roof, 1989.

Einstein, Albert. "The World As I See It." *The World As I See It.* New York: Philosophical Lib., 1949. 1–5.

Elias, Norbert. *The Civilizing Process.* 2 vols. Trans. Edmund Jephcott. New York: Pantheon, 1978–82.

Ellison, Ralph. *Shadow and Act*. 1954. New York: Vintage, 1995.

Erni, John Nguyet. *Unstable Frontiers: Technomedicine and the Cultural Politics of "Curing" AIDS*. Minneapolis: U of Minnesota P, 1994.

Fanon, Frantz. *The Wretched of the Earth*. New York: Grove, 1963.

Farrell, Gabriel. *The Story of Blindness*. Cambridge: Harvard UP, 1956.

Faulkner, William. Light in August: *The Corrected Text*. New York: Vintage, 1991.

Fichten, Catherine S., and Rhonda Amsel. "Thoughts Concerning Interaction between College Students Who Have a Physical Disability and Their Nondisabled Peers." *Rehabilitation Counseling Bulletin* 32 (1988): 22–40.

Finger, Anne. *Bone Truth: A Novel*. Minneapolis: Coffee House, 1994.

———. "Helen and Frida." Fries, *Staring* 255–63.

———. *Past Due: A Story of Disability, Pregnancy, and Birth*. Seattle: Seal, 1990.

Fishkin, Shelley Fisher. *Was Huck Black? Mark Twain and African-American Voices*. New York: Oxford UP, 1993.

Foster, Susan Leigh, ed. *Choreographing History*. Bloomington: Indiana UP, 1995.

Foucault, Michel. *The Birth of the Clinic: An Archaeology of Medical Perception*. Trans. A. M. Sheridan Smith. New York: Vintage, 1975.

———. *Discipline and Punish: The Birth of the Prison*. Trans. Alan Sheridan. New York: Vintage-Random, 1977.

———. *The History of Sexuality*. Vol. 1. Trans. Robert Hurley. New York: Vintage-Random, 1978.

———. *Technologies of the Self: A Seminar with Michel Foucault*. Ed. Luther H. Martin, Huck Gutman, and Patrick H. Hutton. Amherst: U of Massachusetts P, 1988.

———. *The Use of Pleasure*. Trans. Robert Hurley. New York: Vintage, 1990.

Fox, H., M. Daniels, and H. Wermer. "Applicants Rejected for Psychoanalytic Training." *Journal of the American Psychoanalytic Association* 12 (1964): 692–716.

Frank, Arthur W. *The Wounded Storyteller: Body, Illness, and Ethics*. Chicago: U of Chicago P, 1995.

Freire, Paulo. *Pedagogy of the Oppressed*. New York: Seabury, 1971.

Freud, Sigmund. *The Standard Edition*. Ed. James Strachey. 24 vols. London: Hogarth, 1953–74.

Fries, Kenny. *Anesthesia*. Louisville: Advocado, 1996.

———. *Body, Remember: A Memoir*. New York: Plume, 1998.

———. Introduction. Fries, *Staring* 1–10.

———, ed. *Staring Back: The Disability Experience from the Inside Out*. New York: Plume, 1997.

Funk, Robert. "Disability Rights: From Caste to Class in the Context of Civil Rights." Gartner and Joe 7–30.

Gallagher, Catherine. *Nobody's Story: The Vanishing Acts of Women Writers in the Marketplace, 1670–1820*. Berkeley: U of California P, 1994.

Gallagher, Hugh Gregory. *FDR's Splendid Deception*. New York: Dodd, 1985.

Gannon, Jack R. *Deaf Heritage: A Narrative History of Deaf America*. Silver Spring: Natl. Assn. of the Deaf, 1981.

———. *The Week the World Heard Gallaudet*. Washington: Gallaudet UP, 1989.

Garland-Thomson, Rosemarie. "Benevolent Maternalism and Physically Disabled Figures: Dilemmas of Female Embodiment in Stowe, Davis, and Phelps." *American Literature* 68 (1996): 555–86.

———. "Crippled Little Girls and Lame Old Women: Sentimental Spectacles of Sympathy with Rhetorics of Reform in Nineteenth-Century American Women's Writing." *Nineteenth-Century American Women Writers: A Critical Collection*. Ed. Karen Kilcup. New York: Blackwell, 1988. 128–45.

———. *Extraordinary Bodies: Figuring Physical Disability in American Culture and Literature*. New York: Columbia UP, 1997.

———, ed. *Freakery: Cultural Spectacles of the Extraordinary Body*. New York: New York UP, 1996.

———. "From Wonder to Error: A Genealogy of Freak Discourse in Modernity." Garland-Thomson, *Freakery* 1–22.

———. "Integrating Disability Studies into the Existing Curriculum: The Example of 'Women and Literature' at Howard University." *Radical Teacher* 47 (1995): 15–21.

Gartner, Alan, and Tom Joe, eds. *Images of the Disabled, Disabling Images*. New York: Praeger, 1987.

Gates, Henry Louis, Jr. *The Signifying Monkey: A Theory of African-American Literary Criticism*. New York: Oxford UP, 1988.

Gerhardt, Mia I. "'Homicide West': Some Observations on the Nero Wolfe Stories of Rex Stout." *English Studies* 49 (1968): 107–27.

Gilman, Sander L. *Seeing the Insane*. New York: Wiley; Brunner, 1982.

Gitter, Elizabeth A. "The Blind Daughter in Charles Dickens's *Cricket on the Hearth*." *Studies in English Literature* 39 (1999): 675–89.

———. "Deaf-Mutes and Heroines in the Victorian Era." *Victorian Literature and Culture* 20 (1992): 179–96.

Glazer, Nathan. *We Are All Multiculturalists Now*. Cambridge: Harvard UP, 1997.

Gledhill, Christine. "The Melodramatic Field: An Investigation." *Home Is Where the Heart Is: Studies in Melodrama and the Woman's Film*. Ed. Gledhill. London: British Film Inst., 1987.

Goffman, Erving. *The Presentation of Self in Everyday Life*. 1959. Woodstock: Overlook, 1973.

———. *Stigma: Notes on the Management of Spoiled Identity*. New York: Simon, 1963.

Goldhagen, Daniel Jonah. *Hitler's Willing Executioners: Ordinary Germans and the Holocaust.* New York: Knopf, 1996.

Golfus, Billy. *When Billy Broke His Head . . . and Other Tales of Wonder.* Dir. Golfus and David E. Simpson. Videocassette. Independent Television Service, 1995.

Goode, David. *A World without Words: The Social Construction of Children Born Deaf and Blind.* Philadelphia: Temple UP, 1994.

Graves, Algernon, and William Vine Cronin. *A History of the Works of Sir Joshua Reynolds.* 4 vols. London: Graves, 1899–1901.

Grealy, Lucy. *Autobiography of a Face.* Boston: Houghton, 1994.

Great Britain. Royal Commission on the Blind, the Deaf and Dumb, et Cetera, of the United Kingdom. *Report.* London: HMSO, 1889.

Greenacre, Phyllis. "Early Physical Determinants in the Development of the Sense of Identity." *Journal of American Psychoanalytic Association* 6 (1958): 612–27.

Greenblatt, Stephen. *Marvelous Possessions: The Wonder of the New World.* Chicago: U of Chicago P, 1991.

———. "Toward a Universal Language of Motion: Reflections on a Seventeenth-Century Muscle Man." Foster 25–31.

Grier, William H. "When the Therapist Is Negro: Some Effects on the Treatment Process." *American Journal of Psychiatry* 123 (1967): 1587–92.

Gunning, Tom. "Tracing the Individual Body: Photography, Detectives, and Early Cinema." *Cinema and the Invention of Modern Life.* Ed. Leo Charney and Vanessa R. Schwartz. Berkeley: U of California P, 1995. 15–45.

Gutierrez, Kris, Betsy Rymes, and Joanne Larson. "Script, Counterscript, and Underlife in the Classroom: James Brown versus Brown v. Board of Education." *Harvard Educational Review* 65 (1995): 445–71.

Gutierrez-Jones, Carl. "Injury by Design." *Cultural Critique: The Future of American Studies* 40 (1998): 73–102.

Hahn, Harlan. "Civil Rights for Disabled Americans: The Foundation of a Political Agenda." Gartner and Joe 181–203.

Halberstam, Judith, and Ira Livingston, eds. *Posthuman Bodies.* Bloomington: Indiana UP, 1995.

Halperin, David M. *Saint Foucault: Towards a Gay Hagiography.* New York: Oxford UP, 1995.

Halttunen, Karen. "Humanitarianism and the Pornography of Pain in Anglo-American Culture." *American Historical Review* 100 (1995): 303–34.

Hamilton, Elizabeth. "From Social Welfare to Civil Rights: The Representation of Disability in Twentieth-Century German Literature." Mitchell and Snyder, *Body* 223–39.

Hamlin, Christopher. "Predisposing Causes and Public Health in Early Nineteenth-Century Medical Thought." *Social History of Medicine* 5 (1992): 43–70.

Handler, Lowell. *Twitch and Shout: A Touretter's Tale.* New York: Dutton, 1998.

Haraway, Donna. "A Manifesto for Cyborgs: Science, Technology, and Socialist Feminism in the 1980s." *Socialist Review* 15.2 (1985): 65–108. Rpt. as "A Cyborg Manifesto." *Simians, Cyborgs, and Women.* By Haraway. New York: Routledge, 1991. 149–81.

Harris, Adrienne, and Dana Wideman. "The Construction of Gender and Disability in Early Attachment." *Women with Disabilities: Essays in Psychology, Culture, and Politics.* Ed. Michelle Fine and Adrienne Asch. Philadelphia: Temple UP, 1988. 115–38.

Harris, Benjamin, ed. *The Fables of Young Aesop, with Their Morals: With a Moral History of His Life and Death, Illustrated with Forty Curious Cuts Applicable to Each Fable.* London: Harris, 1671.

Harrowitz, Nancy. "The Body of the Detective Model: Charles S. Peirce and Edgar Allan Poe." *The Sign of Three: Dupin, Holmes, Peirce.* Ed. Umberto Eco and Thomas A. Sebeok. Bloomington: Indiana UP, 1983. 179–97.

Hawkins, Ann Hunsaker. *Reconstructing Illness: Studies in Pathography.* West Lafayette: Purdue UP, 1993.

Heine, Helme. *The Marvelous Journey through the Night.* Trans. Ralph Manheim. New York: Farrar, 1989.

Hemingway, Ernest. *The Sun Also Rises.* 1926. New York: Scribner's, 1986.

Herman, Didi. *The Antigay Agenda: Orthodox Vision and the Christian Right.* Chicago: U of Chicago P, 1997.

Hermand, Jost. *Arnold Zweig.* Reinbek: Rowohlt, 1990.

———. *Engagement als Lebensform: Über Arnold Zweig.* Berlin: Sigma, 1992.

Herndl, Diane Price. *Invalid Women: Figuring Feminine Illness in American Fiction and Culture, 1840–1940.* Chapel Hill: U of North Carolina P, 1993.

"Heterosexual." *Oxford English Dictionary Supplement.* 1971.

"Higher Education and Disability Law: Emerging Issues." *Heath: National Clearinghouse on Postsecondary Education for Individuals with Disabilities* 14 (1995): 1–3.

Hill, George Birkbeck, ed. *Johnsonian Miscellanies.* 2 vols. Oxford: Clarendon, 1897.

Howe, Elisabeth Teresa. "Sor Teresa de Cartagena and Entendimiento." *Romanische Forschungen* 108 (1996): 133–45.

Hull, John M. *Touching the Rock: An Experience of Blindness.* New York: Pantheon, 1990.

Humphreys, Tom, and Carol Padden. *Deaf in America: Voices from a Culture.* Cambridge: Harvard UP, 1988.

Hunter, Kathryn Montgomery. *Doctors' Stories: The Narrative Structure of Medical Knowledge.* Princeton: Princeton UP, 1991.

Hutton, Lewis J. Introduction. Teresa de Cartagena 7–36.

Ingrams, Richard, ed. *Dr. Johnson by Mrs. Thrale.* London: Hogarth, 1984.

In the Gloaming. Dir. Christopher Reeve. Perf. Glenn Close, Robert Sean Leonard, and David Strathairn. HBO, 1997.

Isaac, Frederick. "Enter the Fat Man: Rex Stout's *Fer-de-Lance.*" *In the Beginning: First Novels in Mystery Series.* Ed. Mary Jean DeMarr. Bowling Green: Popular, 1995. 59–68.

Jackson, Peter. *Maps of Meaning.* London: Unwin, 1989.

Jacobson, Edith. "The 'Exceptions': An Elaboration of Freud's Character Study." *Psychoanalytic Study of the Child* 20 (1965): 135–54.

Jay, Martin. *Downcast Eyes: The Denigration of Vision in Twentieth-Century Thought.* Berkeley: U of California P, 1993.

Johnson, James Weldon. *The Autobiography of an Ex-Coloured Man.* 1912. New York: Vintage, 1989.

Johnson, Kirk. "Looking Inward, Understanding Strange Worlds." *New York Times* 23 Oct. 1996: C6.

Katz, Jonathan Ned. "The Invention of Heterosexuality." *Socialist Review* 1 (1990): 7–34.

———. *The Invention of Heterosexuality.* New York: Dutton, 1995.

Kauffman, Linda. *Bad Girls and Sick Boys: Fantasies in Contemporary Art and Culture.* Berkeley: U of California P, 1998.

Kawash, Samira. "*The Autobiography of an Ex-Coloured Man:* (Passing for) Black Passing for White." *Passing and the Fictions of Identity.* Ed. Elaine K. Ginsberg. Durham: Duke UP, 1996. 59–74.

Keller, Helen. "Our Mark Twain." *Midstream: My Later Life.* Garden City: Doubleday, 1929. 47–69.

———. *The Story of My Life.* New York: Doubleday, 1903.

Kelley, Robert E., and O M Brack, Jr. *Samuel Johnson's Early Biographers.* Iowa City: U of Iowa P, 1971.

Kisor, Henry. *What's That Pig Outdoors? A Memoir of Deafness.* New York: Hill, 1990.

Klages, Mary. *Woeful Afflictions: Disability and Sentimentality in Victorian America.* Philadelphia: U of Pennsylvania P, 1999.

Kleck, Robert, Hiroshi Ono, and Albert H. Hastorf. "The Effects of Physical Deviance upon Face-to-Face Interaction." *Human Relations* 19 (1966): 425–36.

Kuhn, Thomas S. *The Structure of Scientific Revolutions.* 3rd ed. Chicago: U of Chicago P, 1996.

Kushner, Tony. "Foreword: Notes toward a Theater of the Fabulous." *Staging Lives: An Anthology of Contemporary Gay Theater.* Ed. John M. Clum. Boulder: Westview, 1996. vii–ix.

LaCom, Cindy. "'It Is More than Lame': Infirmity and Maternity in Victorian Fiction." *Mitchell and Snyder, Body* 189–201.

Lakoff, George. *Women, Fire, and Dangerous Things: What Categories Reveal about the Mind.* Chicago: U of Chicago P, 1987.

Lane, Harlan. *The Mask of Benevolence: Disabling the Deaf Community.* New York: Knopf, 1992.

Lasch, Christopher. *The Culture of Narcissism: American Life in an Age of Diminishing Expectations.* New York: Warner, 1979.

Lavater, Johan Caspar. *Essays on Physiognomy, Designed to Promote the Knowledge and Love of Mankind.* 3 vols in 5. Trans. Henry Hunter. London, 1789–98.

Lawrence, William. "Lectures on the Anatomy, Physiology, and Diseases of the Eye." *Lancet* Feb. 1826: 628–30.

Leitner, Maria. *Elisabeth, ein Hitlermädchen.* 1937. Berlin: Aufbau, 1985.

Lejeune, Philippe. *On Autobiography.* Minneapolis: U of Minnesota P, 1989.

Lentz, Ella Mae. *The Treasure.* Videocassette. In Motion, 1995.

Lewes, George Henry. "The Lady Novelists." *Westminster Review* 58 (1852): 129–41.

Limon, John. *The Place of Fiction in the Time of Science: A Disciplinary History of American Writing.* New York: Cambridge UP, 1990.

Linton, Simi. *Claiming Disability: Knowledge and Identity.* New York: New York UP, 1998.

Linton, Simi, Susan Mello, and John O'Neill. "Disability Studies: Expanding the Parameters of Diversity." *Radical Teacher* 47 (1995): 4–10.

Lionnet, Françoise. *Autobiographical Voices: Race, Gender, Self-Portraiture.* Ithaca: Cornell UP, 1989.

Lomax, Elizabeth. "Infantile Syphilis as an Example of Nineteenth-Century Belief in the Inheritance of Acquired Characteristics." *Journal of the History of Medicine* 34 (1979): 23–39.

Longmore, Paul. "Screening Stereotypes: Images of Disabled People in Television and Motion Pictures." *Social Policy* 15 (1985): 31–38.

Lönne, Birgit. "Entstehung und Wirkung." Zweig, *Beil* 631–47.

López Estrada, Francisco. "Las mujeres escritoras en la Edad Media castellana." *La condición de la mujer en la Edad Media: Actas del Coloquio celebrado en la casa Velázquez del 5 al 7 de noviembre de 1984.* Madrid: U Complutense, 1986. 9–38.

Lorde, Audre. *The Cancer Journals.* San Francisco: Aunt Lute, 1980.

Lott, Eric. *Love and Theft: Blackface Minstrelsy and the American Working Class.* New York: Oxford, 1993.

———. "Mr. Clemens and Jim Crow: Twain, Race, and Blackface." *Criticism and the Color Line: Desegregating American Literary Studies.* Ed. Henry B. Wonham. New Brunswick: Rutgers UP, 1996. 30–42.

Love, Susan, with Karen Lindsey. *Dr. Susan Love's Breast Book.* 2nd ed. Reading: Addison, 1995.

Lunsford, Andrea A. *The Everyday Writer.* Boston: Bedford–St. Martin's, 2001.

Lussier, André. "The Physical Handicap and the Body Ego." *International Journal of Psycho-analysis* 61 (1980): 179–85.

Lynch, Deidre. *The Economy of Character: Novels, Market Culture, and the Business of Inner Meaning.* Chicago: U of Chicago P, 1998.

Mack, Maynard. *Alexander Pope: A Life.* New York: Norton, 1986.

Mairs, Nancy. "Carnal Acts." Fries, *Staring* 51–61.

———. "On Being Crippled." *With Wings: An Anthology of Literature by and about Women with Disabilities.* Ed. Marsha Saxton and Florence Howe. New York: Feminist, 1987. 118–27.

———. *Waist-High in the World: A Life among the Nondisabled.* Boston: Beacon, 1996.

Mann, Edwin John, ed. *The Deaf and Dumb; or, A Collection of Articles Relating to the Condition of Deaf Mutes; Their Education, and the Principal Asylums Devoted to Their Instruction.* Boston: Hitchcock, 1836.

Marcus, Neil. *Storm Reading.* Storm Reading Video Production, 1996.

Martin, Frances. *Elizabeth Gilbert and Her Work for the Blind.* London: Macmillan, 1884.

Mazzeo, Joseph Anthony. "St. Augustine's Rhetoric of Silence." *Journal of the History of Ideas* 23 (1962): 175–96.

McAleer, John. *Rex Stout: A Biography.* Boston: Little, 1977.

McHenry, Lawrence C., Jr. "Samuel Johnson's Tics and Gesticulations." *Journal of the History of Medicine and Allied Sciences* 22 (1967): 152–68.

McKeon, Michael. "Writer as Hero: Novelistic Prefigurations and the Emergence of Literary Biography." *Contesting the Subject.* Ed. William Epstein. West Lafayette: Purdue UP, 1991. 17–41.

McRuer, Robert. "As Good As It Gets: Queer Theory and Critical Disability." *GLQ: A Journal of Lesbian and Gay Studies,* 9 (2002), forthcoming.

———. *The Queer Renaissance: Contemporary American Literature and the Reinvention of Lesbian and Gay Identities.* New York: New York UP, 1997.

Medoff, Mark. *Children of a Lesser God.* New York: Dramatists Play Service, 1998.

Michalko, Rod, and Tanya Titchkosky. "Putting Disability in Its Place: It's Not a Joking Matter." Wilson and Lewiecki-Wilson 200–28.

Michie, Helena. "'Who Is This in Pain?': Scarring, Disfigurement, and Female Identity in *Bleak House* and *Our Mutual Friend.*" *Novel* 22 (1989): 199–212.

Mitchell, David T., and Sharon L. Snyder, eds. *The Body and Physical Difference: Discourses of Disability in the Humanities.* The Body, in Theory: Histories of Cultural Materialism. Ann Arbor: U of Michigan P, 1997.

———eds. *Disability in the Humanities.* Spec. issue of *Disability Studies Quarterly* 17.4 (1998): 237–340.

————. *Narrative Prosthesis: Disability and the Dependencies of Discourse*. Ann Arbor: U of Michigan P, 2001.

————. "Re-engaging the Body: Disability Studies and the Resistance to Embodiment." *Public Culture* 13.3 (2001): 367–90.

————. "Representation and Its Discontents: The Uneasy Home of Disability in Literature and Film." *Handbook of Disability Studies*. Ed. Gary L. Albrecht, Katherine D. Seelman, and Michael Bury. Thousand Oaks: Sage, 2001. 195–218.

————. "Transforming Deformity / Performing Disability." *Bodies in Commotion*. Ed. Carrie Sandhal and Philip Auslander. Ann Arbor: U of Michigan P, forthcoming.

Moi, Toril. *Sexual/Textual Politics: Feminist Literary Theory*. London: Routledge, 1985.

Molina, Irene Alejandra. "*La arboleda de los enfermos* de Teresa de Cartagena: Un sermón olvidado." Masters thesis. U of Texas, Austin, 1990.

Montaigne, Michel de. *The Complete Essays of Montaigne*. Trans. Donald M. Frame. 9th ed. Stanford: Stanford UP, 1986.

Montgomery, Martin, and Stuart Allan. "Ideology, Discourse, and Cultural Studies: The Contribution of Michel Pêcheux." *Canadian Journal of Communications* 17.2 (1992). 27 Aug. 2001 <http://www.cjc-online.ca/title.php3?page = 4&journal_id = 9>.

Morrison, Toni. *Playing in the Dark: Whiteness and the Literary Imagination*. New York: Vintage, 1990.

Murphy, Robert. *The Body Silent*. New York: Henry Holt, 1987.

Nelson, Jennifer L., and Bradley S. Berens. "Spoken Daggers, Deaf Ears, and Silent Mouths: Fantasies of Deafness in Early Modern England." Davis, *Reader* 52–74.

Niederland, William G. "Narcissistic Ego Impairment in Patients with Early Physical Malformations." *Psychoanalytic Study of the Child* 20 (1965): 518–34.

Norden, Martin F. *The Cinema of Isolation: A History of Physical Disability in the Movies*. New Brunswick: Rutgers UP, 1994.

Northcote, James. *The Life of Sir Joshua Reynolds*. 1819. London: Cornmarket, 1971.

Not As Deaf As He Seems: An Ethiopean Farce. Clyde: Ames, 1865.

Nussbaum, Felicity A. "Feminotopias: The Pleasures of 'Deformity' in Mid-Eighteenth-Century England." Mitchell and Snyder, *Body* 161–73.

Nussbaum, Susan. *Mishuganismo*. Fries, *Staring* 367–402.

O'Connor, Flannery. "A Good Man Is Hard to Find." *The Heath Anthology of American Literature*. 2nd ed. Ed. Paul Lauter et al. Vol. 2. Lexington: Heath, 2147–58.

Oe, Kenzaburo. *A Healing Family: A Candid Account of Life with a Handicapped Son*. Trans. Stephen Snyder. New York: Kodansha Intl., 1996.

Ogden, Thomas Henry. "A Psychoanalytic Psychotherapy of a Patient with Cerebral Palsy: The Relation of Aggression to Self and Body Representation." *International Journal of Psychoanalytic Psychotherapy* 3 (1974): 419–23.

Olney, James. "Autobiography and the Cultural Moment." *Autobiography: Essays Theoretical and Critical.* Ed. Olney. Princeton: Princeton UP, 1980. 3–27.

Olsen, Tillie. *Silences.* New York: Delacorte, 1978.

The Oxford English Dictionary. 2nd ed. 1989.

Page, Norman, ed. *Dr. Johnson: Interviews and Recollections.* London: Macmillan, 1987.

Paglia, Camille. *Sex, Art, and American Culture.* New York: Vintage, 1992.

———. *Vamps and Tramps.* New York: Vintage, 1994.

Park, Katherine, and Lorraine J. Daston. "Unnatural Conceptions: The Study of Monsters in Sixteenth- and Seventeenth-Century France and England." *Past and Present* 92 (1981): 20–54.

Pasley, Robert S. "The Greek Interpreter Interpreted: A Revisionist Essay." *Baker Street Journal* 35 (1985): 106–11.

Patton, Cindy. *Fatal Advice: How Safe-Sex Education Went Wrong.* Durham: Duke UP, 1997.

Payne, Linda R. "An Annotated Life of Johnson: Dr. William Cadogan on 'Bozzy' and His 'Bear.'" *Collections* 2 (1987): 1–25.

Pender, Stephen. "'No Monsters at the Resurrection': Inside Some Conjoined Twins." *Monster Theory.* Ed. Jeffrey Jerome Cohen. Minneapolis: U of Minnesota P, 1996. 143–67.

Pernick, Martin S. *The Black Stork: Eugenics and the Death of "Defective" Babies in American Medicine and Motion Pictures since 1915.* New York: Oxford UP, 1996.

Plann, Susan. *A Silent Minority: Deaf Education in Spain, 1550–1835.* Berkeley: U of California P, 1997.

Pope, Alexander. *The Poetical Works of Alexander Pope with Memoir, Explanatory Notes, Etc. By the Author, Warburton, and Others.* New York: Hurst, 1888.

Porter, James I. Foreword. Mitchell and Snyder, *Body* xiii–xiv.

Pratt, Mary Louise. *Imperial Eyes: Travel Writing and Transculturation.* London: Routledge, 1992.

Price, Reynolds. *A Whole New Life: An Illness and a Healing.* New York: Atheneum, 1994.

Projektgruppe für die vergessenen Opfern des NS-Regimes in Hamburg e. V., ed. *Verachtet—verfolgt—vernichtet: Zu den "vergessenen" Opfern des NS-Regimes.* Hamburg: VSA, 1986.

Propp, William W. "A Study in Similarity: Mycroft Holmes and C. Auguste Dupin." *Baker Street Journal* 28 (1978): 32–35.

Pykett, Lyn. *The "Improper" Feminine: The Women's Sensation Novel and the New Woman Writing.* London: Routledge, 1992.

Rabinowitz, Paula. "Soft Fictions and Intimate Documents: Can Feminism Be Posthuman?" Halberstam and Livingston 97–112.

Rauber, D. F. "Sherlock Holmes and Nero Wolfe: The Role of the 'Great Detective' in Intellectual History." *Journal of Popular Culture* 6 (1972): 483–95.

Raubicheck, Walter. "Father Brown and the 'Performance' of Crime." *Chesterton Review* 19 (1993): 39–45.

The Real Mother Goose. Illus. Blanche Fisher Wright. New York: Scholastic, 1994.

Reiter, Raimond. "Die 'Kinderfachabteilung' in Lüneburg." *1999* 11.3 (1996): 55–67.

Rennie, Debbie. *Poetry in Motion: Original Works in ASL*. Videocassette. Sign Media, 1990.

Reyde, Aleyn Lyall. *Johnsonian Gleanings*. 11 vols. London: Francis, 1909–52.

Rich, Adrienne. "Compulsory Heterosexuality and Lesbian Existence." *Powers of Desire: The Politics of Sexuality*. Ed. Ann Snitow, Christine Stansell, and Sharon Thompson. New York: Monthly Rev., 1983. 177–205.

———. *On Lies, Secrets, and Silences: Selected Prose, 1966–1978*. New York: Norton, 1979.

Richards, Greg. *Growth Charts for Children with Down Syndrome*. 28 Aug. 2001. 29 Aug. 2001 <http://www.growthcharts.com>, under "Terminology."

"Richmond News and Gossip." *Charleston Mercury* 15 Mar. 1862: 1.

Riis, Jacob. *How the Other Half Lives: Studies among the Tenements of New York*. New York: Scribner's, 1890.

Robinson, Duncan. "Giuseppe Baretti as 'A Man of Great Humanity.'" *British Art, 1740–1820: Essays in Honor of Robert R. Wark*. Ed. Guilland Sutherland. San Marino: Huntington Lib., 1992. 81–94.

Rodríguez Rivas, Gregorio. "*La arboleda de los enfermos* de Teresa de Cartagena, literatura ascética en el siglo XV." *Entemu* (Centro Asociado de Asturias) 3 (1991): 117–30.

Rosenberg, Charles. "The Bitter Fruit: Heredity, Disease, and Social Thought in Nineteenth-Century America." *Perspectives in American History* 8 (1974): 189–235.

———. *No Other Gods: On Science and American Social Thought*. Baltimore: Johns Hopkins UP, 1976.

Rosenberg, John R. *The Circular Pilgrimage: An Anatomy of Confessional Autobiography in Spain*. New York: Lang, 1994.

Rosenblum, Barbara. "Living in an Unstable Body." *Cancer in Two Voices*. By Sandra Butler and Rosenblum. San Francisco: Spinsters, 1991. Rpt. in Fries, *Staring* 93–104.

Rosenblum, Walter, Naomi Rosenblum, and Alan Trachtenberg. *America and Lewis Hine*. Millerton: Aperture, 1977.

Rothman, Juliet Cassuto. *Saying Goodbye to Daniel: When Death Is the Best Choice*. New York: Continuum, 1995.

Rubin, Gayle. "The Traffic in Women: Notes on the 'Political Economy' of Sex." *Toward an Anthropology of Women*. Ed. Rayna R. Reiter. New York: Monthly Rev., 1975. 157–210.

Ruthrof, Horst. *Semantics and the Body: Meaning from Frege to the Postmodern.* Toronto: U of Toronto P, 1997.

Sacks, Oliver. *An Anthropologist on Mars.* New York: Vintage, 1995.

———. *Awakenings.* Rev. ed. New York: Harper, 1990.

———. *Island of the Colour-Blind and Cycad Island.* New York: Picador, 1996.

———. *A Leg to Stand On.* New York: Summit, 1984.

———. *"The Man Who Mistook His Wife for a Hat" and Other Clinical Tales.* New York: Summit, 1985.

———. *The Mind Traveler.* Dir. Christopher Rawlence. PBS–Rosetta Pictures. Sept. 1998.

———. *Seeing Voices.* New York: Harper, 1990.

———. *Uncle Tungsten: Memories of a Chemical Boyhood.* New York: Knopf, 2001.

Scarry, Elaine. *The Body in Pain: The Making and Unmaking of the World.* Ox

Schor, Naomi. *Bad Objects: Essays Popular and Unpopular.* Durham: Duke UP, 1995.

Seidenspinner-Núñez, Dayle. "'El solo me leyó': Gendered Hermeneutics and Subversive Poetics in *Admiraçion operum Dey* of Teresa de Cartagena." *Medievalia* 15 (1993): 14–23.

———, trans. and ed. *The Writings of Teresa de Cartagena.* Cambridge: Boydell, 1998.

Shakespeare, Tom. Rev. of *An Anthropologist on Mars*, by Oliver Sacks. *Disability and Society* 11.1 (1996): 137–39.

Shakespeare, William. *The Riverside Shakespeare.* Ed. G. Blakemore Evans et al. Boston: Houghton, 1974.

Shapin, Steven. "The Philosopher and the Chicken: On the Dietetics of Disembodied Knowledge." *Science Incarnate: Historical Embodiments of Natural Knowledge.* Ed. Shapin and Christopher Lawrence. Chicago: U of Chicago P, 1998. 21–50.

Shapiro, Joseph P. *No Pity: People with Disabilities Forging a New Civil Rights Movement.* New York: Times, 1993.

Shaw, Barrett, ed. *The Ragged Edge: The Disability Experience from the Pages of the First Fifteen Years of the Disability Rag.* Louisville: Advocado, 1994.

Shaw, Cuthbert. *The Race.* 2nd ed. London, 1766.

Sidransky, Ruth. *In Silence: Growing Up Hearing in a Deaf World.* New York: St. Martin's, 1990.

Siebers, Tobin. "Kant and the Politics of Beauty." *Philosophy and Literature* 22.1 (1998): 31–50.

———. *The Mirror of Medusa.* 1983. Christchurch, NZ: Cybereditions, 2000.

————. "My Withered Limb." *Michigan Quarterly Review* 37.2 (1998): 196–205.

————. *The Subject and Other Subjects: On Ethical, Aesthetic, and Political Identity.* Ann Arbor: U of Michigan P, 1998.

Sienkiewicz-Mercer, Ruth, and Steven B. Kaplan. *I Raise My Eyes to Say Yes.* Boston: Houghton, 1989.

Smead, James D. "The Landscape of Modernity: Rationality and the Detective." *Digging into Popular Culture: Theories and Methodologies in Archeology, Anthropology, and Other Fields.* Ed. Ray B. Browne and Pat Browne. Bowling Green: Popular, 1991. 165–71.

Snyder, Sharon. "Performing Deformity in Shakespeare's *Richard III.*" Enabling the Humanities Conf. Ohio State U. 18 Apr. 1998.

Snyder, Sharon L., and David T. Mitchell, dirs. *Vital Signs: Crip Culture Talks Back.* Videocassette. Brace Yourselves, 1997.

Sobottke, Thomas M. "Speculations on the Further Career of Mycroft Holmes." *Baker Street Journal* 2 (1990): 75–77.

Sontag, Susan. Illness as Metaphor *and* AIDS and Its Metaphors. New York: Anchor-Doubleday, 1990.

Sophocles. *Philoctetes. Sophocles II.* Trans. David Grene and Richmond Lattimore. New York: Washington Square, 1967. 198–264.

Spenser, Edmund. *The Faerie Queene.* Ed. A. C. Hamilton. London: Longman, 1977.

Spradley, Lynn. Epilogue. Spradley and Spradley 279–82.

Spradley, Thomas S., and James P. Spradley. *Deaf like Me.* 1978. Washington: Gallaudet UP, 1985.

Stafford, Barbara Maria. *Body Criticism: Imaging the Unseen in Enlightenment Art and Medicine.* Cambridge: MIT P, 1994.

Stange, Maren. *Symbols of Ideal Life: Social Documentary Photography in America, 1890–1950.* New York: Cambridge UP, 1989.

Starr, Paul. *The Social Transformation of American Medicine.* New York: Basic, 1982.

Stewart, Susan. "Letter on Sound." *Close Listening: Poetry and the Performed Word.* Ed. Charles Bernstein. New York: Oxford UP, 1998. 29–52.

————. "Lyric Possession." *Critical Inquiry* 22 (1995): 34–63.

Stiller, Jerome. "The Role of Personality in Attitudes toward Those with Physical Disabilities." *Current Topics in Rehabilitation Psychology.* Ed. C. J. Golden. Orlando: Grune, 1984. 201–26.

Stone, Deborah. *The Disabled State.* Philadelphia: Temple UP, 1984.

Stout, Rex. *Fer-de-Lance.* New York: Bantam, 1984.

————. *Over My Dead Body.* 1939. New York: Bantam, 1994.

The Suicide Machine. Detroit Free Press. 1997. 20 Aug. 2001 <http://www .freep.com/suicide/>.

Surtz, Ronald E. "Image Patterns in Teresa de Cartagena's *Arboleda de los enfermos." La Chispa '87: Selected Proceedings*. Ed. Gilbert Paolini. New Orleans: Tulane U, 1987. 297–304.

Swan, Jim. "Touching Words: Helen Keller, Plagiarism, Authorship." *The Construction of Authorship: Textual Appropriation in Law and Literature*. Ed. Martha Woodmansee and Peter Jaszi. Durham: Duke UP, 1994. 57–100.

Swett, William B. "Life and Adventures of William B. Swett." Trans. from sign language by William Chamberlain. *The Deaf-Mutes' Friend* 1 (1869): 1–6.

Tanner, Tony. *Adultery in the Novel: Contract and Transgression*. Baltimore: Johns Hopkins UP, 1979.

Taylor, Humphrey. "Americans with Disabilities Still Pervasively Disadvantaged on a Broad Range of Key Indicators." *Harris Poll Library*. Harris Interactive. Poll 56. 14 Oct. 1998. 28 Aug. 2001 <http://www.harrisinteractive.com/harris_poll/index.asp?PID=152>.

Teresa de Cartagena. Arboleda de los enfermos y Admiraçión operum Dey. Ed. Lewis J. Hutton. Madrid: Anejos de la Real Academia Española, 1967.

Thomas, Kenneth R. "Countertransference and Disability: Some Observations." *Journal of Melanie Klein and Object Relations* 15.1 (1997): 145–61.

Thomas, Ronald R. "Minding the Body Politic: The Romance of Science and the Revision of History in Victorian Detective Fiction." *Victorian Literature and Culture* 19 (1991): 233–54.

Thomson, Rosemarie. *See* Garland-Thomson, Rosemarie.

Timbs, John. *Anecdote Biography*. London, 1860.

Trachtenberg, Alan. *The Incorporation of America: Culture and Society in the Gilded Age*. New York: Hill, 1982.

———. *Reading American Photographs: Images as History, Mathew Brady to Walker Evans*. New York: Hill, 1989.

Turner, R. Jay, and P. D. McLean. "Physical Disability and Psychological Distress." *Rehabilitation Psychology* 34.4 (1989): 225–42.

Twain, Mark. *Adventures of Huckleberry Finn*. 1885. Boston: Bedford, 1995.

———. *The Adventures of Tom Sawyer*. 1876. London: Octopus, 1978.

———. *The Autobiography of Mark Twain*. Ed. Charles Neider. 1924. New York: Harper, 1959.

———. "How the Author Was Sold in Newark." *Sketches New and Old*. Hartford: Amer., 1893. 103–05. Project Gutenberg Etext. 9 Apr. 2002 <http://www2.cddc.vt.edu/gutenberg/etext02/mtsno10.txt>.

———. *Life on the Mississippi*. 1875–83. New York: Lib. of Amer., 1985.

———. "A Little Note to M. Paul Bourget." *"How to Tell a Story" and Other Essays*. 1897. Saint Clair Shores: Scholarly, 1977.

———. *Roughing It*. 1871. Hartford: Amer., 1891.

United Colors of Benetton. *The Sunflowers*. Bergamo, It.: Nuovo Instituto Italiano, 1998.

Valli, Clayton. *ASL Poetry: Selected Works of Clayton Valli*. Videocassette. Dawn Pictures, 1995.

———. "The Nature of the Line in ASL Poetry." *SLR '87 Papers from the Fourth International Symposium on Sign Language Research*. Ed. W. H. Edmondson and F. Karlsson. Hamburg: Signum, 1990.

———. *Poetry in Motion: Original Works in ASL*. Videocassette. Sign Media, 1990.

Vicente García, Luis Miguel. "La defensa de la mujer como intelectual en Teresa de Cartagena y Sor Juana Inés de la Cruz." *Mester* 18.2 (1989): 95–103.

Vincent, Nora. "Disability Chic: Yet Another Academic Fad." *New York Press* 11–17 Feb. 1998: 40–41.

———. "Enabling Disabled Scholarship." *Salon*. 18 Aug. 1999 <http://www.salon.com/books/it/1999/08/18/disability>.

———. "The Future of Queer: Wedded to Orthodoxy." *Village Voice* 22 Feb. 2000: 16.

Vormweg, Heinrich. "Gerechtigkeit über sich fühlend: Arnold Zweig's Roman *Das Beil von Wandsbek*." *Deutsche Exilliteratur, 1933–1945*. Ed. Manfred Durzak. Stuttgart: Reclam, 1973.

Walker, Lou Ann. *A Loss for Words*. New York: Harper, 1986.

Walter, Hans-Albert. "Die Geschäfte des Herrn Albert Teetjen: Das faschistische Deutschland in Arnold Zweig's Exilroman *Das Beil von Wandsbek*." *Frankfurter Hefte* 36.4 (1981): 49–62.

Warner, Michael. "Normal and Normaller: Beyond Gay Marriage." *GLQ: A Journal of Lesbian and Gay Studies* 5.2 (1999): 119–71.

———. *The Trouble with Normal: Sex, Politics, and the Ethics of Queer Life*. New York: Free, 1999.

Watney, Simon. *Policing Desire: Pornography, AIDS, and the Media*. 2nd ed. Minneapolis: U of Minnesota P, 1989.

Wendell, Susan. *The Rejected Body: Feminist Philosophical Reflections on Disability*. London: Routledge, 1996.

West, Paul. Preface. Words for a Deaf Daughter *and* Gala: A Fictional Sequel. Normal: Dalkey Archive, 1993. vii–xii.

———. *Words for a Deaf Daughter*. New York: Harper, 1970.

West, Shearer. "Wilkes's Squint: Synecdochic Physiognomy and Political Identity in Eighteenth-Century Print Culture." *Eighteenth-Century Studies* 33.1 (1999): 65–84.

Whitman, Walt. *The Eighteenth Presidency!* Whitman, *Poetry* 1331–49.

———. *The Journalism: 1834–1846*. Ed. Herbert Bergman et al. New York: Lang, 1998. Vol. 1 of *The Collected Writings*.

———. Leaves of Grass: *Facsimile of 1856 Edition*. N.p.: Norwood, 1976.

———. *Poetry and Prose*. New York: Lib. of Amer., 1996.

Wiggin, Kate Douglas. *The Birds' Christmas Carol.* 1886. Boston: Houghton, 1891.

Williams, John M. "And Here's the Pitch: Madison Avenue Discovers the Invisible Consumer." *We Magazine* 3.4 (1999): 28–31.

Williams, Raymond. *Keywords: A Vocabulary of Culture and Society.* Rev. ed. New York: Oxford UP, 1983.

Williamson, Aaron. E-mail to Michael Davidson. 18 Jan. 2000.

———. "Hearing Things." *Animated* (Spring 1999): 17–18.

———. Lecture. U of California, San Diego. 3 Mar. 2000.

Wills, David. *Prosthesis.* Meridian: Crossing Aesthetics. Stanford: Stanford UP, 1995.

Wilson, Dudley. *Signs and Portents: Monstrous Births from the Middle Ages to the Enlightenment.* London: Routledge, 1993.

Wilson, James C., and Cynthia Lewiecki-Wilson, eds. *Embodied Rhetorics: Disability in Language and Culture.* Carbondale: Southern Illinois UP, 2001.

Wilson, Thomas. *Arte of Rhetorique: The Renaissance Imagination.* Ed. Thomas J. Derrick. New York: Garland, 1982.

World Health Organization. *ICIDH-2: International Classification of Impairments, Activities and Participation: A Manual of Dimensions of Disablement and Functioning: Beta-1 Draft for Field Trials, June 1997.* Geneva: World Health Org., 1997. 29 Nov. 1998 <http//:www.who.ch/icidh>.

Wrigley, Owen. *The Politics of Deafness.* Washington: Gallaudet UP, 1996.

Yeazell, Ruth Bernard. "Henry James." *Columbia Literary History of the United States.* Ed. Emory Elliott. New York: Columbia UP, 1988. 668–89.

Yonge, Charlotte Mary. *The Clever Woman of the Family.* 1865. New York: Penguin, 1986.

Yorke, Clifford. "Some Comments on the Psychoanalytic Treatment of Patients with Physical Disabilities." *International Journal of Psycho-analysis* 61 (1980): 187–93.

Yung, Kai Kin. *Samuel Johnson, 1709–84: A Bicentenary Exhibition.* London: Arts Council of Great Britain; Herbert, 1984.

Žižek, Slavoj. *The Sublime Object of Ideology.* London: Verso, 1989.

Zola, Irving. "'Any Distinguishing Features?' The Portrayal of Disability in the Crime-Mystery Genre." *Policy Studies Journal* 15 (1987): 485–513.

———. *Missing Pieces: A Chronicle of Living with a Disability.* Philadelphia: Temple UP, 1982.

———. "The Portrayal of Disability in the Crime Mystery Genre." *Social Policy* 17 (1987): 34–39.

Zweig, Arnold. *The Axe of Wandsbek.* Trans. Eric Sutton. New York: Hutchinson, 1948.

———. *Das Beil von Wandsbek.* Berlin: Aufbau, 1996.

INDEX

abandonment, fear of, 53
able-bodiedness
  compulsory, 89, 91, 92–94, 96–97
  definitions of term, 91–92
ableism, 101–02, 286
abortion, 328
accommodations, 300–02, 332
Access Theater, 322
Ackerknecht, Erwin, 233n7
activity, definitions of, 293
ACT UP, 96, 99n10
ADA (Americans with Disabilities Act;
    1990), 1–2, 41, 47, 72, 283, 292,
    297, 312
Adams, Scott, 278
Adventures of Huckleberry Finn, The
    (Twain), 234, 238–39, 241–46
advertising
  and charity, 63–65
  and public awareness campaigns,
    63–65, 66–69, 70–72
advocacy
  politics of, 41–42
  See also disability rights movement
Aesop, 192–93
Allan, Stuart, 285
Allen, Gay Wilson, 248, 254, 257
Altick, Richard, 75n1
American Sign Language. *See* ASL
Americans with Disabilities Act. *See* ADA
amputation, 25, 145–46, 151, 174
Amsel, Rhonda, 55n8, n12
Anderson, Benedict, 101
Anderson, David R., 273, 276

Anderson, Laurie, 87, 148, 150
Anthropologist on Mars, An (Sacks),
    121–22, 125–27
antidepressants, 164–65
Antin, Eleanor, 87
Anzaldúa, Gloria, 87, 99n9
Arboleda de los enfermos (Teresa de
    Cartagena), 131–43, 343
Are You Fit to Marry? (film), 189
Aristophanes, 246n1
arts, disability related to, 173, 174,
    182–87, 189–91, 193–94, 260–61
Asch, Adrienne, 45, 47, 55n13
As Good As It Gets (film), 94–95, 97,
    99n8
ASL (American Sign Language), 77–78,
    308
  as ancillary to English, 87
  Flying Words Project, 78–82, 87, 343
  gestural potentiality of, 78, 211–17
  institutional use of, 221, 236
  in poetry, 78, 81–82, 87n1, 343
  rhetoric of, 211–21
Aspiz, Harold, 250, 252, 254
Astill, Craig, 82
audism, 77, 78
Augustine, Saint, 127, 134, 135
autobiography, 50, 78, 117n3
  of aching body, 131–43
  as confessional, 132–33
  as disability narrative, 109–17, 319
  in medical case study, 118–30
autoethnography, 116–17
Awakenings (Sacks), 120–21

death, 164–70
  assisted suicide, 160, 165–70
  cure-or-kill mindset, 180–81
  and damnation, 165
  as moral issue, 165–67, 170
  sex and, 156–64
  suicidal tendencies, 165, 170
death mask, analysis of, 203
Debord, Guy, 75n2
Dennett, Andrea Stulman, 75n1
Deformed Transformed, The (Byron), 176, 195n5, 343
Deitch, Jeffrey, 155n4
Dekesel, Kristiaan, 213, 214, 219, 221
democracy
  equality in, 105
  individualism in, 104
  representative, 102–05
D'Ennery, Adolphe Philippe, 222, 232n1
Dennett, Andrea Stulman, 75n1
Derrida, Jacques, 86, 135, 142n14
DeSalvo, Louise, 196n13
Descartes, René, 289
Deutsch, Helen, 9, 195n7, 196n10, 198, 209n6, 232n3, 346
Deyermond, Alan, 142nn3–5, 142n8
Dickens, Charles, 9, 182, 224, 225–27, 228, 231, 232n2, 232–33n4, 239, 261
Didion, Joan, 1, 194n4
difference, display of, 22
disability
  in the arts, 173, 174, 182–87, 188–91, 193–94, 260–61
  contextualization of, 88–89
  continuum of, 285–86
  and courage, 61–63
  critical insight from, 178
  cultural accommodations to, 15, 53, 301–02
  as cultural condition, 32–33, 50, 110, 112, 116, 169
  cultural representations of, 109–10, 224–25, 272, 293, 339
  definition of, 271
  as deviance from norms, 20–21, 23, 29n1, 33, 63–64, 161, 191
  fears of, 53, 235–36
  as fundamental human experience, 3, 72, 74–75, 96, 338

and genius, 198–200
and helplessness, 161–62, 323
hierarchies of, 324
and hopelessness, 168
as identity, 113, 308–16, 317–18, 319–21
individualization of, 48–49, 51, 110, 198–200, 208, 340, 342
insight via, 321–23, 332, 335
in literature, 15–24, 27, 173–82, 188–89, 208, 222–33, 234–47, 248–59, 319–20, 321–26
as loss, 111
as mark of distinction, 59
mechanical model of, 169
media portrayals of, 110–11, 319, 335
medical model of, 169, 293, 341
as metaphor, 16, 17, 24–29, 51, 221, 261, 324, 342
as moral condition, 112
and narcissism, 40, 41, 43–47, 50, 53
open discussions about, 301, 315
otherness in, 51, 66, 111, 131–32, 139–41, 193, 229, 299
pathologization of, 56, 160–61, 200
photographs of, 57–74
physical barriers to, 53, 318–19, 330
and power, 261
as problem in need of solution, 15, 63–64, 111–13, 161, 169
and psychoanalysis, 45–47
as spectacle, 56–75
theorization of, 49
transformational, 134
transmission of, 229–32, 252
uses of term, 74–75, 271, 292–93, 338
virtual, 95–97
visual rhetorics of, 58–59, 63, 65, 69, 72, 74, 75n6
disability law, 297–302, 303
disability market, advertising to, 66
disability rights movement, 2, 116, 141
  consciousness raising via, 41, 43, 261, 283–85, 342
  individualization in, 49
  normalcy critiqued in, 91
  related to other movements, 93–97, 112, 170, 303